SOCIALIST REGISTER 2017

THE SOCIALIST REGISTER

Founded in 1964

EDITORS

LEO PANITCH
GREG ALBO

FOUNDING EDITORS
RALPH MILIBAND (1924-1994)
JOHN SAVILLE (1916-2009)

ASSOCIATE EDITORS
COLIN LEYS
ALFREDO SAAD-FILHO

ASSISTANT EDITOR
ALAN ZUEGE

EDITORIAL ASSISTANT
STEPHEN MAHER

CONTRIBUTING EDITORS
BASHIR ABU-MANNEH
GILBERT ACHCAR
AIJAZ AHMAD
ELMAR ALTVATER
HENRY BERNSTEIN
PATRICK BOND
ATILIO BORON
JOHANNA BRENNER
PAUL CAMMACK
VIVEK CHIBBER
GEORGE COMNINEL
MADELEINE DAVIS
BARBARA EPSTEIN
BILL FLETCHER JR
SAM GINDIN
BARBARA HARRISS-WHITE
DAVID HARVEY
JUDITH ADLER HELLMAN
CHRISTOPH HERMANN
NANCY HOLMSTROM
URSULA HUWS
RAY KIELY
MARTIJN KONINGS
HANNES LACHER
LIN CHUN
MICHAEL LOWY
ŞEBNEM OĞUZ
CHARLES POST
ADOLPH REED JR
STEPHANIE ROSS
SHEILA ROWBOTHAM
JOHN S. SAUL
MICHALIS SPOURDALAKIS
HILARY WAINWRIGHT

To get online access to all Register volumes visit our website
http://www.socialistregister.com

SOCIALIST REGISTER 2017

RETHINKING REVOLUTION

Edited by LEO PANITCH and GREG ALBO

THE MERLIN PRESS
MONTHLY REVIEW PRESS
FERNWOOD PUBLISHING

First published in 2016
by The Merlin Press Ltd.
Central Books Building
Freshwater Road
London
RM8 1RX

www.merlinpress.co.uk

© The Merlin Press, 2016

British Library Cataloguing in Publication Data is available from the British Library

ISSN. 0081-0606

Published in the UK by The Merlin Press
ISBN. 978-0-85036-725-6 Paperback
ISBN. 978-0-85036-724-9 Hardback

Published in the USA by Monthly Review Press
ISBN. 978-1-58367-633-2 Paperback

Published in Canada by Fernwood Publishing
ISBN. 978-1-55266-911-2 Paperback

Printed in the EU on behalf of Stanton Book Services, Wellingborough, Northants

CONTENTS

Leo Panitch Greg Albo	Preface	ix
Bryan D Palmer Joan Sangster	The distinctive heritage of 1917: resuscitating revolution's *longue durée*	1
Leo Panitch Sam Gindin	Class, party and the challenge of state transformation	35
Jodi Dean	The actuality of revolution	59
Hilary Wainwright	Radicalizing the party-movement relationship: from Ralph Miliband to Jeremy Corbyn and beyond	80
Fabien Escalona	The heritage of Eurocommunism in the contemporary radical left	102
Andreas Malm	Revolution in a warming world: lessons from the Russian to the Syrian revolutions	120
David Schwartzman	Beyond eco-catastrophism: the conditions for solar communism	143
Patrick Bond	South Africa's next revolt: eco-socialist opportunities	161
Robert Cavooris	Turning the tide: revolutionary potential and the limits of Bolivia's 'process of change'	186

Steve Striffler	Something left in Latin America: Venezuela and the struggle for twenty-first century socialism	207
Pierre Beaudet	In search of the 'modern prince': the new Québec rebellion	230
August H Nimtz	Marx and Engels on the revolutionary party	247
A W Zurbrugg	1917 and the 'workers' state': looking back	265
Wang Hui	The 'people's war' and the legacy of the Chinese revolution	286
Adolph Reed, Jr	Revolution as 'national liberation'? the origins of neoliberal antiracism	299
Walter Benn Michaels	Picturing the whole: form, reform, revolution	323
Slavoj Žižek	Addressing the impossible	339
Leo Panitch	On revolutionary optimism of the intellect	356

CONTRIBUTORS

Pierre Beaudet teaches International Development and Global Studies at the University of Ottawa, and is the founder of the Quebec NGO Alternatives, and Editor of the *Nouveaux cahiers du socialisme*.

Patrick Bond, who directed the Centre for Civil Society at the University of KwaZulu-Natal since 2004, is now professor in the School of Governance at the University of Witwatersrand. Johannesburg, South Africa.

Robert Cavooris is a graduate student in the History of Consciousness Department, University of California, Santa Cruz.

Jodi Dean teaches political philosophy in the Political Science department at Hobart and William Smith Colleges in Geneva, New York.

Fabien Escalona is a teacher and researcher at Sciences Po, Grenoble and the *Centre d'étude de la vie politique* (Cevipol) at Université libre de Bruxelles.

Wang Hui is a professor in the Department of Chinese Language and Literature, Tsinghua University, Beijing.

Sam Gindin, the former chief economist and director of research for the Canadian Auto Workers union, is an adjunct professor in the political science department at York University, Toronto.

Andreas Malm teaches human ecology at Lund University, Sweden.

Walter Benn Michaels is an American literary theorist who teaches at the University of Illinois at Chicago.

August Nimtz, Jr is a professor of political science at the University of Minnesota in Minneapolis.

Bryan Palmer is emeritus professor of history at Trent University, Peterborough, Ontario and editor of the journal *Labour/Le Travail*.

Leo Panitch is emeritus professor of political science at York University, Toronto. Since 1985, he has served as co-editor of the *Socialist Register*.

Adolph L. Reed, Jr is a professor of political science at the University of Pennsylvania, specializing in race and American politics.

Joan Sangster holds the Morton Chair in History at Trent University, Peterborough, Ontario.

David Schwartzman is Professor Emeritus in the Department of Biology at Howard University, Washington, D.C.

Steve Striffler is the Doris Zemurray Stone Chair in Latin American Studies and Professor of Anthropology at the University of New Orleans.

Hilary Wainwright, editor of Red Pepper magazine, is a Fellow of the New Politics Project of the Transnational Institute in Amsterdam.

Slavoj Žižek is senior researcher at the Institute for Sociology and Philosophy at the University of Ljubljana, Global Distinguished Professor of German at New York University, and international director of the Birkbeck Institute for the Humanities of the University of London.

A.W. Zurbrugg is publisher at The Merlin Press, London.

PREFACE

This 53rd volume of the *Socialist Register* addresses the question of the meaning of revolution in the twenty-first century. Coming to terms with the legacy of 1917 is obviously one aspect of this. 'October' was a unique event that provided inspiration for millions of oppressed people, and also became an inevitable point of reference for socialist politics in the twentieth century. The twenty-first century left needs to both understand and transcend this legacy through a critical reappraisal of its broad effects – both positive and negative – on political, intellectual and cultural life everywhere as well as on the other revolutions that took place over the last century. But the main point of the volume is to look forward more than back.

All revolutions emerge in conjunctures saturated with unique contradictions, contingencies, class alignments and struggles. This concrete confluence of forces constitutes the political conditions that revolutionaries must not only understand, but also act and organize within. The 'political event' of gaining state power, whether by taking parliament or in a collapse of the existing political regime, has proven time and again to be less crucial than the social revolution of building capacities for self-government and the democratization and socialization of institutional resources. The 'event', in itself, may be a dramatic rupture that opens up new political possibilities and imaginaries bursting beyond the limited horizons of capitalist market calculation. But it will never be a sufficient condition for the exploited and oppressed to build their own capacities for establishing collective, rather than competitive, ways of living through developing socialist democracy. There is a need, in this context, for the left to maintain an openness to, and patience with, the quite varied experiments in social alternatives to neoliberalism as they emerge in the current period. It is anything but clear where new space for projects of structural reform might open up, or more profound ruptures might suddenly burst onto the political scene.

In this sense, even if the anniversary of 1917 occasions it, this volume is not a history of revolutions, or a collection of recipes for making revolution today. At a time when reform as it was understood in the twentieth century appears as impossible as revolution in the foreseeable future, it is necessary to try to rethink yet again the relationship between capitalist crises and both revolution and reform, and to do this in relation to the current conjuncture as well as the trajectories of radical politics in various regions. The volume also addresses the processes at work in the remaking of the socialist movement today and how far this may help in placing revolutionary transformations and democratization of the social order back on the agenda. This includes assessing the salience of the concept of the revolutionary party *and* of the working class as a revolutionary agency today. What both of these mean not only for political practice but also for revolutionary vision, including its artistic expression, has also been our remit, as has the meaning of revolution in the context of the immense ecological challenges the twenty-first century faces.

Of course, the *Socialist Register* has always been concerned to interrogate the shifting meaning of and prospects for revolutionary ruptures from capitalism, recognizing that revolutionary moments of the past continue to shape the terrain of the present, but that there are no blueprints that would guarantee the successful making of democratic socialism in the future. As Ralph Miliband put it in the first volume in 1964: 'The most obvious lesson provided by past socialist experience in the countries of advanced capitalism concerns the relationship between economic crisis and socialist commitment – or rather the lack of such relationship … The repetition today of the depression of the early 'thirties, in countries like Britain and the United States, would probably have far more dramatic consequences. But it is by no means certain that the consequences would necessarily flow in socialist directions.' And if it was for this reason that so many essays in the *Register* undertook a critical analysis of what Lenin had called social democracy's 'parliamentary cretinism', there was at the same time an acute awareness of Leninism's inadequacies. Miliband's famous 'Moving On' essay in 1976 opened by noting that 'the main problem for the socialist left in Britain is still that of its own organisation into an effective political formation, able to attract a substantial measure of support and to hold out a genuine promise of further growth'. One reason for this was the persistence among so much of the radical left of 'a common perception of socialist change in terms of a revolutionary seizure of power on the Bolshevik model of October 1917. This is their common point of departure and of arrival, the script and scenario which determines their whole mode of being. But this Bolshevik model has very little appeal in the working class movements of bourgeois democratic regimes in general … [which] imposes upon revolutionary socialists a strategy of advance which has to include a real measure of electoral legitimation.'

How to achieve this without falling back into social democratic gradualist illusions, how to combine 'Reform and Revolution', the title of Andre Gorz's brilliant essay in the 1968 volume was, and remains, the *Register*'s primary concern: 'A socialist strategy of progressive reforms does not mean the installation of islands of socialism in a capitalist ocean. But it does mean ... an intensification and deepening of the antagonism between the logic of social production according to the needs and aspirations of men, and the logic of capitalist accumulation and the power of management.' A key concern of the *Register*, therefore, has been assessing whether the conditions for this were being enhanced, or rather undermined, precisely in the face of what Elmar Altvater, in a remarkably prescient essay in the 1979 volume, identified as the 'dual line of attack – authoritarian structuring of government policy, which no longer seeks social and political compromise with the workers' movement, and the release of the economy to market forces – [which] presents the workers' movement with a historic challenge, and will gradually compel the formulation of alternatives to the prevailing policy.'

As the release of these 'market forces' around the globe through the ensuing decade enveloped even those Communist regimes which had claimed the legacy of 1917, the Preface to the 1989 *Register*, on the theme of 'Revolution Today: Aspirations and Realities', opened with these words: 'The socialist aspiration to create a cooperative, egalitarian, democratic and classless society entails, for its realization, a fundamental transformation of the social and political order, in a word, a revolution. But what does the idea of revolution itself entail today? To ask this question as we approach the end of this century immediately raises a host of issues concerning whether and how socialist aspirations can be realized, and poses problems and dilemmas over the very ways we can think about these issues, as well as over the ways in which they might be resolved.' The *Register* has continued to address these questions ever since – even devoting entire volumes to them, such as the 2000 volume on 'Necessary and Unnecessary Utopias' – while increasingly seeking to bring socialist-feminist and eco-socialist perspectives to bear on them.

Yet we were swimming against the tide, even on the left. As one of our most prominent contributors, who for many years was also a member of the *Register*'s editorial collective, Ellen Meiksins Wood, put it in the 1990 volume on 'The Retreat of the Intellectuals': 'We live in curious times. Just when intellectuals of the Left in the West have a rare opportunity to do something useful, if not actually world-historic, they – or large sections of them – are in full retreat. Just when reformers in the Soviet Union and

Eastern Europe are looking to Western capitalism for paradigms of economic and political success, many of us appear to be abdicating the traditional role of the Western left as critic of capitalism. Just when more than ever we need a Karl Marx to reveal the inner workings of the capitalist system, or a Friedrich Engels to expose its ugly realities "on the ground", what we are getting is an army of "post-Marxists" one of whose principal functions is apparently to conceptualize away the problem of capitalism.'

Even in mourning Ellen's death this past year, we are mindful that she lived to see the tide turn back, to see that the era of conceptualizing away the problem of capitalism was well and truly over. Recognition that the consequence of this 'will not necessarily flow in socialist directions' was what led to the 2016 volume on 'The Politics of the Right', and we very much hope that this year's volume will help in rethinking how to shift the flow in socialist directions (as we hope our subsequent volumes on rethinking democracy and eco-socialist ways of living in the twenty-first century will as well). As always, we want to thank all our contributors for their essays, and for the eagerness as well as comradeship with which they approached thinking through such a difficult, and most often sharply contentious, topic.

Since its inception, the *Register*'s editors have had the considerable good fortune to work with the highly progressive publishers at Merlin Press, and we are especially happy that Tony Zurbrugg, with his essay in this volume, follows in the footsteps of his predecessor, Martin Eve, who contributed an essay to the 1983 *Register*. We are also very grateful for his and for his colleague Adrian Howe's help, support and patience in producing this volume, as we are for Louis Mackay's great cover art. We would also like to thank Lin Chun, who was extremely generous as a contributing editor in securing and editing Wang Hui's essay; Mathew Flisfeder for his help with securing Slavoj Zizek's essay; and Bernard Gibbons for his translation of Fabien Escalona's essay. Finally, we want to express our appreciation to our long-serving assistant editor, Alan Zuege, and to Steve Maher, without whose hard and creative editorial work this volume would not have come to fruition.

LP
GA
July 2016

THE DISTINCTIVE HERITAGE OF 1917: RESUSCITATING REVOLUTION'S *LONGUE DURÉE*

BRYAN D. PALMER AND JOAN SANGSTER

For many on the revolutionary left, 1917 is an unpleasant apparition, a ghost that haunts us still. Our perspective is different: 1917 lives in our thoughts and actions, our theories and our sensibilities, because it remains a testimony to human agency and the irrepressible potential of revolution. The Bolsheviks, so often castigated as incarcerated in their slavish adherence to the determination of objective conditions, were nothing if not believers in the importance of the subjective factor in the making of history, evident in their own trajectory. The revolution that catapulted the Bolsheviks to power contradicted the prevailing European Marxist orthodoxy which mapped an evolutionary path to revolution based on the logic of capitalist development, and followed on the heels of disastrous dissolution of the Second International as its leaders chose to abandon their anti-war stance to align themselves with their own national bourgeois states.

It is today more important than ever for revolutionary leftists to confront both the possibilities posed by the Revolution of 1917 and the ways in which its outcomes seem to have soured the meaning of socialism in the mouths of those with an appetite for a politics of emancipatory transformation. On the one hand, our times cry out for the need to transcend capitalist oppression, exploitation, and degradation. Those same needs galvanized the pre-First World War revolutionary left in Russia and elsewhere, and structured the early years of the Bolshevik Revolution. On the other hand, Revolution's current capacities and claims, associated with 1917 being overtaken by a Thermidorian Stalinization, have seldom been held in disregard by so many, including a considerable section of the ostensible left.

As Geoff Eley writes: 'Revolutions no longer receive a good press. The calamity of Stalinism and the ignominious demise of the Soviet Union have been allowed to erase almost entirely the Russian Revolution's emancipatory effects.'[1] Against the sense that revolution might transform the human condition has come resignation, articulated by one militant '68er, Régis Debray, whose sad autobiography declared that '*Revolution now arouses among us, not just in the lineage of its victims but that of its authors and beneficiaries too, the same repulsive images as revolt or jacquerie in eighteenth-century drawing rooms*'. The revolutionary project was now written off curtly: 'Two centuries, millions of corpses, one complete rotation: for nothing.'[2]

Our view of the 'long revolution', needless to say, differs from Debray. We also recognize that the heritage of revolution is highly differentiated: it both precedes and follows 1917, and cannot be characterized by a unitary and homogenous mobilization across time and space, for political differences between and within communism, socialism, anarchism and syndicalism, were not unimportant. Anarchism itself fragmented into disparate tendencies, some embracing revolutionary collectivist ideas, others stressing individual freedom and autonomy, though Emma Goldman perhaps embodied the coalescing of these strands. Marx and Engels railed against utopian socialists, but others combined elements of the scientific and the utopian in both analytic accents and practical orientations.

William Morris captured something of this combination in his defence of revolution in the 1880s. It was Morris's purpose, whether he addressed audiences large or small, to 'stir [them] up not to be contented with a little,' to persuade them that they must either struggle to be free or remain mired in enslavement.[3] It was the duty of those 'who believe in the necessity of social revolution ... first to express their own discontent', drawing in others, second 'to learn from books and from living people', and third 'to join any body of men honestly striving to give means of expression to revolutionary discontent and hope'. Lenin and the Bolsheviks separated themselves from such utopian socialist appeals, but the world communist movement spawned by 1917 did not entirely abandon these sensibilities. No advocate of Lenin, E.P. Thompson staked out the ground of widening revolutionary struggle in *Out of Apathy* (1960):

> The point of breakthrough is not one more shuffle along the evolutionary path, which suddenly sinks the scales on the socialist side ... Certainly, the transition can be defined, in the widest historical sense, as a transfer of class power: the dislodgment of the power from the 'commanding heights' and the assertion of the power of socialist democracy. But this point cannot be defined in narrow political (least of all parliamentary) terms; nor can we be certain, in advance, in what context the breakthrough will be made. What it is more important to insist upon is that it is necessary to *find out*

the breaking point, not by theoretical speculation alone, but *in practice* by unrelenting reforming pressures in many fields, which are designed to reach a revolutionary culmination. And this will entail a confrontation, throughout society, between two systems, two ways of life.[4]

However divergent the lines between various revolutionary projects, Thompson, like many nineteenth-century socialist figures and twentieth-century dissident communists, embraced revolution as 'immediacy'; as the necessary project of posing radical, root-and-branch, social transformation as essential to human liberation, indeed survival.

In the pages that follow we address the heritage of 1917 and its broadened understanding of revolution, exploring themes such as women's liberation, sexuality, reproduction, and the family, as well as campaigns for racial equality, class mobilizations, and the complex representation of resistance and struggle in various artistic and literary genres. While not everything we discuss bears the direct and unmediated imprint of 1917, it is difficult to imagine the range of resistance and the richness of varied developments without appreciating the heritage of revolution. We explore such themes in specific historical periods where the impact of 1917 registered in different ways. Whatever the peculiarities of these local manifestations, however, our outline could well be generalized to other national and regional contexts. As co-authors we actually disagree on important aspects of what might fall under the discussion of 1917's meanings,[5] but in such contention lies the real political scene of the current left; our differences are an acknowledgement of the theoretical and practical divisions that plague socialists serious about the project of replacing capitalism with a realizable social order that can deliver the necessary utopian promise of revolution.

REVOLUTIONARY REVERBERATIONS I: GENDER

From the time of Flora Tristan, the French socialist and feminist who in 1840 lamented her exile from civil society as a 'pariah' because she believed in the emancipation of both women and the working class, to later experimentation within socialist communes and organizing by anarchists, syndicalists, communists and defiant sex radicals, revolution provided a hopeful pathway to sexual and gender equality. After 1917, Russia was initially a model against which all defined themselves. Without experiencing an intense bourgeois or social democratic struggle for suffrage, as happened in many European countries, the Bolsheviks moved swiftly from proclaiming women's equal citizenship to a social revolution. In no small part because of pressure from feminist revolutionaries like Alexandra Kollontai, who saw familial and sexual liberation as a *sine qua non* of social emancipation, and Clara Zetkin's previous success with semi-autonomous organizations of socialist women, the Bolsheviks set in motion a massive educational campaign to bring women to political consciousness through a Women's Commission or *Zhenotdel*.

By 1920, this work was also internationalized when women from nineteen countries met to discuss a lengthy set of 'Theses on the Communist Women's Movement', a blueprint for the emancipation of women within communism. Soviet reforms abolished illegitimacy and provided women with access to divorce, birth control, abortion, equal pay, and land and property rights. There were even legislative changes that advanced sexual freedoms dramatically, such as the decriminalization of sodomy in 1922, a remarkably progressive attitude to homosexuality given the prevailing European repression of same-sex practices. At the core of this revolutionary programme was the understanding that sexual practices had to be freed from the conservatizing clutches of church and state and that fundamental to the liberation of humanity was the alteration of women's labour: women's paid work was a means to economic independence and socialized domestic labour – communal kitchens, laundries, and crèches – would challenge women's oppression within the family.

Extensive studies have examined the rise and demise of women's Soviet emancipation, including the immense barriers to any transformation of gender roles: the resilience of patriarchal social norms and religious belief, the hard reality of civil war and lack of economic resources, and the prioritization of other political issues over gender equality. By the end of the 1920s, equality, other than encouraging women's labour force participation, was on the backburner; the Zhenotdel was abolished, and the International Women's Secretariat came under the rigid control of an increasingly Stalinized Comintern Executive. A singular emphasis on women's integration into productive labour left Russian women with both a double day and a double sexual standard.

Yet as Eley notes, the Bolshevik reforms initially conveyed a salutary lesson: this was 'Western feminism's maximum program to which no government in the West ever came close' to realization.[6] Even if the revolutionary left's faith in change ultimately exceeded what had been achieved, the Bolshevik Revolution unleashed an unprecedented debate both within the wider left and throughout communist parties themselves. The apparent Soviet commitment to thoroughgoing change, especially the recognition that housework had to be transformed and sexual freedom addressed, was seen as an important feminist 'breakthrough'.[7] The revolution electrified socialist, communist, and even some liberal women who saw it as proof that transformative change *was* possible: if an underdeveloped country could take such extraordinary steps, why not Western industrialized ones?

Political tourists to the Soviet Union already committed to communism were usually uncritical acolytes of changes to women's status, but socialist and liberal women also wrote convincingly about the possibilities they glimpsed inside the new Russian society, from socialized childcare to family planning and opportunities for higher education. This positive assessment, even on the part of liberals, galvanized right-wing opponents in the United States, including a contingent of conservative women who took up the political cudgels of antifeminism paired with gendered understandings of class struggle: 'Miss Bolsheviki has come to town, / With a Russian cap and a German gown, / In women's clubs she's sure to be found, / For she's come to disarm America.' Assaults on the ostensible 'nationalization of women' and stereotypical Soviet-inspired 'Bureaus of Free Love' were of a piece with the infamous 'Spider Web Chart', first published in Henry Ford's *Dearborn Independent* (1924), that linked liberal women's groups to a network of Bolshevik-connected clubs, causes and campaigns.[8] Right-wing women's anti-Bolshevik, anti-socialist and anti-pacifist mobilizations had some success stalling and rolling back moderate feminist social reforms.

The equality ledger in the USSR was increasingly contested as Stalinism was consolidated, but the revolution nonetheless inspired imitations, departures and elaborations. Interpretation of women's emancipation varied according to different national contexts, histories, cultures, and the strength of particular national communist parties, as well as their relationship to rivals on the social democratic left. In Mexico, the Communist Party did not even attempt to establish a women's department until 1931 due to other organizing priorities and Mexican communists' complex tussle for 'revolutionary authenticity' with the nationalistic Partido Revolucionario Institucional [PRI] and its 'revolutionary' state.[9]

In the smaller Canadian and American parties, directives from the International Women's Secretariat were seen as welcome advice from seasoned revolutionaries, though instructions were refracted through local conditions and needs, and sometimes stymied by leadership apathy. Nonetheless, for women recruited from previous suffrage and socialist activism, international revolutionary direction provided hope for those who longed for a new politics that promised to transcend a past littered with the dead ends of bourgeois or social democratic feminisms, constrained as they were by discourses of individual liberal rights or a parliamentary preoccupation with protecting the working-class family through legislative enactments.

Soviet inspiration, advice, and prodding helped to bring into being a new semi-autonomous Canadian organization of left-wing women, the Women's Labor Leagues; an agitational women's paper, *The Woman Worker*, that addressed issues of social/sexual as well as material subordination; and perhaps most importantly, advocacy for the legalization of abortion and birth control, issues largely side-stepped by the earlier Canadian socialist left. Birth control issues were similarly brought to the fore in the UK by birth-control advocate and communist Stella Browne, who was ultimately disappointed to discover that the British Communist Party did not welcome a revolution in familial and sexual roles as promoted by Alexandra Kollantai.

Many American feminist historians have been highly critical of the revolution's impact on the women's equality debate within the Communist Party USA, claiming that issues of emancipation and women's special oppression suffered at the hands of an apathetic Party leadership given to sexist denigrations and masculinist understandings of politics. Others, however, concede that the early Bolshevik experiment 'empowered' new female converts to revolutionary communism. Housewives mobilized around cost-of-living issues, women contributed to campaigns of solidarity such as Friends of Soviet Russia, and women workers organized in the needle and garment trades. Moreover, in the 1920s the majority of female communists in the US were immigrants whose first language was not necessarily English; their perspectives and practices have been obscured due to historians' lack of facility with language-based sources.

Internationalism, later corralled and corrupted by the Comintern, offered at first a critical sense of possibility for dialogue, not only through official channels like the International Women's Secretariat, but via a host of other institutions and organs. The Ukrainian paper for communist women, *Robitnystia* (*Working Woman*), published in Winnipeg, Canada after a similar paper closed down in Cleveland, Ohio, circulated through the Ukrainian communist diaspora in the Americas, connecting Russia's revolution to North American women's emancipation. Edited by a communist émigré playwright from the Ukraine, Myroslav Irchan (Andriy Babiuk), it was intended for a working-class female constituency often denigrated and labelled illiterate and backward. It provided working-class women with a voice in the emerging revolutionary milieu, generating an entirely new critical discussion of partriarchy and male chauvinism, dubbed 'porcupinsim',[10] mobilizing engagement with the issue of gender equality through the cultural genres of fiction, drama, and personal storytelling. As in the early days of revolutionary Russia, culture was conceived as a midwife to transformational consciousness. If this kind of cultural production had contradictions, it was not just that it was not 'feminist' enough; the paper was also tied to Soviet priorities and orchestrated nationalist sensibilities as a means of sustaining and deepening communist solidarities, not unlike the immigrant labour upheavals of the First World War era in the United States, which both contributed to intensifying class conflict and sidelined that struggle into problematic mobilizations.

REVOLUTION'S REVERSALS: THE 1920s

The decade of the 1920s witnessed significant setbacks for the revolutionary left, including the defeat of the German Revolution (1923), an event that overdetermined the possibilities for the Communist International and structured the Soviet Union's drift to Stalinization. The failure of the German Revolution, accompanied by setbacks for the revolutionary left in Austria, Hungary, and Italy, occurred before Russia's 1917 revolution had the opportunity to truly free itself from the imperialist encirclement and deforming containments of the First World War and its immediate aftermath. The ravages of a debilitating, Western-supported civil war weakened the Bolshevik Revolution and, with no support forthcoming from a central Europe undergoing capitalist restabilization, the early 1920s saw Soviet industry struggling to rebuild, its working class exhausted. With the agricultural sector decimated, the peasantry was disaffected. The revolutionary state, caught in the vice of crisis, was drifting towards bureaucratism as Lenin's health deteriorated in 1922. With the leadership vacuum created by the leading Bolshevik's death in 1924, the stage was set for Stalin to consolidate power and secure authoritarian rule for a bureaucratic caste, a political apparatus of retrenchment orchestrated by a regime increasingly reliant on brutalizing force. 'Socialism in one country', a programme counter-posed to revolutionary internationalism and the class struggle initiative of 'permanent revolution', was in the making, corresponding to a resurrection of officially-sanctioned chauvinism; the 'show trials' and political purges of the 1930s were the last chapters in a book of banishment first written over the course of the mid-to-late 1920s, which included the enforced marginalization and final exile of Trotsky. Along the way, any revolutionary role the Communist International could have provided to insurgent forces around the world proved spent, as indicated in Stalin's course in China, where revolution was derailed in 1926-1927. As Perry Anderson concluded, the 1920s saw the sorry denouement of classical Bolshevism as 'Marxism was largely reduced to a memento in Russia … The most advanced country in the world in the development of historical materialism, which had outdone all Europe by the variety and vigour of its theorists, was turned within a decade into a semiliterate backwater, formidable only by the weight of its censorship and the crudity of its propaganda.'[11]

Within the advanced capitalist political economies of the west, especially a United States not ravaged by the First World War's destructions, the fortunes of the profit system soared materially and ideologically. Class struggle took a decided turn for the worse. Employers' groups, as Chad Pearson has shown, upped the ante of aggressive rhetorical and practical assault, placing 'dangerous foreigners' and the proverbial 'agitator' in the crosshairs of a direct retaliatory attack. 'Socialism, syndicalism, communism, and other mental and moral diseases are among our inheritance from the cesspools of foreign thought,' declared one authority favoured by the National Association of Manufacturers.[12]

Reaction reigned triumphant, ushering in an era of repressive backlash, components of which included heightened surveillance of targeted dissident groups, mass deportations of 'alien radicals' (the annual count of those expelled from the United States climbing to 38,000 by the end of the 1920s) and a rash of criminal syndicalist trials that, in California alone, netted 500 arrests and 164 convictions by 1924.[13] Such developments accelerated the American Federation of Labor's (AFL) conservatism and anticommunism, and provided critical nails in the ongoing construction of the coffin of revolutionary syndicalism, epitomized in the Industrial Workers of the World, and helped seal the fate of Sacco and Vanzetti in 1927. The orthodox holiday of the international revolutionary working class, May Day, was subjected to counter-mobilization as bodies like the American Defense Society attempted to reclaim 1 May, promoting Loyalty and American Day events: patriotism was cultivated as an antidote to the 'deep-seated conspiracy against civilization' associated with 'communism, IWWism or Bolshevism'.[14] There was even an attempt to re-label May Day a National Child Health Day.

The convergence of these and other trends ensured that trade unions and militant minorities of labour radicals could not sustain the global workers' revolt of 1916-1923 which, by 1929, was a distant memory. The ossified United States craft unions of the late 1920s were pale reflections of the tumultuous trade unions of the First World War era that, even in defeat, had taken on powerful capitalist enterprises, rattling the cage of class containment. By 1928, according to one of the dons of the American Wisconsin School of industrial relations, Selig Perlman, the AFL was governed by a 'psychology of ... "defeatism" and complacency'.[15]

This context, in conjunction with the conservatizing Stalinization of the Communist International, wrote *finis* to much of the revolutionary optimism that infused the immediate post-1917 years with a sense of imminent possibility. Within the Comintern, reliance on an increasingly mechanical Marxism turned ideas towards economism, on the one hand, and a mechanical philosophical 'diamat' on the other, structuring programmatic decisions around the foreign policy needs of the Soviet Union. Stalin's personal authority dovetailed destructively with such developments. And among Marxists who remained committed to developing the revolutionary theoretical arsenal, this context of limitation conditioned a break with the classical nineteenth-century fusion of conceptualization and actual engagement with class struggle. This ushered into being a 1920s retreat into aestheticization that would gather force over the course of the twentieth century, culminating in a 'Western Marxism' animated by philosophy but increasingly distanced from revolutionary political practice.[16] The Comintern's original influence, one of healthy advice to national sections, withered over the course of the 1920s and 1930s: flexibility in the application of socialist analysis and principles hardened into a refusal to allow socialist and feminist ideas to flourish freely in productive tension and debate, stifling revolutionary initiative and innovation.

REVOLUTIONARY REVERBERATIONS II: RACE

Race, like gender, received a new leftward lease on life in the United States in the wake of the Bolshevik Revolution. Socialists in North America, it has long been recognized, failed to give race either its analytic or political due until 1917 pushed communists to the forefront of the revolutionary movement. Guided by the Communist International, communists in the United States began to grapple seriously with what was then called 'the Negro Question'. Like so much else, Stalinism deformed this engagement. It helped frame the discussion about race in non-Marxist, almost absurdly nationalist ways, conceiving of African-Americans not as the most oppressed of a multi-racial, multi-ethnic United States working class, but as a *separate* nation. This was most evident in the discussions at the Negro Commission of the Sixth World Congress of the CI (1928), out of which came the codification of the 'Black Belt Nation' thesis. This posited the need for revolutionary communists in the United States to struggle to build a 'Negro Soviet Republic' in the American South's black belt, where the population density of African Americans supposedly established a claim to nationhood. Aside from a few African American advocates such as Harry Haywood, the notion of a Black Belt Nation had little appeal among the oppressed black population of the United States, whose struggles for jobs, equality, and an end to Lynch Law and Jim Crow structured much of everyday life. That said, the attempt to actually conceptualize the oppression of American blacks in ways that accented the need for revolutionary transformations convinced many that the Communist Party USA, unlike past socialist organizations, was treating the race issue seriously rather than subordinating the struggle for Negro rights to the class question.

The race issue in the United States in the period from 1917-1925 was dominated not so much by Communist Party considerations as by the massive influx of black southerners to the urban-industrial centres of the north. The 'Great Migration' culminated in the explosive growth of Chicago's 'black metropolis' and New York City's Harlem, with segregation contributing to a vibrant black literary and musical aesthetic – dubbed the advent of 'the New Negro' – in which creative understandings of racial oppression and human liberation joined culture and politics in a profoundly anti-capitalist critique of racism that went far beyond calls to improve race relations or allow blacks to pursue the rites of citizenship.

Intensified working-class revolt and a renewed wave of racist violence characterized the immediate postwar period, providing the impetus for what Barbara Foley calls a 'red-black' politics that co-joined critiques of capitalism and racism: 'massive class and antiracist struggles,' she argues, 'erupt[ed] in the wake of the Great War and the Bolshevik Revolution'.[17] The leftward turn in political discussion concerning race was expressed not only in the radical black press but also in more mainstream 'Negro' and white liberal forums, though it found its strongest articulation in left-wing African American publications like *The Messenger,* founded by socialists A. Philip Randolph and Chandler Owen in 1917. This radical editorial duo welcomed the Bolshevik Revolution as 'the Banquo's ghost to the Macbeth capitalists of the world, whether they inhabit Germany, England, America or Japan. It is a foreword of a true world democracy. The Soviets represent the needs and aims of the masses.'[18] Other more 'Afrocentric' publications like *The Crusader*, paper of the African Blood Brotherhood, which would eventually find itself associated with the Communist Party, linked global imperialism to racism and advocated a 'multi-racial revolution'.

Explaining the violence faced by African Americans in their everyday lives, red-black revolutionaries like Cyril Briggs and Richard B. Moore situated racial oppression in an imperialist global system, explored class relations of exploitation, denounced capitalist profit and a regime of expropriation and accumulation, and did what they could to unmask the ideological obscuring of working-class common interest. A unique Harlem figure, Hubert Harrison, was, like so many of these red-black dissidents, a product of the Caribbean diaspora. Arguably the leading left-wing black intellectual in the United States, he embraced an array of causes, including birth control, the IWW, the Socialist Party (as an internal critic) and *The Voice*, a radical First World War era 'race' paper. More than any other figure he galvanized 'race consciousness', insisting that it necessarily had to accompany 'class consciousness' in the making of revolution.[19]

As Foley suggests, however, the revolutionary origins of the 'New Negro' movement would not survive the repression unleashed by the red and black agitations of 1919. Hopes for an interracial movement of opposition were dashed in a rash of racist pogroms. As the postwar strike wave peaked in 1919, over twenty race riots erupted. In Chicago, one of these racially charged urban implosions took the lives of twenty-three African Americans and fifteen whites, leaving the epicentre of black employment, the Chicago Stockyards, under military occupation. A voice of the Harlem Renaissance, Claude McKay, penned an anguished poetic response, capturing an African American mood simultaneously resistant and resilient, but also resigned: 'If we must die, let it not be like hogs / Hunted and penned in an inglorious spot, / While round us bark the mad and hungry dogs, / Making their mock at our accursed lot.'[20]

Just as deportations and a nativist assault on immigrant radicals drove the 'alien' other into retreat, by the mid-1920s the 'New Negro's' revolutionary beginnings faded from view, overtaken by understandable culturalist, pluralist, and nationalist sensibilities. What remained was an artistic attachment to an African American folk experience, tied to southern slavery, but stripped of the oppositional cosmopolitanism that could have challenged the limiting appeal of the kind of race separatism that would animate both Garveyism and the Communist Party's call for a Black Belt Nation. The organic connection of workers' revolution and the eradication of racism would nevertheless prove difficult to disentangle. It surfaced again and again in myriad movements and civil rights struggles, among them the pan-Africanism of Comintern-affiliated George Padmore in the 1930s or the fertile contributions of C.L.R. James to a widening array of issues. Among the contentious topics James addressed over the course of decades of revolutionary reassessment were the 1917 revolution's degeneration and the relation of this denouement to capitalism, colonialism, and anti-imperialist struggles in the Caribbean, as well as the nature and meaning of working-class self-activity.[21] In the 1960s, the dialectic of race/class struggle was wrestling inside the Black Power movement, evident in the development of Malcolm X as well as in sectors of the Black Panthers.[22] Small wonder that, from the early 1920s on right-wing commentators were quick to decry the 'communist conspiracy's' so-called enlistment of the 'negro masses' in its nefarious 'campaign to bring about the overthrow of the government' of the United States 'by violence'.[23]

REVOLUTIONARY REVERBERATIONS III: CRISIS OF CAPITALISM; CULTURE AS CONFLICT

By the time of capitalism's collapse in the Great Depression of the 1930s, revolutionary politics within the Soviet Union and in its many satellite communist parties was withering on the vine of Stalinist programmatic indecision, which lurched from right, to left, to right in the oscillating 'turns' of Comintern directive. With the expulsion of dissident communists and the Soviet declaration of its ultra-left 'Third Period' in 1928, it was difficult for left oppositions of various kinds to gain much ground. This of course did not mean that revolutionary ideals inspired by the Bolshevik Revolution simply evaporated, either inside the official Communist movement or outside of it, on its margins. Revolutionary fervour persisted, nurtured within the small space regional and national parties attempted to carve out for locally relevant organizing. Revolutionary ideals in the Depression decade also took shape in other dissident communist configurations and parties, including Lovestoneites, Trotskyists, anarcho-syndicalists, and even some socialist groups caught between the revolutionary impulses of the 1930s and their continuing adherence to social democratic strategies and tactics. In the latter camp were groups like the American Workers Party, which rallied Conference for Progressive Labor Action intellectuals/activists and was led by the long-time peace campaigner, A.J. Muste.

Revolution's relevance seemed obvious to many amidst the global crisis of world capitalism announced with the startling meltdown of 1929. The collapse of stock markets, the closing of workplaces and the resulting massive, unprecedented unemployment, loss of homes and farms, and the inability of many western governments to face the crisis with anything other than retrenchment and austerity, put capitalism on trial. That the Soviet Union, in spite of its internal domestic repression, seemed to be weathering the storms of economic crisis rather well reinforced the notion that something was obviously wrong with the profit system. Sophia Dixon, an early founder of the Cooperative Commonwealth Federation (CCF), a Canadian party that declared its intent to replace decrepit 'capitalism' with a system of socialist cooperation, articulated the growing sense of impending crisis and the need for political imagination: 'it seemed as if the capitalist system was simply crumbling before us and our task was to find and build a new system which could replace the old.'[24] The shape of global crisis varied across regions and from nation to nation, with the complexity of political cultures and their configurations of race, ethnicity, and gender complicating matters, but the sense that a Marxist analysis of capitalism's inevitable weaknesses and working-class/popular resistance were absolutely necessary animated insurgent groups worldwide.

Established communist parties led struggles of the unemployed in the early 1930s and, with the turn to the Popular Front in 1935, played vital roles in industrial union drives. Too often, however, the labour upheaval of the 1930s in the United States and Canada is tied to the CIO sit-down strikes in the automobile sector in 1936-1937, heralded as orchestrated by the far-seeing break from AFL craft unionism initiated by United Mine Workers of America boss and Congress of Industrial Organization front-man, John L. Lewis. But Lewis, who would rather cynically utilize communist organizers to good effect in the late 1930s and 1940s, had actually taken his cues from a 1934 strike wave organized by revolutionaries active within AFL unions. Their resolute battles against recalcitrant employers and trade union bureaucrats led to bloody conflicts in industrial cities, transport centres, west coast ports, and southern mill towns. These 1934 uprisings had the character of Rosa Luxemburg's mass strike and were led, often with startling success, by Trotskyists of the Communist League of America, Musteites in the American Workers Party, and the Communist Party USA.

With the nationwide attention given to the Trotskyist successes in organizing the previously largely unorganized teamsters and coal yard/market workers of Minneapolis, for instance, Lewis and many others were struck by the fact that an ossified International Brotherhood of Teamsters Local with less than 200 members in 1932-1933 managed, under revolutionary leadership (that included the trio of militant Minneapolis Dunne brothers as well as New York-based Left Oppositionists James Cannon and Max Shachtman) to grow explosively over the course of 1934. It took three strikes within a concentrated seven or so months of intense class struggle, but the Trotskyist-led General Drivers Union stared down a Farmer-Labor Governor, locked horns with an obstinate and hostile municipal administration, ran rings around Washington-dispatched mediators, duked it out with police and vigilantes, mocked National Guardsmen, and finally defeated a cabal of trucking employers. Eventually the union boasted a membership of 7,000.[25]

Revolutionaries in Toledo, under the guidance of Muste, his labor lieutenant Louis Budenz, and a dedicated corps of unemployed organizers and agitators made similar if less spectacular gains in the Toledo auto-parts industry, breaking through organizational impasses the United Automobile Workers had failed to crack previously. On the west coast, Communist Party labour leader Harry Bridges found himself 'swept along in the flood' of Longshoremen's militancy, which resulted in pitched battles with police and National Guardsmen, hospitalizing and injuring hundreds while leaving two strikers and an onlooker dead. The bitter, explosive class struggles of 1934, animated by revolutionaries who in one way or another were inspired by the events of 1917, pitted workers against employers and their reactionary associations; a Rooseveltian façade of liberal governance, with its structures of accommodation and incorporation; and ultimately the armed might of the capitalist state.

Throughout the 1930s, such conflicts inspired and blurred into other campaigns. The Communist Party, for instance, was in the forefront of struggles against racism, although in periods of ultraleft sectarianism, such as those that saw mobilizations against the 'lynch mob' atmosphere surrounding the trials of the Scottsboro Boys, much was squandered in the building of effective united front campaigns. Rank-and-file Communist Party members in Britain, Canada, and the United States constituted the backbone of the volunteer battalions that fought against Franco's forces in Spain, putting their bodies on the line in an armed struggle against fascism and for democracy. On the ground of most advanced western capitalist nations Communists conducted revolutionary educationals, held May Day rallies, celebrated anniversaries of the 1917 Revolution and the Paris Commune, walked picket lines, defended those arrested and serving time as class war prisoners (and supported the families of incarcerated victims of bourgeois 'justice'), and demonstrated for the causes they believed in.

It is impossible to miss the widening reach of international communism and the Revolution of 1917, as well as the interest in all things Soviet, in glancing at some of the 1930s titles of the Left Book Club, a London popular frontist endeavour; these publications ranged from *The Paris Commune of 1871* (1937) to *The Position of Women in the USSR* (1937) to *I Went To the Soviet Arctic* (1939). Indeed, art, literature, theatre, poetry, music, and representation became an increasingly contested area for the articulation of revolutionary anti-capitalism, so much so that Michael Denning considers what he calls 'the cultural front' in the United States a more important mobilization than the Comintern-declared Popular Front policy that helped frame the radical aesthetic of the 1930s.[26] Some of the Depression-era recruits to revolutionary communism, both children of working-class immigrants and middle-class intellectuals, returned to questions associated with the revolutionary avant-garde of 1917, addressing how art and politics were related: how might culture stimulate the revolutionary imagination and inspire anti-capitalist thinking? Workers' theatre, from its early incarnation as the amateur self-activity of unemployed workers, to later, more professional left-wing theatre groups, flourished as a reflection of 1930s dissent.

During the Congress of Industrial Organization upsurge of 1937, for instance, life seemed to be imitating art. Mark Blitzstein's 'proletarian opera' *The Cradle Will Rock* staged an impromptu performance about organizing in 'Steeltown, USA' in defiance of Works Project Administration [WPA] cuts to relief funding, and Clifford Odets' *Waiting for Lefty* opened at New York's Group Theatre, its rallying cry, 'STRIKE, STRIKE, STRIKE!!!' echoing picket line chants. These themes of working-class upsurge reverberated as never before in a growing body of left-wing fiction, poetry, art, photography and cultural criticism.[27] Commercially successful and eminently Popular Front productions had often been preceded by militant Third Period agit-prop performances, such as the Progressive Arts Clubs of Canada's *Eight Men Speak*, which took direct aim at the political persecution of the Canadian Communist Party in the early 1930s.

This cultural arena, especially as expressed in Canadian journals like *Masses* and *New Frontiers*, was also a particular focus of women's revolutionary activity, stimulating new discussion about socialism and women's emancipation. Writer and later renowned poet Dorothy Livesay, and theatre director 'Jim' (Eugenia) Watts tried to create a revolutionary alternative culture that exposed the exploitation, suffering and oppression of capitalism – for workers and families – contrasting the profit system's impoverishing impulses to the possibilities of communist collectivism. The means to this end was the creation of a class 'for itself', this consciousness developed by resistance nurtured in unions, welfare rights organizations, anti-fascist agitation, peace mobilizations, and cultural activities and productions of all kinds.

Not dissimilarly, in the United States communist women's cultural production also flourished in the form of poetry, fiction, journalism and political commentary, from better known authors like Meridel LeSueur, Agnes Smedley and Tillie Olsen to lesser-known writers documenting particular local struggles and issues. While communist women's cultural production was subsequently critiqued by feminists for its containment within a workerist 'male-dominated' paradigm, a 'masculine-modeled Marxism',[28] the attachment to and embrace of the possibility of revolutionary change, including a vision more attuned to women's domestic and sexual liberation, was very much part of this dissident oeuvre.

In Mexico, a cultural front also took shape in the 1920s, gathering ideological power during the Depression: the influence of Mexican communism was enhanced, according to Barry Carr, because of a vibrant circle of 'vanguard artistic and cultural movements, especially the revolutionary mural movement'.[29] By the time of the Popular Front, when Mexican communist women transitioned from the sectarian isolation of the Third Period to make common cause with (ruling party) PRI women in building an alliance against fascism and for women's suffrage and demands for secure livelihoods, a feminist political-cultural rapprochement was emerging. Communist women accustomed to singing the Internationale at their own meetings created a new hybrid culture that integrated the symbols and sensibilities from the internal Mexican revolution with established and long-understood forms of identification with the external socialist revolution, a process that temporarily, at least, facilitated a distinctly revolutionary 'culture of feeling' specific to the Mexican locale.[30]

CAPITALISM'S TRIUMPHS AND REVOLUTION'S PERSISTENCE: THE INSURGENT 'THIRD WORLD', 1945-1965

Capitalism weathered difficult storms in the 1930s and 1940s, triumphing, seemingly, over the crisis of production/accumulation/unemployment signaled by the global depression of the 1930s. One part of the solution to that devastating collapse was the international conflict of the Second World War, which resolved a crisis in the productive sphere of capitalist social relations only through the accelerated growth in economic activities related to armed confrontations among nations. That said, armament Keynesianism alone could provide no long-term fix for capitalism's internal contradictions. But it showed the way forward.

Arms production did help bankroll, in the advanced capitalist west, the emergence of a welfare state that, if never as all-encompassing as it was proclaimed to be, nonetheless closed some of the cracks through which too many of the disadvantaged had historically fallen. It also promoted the first truly far-seeing acknowledgement (never, of course, generalized among all employers) of the need for a state-orchestrated system mediating the relations of antagonistic capital and labour, now referred to as the postwar settlement. Not surprisingly, as the hot war of 1939-1945 cooled in armistice, and the longer deep-freeze of capitalism vs. communism hardened global relations into a new Cold War, one part of this postwar settlement was an intensified domestic war on communist dissidents inside the capitalist economies of the west, the nadir of this process reached in American McCarthyism. One crucial area of this political house cleaning was, understandably, the increasingly important trade unions. By the 1950s, revolutionary dissidents, be they Communist Party militants or adherents to smaller organizations of opposition like those of the fractured landscape of Trotskyism, were largely exiled from the labour movement.

If western capitalism gave the outward appearance of a settled stabilization, this 1945-1965 period would see revolution resurgent in what was then commonly referred to as the 'Third World'.[31] Anticolonial revolutionary movements in this 'Third World' were inextricably linked to the Bolshevik Revolution of 1917. A Tartar Muslim minority within Russia, led by the secular socialist Sultan Galiev, charted a course for an independent Muslim Communist Party and a predominantly Muslim state in the Middle Volga and the Southern Urals. Galiev championed a revolution that challenged the Great Russian chauvinism of Czarist Russia in the hopes of creating an alternative that trod lightly on religious freedom, but ultimately facilitated the gradual secularization of the Muslim masses whom he believed were trapped within an impoverished Islamic traditionalism. He initially proved useful to Joseph Stalin, but his ideas were soon cast aside; the Muslim Communist Party was stripped of its autonomy, and the promise of a large Muslim Republic rescinded. Eventually Galiev would come to believe that the socialist revolution would not necessarily resolve the problem of nationalities; that Muslim oppression had simply been reconfigured under Stalin; and that a Communist Colonial International, independent from the Soviet Third Communist International, was needed. Driven into a more nationalist Muslim position by Stalin's policies, he distanced himself from the dialectical, Bolshevik understandings of class and nationalism. Galiev soon found himself banished from Stalin's inner circle. He was the first high-ranking Communist Party figure ordered arrested in the Stalinist repression of the 1920s. Marginalized, rearrested, and eventually sentenced to ten years hard labour, Galiev had disappeared by 1940.[32]

The anti-colonialism of the 1945-1965 years was born under the shadow of this mixed legacy. On the one hand, as Tariq Ali and Fred Halliday have argued, the struggles for national liberation characteristic of the colonial world in this period had in fact been made possible in some ways by the promise of 1917. The making of a revolutionary workers' state, however transitory, had declared that capitalism's hegemony might well be broken at its weakest link. Increasingly, in the post-Second World War period, that vulnerable point was exposed: revolution might be reborn, in an age of triumphant capitalism, at precisely that corroding conjuncture where imperialism consolidated relations of super-exploitation incapable of rooting oppressed populations in allegiance to regimes of accumulation that drained and dispossessed far more than they developed. On the other hand, the very timing of this anti-colonial insurgency, poised as it was between the devastation of Europe during the Second World War and the escalating Cold War, ensured that the postwar American Empire took shape in part through its ideological counterrevolutionary overdrive. As the colonial revolution took inspiration and in some cases material support from the homeland of the original Bolshevik experiment, the legacies of 1917 worked themselves into a profusion of 'Third World' conflicts in new and complex Cold War ways. The United States, previously animated by a more localized view of its sphere of influence under the Monroe Doctrine, now broadened its post-Second World War Cold War reach to a global containment of communism.[33] Revolution's persistence conditioned counter-revolution's reaction which, in the case of the US, was considerably widened.

If the Bolsheviks had struggled and failed to resolve simultaneously the inextricably entwined dilemma of revolution – class exploitation *and* national oppression – the anti-colonial insurgencies of three decades later were often cast in terms that promised a reckoning with the older Bolshevik project. Thus, Régis Debray, surveying the long march of revolution in Latin America which encompassed unsuccessful guerrilla struggles in Argentina, Paraguay, Santo Domingo, Columbia, Ecuador, Venezuela, Peru, and Brazil (1959-1964), as well as the victorious Fidelista Cuban Revolution (1959), concluded (somewhat incongruously) that if Soviet-inspired communist parties were often a brake on the creation of Guevara-like revolutionary *foco* in the countryside of the rebellious peasantry, there was nonetheless an organic link between 'Third World' uprisings and Leninism.

It is impossible to disconnect the waves of revolutionary, anti-colonial struggle that convulsed not only Latin America, but also China, Korea, and Indochina in the immediate post-Second World War period from the influence of 1917 and the Soviet Union, even if Stalinism continued, as it had for decades, to squander revolutionary possibilities and bear responsibility for catastrophic defeats. Yet there were advances. If capitalism remained entrenched in Taiwan, South Korea, and South Vietnam, post-revolutionary societies were established, and their influence – particularly in the case of China and North Vietnam – on the emergence of western youth movements of a revolutionary bent in future decades would be extraordinary. Other radical mobilizations in the Far East were put down with brutal suppression, including in the Philippines and Malaya. Particularly violent was the case of Indonesia, where an anti-communist bloodbath led by right-wing General Suharto and aided by CIA intelligence resulted in the decimation of the Soviet-aligned Communist Party, with hundreds of thousands of PKI members and sympathizers slaughtered and President Sukarno placed under permanent house arrest.

In Africa, the Algerian independence struggle, victorious in 1962 and memorialized in Frantz Fanon's psychoanalytic advocacy of the cathartic consequences of revolutionary violence, was but one of a number of revolts – anti-colonial, nationalist, and socialist. These included struggles in Kenya and the extended Emergency during the 1950s; the independence struggle led by Patrice Lumumba in the Belgian Congo in 1960; the rise of Gamal Abdel Nasser in Egypt, where monarchy was overthrown, the Suez Canal nationalized, and a pan-Arab unity movement born; the most explicit anti-imperialist and African socialist initiative, the Ghanaian Revolution associated with Kwame Nkrumah, a founder of the Organization of African Unity and committed Pan-Africanist; and the long-drawn out wars of national liberation associated with Portugal's disintegrating colonial presence in Angola, Mozambique, Guinea-Bissau, Cape Verde, and São Tome.

The significance of the anticolonial struggles of this era was thus evident as early as 1955 with the Bandung Conference of Asian and African countries, where decolonization topped the list of concerns. By the time of the Accra Conferences of 1958, there could be no mistaking the extent to which an ongoing struggle against colonialism linked 'the new and politically self-conscious Africa' to comrades in progressive European movements.[34] The struggle for Africa would figure importantly in the tumultuous 1960s.

This set the stage for an experiment in African socialism. Jitendra Mohan outlined in the 1966 *Socialist Register* how this ferment was an affirmation of 'orginality', 'distinctiveness', and 'independence'. But there was also often a rejection of 'ideology' and refusal of the 'tyranny of concepts', perhaps too easily represented as European colonial imports. Mohan suggested that in the explosion of 1950s and 1960s African socialism, developments often dominated by indigenous elites pressured struggle in the direction of non-alignment with either capitalism or communism. The claim was routinely made among such African elites that their societies were 'classless'. This in Mohan's view tended to produce a 'socialism' that was at best an 'ill-tempered alloy of good intentions and bad plans'.[35]

The results were often less than exemplary: military coups decapitated the path to socialism in Ghana and elsewhere; the beginnings of an independence struggle in Malawi were truncated by Prime Minister Dr. H. K. Banda, who cultivated ties to imperial Britain and white South Africa; while in Congo-Brazzaville a rhetoric of 'champagne Marxism' coexisted with corruption and close ties with colonial power in France. Nonetheless, as the Arusha Declaration of 1967 in Tanzania suggested, and much of the history of struggle in South Africa confirmed, anti-colonialism in Africa was often inseparable from calls for self-reliance, greater democratic participation, mobilization of the poor landed and urban masses, and an expansive theorizing, culminating in movements and even uprisings that marched under the flag of socialist possibility. Too often, to be sure, and especially as the global capitalist economy constricted in crisis as the 1970s unfolded, this socialist sensibility seemed strangled as the material foundations of neocolonial production and exchange withered under pressures of declining markets for Africa's raw materials and massive increases in the costs of import necessities, especially pronounced with the 'oil shock' of 1973.

This objective limitation was mirrored by similar constraints in the subjective sphere, especially where armed insurrection consolidated vanguard forces, such as the Mozambique Liberation Front, or Frelimo. Frelimo has been interpreted as verification of the validity of Frantz Fanon's theories on the salutary consequences of anti-colonial violence. As the leading contingent in the struggle for independence in Mozambique, Frelimo fought a protracted war against opponents, including South African advocates of apartheid, eventually declaring itself a Marxist-Leninist Party and consolidating a one-party state in which the danger of authoritarianism was ever-present. Yet Frelimo, as John Saul suggests, did not so much stifle popular initiative as fail to encourage it sufficiently:

> After independence the scale became infinitely vaster, the stratum of middle-level cadre too thin on the ground and too ill-trained, the challenges – not least South Africa's ongoing war – literally overwhelming ... Not surprisingly, even the most solid senior leaders have been reduced under such circumstances to fire-fighting a seemingly endless series of emergencies rather than finding time to concentrate on the slow, patient, ongoing political work which would serve to consolidate a firmer political basis for the revolution.[36]

Jean-Paul Sartre's famous preface to Frantz Fanon's *The Wretched of the Earth* (1961) captured well how exploitation and oppression had come together under the anti-colonial banner, 'Natives of all under-developed countries, unite!' While cognizant of the advanced capitalist world's exploitation of the resources and labour of the 'Third World', Sartre also wrote of the abstract philosophical assumption of universality which served as cover for this plunder: 'On the other side of the ocean there was a race of less-than-humans, who, thanks to us, might reach our status a thousand years hence ...' This history of colonialism enslaved some and allowed others 'a simulacrum of phoney independence'. Capitalist colonization has 'multiplied divisions and opposing groups, fashioned classes and sometimes even racial prejudices, and has endeavoured by every means to bring about and intensify the stratification of colonized societies'. Fanon's book, Sartre concluded, announced the inevitable making of 'Third World unity', a work in progress that would culminate in a 'national revolution' that 'must be socialist'.[37]

This message resounded throughout the 'Third World', but it also boomeranged back on the 'First World', as Sartre (if not, perhaps, Fanon) intended, especially via the 'Black' and 'Red Power' movements of African American and Indigenous resistance that exploded into prominence in the United States and Canada in the 1960s. Both Stokely Carmichael and Eldridge Cleaver venerated Fanon, as did Pierre Vallières, theoretician of Quebec's Front de Libération du Québec [FLQ]. And Indigenous activists of the era, from Lee Maracle [Bobbi Lee] to Harold Adams, were unequivocal in seeing Fanon as central to their recognition of the need for a revolutionary challenge to colonialism.[38]

Perry Anderson once summed up the conjuncture of the 1950s as encompassing four structural components: 'a struggle between capitalist and socialist economic systems, a contest between imperialist and indigenous national systems, a conflict between parliamentary and authoritarian political systems, and a confrontation between technologically equivalent and reciprocally suicidal military systems.' Thus, 'International class struggle, defence of democracy, revolt against colonialism, arms race: each slogan indicates one "moment" in the Cold War and denies the other. The reality is their infinite imbrication and interpenetration.'[39]

Revolution signalled the nature of this constellation of structural impasse. As the Swedish New Leftist Göran Therborn suggested insightfully in a brief 1968 essay, 'From Petrograd to Saigon', the ties that bound developments of this period inextricably together were inevitably located along the axis of revolutionary thought and practice that reached across the span of capitalism vs. socialism, testing the triumphalism of a post-Second World War ideological acquisitive individualism ensconced in the nation states of the developed northern hemisphere *and* the increasingly constricted material base of actually existing socialism, now claustrophobically contained within the obvious limitations of Stalinism.[40]

Untainted by troubling attachment to Stalinism's debilitating influence, this reigniting of the fires of revolutionary possibility had been evident in the emergence of the first British New Left in the late 1950s. The Suez Crisis was then seen as evidence of an ossified capitalist imperialism and its reluctance to give up the ghost of empire, while the USSR's 1956 invasion of Hungry and the subsequent suppression of dissent tarred the Stalinist state with a like brush of brutalizing 'First World' subordination. A few years later, the second American New Left unfurled its 1962 banner, the Port Huron Statement, breaking from complacency, refusing the perverted dreams of Stalinism, decrying poverty and deprivation amidst affluence, insisting on an end to the policies of nuclear arms deterrence, embracing both the colonial revolution abroad and the civil rights revolution at home, and shunning the ideologies of anti-communism and the consumerism of the marketplace. Seeking 'the unattainable,' this New Left proclaimed it was doing nothing less than avoiding 'the unimaginable'.[41]

1968 AND THE NEW (LEFT) REVOLUTION

The birth of the New Left, whether in Britain or America, was thus inseparable from the ossified structures of a Cold War world frozen in rigid oppositional blocs. But 'Third World' movements of national liberation unsettled Marxist-Leninist understandings of class struggle just as they challenged the hegemonic hold of imperialism and capitalism throughout the global South. In this changed political climate, the language of revolution shifted gears. While it referenced 1917 and its antecedents, refusing the logic of a post-Second World War 'free world' animated by a regime of accumulation and an ideology of acquisitive individualism, it simultaneously rejected the bureaucratized 'Soviet Marxism' of a USSR now associated with Stalinist atrocity, laid bare for all to see in Khrushchev's revelations and the tanks that rolled into Budapest in 1956 and Prague in 1968. As Herbert Marcuse noted in *Soviet Marxism,* the machinery of state power, West and East, was now 'bereft of any emancipatory dimension'.[42]

As the Vietnam imbroglio, with its pressures on both the ethical-moral standing of the state and the Keynesian balance of guns or butter, propelled the domestic American political economy towards crisis, the United States was impaled on the ever-sharpening horns of youthful protests, inner-city black insurgencies, and a war across the world that it could not win. For the first time since the mass industrial-union struggles that reached from the late 1930s into the late 1940s, young workers exploded in rebellious antagonism, upping the decibel level of class struggle in articulations of alienation that were followed, in the next decade, by mobilizations of racialized and women workers intent on securing some of the benefits of labour organization.[43]

The Soviets fared no better. Their backing of 'Third World' liberation movements rang most hollow in European satellites such as Czechoslovakia, faced with 'Moscow Diktats' suppressing workers' strikes or student protests, while stifling a rising tide of nationalist resentment at Soviet subordination. As workers and students organized job actions and sit-ins, the demonstrations of discontent took on the trappings of a rebellion: the USSR responded ultimately with repression and its own 'occupation', military-style. Harkening back to 1917, revolutionary graffiti proclaimed, 'Lenin awake, Brezhnev has gone mad!' With the Soviet Union, like its capitalist counterpart the United States, plunged into escalating crises culminating, by the opening of the 1980s, in the layers of challenge associated with Poland's

Solidarnosc, the stage was set for the implosion of 'actually existing socialism' in the late 1980s and 1990s.[44]

By that time the ideological arsenal of counter-revolution had been well stocked with the defection, over the course of the 1970s and 1980s, of a significant cohort of erstwhile leftists to the camp of a *revanchist* right. This 'turn' was, of course, reinforced and sustained by the myriad ways capitalist hegemony consolidated amidst the disciplinary regime of routine crises that reached from the fiscal distress of western capitalist states in 1973 to the financial meltdown of 2007-2008. Trade unions were assaulted, social movements driven inward in their embrace of particularity, and critical analysis retreated into an eschewing of the very 'master narratives' necessary to make sense of a new world order that proclaimed 'an end of history', a coded erasure of revolutionary possibility.

This four-decade long retreat, coerced on the one hand and acquiesced to on the other, now blinds us to the extent that revolution remained very much on the agenda throughout the 1960s and into the 1970s despite the tarnishing of 1917's accomplishments through Stalinization. Revolution seemed the antidote, at times like May 1968, not only to capitalism and its discontents, but to actually existing socialism and its shortcomings, with students *and* workers, feminists *and* Marxists, drawn to the legacies of revolt associated with 1917 and other instances of insurgent upheaval. The umbilical cord reaching from 1917 to 1968 was easily discernible, even in the post-mortems. Thus the *New Left Review* introduced an issue devoted entirely to the 1968 events, with essays by Ernest Mandel, Jean-Marie Vincent, André Gorz, André Glucksmann, and a reprinted 1908 essay of Lenin's on the student movement, with a statement that confirmed how revolution, lived out in anti-colonial uprisings and wars of national liberation in the 1950s and early-to-mid 1960s, was now grasped as necessary, even possible, in the heart of the imperialist metropoles.[45]

The events of May '68, moreover, while often associated with Paris alone, were but one of a number of 1968-1969 socio-political explosions that reverberated throughout the world, and that included mass protests, often quite violent, in London, Rome, Berlin, Chicago, New York, various central and eastern European countries behind the Iron Curtain, and throughout the developing world. In Kingston, Jamaica riots broke out as the government refused to allow the Marxist historian Walter Rodney to return to his teaching post at the University of the West Indies; student protests in Mexico City culminated in the Tlateloko massacre; Brazilian guerrillas escalated their war against the military dictatorship; and in Pakistan the People's Party opposition movement of oft-jailed Zulfikar Ali Bhutto, guided by an ostensibly socialist platform, galvanized students and workers in struggles that routinely broke out into the streets and proved deadly.

New concerns animated many such struggles. Bureaucracy, suggested Isaac Deutscher in the 1969 *Socialist Register*, now occupied a pivotal place in the analytic imperatives of socialist thought since it was impossible to deny that the apparatus of governance in all societies, regardless of their social and political organization, was contributing to widespread malaise, now fashionably described as 'alienation'. This was something Marx had not anticipated, stressed Marcuse, who concluded that revolution was now more than ever before mandatory. Its 're-examination' as something more than 'a merely abstract and speculative undertaking' was critical if the 'subordination of man to the instruments of his labour, to the total, overwhelming apparatus of production and destruction' was not to reach the point 'of an all but incontrollable power' that was 'objectified' and 'self-propelling', dragging the 'indoctrinated and integrated people along' behind a 'mobilized national interest'. Deutscher, too, recognized revolution's ongoing significance, stressing that in spite of Stalinization and ostensible de-Stalinization, 'Whatever may be the malaise, the heartsearchings and the gropings of the post-Stalin era testify in their own way to the continuity of the revolutionary epoch'. For Deutscher, decades of totalitarian rule inside the Soviet Union had 'robbed the people of their capacity for self-expression, spontaneous action, and self-organization'. That said, Deutscher acknowledged that even Trotsky, just before his assassination by a Stalinist agent, insisted that 'the revolution had not come to an end', concluding that, 'The great divide of 1917 still looms as large as ever in the consciousness of mankind'.[46]

What of womankind? A revitalized women's movement, which burst on the scene with considerable force in the late 1960s, had been galvanized within the New Left, but also in the house of labour and the anti-nuclear movement that began in the late 1950s and soon morphed into anti-war protests and support for anti-colonial revolutionary movements in Vietnam and elsewhere. Many histories gloss over or marginalize these multiple origins, their understandings constrained by what is often mislabelled 'second wave feminism'. Given that the wave terminology fundamentally ignores communist, anarchist and socialist women's organizing, especially between the interwar period and the 1960s, it is not just historically flawed but deeply biased against forms of revolutionary feminism, which remained globally vibrant in these decades.

Nonetheless, a renewal in women's self-organization and a more expansive theorizing about colonialism, socialism and feminism was apparent by the late

1960s. As much as this push for a theory and practice of women's liberation was indeed indebted to Marxism and the struggles of revolutionaries in the past, feminism's development in this period was not unambiguously sympathetic to older communist traditions: if anything, revolution in this realm was situated ambivalently with respect to the heritage of 1917.

Thus Juliet Mitchell's decisively important 'Women: The Longest Revolution', published in the *New Left Review* in 1966, was premised on the notion that 'The struggle for women's equality has always been seen by socialists as part of the struggle for socialism'. Mitchell alluded lightly to 1917, drawing far more on the writings of Marx and Engels and juxtaposing them to the utopianism of Charles Fourier, Wilhelm Reich, and Herbert Marcuse. She did reference Lenin's remarks to Clara Zetkin, accepting that inasmuch as the struggle for sexual freedom was an important component of a 'wild and revolutionary' encounter with repression, it was nonetheless perceived by many orthodox Marxists as 'quite bourgeois ... a hobby of the intellectuals' and thus foreign to the 'class conscious, fighting, proletariat'. This did not curb masculinist New Left critiques of socialist feminism, rooted in confident assertions that the emancipation of women would only take place through 'class struggle, subsuming feminism and at the same time transcending it'.[47]

The 1960s women's liberation movement, conceived in part within the New Left but also born in a proliferation of feminist consciousness-raising groups, women's collectives, and mobilizations/campaigns for abortion, workplace and other rights, grappled from its beginnings with revolution and its contradictory heritage. Canadian socialist-feminist Margaret Benston, a member of the Vancouver Women's Caucus, was prompted by her readings of Marx, Mitchell, Marcuse, and the Trotskyist economist Ernest Mandel to pen what would become one of the most influential short texts of socialist feminism, 'The Political Economy of Women's Liberation'. Travelling across Canada in mimeographed versions, Benston's essay, once in print, leapfrogged around the globe, translated into Spanish, French, Italian, Swedish, German, and Japanese. It resonated internationally with the writings of Selma James and Mariarosa Della Costa about wages, housework, and the capitalist mode of production. In Italy sections of the women's movement called themselves Benstonistas.[48]

But the tensions in the New Left around feminism were nonetheless acute, and prompted women to ponder their relations with male brothers and lovers as well as the revolutionary heritage that all such activists inevitably found themselves debating. The Canadian New Left grouping, the Student Union for Peace Action (SUPA), gave rise to a quintessential feminist document, 'Sisters, Brothers, Lovers ... Listen'.[49] Accenting liberation and love, alienation and anger, conformism and creativity, the document insisted on the necessity to 'act as though the revolution had occurred by our relationships with one another'. Those relationships, inside SUPA, were anything but egalitarian.

How this emerging feminism related to the implosion of the New Left at the end of the 1960s and into the 1970s is an important international history largely still untold. By the early 1970s, the New Left was in disarray and some socialist feminists who had struggled within it had gravitated to vanguard organizations, either Trotyskist or 'new communist' (often Maoist). Today's conventional wisdom, so hostile to the revolutionary left, suggests that attention to gender and sexuality received a hearing in such parties but over time seemed destined to get short, revolutionary shrift. That said, there is no denying the extent to which the politics of women's liberation fused with the legacies of revolution in a rebellious era.[50]

The theoretical and practical linkages between anti-colonial, Marxist and feminist thinking were articulated most visibly by feminists involved in the anti-war movement, some of whom made common cause across international borders with Indochinese women, arranging anti-war conferences on neutral ground in Canada or travelling to Vietnam to express their support. Revolutionary strivings were also visible in the Black women's liberation movement which used theoretical touchstones from anti-colonial thought in their organizing, and in Quebec's feminist movement, which by 1968 was linked to the impulses of revolutionary nationalism in francophone Canada as well as developments in 'France, global anti-colonial liberation struggles, the cultural revolution in China, and American Black liberation struggles'.[51] In their paper, *Quebecoise Deboutte!*, feminists analyzed the subjection of women as a product of capitalist and imperialist structures as well as gender ideologies, particularly the oppression of the private, patriarchal, heterosexual family. Revolutionary feminists not only drew on anti-colonial ideas, but subjected their own attachment to nation to the same indictment, critiquing the dispossession of Indigenous peoples as a project of primitive accumulation and a white Christian assault on Indigenous gender relations, presented as far more egalitarian than conventional contemporary socio-sexual norms.

The marriage of anti-colonial politics with women's liberation might seem more clear-cut in African-American and Chicana organizing, or in Quebec, but efforts to create a revolutionary women's liberation that recognized class exploitation and imperialism were also expressed in other women's newspapers, writing, and organizing. Revolutionary ideals and heroic antecedents were routinely discussed, not necessarily favouring any specific tradition, but through exploring them all: anarchism, syndicalism, Marxism, socialism. However heterogeneous their definitions of 'left', there was a profound desire to develop theory that advanced the analysis of capitalism, colonialism, patriarchy, racism, and social reproduction, making the transformation of gender and sexual roles as earth shattering a prospect as the abolition of classes.

Rowbotham's *Women, Resistance and Revolution* was an exemplar of this kind of popular intervention. A rapprochement with Marxist and socialist ideas was sought, but without abandoning new insights on gender oppression, domestic labour, and sexual liberation. While women and the colonized shared certain features of cultural, symbolic and psychological marginalization, Rowbotham wrote, the 'analogy' of 'sexual and racial imperialism stops there, partly because the colonizer's women have themselves enjoyed the spoils of imperial domination'.[52] The explosion of writing about various marriages, divorces and integrations of Marxism and feminism, along with the historical recuperation of the revolutionary thought of women like Emma Goldman and Alexandra Kollantai, exemplifies such strivings for revolutionary recovery, the search for a reconciliation seemingly severed in Marxism's and feminism's New Left rupture.

The resurgence in such revolutionary thinking appeared to decline by the late 1980s. Certainly, American histories of feminism often appear to be built around a common narrative of feminists 'leaving the left,' abandoning masculine Marxism and its many flaws; even efforts to develop a socialist-feminist praxis were decreed 'decimated' by the 1980s, with the ultra-left cited as the villain. While it is incontrovertible that Marxism and the revolutionary left were politically and theoretically marginalized by the 1980s, this declension story ignores the complexity of the politico-intellectual climate. First, revolutionary streams of anti-imperialist, left feminism persisted in theory and practice, though they were less popularly known or promoted. Dilemmas that women revolutionaries struggled with since 1917, such as the transformation of social reproduction, remained very much alive. Second, the resilient resurgence of liberal and radical feminism has always been an American story, overshadowing but not necessary reflecting global feminist politics. Third, feminist revolutionary ideas were re-shaped within cultural paradigms that were appealing in terms of sexual liberation and identity politics, but which Marxist-feminists have argued reflected the dominant suppositions of ever more powerful forces of neoliberalism. As in so much, the 'woman question' in our times mirrors the trajectory of revolution's reception.

CONCLUSION: REVOLUTION'S CURRENCY AND THE CONTEMPORARY CRISIS OF CAPITALISM

How do we assess revolution's currency in our particular moment? It is difficult not to accent the contradictory nature of recent developments.

To be sure, there are abundant signs that the revolutionary left and its attachment to the legacies of 1917 are on the decline. This has been evident not only with respect to the fortunes of socialist-feminism, but in terms of the general waning influence of revolutionaries and even leftists of all stripes in the labour movement, and of Marxism within the academy where, aside from pockets of influence, it is a marginalized voice. The implosion and decline of revolutionary organizations of the 'new communist' and Trotskyist kind, first evident in the 1970s and continuing over the next decades, is but one expression of this, as is the collapse of 'actually existing socialism' in the Soviet Union, now gone, and throughout once-Soviet central and eastern Europe, largely incorporated into the European Union (EU). In outposts of the planned economy, such as China and Cuba, moreover, the drift to capitalist restoration is discernible, if not yet able to be judged irreversible. The experiment of African Socialism, in which so much hope was invested in the 1960s, has slowly spiraled downward, the arc of politics trending towards authoritarianism. The long march of the Brazilian left to power, and the subsequent reckoning with the terror of right-wing military dictatorship, stalled in the morass of populism, concessions to austerity, and corruption that constituted Workers' Party governance, a development hardly unique throughout Latin America. The promise of the Arab Spring, so electrifying in 2011, is in an undeniable blackout. Within an unstable EU, Greece's Syriza, a coalition of the radical left constituted under the colours of revolutionary politics (red), ecological commitments (green), and diverse social movements (purple), suffered humiliation at the hands of the large national capitalist power brokers, headed by Germany. Even at the point of resistance, the mercurial politics of anarchist-inflected anti-globalization struggles that erupted in the years reaching from the Battle for Seattle in 1998 to the Occupy Wall Street mobilizations of 2011 fit uneasily, at the juncture of theory and practice, with the legacies of 1917. In any case, their concrete achievements have been ambiguous.

This however is not the sum total of what needs to be addressed, for capitalism *will,* inevitably, push people toward resistance. Within the advanced capitalist political economies of the West, for instance, economic crises have now become so routine – their calendar of catastrophe squeezed into shorter and shorter time-frames – as to be part of the fabric of everyday life. Arguably at no time since the Great Depression have the material conditions of so many been so bad. Precariousness and underemployment define the lives of youth, women, and peoples of colour; rampant unemployment erodes the prospects of the masses; and the 'freedoms' demanded in the name of globalization and privatization run rampant within states that have gone into ideological overdrive, taking their toll in the disruptions of a relentless restructuring. Adding insult to injury, racist, homophobic, and misogynist mobilizations are disfiguring political culture. Combined with the assault on trade union freedoms and the dismantling of the welfare state, the threat to hard-won material entitlements in the economic sphere and within the arenas of civil and reproductive rights is so staggering that it has prompted periodic populist and left-wing upheavals even within the conventional mainstream of political life.

These have shaken to the core the seemingly settled regimes of both the Republican and Democratic Parties in the United States, where the presidential nomination process in 2016 was marked by tumultuous rallies, repudiation of 'the Establishment', and claims that a 'political revolution' is in the making. Popular discontent does not necessarily develop in left-wing ways, of course, and even when it unfurls under the banner of progressivism it is unlikely, without the kind of unambiguous socialist interventions decidedly lacking in our times, to take a path that is distinguishable from a politics of liberal platitude. Nonetheless, discontent is, in specific political formations of our times, leaning left, as indicated in many developments in the global South, within the Labour Party in Britain, and in Canada's New Democratic Party, as dissenters have recently urged an ambiguous leap to counteract the party's rightward shift and disastrous 2015 electoral showing. Across Europe there are unmistakable signs of this reconfiguration, although Spain's Podemos and Greece's Syriza must be set alongside the disturbing rise of anti-system parties of the extreme (even fascistic) right. As China's bureaucratic elite charts an uncertain course in its intensifying industrialization and aggressive attempt to corner global markets, there are unmistakable signs that an insurgent working class is struggling to break free from the chains of its peculiar exploitation and oppression.

The point is not that we are on the verge of revolutionary breakthroughs. Far from it. But the volatility of the current moment, and mounting evidence that capitalism cannot forever balance the books of its antagonistic class relations, just as the contradictory essence of regimes straddling the socialist/capitalist divide unsteadily must eventually topple into one camp or the other, suggests not only the need for new political options, but the possibility that they might gain traction in wider circles of the dispossessed and the discontented. The task for the left is daunting, but one small part of what must be done is to make sure that the current conjuncture is in fact cognizant of the history of revolution and what it offers us in terms of political insight.

This is a daunting challenge since a central component of neoliberalism's ideological project has been to stifle, suppress, and suffocate the heritage of 1917 and its commitment to ongoing revolutionary change. This is one of neoliberalism's most significant successes: the extent to which it has extinguished revolution's *longue durée*, the articulation of a commitment to the project that was first realized, albeit briefly and incompletely, in 1917, and that remains central to reconstructing the world in humanity's best interests. For decades, even in the face of considerable anguished reassessment of the Soviet revolution, it proved impossible for the left to abandon understandings associated with the emancipatory aspects of 1917's promise. This carried through into the upheavals of the 1960s, even as a 'New' Left distanced itself from much that was seemingly old, an endeavour that ultimately proved impossible.

As the global capitalist economy crashed in the 1970s, the anti-colonial independence struggles of the post-Second World War wound down, as did the spirit of '68. As strike waves crested in the mid-1970s, trade unionism stalled, its generalized transnational momentum running headlong into a wall of material constraint, critical bricks of that barrier being widespread economic stagnation, soaring inflation, and mass unemployment. Further heightening the challenge to combativity was a resurgent right, which took to the hustings of mass politics with the message of neoliberalism, soon to be the reigning orthodoxy within the corridors of state power. This combined with other developments more internal to the platform, politics, and parties of revolution, eviscerated labour and the extra-parliamentary left.

Many erstwhile dissidents, reeling from the failures of the New Left and growing increasingly disillusioned with Marxist 'statism', found themselves drawn to the tenets of this new 'post', neoliberal ideology, with its claim that all authoritarianisms – of the left or the right – could be curbed by invoking the self-management of the deregulated marketplace. Foucault was but one of many voices emanating from the ostensible left championing 'the disappearance of terrorism, of theoretical monopolies, and of the monarchy of accepted thinking', one part of which was revolution. Not for nothing had Jean-Paul Sartre said of Michel Foucault, as early as 1966, that he constituted, 'the last barrier that the bourgeoisie can still raise against Marx'.[53]

André Glucksmann's accelerated devolution from a May '68 militant to an early 1970s member of the Maoist group Gauche Prolétarienne, to the author of the 'new philosophy' text *The Master Thinkers* (1977) which pilloried Marx, Hegel, Fichte, and Nietzsche as architects of the ostensible state-science-reason-knowledge-socialism complex that supposedly prefigured the gulag and the concentration camp, was but the most dramatic individual display of an influential politics indiscriminately congealing the Nazi and Soviet experiences – a position long associated with liberal Cold War repudiations of a rather elastic 'totalitarianism'. Foucault, as Michael Scott Christofferson has recently argued, played a not insignificant role in shoring up the fortunes of Glucksmann and facilitating the wider drift of this new politics assailing 'the state-revolution with all its final solutions' in general.[54] If French intellectual life seemed to take longer and more wildly venturesome strides in this direction, across the expanse of 'critical theory' in the 1970s and beyond, these positions gained a certain understated credence, lessening Marxism's appeal. As Stephano Azzara has noted, 'the victory of neoliberalism can be measured by the degree to which it has been able – sometimes explicitly but more often without anyone realizing it – to penetrate and restructure the vision of its opponents'.[55]

Bringing revolution and the emancipatory vision of socialist-feminism back in to the theory and practice of the left, reconnecting thinking and struggles with the legacies of 1917 and their *longue durée*, is thus one component of the contemporary challenge of our times. With neoliberalism so ascendant, continuity between the present of the left and its pasts has not only been broken, but has also in some measure been forgotten. Historical recovery is a small but important part of the renewal of the left. This does not mean repeating the mistakes and shortcomings of the past, condemning our practice and our analysis to remain in the shadows of earlier deficiency. Rather, revolution's present, like its past, is necessarily subject to the same expansive understandings that have always animated the best in the conceptualization and concrete struggles of those who, like William Morris, imagine their purpose as revolutionaries to be to stir the people up and 'not to be contented with a little'. We need, in our current times, a reinvigorated left agency, one that will turn the tides of destructive change – which for too long have been crashing humanity's beleaguered shorelines – in entirely new, and socialist, directions. To do this is to extend the distinctive heritage of 1917, making it resonate with our present.

NOTES

1 Geoff Eley, *Forging Democracy: The History of the Left in Europe, 1850-2000*, New York: Oxford University Press, 2002, p. ix.
2 Régis Debray, *Praised Be Our Lords: The Autobiography,* New York: Verso, 2007, p. 75.
3 Quotes from E.P. Thompson, *William Morris: Romantic to Revolutionary,* New York: Pantheon, 1977, pp. 305, 311.

4   E.P. Thompson, 'Revolution', *Out of Apathy,* Thompson et al., eds., London: Steeves and Sons, 1960, pp. 302-5.
5   We diverge, for instance, on the not inconsequential question of socialist organization. One of us, a socialist-feminist, is more sceptical of Leninist understandings of mobilization, sympathizing with critiques put forward by Sheila Rowbotham and others in the 1970s. The other, a historian of Trotskyism, sides more with Neil Davidson's recent position that we might do well to take Lenin more seriously. See Sheila Rowbotham, Lynne Segal, and Hilary Wainright, *Beyond the Fragments: Feminism and the Making of Socialism,* London: Merlin, 2013 (with new introductions to this third edition by each of the co-authors); Neil Davidson, "Is Social Revolution Still Possible in the Twenty-First Century," *Journal of Contemporary Central and Eastern Europe,* 23, 2015, p. 144.
6   Eley, *Forging Democracy,* 188.
7   Elizabeth Waters, 'In the Shadow of the Comintern: The Communist Women's Movement, 1920-43,' in Sonia Kruks, Rayna Rapp, Marilyn B. Young, eds., *Promissory Notes: Women in the Transition to Socialism,* New York: Monthly Review Press, 1989, p. 33.
8   Kirsten Marie Delegard, *Battling Miss Bolsheviki: The Origins of Female Conservatism in the United States,* Philadelphia: University of Pennsylvania Press, 2012, esp. pp. 47-51.
9   Jocelyn Olcott, *Revolutionary Women in Postrevolutionary Mexico,* Durham: Duke University Press, 2005, p. 50.
10 Joan Sangster, '*Robitnystia* and the Porcupinism Debate: Reassessing Ethnicity, Gender and Class in Early Canadian Communism,' *Labour/Le Travail,* 56(Fall), 2005, pp. 51-89.
11 Perry Anderson, *Considerations on Western Marxism,* London: NLB, 1976, p. 20.
12 Chad Pearson, 'Fighting the "Red Danger": Employers and Anti-Communism,' in Robert Justin Goldstein, ed., *Little 'Red Scares': Anticommunism and Political Repression in the United States, 1921-1946,* Burlington, Vermont: Ashgate, 2014, pp. 135-64, with quote at p. 143.
13 William Preston, Jr., *Aliens and Dissenters: Federal Suppression of Radicals, 1903-1933,* Cambridge, Massachusetts: Harvard University Press, 1963, pp. 181-272.
14 Donna T. Haverty-Stacke, *America's Forgotten Holiday: May Day and Nationalism, 1867-1960,* New York: New York University Press, 2009, pp. 105-41.
15 Selig Perlman, *A Theory of the Labor Movement,* New York, 1928, pp. 204, 232, quoted in David Montgomery, *The Fall of the House of Labor,* New York: Cambridge University Press, 1987, 453-4.
16 Anderson, *Considerations on Western Marxism;* Georg Lukács, *A Defence of History and Class Consciousness: Tailism and the Dialectic,* New York: Verso, 2000.
17 Barbara Foley, *Spectres of 1919: Class and Nation in the Making Of The New Negro,* Chicago: University of Illinois Press, 2003, p. 7.
18 Foley, *Spectres of 1919,* p. 50.
19 Jeffrey B. Perry, *Hubert Harrison: The Voice of Harlem Radicalism, 1883-1918,* New York: Columbia University Press, 2009.
20 Claude McKay, "If We Must Die," *Liberator,* 2(July), 1919, p. 21.
21 Much of this history can be gleaned from Cedric J. Robinson, *Black Marxism: The Making of the Black Radical Tradition,* London: Zed Books, 1983.
22 See Manning Marable, *Malcolm X: A Life of Reinvention,* New York: Viking, 2011; Jeffrey Haas, *The Assassination of Fred Hampton: How the FBI and the Chicago Police Murdered a Black Panther,* Chicago: Chicago Review Press, 2009.
23 R. B. Whitney, *Reds in America,* New York: Beckwith Press, 1924, p. 189.
24 Quoted in Joan Sangster, *Dreams of Equality: Women on the Canadian Left, 1920-1950,* Toronto: McClelland and Stewart, 1989, p. 94.
25 Bryan D. Palmer, *Revolutionary Teamsters: The Minneapolis Truckers' Strikes of 1934,*

Chicago: Haymarket, 2014.
26 Michael Denning, *The Cultural Front: The Laboring of American Culture in the Twentieth Century*, London and New York: Verso, 1996.
27 There is no better entre to this literary left than Alan Wald's trilogy: *Exiles from a Future Time: The Forging of a Mid-Twentieth Century Literary Left*, Chapel Hill: University of North Carolina Press, 2002; *Trinity of Passion: The Literary Left and the Antifascist Crusade*, Chapel Hill: University of North Carolina Press, 2007; *American Night: The Literary Left in the Era of the Cold War*, Chapel Hill: University of North Carolina Press, 2012.
28 Kathleen Brown, '"The Savagely Fathered and Un-Mothered" World of the Communist Party, USA: Feminism, Maternalism, and Mother Bloor,' *Feminist Studies*, 25(Autumn 1999), p. 539; Paula Rabinowitz, 'Women and U.S. Literary Radicalism,' in Charlotte Nekola and Paula Rabinowitz, eds., *Writing Red: An Anthology of American Women Writers, 1930-1940*, New York: The Feminist Press, 1987, p. 5.
29 Barry Carr, *Marxism and Communism in Twentieth Century Mexico*, Lincoln: University of Nebraska Press, 1992, p. 35.
30 Olcott, *Revolutionary Women*, p. 135.
31 See, for instance, Peter Worsley, *The Third World*, London: Weidenfeld and Nicolson, 1964.
32 Maxime Rodinson, *Marxism and the Muslim World*, London: Zed Press, 1979, pp. 133-41.
33 Fred Halliday, *The Making of the Second Cold War*, London: Verso, 1983, pp. 81-133; Tariq Ali, *Speaking of Empire and Resistance: Conversations with Tariq Ali*, New York: New Press, 2005, pp. 15, 28.
34 Seng Tan and Amitav Acharya, eds., *Bandung Revisited: The Legacy of the 1955 Asian-African Conference for International Order*, Singapore: National University of Singapore, 2008; John Rex, "The Meaning of the Accra Conferences," *New Reasoner*, 9(Summer), 1959, pp. 84-9.
35 Mohan 'Varieties of African Socialism', in Ralph Miliband and John Saville, eds., *The Socialist Register 1966*, London: Merlin, 1966, pp. 228, 232.
36 John Saul, ed., *A Difficult Road: The Transition to Socialism in Mozambique*, New York: Monthly Review Press, 1985, p. 101.
37 Jean-Paul Sartre, 'Preface', *The Wretched of the Earth*, New York: Grove, 1966, pp. 7-26.
38 Bryan D. Palmer, *Canada's 1960s: The Ironies of Identity in a Rebellious Era*, Toronto: University of Toronto Press, 2009, pp. 14, 197, 235; Sean Mills, *The Empire Within: Postcolonial Thought and Political Activism in Sixties Montreal*, Montreal and Kingston: McGill-Queen's University Press, esp. pp. 30-34.
39 Perry Anderson, 'The Left in the Fifties', *New Left Review*, 29(January-February), 1965, p. 12.
40 Göran Therborn, 'From Petrograd to Saigon', *New Left Review*, 48(March-April), 1968, pp. 3-11.
41 Tom Hayden, *The Port Huron Statement: The Visionary Call of the 1960s Revolution*, New York: Thunder's Mouth Press, 2005.
42 Herbert Marcuse, *Soviet Marxism: A Critical Analysis,* New York: Columbia University Press, 1958.
43 Ernest Mandel, 'Where is America Going?' *New Left Review*, 54(March-April), 1969, pp. 3-16; Ernest Mandel, *Late Capitalism*, London: Verso, 1978, pp. 584-5; Peter B. Levy, *The New Left and Labor in the 1960s,* Chicago: University of Illinois Press, 1994; Jefferson Cowie, *Stayin' Alive: The 1970s and the Last Days of the Working Class*, New York: New Press, 2010.

44 Tamara Deutscher, 'Voices of Dissent', in Ralph Miliband and John Saville, eds., *The Socialist Register 1978*, London: Merlin, 1978, pp. 22-43; Pavel Tomalek, 'The Student Action', *New Left Review*, 53(January-February), 1969, pp. 13-22.
45 'Introduction', *New Left Review*, 52(November-December 1968), pp. 1-8.
46 Isaac Deutscher, 'Roots of Bureaucracy,' in Ralph Milliband and John Saville, eds., *The Socialist Register 1969*, London: Merlin, 1969, pp. 9-28; Herbert Marcuse, 'Re-Examination of the Concept of Revolution', *New Left Review*, 56(July-August), 1969, pp. 27-34; Isaac Deutscher, '1917-1967: The Unfinished Revolution', *New Left Review*, 43 (May-June), 1967, pp. 27-39.
47 Juliet Mitchell, 'Women: The Longest Revolution', *New Left Review*, 40(November-December), 1966, pp. 11-37; Quintin Hoare, 'On Women: The Longest Revolution,' and Juliet Mitchell, 'Reply,' *New Left Review*, 41(January-February), 1967, pp. 78-83.
48 Palmer, *Canada's 1960s*, pp. 297-9.
49 Judy Bernstein, Peggy Morton, Linda Seese, Myrna Wood, 'Sisters, Brothers, Lovers … Listen,' in *Women Unite! An Anthology of the Canadian Women's Movement*, Toronto: Women's Educational Press, 1972, pp. 31-9.
50 Sheila Rowbotham, *Remembering the Sixties*, London: Verso, 2001; Max Elbaum, *Revolution in the Air: Radicals Turn to Lenin, Mao, and Che*, London: Verso, 2002.
51 Veronica O'Leary, ed., *Québécois Deboutte! Une anthologie de textes du Front de Libération des Femmes (1969-1971) et du Centre des Femmes (1972-1975)*, Montreal: Rémue-Menage, 1982.
52 Sheila Rowbotham, *Women, Resistance and Revolution: A History of Women and Revolution in the Modern World*, London: Penguin, 1972, p. 201.
53 Jean-Paul Sartre, 'Jean-Paul Sartre répond', *L'Arc*, 30, 1966, p. 88, quoted in Michael C. Behrent, 'Liberalism without Humanism: Michel Foucault and the Free Market Creed, 1976-1979', in Daniel Zamora and Michael C. Behrent, eds., *Foucault and Neoliberalism*, London: Polity, 2016, p. 25.
54 Foucault, 'Une mobilization culturelle', *Le Nouvelle Observateur*, 670(September), 1977, p. 49, quoted in Behrent, 'Liberalism without Humanism', p. 38.
55 Stephano G. Azzara, *L'Humanité commune*, Paris: Delga, 2011, p. 12, quoted in Daniel Zamora, 'When Exclusion Replaces Exploitation: The Condition of the Surplus-Population Under Neoliberalism', *nonsite.org*, 10, 2013, p. 24.

CLASS, PARTY AND THE CHALLENGE OF STATE TRANSFORMATION

LEO PANITCH AND SAM GINDIN

In 1917, not only those parties engaged in insurrectionary revolution but even those committed to gradual reform still spoke of eventually transcending capitalism. Half a century later social democrats had explicitly come to define their political goals as compatible with a welfare-state variety of capitalism; and well before the end of the century many who had formerly embraced the legacy of 1917 would join them in this. Yet this occurred just as the universalization of neoliberalism rendered threadbare any notion of distinct varieties of capitalism. The realism without imagination of the so-called 'Third Way' was shown to lack realism as well as imagination.

However reactionary the era of neoliberal globalization has been, it has seemed to confirm the continuing revolutionary nature of the bourgeoisie, at least in terms of creating 'a world after its own image'.[1] Nevertheless, the financialized form of capitalism that greased the wheels not only of global investment and trade, but also of globally integrated production and consumption, was clearly crisis prone.[2] The first global capitalist crisis of the twenty-first century was rooted in the contradictions attending the new credit-dependent forms through which, amidst stagnant wages in the neoliberal era, mass consumption was sustained. Yet in sharp contrast to the two great capitalist crises of the twentieth century, as the crisis has unfolded over the past decade it did not lead to a replacement of the regime of accumulation that gave rise to it. Unlike the break with the Gold Standard regime in the 1930s and the Bretton Woods regime in the 1970s, neoliberalism persisted. This could be seen in the rescue and reproduction of financial capital, the reassertion of austerity in fiscal policy, the dependence on monetary policy for stimulus, and the further aggravation of income and wealth inequality – all of which was made possible by the continuing economic and political weaknesses of global working classes through this period.

We are now in a new conjuncture. It is a very different conjuncture than the one which led to the perception that neoliberalism, at the height of its embrace by Third Way social democracy, was 'the most successful ideology in world history'.[3] While neoliberal economic practices have been reproduced – as has the American empire's centrality in global capitalism – neoliberalism's *legitimacy* has been undermined. As the aftershocks of the US financial crash reverberated across the eurozone and the BRICS, this deepened the multiple economic, ecological, and migratory crises that characterize this new conjuncture. At the same time, neoliberalism's ideological delegitimation has enveloped many political institutions that have sustained its practices, from the European Union to political parties at the national level. What makes the current conjuncture so dangerous is the space this has opened for the far right, with its ultra-nationalist, racist, sexist and homophobic overtones, to capture popular frustrations with liberal democratic politics in the neoliberal era.

The delegitimation of neoliberalism has restored some credibility to the radical socialist case for transcending capitalism as necessary to realize the collective, democratic, egalitarian and ecological aspirations of humanity. It spawned a growing sense that capitalism could no longer continue to be bracketed when protesting the multiple oppressions and ecological threats of our time. And as austerity took top billing over free trade, the spirit of anti-neoliberal protest also shifted. Whereas capitalist globalization had defined the primary focus of oppositional forces in the first decade of the new millennium, the second decade opened with Occupy and the Indignados dramatically highlighting capitalism's gross class inequalities. Yet with this, the insurrectionary flavour of protest without revolutionary effect quickly revealed the limits of forever standing outside the state.

A marked turn on the left from protest to politics has consequently come to define the new conjuncture, as opposition to capitalist globalization shifted from the streets to the state theatres of neoliberal practice. This is in good part what the election of Syriza in Greece and the sudden emergence of Podemos in Spain signified. Corbyn's election as leader of the British Labour Party attracted hundreds of thousands of new members with the promise to sustain activism rather than undermine it. And even in the heartland of the global capitalist empire, the short bridge that spanned Occupy and Sanders' left populist promise for a political revolution 'to create a government which represents all Americans and not just the 1%' was reflected in polls indicating that half of all millennials did not support capitalism and held a positive view of socialism.

This transition from protest to politics has been remarkably class oriented in terms of addressing inequality in income and wealth distribution, as well as in economic and political power relations. Yet as Andrew Murray has so incisively noted, 'this new politics is generally more class-focused than class-rooted. While it places issues of social inequality and global economic power front and center, it neither emerges from the organic institutions of the class-in-itself nor advances the socialist perspective of the class-for-itself.'[4] The strategic questions raised by this pertain not only to all the old difficulties of left parties maintaining a class focus once elected; they also pertain to how a class-rooted politics – in the old sense of the connection between working-class formation and political organization – could become revolutionary today. Given the manifold changes in class composition and identity, as well as the limits and failures of the old working-class parties and unions in light of these changes, what could this mean in terms of new organizational forms and practices? And what would a class-focused *and* class-rooted transformation of the capitalist state actually entail?

While leaders like Tsipras, Iglesias, Corbyn and Sanders all have pointed beyond Third Way social democracy, their capacity to actually move beyond it is another matter. This partly has to do with their personal limitations, but much more with the specific limitations of each of their political parties, including even the strongest left currents within them not preparing adequately for the challenge of actually transforming state apparatuses. The experience of the Syriza government in Greece highlights this, as well as how difficult it is for governments to extricate their state apparatuses from transnational ones.

All this compels a fundamental rethink of the relationship between class, party and state transformation. If Bolshevik revolutionary discourse seems archaic a hundred years after 1917, it is not just because the legacy of its historic demonstration that revolution was possible has faded. It is also because Gramsci's reframing, so soon after 1917, of the key issues of revolutionary strategy – especially regarding the impossibility of an insurrectionary path to power in states deeply embedded in capitalist societies – rings ever more true. What this means for socialists, however, as we face up to a long war of position in the twenty-first century, is not only the recognition of the limitations of twentieth-century Leninism. It above all requires discovering how to avoid the social democratization even of those committed to transcending capitalism. This is the central challenge for socialists today.

CLASS STRUGGLE BEFORE CLASS: THEN AND NOW

The *Communist Manifesto* of 1848 introduced a new theory of revolution. Against the conspiracies of the few and the experiments of the dreamers, an emerging proletariat was heralded with the potential to usher in a new world. The argument was not that these dispossessed labourers carried revolution in their genes; rather it pointed to their potential for organization, which was facilitated by modern means of communication as well as by the way capitalists collectivized labour. Even though their organization would be 'disrupted time and again by competition amongst the workers themselves', it indeed proved to be the case that 'the ever expanding union of the workers' would lead to 'the organization of workers into a class, and consequently into a political party'.[5]

It was this sense of class formation as process that led E.P. Thompson to argue so powerfully that class was not a static social category but a changing social relationship, which historically took shape in the form of class struggle *before* class. Out of the struggles of the dispossessed labourers against the new capitalist order in England in the last half of the eighteenth century and the first half of the nineteenth came the growing collective identity and community of the working class as a social force.[6] Moreover, as Hobsbawm subsequently emphasized, it was really only in the years from 1870 to 1914 – as proletarianization reached a critical mass, and as workers' organizational presence developed on a national and international scale through mass socialist parties and unions – that the revolutionary potential in the working class that Marx had identified looked set to be realized.[7] However arcane the very term 'workers' state' now may seem, it made sense to people in 1917 – and not least to nervous bourgeoisies.

Yet there was much that made this problematic even then. The fact that so many new trade unions and workers' parties had emerged that did not aim to create socialism reflected how far even the newly organized industrial proletariat stood from revolutionary ambitions. And where there was a commitment to socialist purposes, as was ostensibly the case with the social democratic parties of the Second International, this was compromised in serious ways. The winning of workers' full franchise rights had the contradictory effect of integrating them into the nation state, while the growing separation of leaders from led inside workers' organizations undermined not only accountability, but also the capacity to develop workers' revolutionary potentials. This was of course contested in these organizations even before Roberto Michels' famous book outlined their oligarchic tendencies.[8] But these two factors – a class-inclusive nationalism and a non-revolutionary relationship between leaders and led in class organizations – combined to determine why the catastrophic outcome of inter-imperial rivalry announced with the guns of August 1914, far from bringing about the international proletarian revolution, rather ambushed European social democracy into joining the great patriotic war and making truce in the domestic class struggle.

What made proletarian revolution ushering in a workers state still credible after this – perhaps all the more credible – was the Russian Revolution. But what Rosa Luxemburg discerned within its first year would definitively mark the outcome: a revolutionary process which in breaking with liberal democracy quickly narrowed rather than broadened the scope of public participation, ending as a 'clique affair'. Lenin, she noted, saw the capitalist state as 'an instrument of oppression of the working class; the socialist state, of the bourgeoisie', but this 'misses the most essential thing: bourgeois class rule has no need of the political training and education of the entire mass of the people, at least not beyond certain narrow limits'. The great danger was that:

> Without general elections, without unrestricted freedom of press and assembly, without a free struggle of opinion, life dies out in every public institution, becomes a mere semblance of life, in which only the bureaucracy remains as the active element. Public life gradually falls asleep, a few dozen party leaders of inexhaustible energy and boundless experience direct and rule. Among them, in reality only a dozen outstanding heads do the leading and an elite of the working class is invited from time to time to meetings where they are to applaud the speeches of the leaders, and to approve proposed resolutions unanimously – at bottom then, a clique affair.[9]

Isaac Deutscher, looking back some three decades later, succinctly captured the dilemma which had led the Bolsheviks to bring about a dictatorship that would 'at best represent the idea of the class, not the class itself'. He insisted that in consolidating the new regime the Bolsheviks had not 'clung to power for its own sake', but rather that this reflected a deeper quandary. Even though anarcho-syndicalists seemed 'far more popular among the working class', the fact that they 'possessed no positive political programme, no serious organization, national or even local' only reinforced the Bolsheviks identification of the new republic's fate with their own, as 'the only force capable of safeguarding the revolution'.

> Lenin's party refused to allow the famished and emotionally unhinged country to vote their party out of power and itself into a bloody chaos. For this strange sequel to their victory the Bolsheviks were mentally quite unprepared. They had always tacitly assumed that the majority of the working class, having backed them in the revolution, would go on to support them unswervingly until they had carried out the full programme

of socialism. Naive as the assumption was, it sprang from the notion that socialism was the proletarian idea par excellence and that the proletariat, having once adhered to it, would not abandon it … It had never occurred to Marxists to reflect whether it was possible or admissible to try to establish socialism regardless of the will of the working class.[10]

The long term effects of what Luxemburg had so quickly understood would contribute to reproducing a dictatorial regime regardless of the will of the working class – and relatedly, also to the gaps in the 'political training and education of the entire mass of the people' – were chillingly captured by what a leader of the local trade union committee at the Volga Automobile Plant said to us in an interview in 1990 just before the regime established in 1917 collapsed: 'Insofar as workers were backward and underdeveloped, this is because there has in fact been no real political education since 1924. The workers were made fools of by the party.'[11] The words here need to be taken literally: the workers were not merely fooled, but *made* into fools; their revolutionary understanding and capacity was undermined.

The fillip that 1917 had given to fueling workers' revolutionary ambitions worldwide was more than offset by the failure of the revolution in Germany and the Stalinist response to an isolated and beleaguered Soviet Union after Lenin's death, with all the adverse consequences this entailed. Though the spectre of Bolshevism hardly faded, it was the spectre of fascism that dominated radical change in the interwar years. Nevertheless, there was also widespread recognition of the potential of the working class as the social force most capable of transforming state and society. This perception was not least based on worker organization and class formation in the US during the Great Depression. As the US already was the new world centre of capitalism, even before the Second World War, this contributed to the sense on the part of leading American capitalists and state officials that among the barriers to the remaking of a liberal capitalist international order, 'the uprising of [the] international proletariat … [was] the most significant fact of the last twenty years'.[12]

The strength of the organized working class as it had formed up to the 1950s was registered in the institutionalization of collective bargaining and welfare reforms. The effects of this were highly contradictory. The material gains in terms of individual and family consumption, which workers secured directly or indirectly from collective bargaining for rising wages as well as from a social wage largely designed to secure and supplement that consumption, were purchased at the cost of union and party practices that attenuated working class identity and community – especially in light of the restructuring of employment, residency and education that accompanied these developments. To be sure, the continuing salience of working-class organization was palpable. This was increasingly so in the public sector, but it was also measurable in class struggles in the private sector which resisted workplace restructuring, as well as in the wage-led inflation that contributed to the capitalist profitability crisis of the 1970s. Yet the failure to renew and extend working-class identity and community through these struggles opened the way to the neoliberal resolution of the crises of the 1970s through a widespread assault on trade unionism and the welfare state, and the interpellation of workers themselves as 'taxpayers'.

By the beginning of the twenty-first century, aided by the realization of a fully global capitalism and the networked structures of production, finance and consumption that constitute it, there were more workers on the face of the earth than ever before. New technologies certainly restricted job growth in certain sectors, but this also introduced entirely new sectors in both manufacturing and especially high tech services. Though this weakened the leverage of class struggles in important ways, it also introduced new points of strategic potential: strikes at component plants or interruptions of supplier chains at warehouses and ports could force shutdowns throughout a globally integrated production network, and whistleblowing could expose vast stores of information hidden by corporations and states.

The precarious conditions workers increasingly face today, even when they belong to unions, speaks not to a new class division between precariat and proletariat. Precariousness rather reflects how previous processes of working-class formation and organization have become undone. Precariousness is not something new in capitalism: employers have always tried to gain access to labour when they want, dispose of it as they want and, in between, use it with as little restrictions as possible. There is in this context limited value in drawing new sociological nets of who is or is not in the working class. Rather than categorizing workers into different strata – nurses or baristas, teachers or software developers, farmhands or truckers, salespeople or bank-tellers – what needs to preoccupy our imaginations and inform our strategic calculations is how to visualize and how to develop the potential of new forms of working-class organization and formation in the twenty-first century.

There are indeed multitudes of workers' struggles taking place today in the face of an increasingly exploitative and chaotic capitalism. Yet there is no denying that prospects for working-class revolutionary agency seem dim. It was factors internal to working-class institutions, their contradictions and weaknesses, which allowed, in the developing as well as the developed countries, for the passage of free trade, the liberalization of finance, the persistence of austerity, the further commodification of labour power, the restructuring of all dimensions of economic and social life in today's global capitalism. The inability of the working class to renew itself and discover new organizational forms in light of the dynamism of capital and capacities of the state to contain worker resistance has allowed the far right today to articulate and contextualize a set of common sentiments linked to the crisis – frustrations with insecurity and inequality, and anger with parties that once claimed to represent workers' interests. Escaping this crisis of the working class is not primarily a matter of better policies or better tactics. It is primarily an *organizational* challenge to facilitate new processes of class formation rooted in the multiple dimensions of workers' lives that encompass so many identities and communities.

This organizational challenge will have to include developing socialist parties of a new kind. As can be seen from the two examples to which we now turn, the recent shift from protest to politics has already shown the popular resonance which a renewed socialist appeal can have today, even if it has only begun to probe what a consistent socialist politics would actually entail and the barriers that will be encountered.

POLITICAL REVOLUTION TODAY?
FROM SANDERS TO SYRIZA

'Election days come and go. But political and social revolutions that attempt to transform our society never end.' The speech with which Bernie Sanders closed his Democratic primary election campaign began with these sentences; it ended by pointing to future historians who would trace the success of the long effort to transform American society from oligarchy to social justice as beginning with the 'the political revolution of 2016'.[13] It is tempting to treat as ersatz the rhetoric of revolution deployed here, taking the meaning of the word from the sublime to the ridiculous, or from tragedy to farce. The last time an American politician vying for the presidency issued a call for a political revolution it came from Ronald Reagan. But for all the limits of Sanders' populist campaign, the national attention and massive support garnered by a self-styled democratic socialist who positively associated the term revolution with the struggle against class inequality in fact represented a major discursive departure in American political life, which can be a resource for further socialist organizing.

Of course, the specific policy measures advanced by Sanders were, as he constantly insisted, reforms that had at some point been introduced in other capitalist societies. But when the call for public medicare for all, or free college tuition, or infrastructure renewal through direct public employment, is explicitly attached to a critique of a ruling class which wields corporate and financial power through the direct control of parties, elections and the media, this goes beyond the bounds of what can properly be dismissed as mere reformism, even if the demands hardly evoke what the call for bread, land and peace did in 1917. And it is no less a significant departure, especially in the US, to make class inequality the central theme of a political campaign in a manner designed to span and penetrate race and gender divisions in a way that explicitly poses the question of who stands to benefit more from high quality public health care and education and well compensated work opportunities than African-Americans and Latinos, while pointing to the need to move beyond the ghettoes of identity towards building a more coherent class force.

The key question is whether Sanders' campaign really could lay the grounds for an ongoing political movement capable of effecting this 'political revolution'. Sanders' argument during the campaign that he could be sustained in the White House amidst a hostile Congress and imperial state apparatus by a 'mass movement' marching on Washington D.C. was not very convincing. Much more serious was his call after he lost the primary campaign for a shift from protest to politics at every level, including 'school boards, city councils, county commissions, state legislatures and governorships'. But even if this happened, such engagement would also have to be directed at the institutions in which workers have heretofore been organized.

The very fact that the Sanders campaign was class-focused rather than class-rooted may be an advantage here. It opens space for a new politics that can become 'rooted' in the sense of being grounded in working-class struggles but committed to the radical transformation of the generally exhausted institutions of the labour movement. This ranges across turning union branches into centres of working-class life, leading the fight for collective public services, breaking down the oligarchic relationship between leaders and led, contributing to building the broadest member capacities, emphasizing the importance of expressing a clearer class sensibility, and even becoming ambitious enough to introduce socialist ideas. This also applies to Workers Action Centers, which have spread across the US but which are so often overwhelmed by having to reproduce themselves financially in order to continue providing vital services to Black, Latino, immigrant and women workers. Becoming more class-rooted and effective would require building the institutional capacities to creatively organize workers in different sectors into new city-wide organizations, as well as develop a coordinating national infrastructure.

Similar challenges would need to be put to consumer and credit cooperatives, which are broadly identified with the left, but whose primarily narrow economic activities need to be politicized, above all in the sense of opening their spaces to radical education about the capitalist context in which they operate, actively participating in left campaigns, and contributing a portion of their revenue to funding organizers to carry out such tasks. And to get beyond the frustrations so often voiced in the environmental movement with workers' defensive prioritization of their jobs, turning this into a positive rather than negative class focus by speaking in terms of 'just transitions' to a clean energy economy would also mean raising the necessity for economic planning to address both environmental and social crises, with the corollary of challenging the prerogatives of private property and capitalist power structures.

A new class politics cannot emerge *ex nihilo*, however. The Sanders campaign, initiated by an outsider in the Democratic Party, confirmed that if you are not heard in the media you are not broadly heard. But whatever the advantages of initially mobilizing from within established institutions in this respect, the impossibility of a political revolution taking place under the auspices of the Democratic Party needs to be directly faced (even in the Labour Party, it is hard enough to imagine that what Corbyn represents could be sustained without major institutional recalibration). After it had become clear he would not clinch the nomination, Sanders and the movement that had begun to take shape around him appeared at risk of falling into a myopic strategy of internally transforming and democratizing the Democratic Party. In part, this is one of the contradictions in Sanders' choice to run as a Democrat. While the Sanders campaign showed that Democratic Party institutions offer certain bases from which to advance a left politics – lending his campaign a certain legitimacy and credibility within mainstream discourse – in the long run, an alternative political pole will have to be constructed around which social struggles can condense.

It was far from surprising that the thousands of Sanders supporters who gathered at the People's Summit in Chicago after the primary campaign ended did not come to found a new party. What happened there, as Dan La Botz described it, 'was about vision, not organization or strategy', so that one could at best only hear 'the sound made by the *Zeitgeist* passing though the meeting rooms and the halls, brushing up against us, making its way, sometimes gracefully, sometimes clumsily, to the future'.[14] One key test will be whether, as it 'makes its way', lessons are learned from the US Labor Party project of the 1990s, links are made with attempts already underway to spawn new socialist political formations, and traces of either Bolshevik sectarianism or 'Third World' romanticism are avoided while nevertheless also abandoning the naïve admiration for Canadian and European social democracy that has long characterized so much of the US left.[15]

This takes us from Sanders to Syriza, the only party to the left of traditional social democracy in Europe that has actually succeeded in winning a national election since the current economic crisis began. Syriza's roots go back to the formation of Synaspismos, first as an electoral alliance in the 1980s, and then as an independent, although factionalized, new party in the early 1990s. This was part of the broader institutional reconfiguration inaugurated by the Eurocommunist strategic orientation, searching for a way forward in the face of Communist and Social Democratic parties having lost their historic roles and capacities as agencies of working-class political representation and social transformation. This search went all the way back to the 1960s and accelerated after the collapse of the Soviet bloc and social democracy's embrace of the 'Third Way'. In Greece especially the Eurocommunist orientation was characterized by continuing to embrace the tradition of political revolution as experienced in the Civil War after 1945, even while distancing itself from the Soviet regime; and it would increasingly be characterized by the inspiration it took from, and a willingness to work with, new social movements.

Although Synaspismos through the 1990s offered enthusiastic support of European integration, as the neoliberal form of Economic and Monetary Union buried the promises of a European Social Charter the grounds were laid in Greece, as elsewhere on the European radical left, for a more 'Eurosceptical' orientation.[16] This new critical posture towards the European variety of capitalism was a crucial element in Synaspismos explicitly defining, by the turn of the millennium, its strategic goal as 'the socialist transformation of Greek society' while increasingly encouraging 'dialogue and common actions' not only with the alter-globalization movement, but with radical ecologists and political groups of a Trotskyist or Maoist lineage. The goal of the Coalition of the Radical Left, with the acronym Syriza, which emerged out of this as an electoral alliance was designed, as Michalis Spourdalakis put it, 'not so much to unify but rather to connect in a flexible fashion the diverse actions, initiatives and movements ... and to concern itself with developing popular political capacities as much as with changing state policy'. But actually turning Synaspismos, and through it Syriza, into such a party was, as Spourdalakis immediately adds, 'more wishful thinking than realistic prospect'.[17]

As the eurocrisis broke, however, with Greece at the epicentre of the attempt to save the euro through the application of severe austerity at its weakest point, all the elements of Syriza threw themselves into the 2011 wave of protests, occupations and strikes, while supporting the 400 or so community solidarity networks around the country to help the worst affected cope. This prepared the ground for Syriza's electoral breakthrough of 2012. Syriza's active insertion the year before into the massive outbursts across Greece of social protest from below was a source of radical democratic energy that went far beyond what can be generated during an election campaign, however successful. What this meant was eloquently articulated at Syriza's Congress in 2013 when it finally turned itself from an electoral alliance into a single party political organization. The conclusion to its founding resolution called for 'something more' than the programmatic framework that resolution set out. Since 'for a Government of the Left, a parliamentary majority – whatever its size – is not enough', the something more it called for was 'the creation and expression of the widest possible, militant and catalytic political movement of multidimensional subversion'.

> Only such a movement can lead to a Government of the Left and only such a movement can safeguard the course of such a government ... [which] carries out radical reforms, takes on development initiatives and other initiatives of a clear environmental and class orientation, opens up new potentials and opportunities for popular intervention, helps the creation of new forms of popular expression and claims ... Syriza has shouldered the responsibility to contribute decisively to the shaping of this great movement of democratic subversion that will lead the country to a new popular, democratic, and radical changeover.[18]

This sort of language, articulating this sort of understanding, was rare on the European radical left, let alone anywhere else. Yet as the Syriza leadership contemplated the dilemmas it faced as it stood on the doorstep of government, its concern to appear as a viable government in the media's eyes led them to concentrate, as was evident in the Thessalonika Manifesto proclaimed just a year later, on refining and scaling down the policy proposals in the 2013 party programme. This was done with little internal party consultation, with the leadership mainly concerned with there not being enough experienced and efficient personnel in the party to bring into the state to change the notoriously clientelistic and corrupt state apparatus. Little attention was paid to who would be left in the party to act as an organizing cadre in society. The increase in party membership was not at all proportionate to the extent of the electoral breakthrough, and even when new radical activists did join, the leadership generally did very little to support those in the party apparatus

CLASS, PARTY AND THE CHALLENGE OF STATE TRANSFORMATION   47

who wanted to develop these activists' capacities to turn party branches into centres of working-class life and strategically engage with them, preferably in conjunction with the Solidarity Networks, in planning for alternative forms of production and consumption. All this spoke to how far Syriza still was from having discovered how to escape the limits of social democracy.

SYRIZA AND THE PROBLEM OF STATE TRANSFORMATION

[This] is not a 'betrayal'. It's not about the well-known scenario 'they have sold out'. We have seen that there was real confrontation. We have seen the amount of pressure, the blackmailing by the European Central Bank. We have seen that they want to bring the Syriza government to its knees. And they need to do that because it represents a real threat, not some kind of illusion of a reformist type. So the reality is that the representatives of the Greek government did the best they could. But they did it within the wrong framework and with the wrong strategy and, in this sense, the outcome couldn't have been different ... The people who think that 'the reformists will fail' and that somehow in the wings stands the revolutionary vanguard who is waiting to take over somehow and lead the masses to a victory are I think completely outside of reality.[19]

All this was said within a month of Syriza's election at the end of January 2015 by Stathis Kouvelakis, whose interpretation of the dramatic unfolding of events in his country garnered widespread attention on the international left. Himself a member's of Syriza's Central Committee as a partisan of the Left Platform, he was speaking at a meeting in London and addressing the disappointments already felt when the new government agreed to new negotiations with the EU and IMF. Less than five months later, as these negotiations infamously came to a climax, he would, along with many others, leave Syriza in response to what he now called the government's 'capitulation', which indeed became the most common epithet used by the international left. Yet the need to ask whether the outcome could really have been different was now greater than ever. And while the answer did indeed hinge on the adequacy of Syriza's strategy in relation to Europe, that in turn related to deeper issues of party organization, capacity building and state transformation – as well as the adequacy of strategies on the wider European left, at least in terms of shifting the overall balance of forces.

The common criticism of Syriza, strongly advanced by the Left Platform, was that it had not developed a 'Plan B' for leaving the eurozone and adopting an alternate currency as the key condition for rejecting neoliberal austerity and cancelling debt obligations. What this criticism recoiled from admitting was that the capital and import controls this also would require would lead to Greece being forced out of the EU as a whole. After 35 years of integration, the institutional carapace for capitalism in Greece was provided by the manifold ways the state apparatus became entangled with the EU. Breaking out of this would have required Syriza as a party and government to be prepared for an immediate systemic rupture. It could certainly be said that Syriza was naïve to believe that it could stop the European economic torture while remaining in the eurozone, let alone the EU. At the very least, this simultaneously posed two great challenges: could such a state as Greece be fundamentally changed while remaining within the EU, and could the EU itself be fundamentally changed from within at the initiative of that state?

For a small country without significant oil resources, a break with the EU would have entailed economic isolation (along the lines of that endured by the Cuban revolution, yet without the prospect of anything like its geostrategic and economic support from the former USSR). The Syriza government faced the intractable contradiction that to fulfil its promise to stop the EU's economic torture, it would have to leave the EU – which would, given the global as well as European balance of forces and the lack of alternative production and consumption capabilities in place, lead to further economic suffering for an unforeseeable period. Despite the massive popular mobilization the government unleashed by calling the referendum in July to support its position against that of the EU-IMF, the intractable dilemma was the same as it had been when it first entered the state. That the government managed to win re-election in the fall while succumbing to and implementing the diktats of the 'Institutions' indicated that Kouvelakis's observation when it entered into the negotiations back in February still held: 'People support the government because the perception they have is that they couldn't act otherwise in that very specific situation. They really see that the balance of forces was extremely uneven'.

Costas Douzinas, another prominent London-based Greek intellectual newly elected as a Syriza MP in the fall of 2015, hopes the story may not be over. He outlines the 'three different temporalities' through which the radical left must 'simultaneously live' once it enters the state.[20] There is 'the time of the present': the dense and difficult time when the Syriza government – 'held hostage' to the creditors as a 'quasi-protectorate' of the EU and IMF – is required 'to implement what they fought against', and thus 'to legislate and apply the recessional and socially unjust measures it ideologically rejects'. This raises 'grave existential issues and problems of conscience' which cannot go away, but can be 'soothed through the activation of two other temporalities that exist as traces of futurity in the present time'. This begins with 'the medium term of three to five years', when time for the government appears 'slower and longer' as it probes for the space it needs to implement its 'parallel program' so as not only to 'mitigate the effects of the memorandum' but also to advance 'policies with a clear left direction ... in close contact with the party and the social movements'. This is the bridge to the third and longest temporality, 'the time of the radical left vision', which will be reached 'only by continuously and simultaneously implementing and undermining the agreement policies'. As this third temporality starts unfolding, freed from the neoliberal lambast, 'the full programme of the left of the 21st century' will emerge. 'It is a case of escaping into the future, acting now from the perspective of a future perfect, of what will have been. In this sense, the future becomes an active factor of our present.'

It is indeed significant that the Syriza government's continuing ideological rejection of neoliberal logic – even as it implements the measures forced upon it – is precisely what distinguishes Syriza from social democratic governments in the neoliberal era. The crucial condition for the three temporalities to coexist, however, is precisely the 'close contact with the party and the social movements', which Douzinas only mentions in passing. Even in terms of its relations to the party, let alone the social movements, the Syriza government has failed to escape from familiar social democratic patterns as it distanced itself from party pressures, and seemed incapable of appreciating the need for activating party cadre to develop social capacities to lay the grounds for temporality two and eventually three. The neglect of the party turned to offhand dismissal when the government called the second election of 2015. As so many of its leading cadre left the party in the face of this – including even the General Secretary, who also resigned rather than asserting the party's independence from the government – the promise that Syriza might escape the fate of social democracy in neoliberal capitalism was left in tatters. There are still those in Syriza, inside and outside the government, who, operating with something very like the three temporalities in mind, are trying to revive the party outside government as the key agent of transformation. But whether they can manage to create the conditions for 'Syriza to be Syriza again' is now moot indeed.[21]

Yet the problem goes far broader and deeper than with those who still have hopes for Syriza. It was ironically those who advanced the ostensibly more radical Plan B who seemed to treat state power most instrumentally. Little or no attention was paid by them to how to disentangle a very broad range of state apparatuses from budgetary dependence on EU funding, let alone to the transformations the Greek state apparatuses would have to undergo merely to administer the controls and rationing required to manage the black and grey markets that would have expanded inside and outside the state if Greece exited the eurozone. This was especially problematic given the notorious clientelistic and corrupt state practices which Syriza as a party had been vociferously committed to ending, but once in government did not have the time to change, even where the inclination to do so was still there. When confronted with a question on how to deal with this, one Syriza MP who was a leading advocate of Plan B responded privately that in such a moment of rupture it is necessary to shoot people. But this only raised the bigger question of whom the notoriously reactionary coercive apparatuses of the Greek state, as unchanged as they were, would be most likely to listen to, and most likely to shoot.

Perhaps most tellingly, advocates of Plan B showed no more, and often rather less, interest in democratizing state apparatuses by linking them with social movements. This stood in contrast with the minister of social services, who had herself been the key founder of the federation of solidarity networks, Solidairty4All, and openly spoke of her frustrations that Syriza MPs, even while paying over a sizeable portion of their salaries to the networks, insisted that they alone should be the conduits for contact with solidarity activists in their communities. The Minister of Education visited one school a week and told teachers, parents and students that if they wanted to use the school as a base for changing social relations in their communities they would have his support. However, the Ministry of Education itself did not become actively engaged in promoting the use of schools as community hubs, neither providing spaces for activists organizing around food and health services, nor the technical education appropriate to this, nor other special programmes to prepare students to spend periods of time in communities, contributing to adult education and working on community projects.

Yet it must be said that the social movements themselves were largely passive and immobilized in this respect, as if waiting for the government to deliver. Activists from the networks of food solidarity were rightly frustrated they could not even get from the new Minister of Agriculture the information they asked for on the locations of specific crops so they might approach a broader range of farmers. But they did not see it as their responsibility to develop and advance proposals on how the state apparatuses should be changed, even minimally, so as to cope with the economic crisis. How, for instance, could the agriculture ministry have been engaged in identifying idle land to be given over to community food production co-ops, and in coordinating this across sub-regions; or how the defence ministry might have been engaged in directing military trucks (at least those sitting idle between demonstrations) to be used to facilitate the distribution of food through the solidarity networks.

CLASS, PARTY AND THE CHALLENGE OF STATE TRANSFORMATION   51

The point is this. Insofar as the Syriza government has failed the most crucial democratic, let alone revolutionary test, of linking the administration up with popular forces – not just for meeting basic needs but also for planning and implementing the restructuring of economic and social life – there were all too few on the radical left outside the state who really saw this as a priority either.

SIGNPOSTS TOWARDS DEMOCRATIC SOCIALISM

Whatever the final outcome in Greece, it is useful to look back at Nicos Poulantzas's 'Towards a Democratic Socialism', especially given its formative influence on those who founded Synaspismos in the 1980s (Syriza's research institute bears his name to this day).[22] Written in 1978 as the epilogue to his last book, what Poulantzas articulated was reflective of a much broader orientation on the European left, already represented by Gorz, Magri, Benn, Miliband, Rowbotham, Segal, Wainwright, and others, towards trying to discover new strategic directions beyond both the Leninist and Social Democratic 'models' which, despite taking different routes, nevertheless evinced in their practices a common distrust of popular capacities to democratize state structures.[23] As Poulantzas put it: 'There is no longer a question of building "models" of any kind whatsoever. All that is involved is a set of signposts which, drawing lessons of the past, point out the traps to anyone wishing to avoid certain well-known destinations'. For Poulantzas, the 'techno-bureaucratic statism of the experts' was the outcome not only of the instrumentalist strategic conception of social democratic parliamentarism, but also of the 'Leninist dual-power type of strategy which envisages straightforward replacement of the state apparatus with an apparatus of councils ...'

> Transformation of the state apparatus does not really enter into the matter: first of all the existing state power is taken and then another is put in its place. This view of things can no longer be accepted. If taking power denotes a shift in the relationship of forces within the state, and if it is recognized that this will involve a long process of change, then the seizure of state power will entail concomitant transformations of its apparatuses ... In abandoning the dual-power strategy, we do not throw overboard, but pose in a different fashion, the question of the state's materiality as a specific apparatus.[24]

Notably, Poulantzas went back to Luxemburg's critique of Lenin in 1918 to stress the importance of socialists building on liberal democracy, even while transcending it, in order to provide the space for mass struggles to unfold which could 'modify the relationship of forces within the state apparatuses, themselves the strategic site of political struggle'. The very notion *to take* state power 'clearly lacks the strategic vision of a process of transition to socialism – that is of a long stage during which the masses will act to conquer power and transform state apparatuses.' For the working class to displace the old ruling class, in other words, it must develop capacities to democratize the state, which must always rest on 'increased intervention of the popular masses in the state … certainly through their trade union and political forms of representation, but also through their own initiatives within the state itself'. To expect that institutions of direct democracy outside the state can simply displace the old state in a single revolutionary rupture in fact avoided all the difficult questions of political representation and opens the way for a new authoritarian statism.[25]

Indeed, as Andre Gorz had already insisted in his pathbreaking essay on 'Reform and Revolution' a decade earlier, taking off from liberal democracy on 'the peaceful road to socialism' was not a matter of adopting 'an *a priori* option for gradualism; nor of an *a priori* refusal of violent revolution or armed insurrection. It is a consequence of the latter's actual impossibility in the European context.'[26] The advancement of what Gorz called a 'socialist strategy of progressive reforms' did not mean the 'installation of islands of socialism in a capitalist ocean', but rather involved the types of 'structural reforms' or 'non-reformist reforms' which could not be institutionalized so as to close off class antagonism but which allowed for further challenges to the balance of power and logic of capitalism, and thereby introduce a dynamic that allowed the process to go further. In calling for the creation of new 'centres of social control and direct democracy' outside the state, Gorz was far-sighted in terms of what this could contribute to a broad process of new class formation with revolutionary potential, not least by extending to 'the labour of ideological research' and more generally to the transformative capacities of 'cultural labour aiming at the overthrow of norms and schemata of social consciousness'. This would be essential for ensuring that 'the revolutionary movements' capacity for action and hegemony is enriched and confirmed by its capacity to inspire … the autonomous activity of town planners, architects, doctors, teachers and psychologists'.[27]

What this left aside, however, were the crucial changes in state structures that would need to attend this process. Poulantzas went to the heart of the matter, a decade later, stressing that on 'the democratic road to socialism, the long process of taking power essentially consists in the spreading, development, coordination and direction of those diffuse centres of resistance which the masses always possess within the state networks, in such a way that they become real centres of power on the strategic terrain of the state'. Even Gramsci, as Poulantzas pointed out, 'was unable to pose the problem in all its amplitude' since his 'war of position' was conceived as the application of Lenin's model/strategy to the 'different concrete conditions of the West' without actually addressing how to change state apparatuses.[28] Yet it must also be said that Poulantzas, even while highlighting the need for taking up the challenge of state transformation, did not himself get very far in detailing what actually changing the materiality of state apparatuses would entail in specific instances. Lurking here was the theoretical problem Miliband had identified of not differentiating state power from class power, and therefore not specifying sufficiently how the modalities and capacities involved in exercising capitalist state power would be changed into different modalities with structurally transformative capacities.[29] And as Goran Therborn pointed out, in envisaging an important role for unions of state employees in the process of transforming state apparatuses, it was necessary to address the problem that 'state bureaucrats and managers will not thereby disappear, and problems of popular control will remain', thereby continuing to pose 'serious and complicated questions' for the state transformation through socialist democracy.[30]

Socialists have since paid far too little attention to the challenges this poses.[31] While the recognition that neither insurrectionary politics to 'smash the state' nor the social democratic illusion of using the extant state to introduce progressive policies became more and more widespread, this was accompanied with a penchant for developing 'market socialist' models in the late 1980s which has subsequently been succeeded by a spate of radical left literature that – in almost a mirror image of neoliberalism's championing of private corporations and small business firms against the state – weakly points to examples of cooperatives and self-managed enterprises as directly bearing socialist potential.[32] Replicated here is exactly what Poulantzas identified in the conception of those for whom 'the only way to avoid statism is to place oneself outside the state. The way forward would then be, without going as far as dual power simply to block the path of the state from the outside.' Yet by concentrating exclusively on 'breaking power up and scattering it among an infinity of micro-powers', the result is that the 'movement is prevented from intervening in actual transformations of the state, and the two processes are simply kept running along parallel lines'.[33]

CONCLUSIONS

Political hopes are inseparable from notions of what is possible. And possibility is itself intimately related to class formation, the role of parties in this and developing confidence in class institutions, and especially the question of potentials to transform the state. The alliances that socialist parties would have to enter into, not least in face of the growing threat from the far right of the political spectrum, should not just be amongst elites but be directed at new working-class formation of the broadest possible kind; and given the uneven capacities of the class, should also be directed at developing its actual potential to become the transformative agent in a transition to socialism. New socialist parties cannot, however, see themselves as a kind of omnipotent *deus ex machina* in society. Precisely in order not to draw back from the 'prodigious scope of their own aims', as Marx brilliantly wrote in *The Eighteenth Brumaire*, they must 'engage in perpetual self-criticism' and deride 'the inadequacies, weak points and pitiful aspects of their first attempts'.[34] Developing commitments to socialism – getting socialism seriously on the agenda – consequently requires not only addressing the question of political agency, but overcoming a prevailing sense that even sympathetic governments will either be stymied by state apparatuses hostile to the socialist project, and/or that in a globalized world the problem in any case lies beyond the nation state.

To stress the importance of a democratic socialist strategy for entering the state through elections to the end of transforming the state is today less than ever – amidst the deep political and social as well as economic contradictions of the neoliberal era – a matter of discovering a smooth gradual road to socialism. Ruptures, or extended series of ruptures of various intensities, are inescapable. This is so because of the contradictions inherent in reaching beyond capitalism while still being of it, and the virtual inevitability of conditions being premature as the project is attempted in 'circumstances not of our own choosing'. The contradictions for any radical government that would be engaged in this process will include responsibilities for managing a capitalist economy that is likely in crisis while simultaneously trying to satisfy popular expectations for the promised relief, and yet also embarking on the longer-term commitment to transform the state, i.e., not pushing the latter off to an indefinite future.

It is this tension among the various new state responsibilities which makes the role of new socialist parties that will bring such governments to office so fundamental. Given the legitimacy and resources that inevitably will accrue to those party leaders who form the government, the autonomy of the party is crucial in order to counter the pull of those leaders towards social democratization. The party must more than ever keep its feet in the movements and, far from trying to direct them, remain the central site for democratic strategic debate in light of their diverse activities. This is why strategic preparations undertaken well before entering the state on how to avoid replicating the experience with social democracy are so very important. But even with this, the process of transforming the state cannot help but be complex, uncertain, crisis-ridden, with repeated interruptions and possibly even reversals. Beginning with election to local or regional levels of the state would allow for developing capacities of state transformation before coming to national power. Developing alternative means of producing and distributing food, health care and other necessities depends on autonomous movements moving in these directions through takeovers of land, idle buildings, threatened factories and transportation networks. All this in turn would have to be supported and furthered through more radical changes in the state that would range over time from codifying new collective property rights to developing and coordinating agencies of democratic planning. At some points in this process more or less dramatic initiatives of nationalization and socialization of industry and finance would have to take place.

For state apparatuses to be transformed so as to play these roles, their institutional modalities would need to undergo fundamental transformations, given how they are now structured so as to reproduce capitalist social relations. State employees would need to become explicit agents of transformation, aided and sustained in this respect by their unions and the broader labour movement. Rather than expressing defensive particularism, unions themselves would need to be changed fundamentally so as to actively be engaged in developing state workers' transformational capacities, including by establishing councils that link them to the recipients of state services.

Of course, the possibility of such state transformations will not be determined by what happens in one country alone. During the era of neoliberalism state apparatuses have become deeply intertwined with transnational institutions, treaties and regulations to manage and reproduce global capitalism. This has nothing at all to do with capital bypassing the nation state and coming to rely on a transnational state. Both the nature of the current crisis and the responses to it have proved once again how much states still matter. Even in the most elaborate transnational institutional formation, the European Union, the centre of political gravity lies not in the supranational state apparatus headquartered in Brussels. It is, rather, the asymetric economic and political power relations among the states of Europe that really determines what the EU is and does. Any project for democratization at an international scale, such as those being advanced by many of the left for the EU in the wake of the Syriza experience, still depends on the balance of class forces and the particular structures within each nation state. Changes in international institutions are therefore contingent on transformations at the level of nation states. And the changes in international state apparatuses that should be pursued by socialists are those that would allow more room for manoeuvre within each state. What socialist internationalism must mean today is an orientation to shifting the balances of forces in other countries and in international bodies so as to create more space for transformative forces in every country. This was one of the key lessons of 1917, and it is all the more true a century later.

NOTES

1   As *The Communist Manifesto* put it in elaborating on the bourgeoisie's 'highly revolutionary role' historically, 'the bourgeoisie cannot exist without constantly revolutionizing the instruments of production, and thereby relations of production, and with them the whole relations of society ... In a phrase, it creates a world in its own image'. Karl Marx, *Later Political Writings*, edited and translated by Terrell Carver, Cambridge, UK: Cambridge University Press, 1996, pp. 3-5. For a discussion of the continuing implications of this, see Leo Panitch, 'Capitalism, Socialism and Revolution', in Ralph Miliband, Leo Panitch, and John Saville, eds., *The Socialist Register 1989*, London: Merlin Press, 1989; and *Renewing Socialism: Transforming Democracy, Strategy and Imagination*, London: Merlin Press, 2009.

2   Between the 1987 American stock market crash and the investment banking collapse two decades later, there were upwards of a hundred distinct currency and banking crises as a direct outcome of global capital mobility. States were no longer in the business of 'crisis prevention' through regulations that might impede the free flow of capital; rather they were in the business of 'crisis containment', as the US Treasury itself put it in explaining why its central role had become 'firefighting'. See Leo Panitch and Sam Gindin, *The Making of Global Capitalism: The Political Economy of American Empire*, London: Verso, 2012, Chapters 10-12.

3   Perry Anderson, 'Renewals', *New Left Review*, 1(January/February), 2000, pp. 7, 13. 'Whatever limitations persist to its practice, neo-liberalism as a set of principles rules undivided across the globe: the most successful ideology in world history'.

4   Andrew Murray, 'Jeremy Corbyn and the Battle for Socialism', *Jacobin*, 7 February 2016.

5   Marx, *Later Political Writings*, pp. 9-10.

6   See E.P. Thompson, *The Making of the English Working Class*, New York: Pantheon, 1964, pp. 9-11; and 'Eighteenth Century English Society: Class Struggle Without Class', *Social History*, 3(2), May 1978, pp. 133-65.

7   E. H. Hobsbawm, 'The Making of the Working Class, 1870-1914', *Uncommon People: Resistance, Rebellion and Jazz*, New York: The New Press, 1999, pp. 58-9. See especially, Geoff Eley, *Forging Democracy: The History of the Left in Europe, 1850-2000*, New York: OUP, 2002.

8   Robert Michels, *Political Parties: A Sociological Study of the Oligarchical Tendencies of Modern Democracy*, New York: Free Press, 1962.

9   Rosa Luxemburg, 'The Russian Revolution', in Peter Hudis and Kevin Anderson, eds., *The Rosa Luxemburg Reader*, New York: Monthly Review Press, 2004, pp. 304-6.

CLASS, PARTY AND THE CHALLENGE OF STATE TRANSFORMATION   57

10   Isaac Deutscher, *The Prophet Armed*, London: OUP, 1954, pp. 505-6.
11   Quoted in L. Panitch and S. Gindin, 'Moscow, Togliatti, Yaroslavl: Perspectives on Perestroika' in Dan Benedict et al., eds., *Canadians Look at Soviet Auto Workers' Unions*, Toronto: CAW, 1992, p. 19.
12   'An American Proposal', *Fortune*, May 1942. See L. Panitch and S. Gindin, *The Making of Global Capitalism: The Political Economy of American Empire*, London: Verso, 2012, pp. 67-8.
13   Bernie Sanders, 'Prepared Remarks: The Political Revolution Continues', 16 June 2016. Available at: https://berniesanders.com/political-revolution-continues.
14   Dan La Botz, 'Life After Bernie: People's Summit Searches for the Movement's Political Future', *New Politics*, 21 June 2016. Available at: http://newpol.org.
15   See Steve Williams and Rishi Awatramani, 'New Working-Class Organizations and the Social Movement Left', and Mark Dudzic and Adolph Reed, Jr., 'The Crisis of Labour and the Left in the United States', in Leo Panitch and Greg Albo, eds., *Socialist Register 2015: Transforming Classes*, London: Merlin Press, 2014.
16   See Costas Eleftheriou, 'The Uneasy "Symbiosis": Factionalism and Radical Politics in Synaspismos', paper prepared for 4th Hellenic Observatory PhD Symposium, n.d.
17   Michalis Spourdalakis, 'Left Strategy in the Greek Cauldron: Explaining Syriza's Success', in Leo Panitch, Greg Albo, and Vivek Chibber, eds., *Socialist Register 2013: The Question of Strategy*, London: Merlin Press, 2012, p. 102.
18   Available at: https://left.gr/news/political-resolution-1st-congress-syriza.
19   'Syriza and Socialist Strategy', *International Socialism*, No. 146, April 2015 (transcript of a debate between Alec Callinicos and Stathis Kouvelakis, London, 25 February 2015).
20   Costas Douzinas, 'The Left in Power? Notes on Syriza's Rise, Fall and (Possible) Second Rise', *Near Futures Online*, March 2016. Available at: http://nearfuturesonline.org.
21   Michalis Spourdalakis, 'Becoming Syriza Again', *Jacobin*, 31 January 2016.
22   Nicos Poulantzas, 'Towards a Democratic Socialism', *State, Power, Socialism*, London: NLB, 1978.
23   Andre Gorz, 'Reform and Revolution', in Ralph Miliband and John Saville, eds., *The Socialist Register 1968*, London: Merlin Press, 1968; Lucio Magri, 'Problems of the Marxist Theory of the Revolutionary Party', *New Left Review*, 60(March/April), 1970; Tony Benn, *The New Politics: A Socialist Reconnaissance*, Fabian Tract 402, September 1970; Ralph Miliband, 'Moving On', in Ralph Miliband and John Saville, eds., *The Socialist Register 1976*, London: Merlin Press, 1976; Ralph Miliband, *Marxism and Politics*, Oxford: OUP, 1977; Sheila Rowbotham, Lynne Segal, and Hilary Wainwright, *Beyond the Fragments: Feminism and the Making of Socialism*, London: Merlin, 1979.
24   Poulantzas, 'Towards', pp. 257-8, 260-1.
25   Poulantzas, 'Towards', pp. 256, 258, 261.
26   Gorz, 'Reform and Revolution', p. 112.
27   Gorz, 'Reform and Revolution', pp. 132-3. Lucio Magri similarly called for new workers councils 'right across society (factories, offices, schools), with their own structures as mediating organizations between party, union, and state institutions, for which all of the latter needed to act as elements of stimulus and synthesis'. And even though he presented this in terms of the 'need for a creative revival of the theme of *soviets* [as] essential to resolve the theoretical and strategic problems of the Western Revolution', this was directed at offsetting the total dominance of the party, and emphatically did not mean re-endorsing a dual power strategy for smashing the state. Magri, 'Problems', p. 128.
28   Poulantzas, 'Towards', pp. 256, 258.
29   Ralph Miliband, *Class Power and State Power*, London: Verso, 1983, esp. Chapters 2-4.
30   Goran Therborn, *What Does the Ruling Class Do When it Rules? State Apparatuses and*

State Power under Feudalism, Capitalism and Socialism, NLB: London, 1978, pp. 279-80.
31 See however Greg Albo, David Langille and Leo Panitch eds., *A Different Kind of State: Popular Power and Democratic Administration*, Toronto: OUP, 1993.
32 See the critique of recent books in this vein by Alperowitz, Wolff and Wright in Sam Gindin, 'Chasing Utopia', *Jacobin*, 10 March 2016.
33 Poulantzas, 'Towards', p. 262.
34 Marx, *Later Political Writings*, p. 35.

THE ACTUALITY OF REVOLUTION

JODI DEAN

Because it is the party's function to prepare the revolution, it is – simultaneously and equally – both producer and product, both precondition and result of the revolutionary mass movement.

Georg Lukács, *Lenin: The Unity of His Thought*

For a certain North American and European left, revolution today names more a problem than it does a solution. We know that revolutions happen, but we have a hard time believing in revolution. We have a hard time believing in revolution because we are no longer confident that the revolutionary process leads in an emancipatory egalitarian direction. There are revolutions, but they are not for us, not the revolutions we were hoping for, not proletarian revolutions. And even if today there were or could be revolutions of the proletarianized, they would not be enough. Our goals are far grander (or is this grandeur but an inverted form of their diminution?).

I claim we no longer believe in revolution because we no longer adopt the perspective from which we see ourselves as revolutionaries, the perspective of the communist party. Absent this political perspective, only capitalism with its permanent crises, innovations, and transformations appears as capable of effecting revolutionary change. Fortunately, the crowds and demonstrations of the last decade suggest that a new party perspective may be emerging. The collective practices and intensities exhibited in current struggles, as well as the limits against which these struggles falter, are renewing the salience of the party question on the left. As people experience their collective power, the desire for something like a party is re-emerging, a party as the organized site of our belief in revolution.

In this essay I focus on two, seemingly opposed, approaches to organization and revolution. My argument begins with Georg Lukács' account of the Leninist innovation: the realization that the core of historical materialism is the actuality of the proletarian revolution. This enables me to draw out the articulation of revolution, proletariat, party, and state central to the event of 1917. The force of this articulation comes from *anticipation*, the capacity of the future revolution to coordinate the actions that will bring it about. I then turn to our present setting wherein the links between revolution, proletariat, party, and state have dissolved. Here I engage Michael Hardt's and Antonio Negri's discussion in *Commonwealth*, the third volume of their influential Empire trilogy. For Hardt and Negri, revolution involves biopolitics rather than the state, democracy rather than the party, and identity rather than the proletariat. The problem with their account is that it precludes the temporality that would produce revolutionary practice. Revolution is present as *potential*, a possibility that flows out of what we are already doing. Hardt and Negri view revolution as a continuation of the practices of biopolitical production and capitalism's own revolutionary innovation. There is no revolutionary break, no negation of some practices, trajectories, and potentials in the forwarding of emancipatory egalitarian aims. Theirs is thus a 'revolution without revolution'. In contrast, the future projected in Lenin's assumption of the actuality of revolution coordinates political action to bring revolution into being. The party anticipates the revolution, materializing the belief that makes revolution possible not just as an outflow or overflow of present possibilities, but as an effect of the negation of some practices, trajectories, and potentials and the forcing of others.

My argument relies on Jean-Pierre Dupuy's notion of 'projected time'. Dupuy introduces 'projected time' as a name for 'coordination by means of the future', that is, as a term for a temporal metaphysics wherein 'the future counterfactually determines the past, which in turn causally determines it. The future is fixed, but its necessity exists only in retrospect.'[1] From the perspective of the future, what led to it was necessary. It could not have been otherwise because everything that happened led to it. Before an event occurs, there are possibilities, options. After something happens, it appears inevitable, destined. Projected time thus assumes a future inevitability, establishing this inevitability as the fixed point from which to decide upon present actions.

Projected time might seem strange. Dupuy explains that it is actually 'the metaphysics of the ordinary person'. It encompasses ideas of predestination, fate, destiny, 'everything happens for a reason', even psychoanalysis, to an extent. Projected time is also 'the temporality peculiar to someone who carries out a plan that he has given to himself to carry out'.[2] The example of planning makes clear how projected time is not a prediction of what will happen, a fantasy about what one wants to happen, or a set of proposals regarding what should happen.[3] Instead, a certain outcome generates the processes that lead to it. Again, in this temporal metaphysics, the future is not the inevitable effect of a chain of causes. The future is itself the cause. The future produces the past that will give rise to it.

Dupuy developed the metaphysics of projected time in the context of an investigation of catastrophe. People have a hard time believing in imminent disaster, even in the face of abundant information that the worst is about to happen. Dupuy concluded that the obstacle preventing people from acting is not one of knowledge but one of belief. They know what will happen; nevertheless they do not believe that it will happen. Projected time addresses this level of belief. Dupuy wagers that since it is 'more difficult to reject a fate than to avoid a calamity, the threat of catastrophe becomes far more credible if it appears to be something that is inevitable'.[4] That very inevitability can mobilize the determination and imagination necessary for avoiding the inevitable. The logic here is prophetic: the prophet announces the fate of the people so that they will change their ways and thereby escape their destiny. Of course, the tragic rejoinder is that the effort to escape destiny brings about its fulfilment. Yet this logic, too, involves coordination by means of the future insofar as it is still the fixed future whose necessity is retroactively revealed. In Dupuy's words, 'an event becomes possible only in making itself possible'.[5]

A VIEW FROM THE FUTURE

Lenin: A Study on the Unity of His Thought is Lukács' account of the enormity of V.I. Lenin's theoretical contribution: Lenin realized Marxist theory in practice. Written in the immediate aftermath of Lenin's death in 1924, *Lenin* is more than a shorter, livelier account of the party than the one in the better known last chapter of *History and Class Consciousness*, 'Towards a Methodology of the Problem of Organization', written two years earlier. *Lenin* is a presentation of Leninism as a new phase of Marxism. So even as the two works overlap in their emphasis on organization as 'the form of mediation between theory and practice', the latter work positions Lenin as 'the only theoretician equal to Marx'.[6] Lenin's deployment of historical materialism in concrete struggle enables us to recognize, retroactively, Marxism's inner truth: 'historical materialism is the theory of the proletarian revolution.'[7] Not all Marxists share this insight. Vulgar Marxists, Lukács notes, see crises as temporary and rebellion as irrational given the invincibility of the capitalist system. Lenin is unique. Because he grasps 'the actuality of the revolution', Lenin can explain the events around him in its terms. He posits a certain future – the revolution – and lets this future guide action in the present. *Lenin* thus identifies the mechanism through which organization mediates between theory and practice, a point hinted at yet undeveloped in the earlier essay.[8] The projected future of revolution generates the practices that materialize the belief necessary for its realization.

The actuality of revolution could suggest iron laws of history or economistic determinism. This is not Lukács' point – and it could not be his point insofar as he emphasizes that it is only with Lenin that the truth of historical materialism appears. Lenin changes the past, the relation between political economy and class struggle; he activates a different political process. Moreover, Lukács criticizes, repeatedly, mechanistic interpretations of Marx. And while most readers of Lukács emphasize the concept of 'totality' in his work, *Lenin* is striking for its distance from the concept. As Martin Jay notes, Lukács presents in *Lenin* 'a modified "de-centred" or non-genetic view of totality. No longer was the proletariat the meta-subjective totalizer of history.'[9] Jay doesn't tell us what the de-centring force or event might be. I think it is fruitfully understood as the future. The fact that there *will be* a revolution, that proletarian revolution is on the *agenda*, affects the choices, actions, and groups that produce it.

Projected time tells us how to read Lukács' claim that 'the proletarian revolution constitutes the living core of Marxism'.[10] The revolutionary future determines the actions that bring it about. Historical materialism isn't primarily an account of the past. It's a relation to a specific future, one where '*revolution is already on its agenda*'.[11] Lukács observes that the error of Kautsky, Plekhanov, and others lay in their placing the revolution into a future so distant that the actions of the day had no bearing on it. A distant future lacks coordinating capacity. In contrast, he argues that Lenin made the actuality of revolution into the point from which questions are evaluated and individual actions are considered. The revolution functions as 'a reality constituting a norm for our own actions'.[12] This certain future enables choices and decisions. It cuts through multiple tendencies, the manifold conflicts of groups and individuals within the masses, as well as the economic fatalism that contributes to capitalism's own response to crises. The fact of revolution operates as a force of negation within the present that pushes forth the practices necessary to it.

Lukács presents Lenin as making the imminent event of revolution into concrete reality. For Lenin, the actuality of proletarian revolution answers the question of the character of revolution in Russia, it is proletarian rather than bourgeois. This actuality announces as well the class whose role it is to lead the revolution, the proletariat. Lukács observes that most Marxists knew that capitalist developments would lead to proletarian revolution. Lenin, however, was unique in his application of this insight. Lukács notes how

Lenin used it 'to establish firm guide-lines for all questions on the daily agenda, whether they were political or economic, involved theory or tactics, agitation or organization'.[13] With this attention to ongoing struggles, Lenin shifts the register of the question of revolution from knowledge to belief. Concrete practices, tactics, organization, and agitation not only manifest but also produce belief (this materialist notion of belief comes from Žižek who emphasizes that belief is how we act in the face of what we know).[14] A specific vision of the future – proletarian revolution – determines in the present the tactics that will bring the future about.

The projected future of proletarian revolution exhibits coordinating capacity in three interrelated ways: (1) it engenders belief in the revolutionary task of the proletariat; (2) it establishes the role of the revolutionary party; and (3) it determines the proper understanding of the state. In each instance, Lukács brings out Lenin's crucial contribution: Lenin concretizes theory in practice. He approaches practical questions from the perspective of the actuality of revolution. As tactics and organization materialize belief in the revolution, they help bring about the revolution that caused them.

First, Lukács notes that Lenin sees more than the misery of the proletariat. Because he looks at the condition of the proletariat in light of the fact that revolution is 'already on the historical agenda as a practical reality', Lenin detects 'the revolutionary element "which will bring down the old order"'.[15] Lenin doesn't fall prey to economic fatalism. He sees the future in the present and works to bring out belief in that future. The repercussion for practical struggle is that Lenin recognizes that the bourgeoisie is no longer a revolutionary class. The task of revolution has passed to the proletariat.

Recognition of the fact that the bourgeoisie is no longer a revolutionary class enables a concrete understanding of the situation in Russia. Lukács points out that even if it was not clear to participants at the time, the actuality of the revolution was at the core of debates within Russian socialism. Those who projected proletarian revolution into a distant future emphasized the links between economic development and democracy. They thought the bourgeoisie needed to complete its revolution before the proletariat entered the stage. If the proletariat asserted itself too early, the bourgeoisie would ally with Tsarism thereby setting back proletarian progress. In contrast, Lenin understood that the bourgeoisie had already 'ceased to be a revolutionary class'.[16] It was no longer trying to realize its own revolutionary demands, but had instead abandoned them to the proletariat. Lenin's anticipation of the proletarian revolution lets him explain the alliance between the bourgeoisie and Tsarism (both fear the revolutionary proletariat) and demonstrate the illusory nature of the link between 'political democracy' and capitalism (the bourgeoisie could pursue its interests under Tsarism).

Lenin's anticipation also accounts for the proletariat's leading role in the revolution. Because of its alliance with Tsarism, the bourgeoisie was unable to abolish Russian agricultural feudalism. The peasantry was stuck in a situation in which it could revolt, but not pursue a positive alternative. As Lenin presents it, the peasantry has two options: sweep away all medieval practices or gradually adapt to capitalism. The decision between the two is reached through class struggle. The proletariat is the decisive force in this struggle because of the proletariat's own struggle against the bourgeoisie in the cities. So even though the proletariat and the peasantry have different aims, the fact that the bourgeoisie is no longer a revolutionary class creates the basis for their alliance. 'The revolutionary alliance of all the oppressed' develops out of 'a concrete understanding of the conditions of proletarian revolution.'[17]

Lukács acknowledges the significance of Marx's distinction between bourgeois and proletarian revolutions. Yet he condemns the way vulgar Marxism paralyzes this distinction into a 'mechanistic separation'. In its opportunistic version, this paralysis manifests in the insistence that the proletariat discount its own revolutionary aims and support the bourgeois revolution. In its radical left-wing version, the paralysis appears as purity: anything not proletarian is overlooked. Purists ignore the various issues that arise under imperialism (national and colonial questions, for example) and as a result fail to understand the revolutionary environment. The 'real revolution', Lukács insists, 'is the dialectical transformation of the bourgeois revolution into the proletarian revolution'.[18] It's not simply that they are different revolutions appropriate to different levels of capitalist development. One can, and must, become the other.

Second, just as the projected time of proletarian revolution engenders belief in the revolutionary task of the proletariat, so too does it establish the role of the revolutionary party. The actuality of revolution is the presupposition on which Lenin's concept of the party rests. Lukács argues that the dispute between the Bolsheviks and the Mensheviks over party membership has to be understood as a conflict between 'the two different basic attitudes to the possibility, probable course and character, of the revolution'. The projected future of proletarian revolution causes the Bolsheviks to select 'single-minded revolutionaries, prepared to make any sacrifice, from the more or less chaotic mass of the class as a whole'. In contrast, the Mensheviks wanted to count as members those who supported and worked for the party. While the Bolshevik concept has come under sustained criticism, for instance, of the likelihood that professional revolutionaries 'will divorce themselves from their actual class environment and ... degenerate into a sect', Lukács shows how the actuality of revolution produces a set of behavioral norms and expectations that Lenin, uniquely, had the perspicacity to implement.[19]

The party does not make the revolution. Nor does it try to pull along inactive masses and present them with a fait accompli. Instead, it anticipates the revolution. More specifically, the party is 'conceived as an instrument of class struggle in a revolutionary period'.[20] Given that the period is revolutionary, that the proletarian revolution is on the agenda, what form of organization follows? Lenin's answer is the 'strictest selection of party members on the basis of their proletarian class-consciousness, and total solidarity with and support for all the oppressed and exploited within capitalist society'.[21] Why? Because of the way the proletariat develops its own class-consciousness and becomes able to put it to use in the context of revolutionary upheaval.

In the course of its revolutionary movement, the proletariat encounters differences within and without it. The internal differences involve economic differentiation within the proletariat (the infamous 'labour aristocracy'). The external differences refer to the other classes that are part of the revolutionary alliance. Differences within the proletariat hinder class unity. Some workers, perhaps those with more education or experience in union leadership, tend to see their interests as allied with the bourgeoisie. Differences between the proletariat and other social strata create confusion, particularly as crises intensify and the revolutionary period gets nearer. The multiplicity of interests within the revolutionary alliance of the oppressed pulls them in different directions. Not every potential present in the masses forwards the revolution. Figuring out the correct path, and keeping together the alliance through which all can win, becomes increasingly difficult.

Lenin's model of the party responds to the pull of these differences by providing an independent organizational space for the 'fully conscious elements of the proletariat'. Lukács writes: 'It is this that demonstrates *that the Leninist form of organization is inseparably connected with the ability to foresee the approaching revolution.*'[22] In the party, even the most seemingly trivial decision becomes significant, that is, made in light of the projected future of proletarian revolution. A party decision cuts through myriad possibilities, directing action in one way rather than another.

The significance of revolutionary anticipation is born out in Lukács' discussion of the way that Lenin's concept of organization 'means a double break with mechanical fatalism'. The first break is with 'the concept of proletarian class-consciousness as a mechanical product of its class situation'. The second is with the idea that 'the revolution itself was only the mechanical working out of fatalistically explosive economic forces which

– given the sufficient "maturity" of objective revolutionary conditions – would somehow "automatically" lead the proletariat to victory'.[23] Class-consciousness does not follow 'with fatalistic inevitability' from economic situation. Some members of a class will always be passive, always cross sides. Likewise, a combination of forces contributes to the revolutionary situation some 'spontaneous-explosive' actions and some 'consciously-led class actions'.[24] The role of the party is to anticipate this situation: '*The party must prepare the revolution.*'[25] The projected future guides the party to prepare for it. The party must do everything it can to 'prepare the proletarian masses intellectually, materially, and organizationally' for what lies ahead.[26] The party's work is thus coordinated by means of the revolution it anticipates.

Lukács' account makes clear that even as this view of the future provides the party with its organizational form, it is the party that sustains the view. He addresses the debate between Kautsky and Luxemburg. Kautsky argues that the party is the precondition of revolutionary action. Luxemburg argues that it is the product of revolutionary mass movement. Lukács finds each view one-sided: 'Because it is the party's function to prepare the revolution, it is – simultaneously and equally – both *producer* and *product*, both precondition *and* result of the revolutionary mass movement.'[27] The party's role as producer is itself a product of the projected future of proletarian revolution. The party is a product not only of events as they unfold and to which it responds but also of the future that calls it into being, the future that enables it to guides its responses toward it.

Crucial to Lukács' argument is the party's combination of flexibility and consistency. The party has to learn from the struggles of the masses, adjusting its interpretations and practices as necessary. How does it determine when changing itself is necessary? In light of the actuality of revolution: 'Only its relations to the whole, to the fate of the proletarian revolution, makes a thought, a policy decision, etc., right or wrong.'[28] Responses to the present in light of the projected future are inscribed into party structure and theory. Learning from the struggles of the people is possible because of the party's anticipation of the revolution. The party thereby unites the discoveries that arise from the mass struggle with the actuality of the revolution. Belief in revolution arises out of the combination of theory and action: actions appear as revolutionary because the future revolution is calling them into being.

The third way the projected future of proletarian revolution exhibits coordinating capacity involves the understanding of the state. Lukács presents the problem of the state as one that Marxist theory perpetually defers into some indefinite future. He writes, 'Only with Lenin did this "future" become present in the theoretical sense as well.'[29] Lenin makes the question of the state 'immediate' by looking at it in terms of the actuality of revolution. This enables him to discern how the state is a 'weapon of class struggle'. And this clarity further reveals the necessity of political organs beyond those traditionally associated with working-class struggles (unions, cooperatives, parties), organs with a capacity to include all the oppressed. The Soviets are these new organs, 'an anti-government' that disorganizes the bourgeois state apparatus and opens up the struggle for state power.

Understood in terms of the actuality of proletarian revolution, the Soviets as a form for proletarian state power provide the proletariat with practical political insight. For one, they reveal that the assumption that the proletarian revolution can avoid the state is '*an ideological capitulation to the bourgeoisie*'.[30] Those who think that because the proletariat aims to abolish classes it has no need for the organ of class rule are utopian. They send the proletariat down the road to defeat, denying the class the means for defeating the bourgeoisie and establishing socialism. For another, the Soviets uncover '*the bourgeois class character of democracy*'.[31] Many workers fall under the illusion that majority rule is to their benefit since they constitute a majority. Formal democracy, however, treats concrete human beings as abstract individuals. It 'pulverizes' social being, obscures people's position within social belonging, and connects citizens as isolated atoms to the state as a totality. In contrast, the Soviets mark the proletarian attempt '*to counteract this process of disorganization*'.[32] They create the opportunity for proletarian revolutionary leadership by providing the space through which the proletariat can seize ideological leadership from the bourgeoisie and develop an ideology of and for the oppressed classes.

Lukács emphasizes that 'the actuality of the revolution expresses itself in the actuality of the problem of the state for the proletariat'.[33] That the state is a weapon of class war does not mean that the struggle for socialism is won after the proletariat has seized state power. Not only does the struggle against the bourgeoisie continue, now more violently, but also the challenge of the transition to socialism presents itself all the more concretely. In the context of proletarian state power, the projected future of revolution manifests in the ongoing task of building socialism. Proletarian revolution is not a moment. It's a process.

In sum, Lukács presents the actuality of revolution as a projected future. This imminent future suggests norms and standards for action. Every decision, every tactic, every compromise anticipates the revolution. They don't wait until a more propitious time. To the extent that party practices are coordinated by the future, they both manifest belief in it – as opposed to the more abstract knowledge of revolution posited by social democrats – and help bring it about. Lukács insists that the actuality of revolution distinguishes

Lenin's position from both social democrats and left-wing purists. From the perspective of the former, the revolution is always too far off, the proletariat never mature enough, the unions still too weak. From the perspective of the latter, the ripeness of the moment dictates a pure politics, a radical insistence on principles without compromise. Unlike either, the actuality of revolution involves the political time of anticipation and struggle, a time when the future guides the party prepared to usher it in. For Lenin, Lukács writes, it is not enough to evaluate a concrete situation '*in its reality*'.[34] The facts must be related to '*the whole historical process*'; they must be understood in terms of the actuality of revolution. The Lenininst innovation turns on a way of seeing that ties theory to practice by anticipating the future in the present.

REVOLUTION TODAY

Not all communists in 1924 agreed with Lukács' assessment of the Bolshevik revolution. Lukács himself ends his short study of Lenin's thought with a nod to these critics. He provides a dialectical justification for the seemingly contradictory policies of the Russian Communist Party as it returned to capitalism even as it asserted the necessity of revolution on a world scale: the period itself was contradictory. Over the next sixty years, debate over Lenin, the Party, and the success or failure of the 1917 revolution would intensify, pushed in one direction by Stalinist excess, in other directions by the experiences of communist parties elsewhere. By the time of the dissolution of the Soviet Union in 1991, the idea that a proletarian revolution led by a communist party would result in a new state form and successfully transition to socialism was widely discredited.[35] Within the contemporary left, elements of the resulting consensus include the idea that the working class is no longer (if it ever had been) a revolutionary class; the rejection of politics centred on the state; and, the excoriation of vanguardism, hierarchy, and the party form. What, then, of revolution?

In the final volume of their influential trilogy, Hardt and Negri announce: 'Revolution is now, finally, becoming the order of the day.'[36] Their theory of revolution arises out of an account of the biopolitical character of capitalism in the late twentieth century. Networked communications have transformed the process of production, contributing to its homogenization, decentralization/deterritorialization, and informatization. Knowledge, affect, and communication play a greater role; labour has become 'increasingly immaterial'.[37] The result is a fundamental change in the relation between production and the reproduction of life: rather than separate from and subordinated to the demands of productive work, 'life infuses and dominates all production'.[38] As Hardt and Negri argue in *Commonwealth*: 'Today the sites of economic production have spread throughout the social terrain and the production of economic value is increasingly indistinguishable from the production of social relations and forms of life.'[39] With its biopolitical turn, capitalism subsumes the entirety of the social. Social relations don't have to take on the form of the commodity to generate value for capitalism. Capitalism expropriates value from them directly.[40]

On the basis of their analysis of changes in production, Hardt and Negri claim that today 'the perspective of revolutionary action has to be conceived on the biopolitical horizon'.[41] Such a revolution is a 'revolution in life', that is, a revolution that exceeds the range of demands and expectations associated with the labour movement.

Biopolitical revolution has a distinct temporality. In contrast to the projected future provided by the actuality of revolution, revolution today

> ... is no longer imaginable as an event separated from us in the future but has to live in the present, an 'exceeding' present that in some sense already contains the future within it. Revolutionary movement resides on the same horizon of temporality with capitalist control, and its position of being within and against is manifest through a movement of exodus, which poses the exceeding productivity of the multitude against the exceptionality of capitalist command.[42]

Instead of a future with the capacity to coordinate action in the present, revolution coexists with and within non-revolution. Unable to imagine a future revolution, we can't use its actuality to decide our tactics. As a distinct component of political action, tactics fall by the wayside, displaced by potentials within biopolitical production.

Revolution is an excessive element in the present, an element Hardt and Negri associate with the creative, cooperative, communicative labour of the multitude. Revolt involves separation from capitalist control, the liberation of biopolitical production from capitalist dominion. When they say that the 'revolutionary movement resides on the same horizon of temporality with capitalist control', Hardt and Negri are emphasizing a difference between biopolitical and industrial production. Under contemporary conditions, exploitation doesn't involve the capitalist's appropriation of a surplus of labour time that comes after necessary labour time. Necessary and surplus labour happen at the same time, in the same operation of producing social relations and forms of life. The blending of production and reproduction eludes the quantitative measure used to determine necessary and surplus labour time. In the present, therefore, 'the capitalist temporality of valorization and expropriation' can't be understood in terms of measurable sequences but must be viewed as 'a kind of simultaneity'.[43] Hardt and Negri imagine revolution as an analogous 'kind of simultaneity', the excess and limit to capitalist command over the biopolitical production it can never fully capture or control.

Biopolitical exploitation includes accumulation by dispossession and the expropriation of the common. Key to the latter is capitalism's expropriation of the common that biopolitical labour produces – common knowledge, language, culture, and modes of sociality. Hardt and Negri argue that 'rather than providing cooperation, we could even say that capital expropriates cooperation as a central element of exploiting biopolitical labour-power. This expropriation takes place not so much from the individual worker (because cooperation already implies a collectivity) but more clearly from the field of social labour.'[44] Biopolitical labour is generally autonomous from capitalist command, they argue, emerging out of networked cooperative practices. Capital seeks to capture, expropriate, and discipline these practices, even as it itself depends on the creativity that their autonomy unleashes. Bypassing commodification, capital extracts value directly from social relations themselves.

Hardt and Negri highlight the democratic dimension of biopolitical labour: in their view, the same networked, cooperative structures that produce the common generate new democratic capacities, and even 'make possible in the political sphere the development of democratic organizations'.[45] For this reason, Hardt and Negri reject 'vanguard organizations'. The vanguard party corresponds to a different, earlier, structure of labour (a different technical composition of the proletariat). According to Hardt's and Negri's periodization, the vanguard party fits with the early twentieth century's professional factory workers. The deskilled workers of the mid-twentieth century fit with that period's mass party. The political form appropriate to biopolitical labour, the one appropriate to us now, they argue, must be democratic. More specifically, it must be cooperative, autonomous, and horizontally networked. Hardt and Negri concede that 'these democratic capacities of labour do not immediately translate into the creation of democratic political organizations', nevertheless, they are a good basis on which to build them.[46]

Even as they admit that the processes of biopolitical production do not immediately or automatically create the kinds of political organizations we need, and even as they acknowledge that they are not offering a figure adequate to the revolutionary process, Hardt and Negri insist on the distance between their concept of revolution and Lenin's. Reducing Lenin's complex and adaptive approach to political organization via the limited terms of contemporary politics, they treat Lenin's party as 'a new identity'. They argue that Lenin 'conceives the articulation of the social groups in struggle under the hegemony of the party, which forms a counterpower, mirroring in certain respects the identity of the central power it opposes'.[47] Since biopolitical production's networked form takes on the form of power it opposes – the networks of surveillance, international treaties, multinational corporations, and militarized policing – the problem here can't be that the vanguard 'mirrors' the power it opposes. Their periodization makes clear that the problem is precisely that it doesn't. For Hardt and Negri, the vanguard party is inadequate, 'anachronistic', because it doesn't look like the networks of contemporary biopolitical production.

This argument is not convincing. Complex networks are not the horizontal, cooperative, and autonomous forms that Hardt and Negri imagine. As Albert-Laszlo Barabasi's work on complex networks demonstrates, free choice, growth, and preferential attachment produce hierarchies, dramatic differences between the one that is most chosen and preferred and the many that are not.[48] The most popular node or item in a complex network generally has twice as many links as the second most popular, which has more than the third most popular and so, such that there is very little difference among the crowd of those at the bottom but massive differences between top and bottom. This hierarchical structure is pervasive in communicative capitalism. Blockbuster movies, best-selling books, and giant internet hubs like Google, Facebook, YouTube, and China's Baidu, all reflect an effective 'power law' distribution of links in complex networks. The few get a lot; the rest get very little, almost nothing. The idea appears in popular media as the '80/20 rule, the winner-take-all or winner-take-most character of the new economy', and the 'long tail' of the many.[49] The ostensibly creative, cooperative, and democratic character of networked communication doesn't eliminate hierarchy. It entrenches hierarchy by using our own choices against us. And, as Barabasi makes clear, this hierarchy isn't imposed from above. It is an immanent effect of free choice, growth, and preferential attachment.

A political form mirroring biopolitical production would not be horizontal and democratic. Its democracy would produce 'power law' distributions, unequal nodes or outcomes, winners and losers, few and many. We see this phenomenon on Twitter as people fight through trending hashtags: hashtags provide common names that serve as loci of struggle. When they trend, they rise above the long tail of the millions of unread, unloved Tweets coursing through the nets. The democratic element – the very exercise of people's choice to use and forward – produces the inequality that lets some hashtags appear as and even be, for a moment, significant. The fact of emergent hierarchies suggests that an emergent vanguard may well be the political form necessary for struggles under biopolitical conditions. To reject this form in the name of an as yet non-existent democratic organization is both to encourage the conditions that produce the form itself – democratic engagements – and to call for the elimination of whatever these engagements produce, namely, a few out of the many. This rejection has a persistent pattern on the post-68 left: the rejection of leaders and resulting infighting when they emerge and inefficacy when they are condemned.

The structure of the complex networks of biopolitical production indicates that, contra Hardt and Negri, a vanguard party is not anachronistic at all. It is instead a form that corresponds to the dynamics of networked communication. This structure indicates an additional problem with Hardt and Negri's rejection of the vanguard party. They characterize Lenin's party as involving an organizational process that comes from 'above' the movements of the multitude. Historically, this insinuation is clearly false. The Bolsheviks were but one group among multiple parties, tendencies, and factions acting in the tumultuous context of the Russian Revolution. They were active within the movements of the oppressed workers and peasants. The movements themselves, through victories and defeats, short and long-term alliances, new forms of cooperation, and advances in political organization gave rise to the party even as the party furthered the movements. Charles Post writes, 'Leninism cannot be reduced to the post-1923 caricature of "democratic centralism". Instead, the enduring legacy of Leninism remains the goal of constructing an *independent* organization of anti-capitalist organizers and activists who attempt to project a *political* alternative to the forces of official reformism not only in elections, but in mass, extra-parliamentary social struggles.'[50] Lenin's insistence on the actuality of revolution provides the coordination by means of the future at the heart of this projection of a political alternative. The party is a force of anticipation, a temporal force that Hardt's and Negri's concern with the spatial register of top and bottom omits.

Finally, Hardt and Negri criticize Lenin's party on the grounds of identity. For them, the party is a 'new identity', and they think that revolution today must aim at the abolition of identity.[51] Their argument against identity is an important corrective to the advocacy of identity politics still current among some segments of the left. Rejecting the primacy of class, Hardt and Negri draw out radical elements of feminist and anti-racist politics. They argue that the radical core of the politics of sex, race, and class is a self-abolition of identity that results in the proliferation of differences. 'The project for the abolition of identity', Hardt and Negri assert, 'thus fills the traditional role of *the abolition of property and the abolition of the state.*'[52]

Hardt and Negri are right to emphasize the necessity of moving beyond identity politics, bringing us back, in a way, to the broader revolutionary struggles of the oppressed and recognition of the ways capitalism benefits from divisions among the masses. Attachment to identity results in immobilization and subordination, the limiting of what one might become. We should add that insofar as capitalist processes already produce, undermine, and expropriate identities, attempting to hold onto identity is like trying to hold onto air. Identities are already melting away, already vulnerable and unraveling.[53] Nevertheless, Lenin's party is not an identity. On the contrary, the party is a process, in Lukács' version a process whereby the distinctions of what Hardt and Negri associate with identity are smoothed out and a collective revolutionary will is generated.[54] To this extent, the party functions more through the installation and maintenance of a gap within the field in which identity is given than it does as a new identity.

Additional problems accompany Hardt's and Negri's substitution of identity for property and state. These include: leaving exploitative relations intact; leaving state violence intact; leaving processes of proletarianization intact; leaving systems of oppression intact. Capitalism and the state operate through the dissolution of identity just as much as they can through its inscription and amplification. At the level of tactics, a project for the abolition of identity easily flows into the dominant ideology's fixation on fluidity and self-transformation, letting change at the personal level stand in for broader struggles for system change. In fact, when changes at the level of the person become significant, they push up against the limits posed by state and economy, making it clear that these fronts cannot be avoided. This means that fighting over whether and in what form property and the state continue cannot be avoided. Yet Hardt and Negri give us an account of revolution where the endpoint of such fighting cannot be imagined. Revolution envisioned as the abolition of identity fails to provide a perspective that can orient a politics that inevitably comes up against state and economy.

Hardt and Negri reject the goal of working-class power not only on grounds of identity but also on grounds of power. For them the state should not be seized even to serve as an instrument of class struggle (although the multitude might have to engage it). The state is and can only be a seat of domination that guarantees capitalist exploitation and the policing of identity hierarchies. Arguing that revolution must have democracy as its object and that it requires a long and arduous process of transformation, Hardt and Negri misrepresent the dictatorship of the proletariat as nothing more than subservience.[55] Lenin also recognizes that revolutionary transformation does not happen overnight. The dictatorship of the proletariat is nothing but that process of transformation, a process that Lenin, like Hardt and Negri, associates with 'an immense expansion of democracy, which *for the first time* becomes democracy for the poor, democracy for the people, and not democracy for the money-bags'.[56] Unlike Hardt and Negri, however, Lenin recognizes that wresting the power and wealth concentrated in the hands of the few requires more than the extension of democracy. It requires its restriction as well: oppressors, exploiters, and capitalists must be suppressed. There are limits to democratic means.

For Hardt and Negri, the goal of revolution is 'the generation of new forms of social life'.[57] They describe revolutionary struggles as a process of liberation that establishes a common. Such a process, they argue, consolidates insurrection as it institutionalizes new collective habits and practices. Hardt and Negri thus conceive institutions as sites for the management of encounters, extension of social rupture, and transformation of those who compose them.

The resemblance between these institutions and Lukács' depiction of the vanguard party is striking, all the more so given Hardt and Negri's rejection of the party form. The party involves a common name, language, and set of tactics. It has practices that establish ways of being together. Its purpose is occupying and extending the gap within society that class struggle denotes. Moreover, Lukács insists that Lenin's concept of party organization prioritizes flexibility and consistency; the party has and must have a capacity for self-transformation. What Hardt and Negri describe as the extension of insurrection in an institutional process is another way of theorizing the party.

Because they disavow the party, their version of democratic organization lacks a position that can anticipate the revolution and thereby materialize belief in its actuality. The future does not exercise coordinating capacity. Hardt and Negri emphasize that revolution is 'squeezed in the vise between past and future, leaving it very little room for maneuver'. They write, 'even when revolutionaries think their actions are sufficient to launch us into the future, the past bursts through to reimpose itself'. And they conclude, 'Revolution's creation of a new form of government holds off the past and opens toward the future'.[58] Rather than products of the revolution they produce, revolutionaries in Hardt and Negri's version remain at a distance from the future. Their actions seem disconnected from it, uninformed by it, and hence all the more under the sway of the past. Revolution opens to the future, but a projected future does not call into being the forces that will have produced it.

Lacking a vision of the future capable of orienting action, Hardt and Negri outline instead a platform of demands without a carrier, without a body to fight for them. To be sure, their model of institutions suggests that a party or parties could be such a carrier, but rather than presenting their platform as a party platform, Hardt and Negri present them as demands to be made to existing governments and institutions of global governance. The demands are for the provision of basic means of life, global citizenship, and access to the commons. They acknowledge that 'today's ruling powers unfortunately have no intention of granting even these basic demands'.[59] Their response is laughter, 'a laugh of creation and joy, anchored solidly in the present'.[60] No wonder they don't present their demands as the platform of a party. The demands are not to be fought for. They mark potentials present already in the biopolitical production of the common, merely in the form of demands for certain limits to capitalist control.

The identification of egalitarian potential in what generally seems a bleak and miserable present is laudable. But no practices coordinated by means of the future materialize this belief. Absent a party oriented toward its realization, though, it is hard to believe that this potential is stronger than, say, a neo-feudalism of globally connected fortress-cities surrounded by impoverished scavengers competing for access to a better life via networked gaming platforms and desperately defending their last bits of fresh water and arable land from refugees fleeing ever intensifying resource wars, while the tiny class of global billionaires eat caviar in gold-plated jets. Precisely because our setting is one of exploitation, ownership, competition, and struggle, our sense of the present has to be tied to the future that results from the realization of some potentials rather than others. The party is the form for this realization insofar as through it the future can produce the actions that will have brought it about.

CONCLUSION

The global wave of protests associated with the revolutions in Egypt and Tunisia, the mass assemblies in Spain and Greece, the anti-cuts, anti-austerity, and anti-foreclosure protests, the Occupy movement and so on testify to the fact that people are moving together in growing opposition to the policies and practices of states organized in the interest of capital as class. Across the globe, crowds are rupturing the status quo, the actuality of their movement displacing the politics of identity. These mobilized crowds are forcing the left to return again to questions of organization, endurance, and scale. Having come up against the limits of immediacy and horizontality, activists and organizers alike are thinking again about institutional forms like the party.

Their ongoing experiments include radical left coalitions, movement parties, digital parties, and even new and adversarial occupations of established parties. The more people are seeing themselves with a collective capacity to change the world, the more they are working to develop this capacity, to strengthen and institutionalize it.

That the social and activist movements have returned organizational questions to the fore of left politics does not mean that these questions have been clearly answered, however. Even as the movements produce activist vanguards, organizers and militants committed to the struggles of the proletarianized, these movements have not yet produced a new international communist party or international coalition of the radical left.[61] Moreover, it is not clear whether the protests and demonstrations accompanying capitalist crises in the North America and much of Europe auger a revolutionary opening or repeat the gestures of resistance constitutive of the repertoire of left political practice for the last several decades. Lukács lets us understand that these are different formulations of the same problem. Because the party is producer and product, precondition and result, of revolutionary mass movement, solutions and problems appear together and unevenly. The party that lets us see our struggles as revolutionary can only be the product of revolutionary struggles.[62]

To anticipate the party that anticipates the revolution: if revolution is on the agenda, what might this mean for a party today? Hardt and Negri imply that the party form is outmoded. I have argued instead that not only do contemporary networks produce 'power law' distributions of few and many but that emergent hierarchies – particularly when understood in terms of the vanguards and practices that already emerge out of political movement – point to the ways that party organizations emerge. Current examples of this tendency include the adoption of common tactics, names, and symbols that bring together previously separate, disparate, and even competing struggles. When local and issue politics are connected via a common name, successes in one area advance the struggle as a whole. Separate actions become themselves plus all the others. They instill enthusiasm and inspire imitation. They provide a sense of directionality and movement: which way is the struggle going? Simply multiplying fragmented, local actions isn't enough – they have to be felt as more than what any one of them can be in isolation. A common name or set of symbols provides this consistency.

Learning from Lukács and Lenin, we know that consistency must be accompanied by flexibility. There is no reason to assume that every component or branch of the party, particularly an international party, must have the same structure and that this structure must remain constant.

The problem the left encounters today is less a matter of establishing organizational details in advance than it is of solidary political will. As the will emerges, people will figure out the structure in light of the challenges we face. Such challenges include expanding militant pressure in ways that inspire and educate cadres; straining the resources of the state and breaking the confidence of the financial sector; abolishing private property and the capitalist banking system; and advancing international coordination in an uneven environment. The overall goal is to galvanize popular support and develop a program for common management of production, health, transportation, communication, food, housing, and education for the equal benefit of all in the setting of a changing climate, for starters. Responding to these variable challenges generates new knowledge that can be integrated and shared, knowledge that can support and enable flexibility.

If revolution is on the agenda, then it is a revolution of the proletarianized, of those whom capital as a class dispossesses of their labour, lives, and futures. Because capitalism's system of dispossession operates through the wage, debt, privatization, enclosure, theft, colonization, financialization, and racialized state violence, the movements of the proletarianized mobilize a broad, international, array of people and concerns. A global alliance of the radical left, or, better, a new party of communists, can be knit together from the concentrated forces of already existing groups: militants skilled at direct action, artists adept with symbols and slogans, parties experienced at organizing, issue groups knowledgeable about specific areas of concern, mutual aid networks addressing basic needs. If this new party is to be an agent of revolutionary time, it will have to continue to foster and even amplify the common practices and tactics capable of materializing revolutionary belief. This fostering and amplification requires discipline, choices, conscious planning, and decisions regarding what to prioritize and how to allocate resources and energies. Lukács insists, 'Only through discipline can the party be capable of putting the collective will into practice, whereas the introduction of the bourgeois concept of freedom prevents this collective will from forming itself and so transforms the party into a loose aggregate of individuals incapable of action.'[63] Precisely because the movements are many, or, in the language of Occupy, the 99% are not one, precisely because of the multiplicity of the experiences of the oppressed, we need the party as the form through which we discipline ourselves, through which we produce the collective political will that will push revolutionary tendencies in an emancipatory egalitarian direction.

Many of us are convinced that capitalist crises have reached a decisive point. We know that the system is fragile, that it produces its own gravediggers, and that it is held in place by a repressive international state structure. Yet we act as if we did not know this. The party provides a form that can let us believe what we know.

NOTES

1. Jean-Pierre Dupuy, *Economy and the Future*, Translated by M.B. DeBevoise, East Lansing, MI: Michigan State University Press, 2014, p. 110.
2. Dupuy, *Economy*, p. 116.
3. Projected future thus functions differently from the program put forth by Nick Srnicek and Alex Williams in *Inventing the Future*, London: Verso, 2015.
4. Dupuy, *Economy*, p. 129.
5. Dupuy, *Economy*, p. 140.
6. Georg Lukács, 'Towards a Methodology of the Problem of Organization', *History and Class Consciousness*, Translated by Rodney Livingstone, Cambridge, MA: The MIT Press, 1971; Georg Lukács, *Lenin: A Study on the Unity of His Thought*, Translated by Nicholas Jacobs, London: Verso, 2009, p. 13 (italics omitted).
7. Lukács, *Lenin*, p. 9.
8. In 'Towards a Methodology of the Problem of Organization', Lukács describes the tangle of historical, social, and individual factors involved in any organized action. Emphasizing the need to approach an understanding of organized action in light of the historical totality, he writes, 'an analysis that would see an organized action in terms of the lessons it contained for the future, as an answer to the question, "what then shall we do?" sees the problem in terms of organization'. Lukács, 'Towards a Methodology,' p. 300. It is this sense of futurity that is developed in *Lenin*.
9. Martin Jay, *Marxism and Totality*, Berkeley: University of California Press, 1984, p. 122.
10. Lukács, *Lenin*, p. 12.
11. Ibid. (italics in original)
12. Lukács, *Lenin*, p. 18.
13. Lukács, *Lenin*, p. 13.
14. See my discussion in *Žižek's Politics*, New York: Routledge, 2006.
15. Lukács, *Lenin*, p. 11.
16. Lukács, *Lenin*, p. 20.
17. Lukács, *Lenin*, p. 23.
18. Lukács, *Lenin*, p. 47.
19. Lukács, *Lenin*, p. 25.
20. Lukács, *Lenin*, p. 26 (italics omitted).
21. Lukács, *Lenin*, p. 30.
22. Lukács, *Lenin*, p. 29.
23. Lukács, *Lenin*, p. 31.
24. Lukács, *Lenin*, p. 33.
25. Lukács, *Lenin*, p. 32 (italics in original).
26. Lukács, *Lenin*, p. 33.
27. Lukács, *Lenin*, p. 32.
28. Lukács, *Lenin*, p. 36.
29. Lukács, *Lenin*, p. 60.
30. Lukács, *Lenin*, p. 62 (italics in original).
31. Lukács, *Lenin*, p. 63 (italics in original).
32. Lukács, *Lenin*, p. 64 (italics in original).
33. Lukács, *Lenin*, p. 67.

34 Lukács, *Lenin*, p. 80 (italics in original).
35 In an essay written for *The Socialist Register 1989: Revolution Today*, Leo Panitch approaches the loss of confidence in socialist revolution as an effect of the continued revolutionary role of the bourgeoisie. See Leo Panitch, 'Capitalism, Socialism and Revolution: The Contemporary Meaning of Revolution in the West', *The Socialist Register 1989: Revolution Today*, Ralph Miliband, Leo Panitch, and John Saville, eds., London: Merlin, 1989, pp. 1-29.
36 Michael Hardt and Antonio Negri, *Commonwealth*, Cambridge, MA: The Belknap Press of Harvard University Press, 2009, p. 344.
37 Michael Hardt and Antonio Negri, *Empire*, Cambridge, MA: Harvard University Press, 2000, p. 365.
38 Hardt and Negri, *Empire*, p. 365.
39 Hardt and Negri, *Commonwealth*, p. 239.
40 See Jodi Dean, *The Communist Horizon*, London: Verso, 2012, pp. 128-129.
41 Hardt and Negri, *Commonwealth*, p. 239.
42 Hardt and Negri, *Commonwealth*, pp. 242-3.
43 Hardt and Negri, *Commonwealth*, p. 242.
44 Hardt and Negri, *Commonwealth*, p. 140.
45 Hardt and Negri, *Commonwealth*, p. 354.
46 Hardt and Negri, *Commonwealth*, p. 353.
47 Hardt and Negri, *Commonwealth*, p. 351.
48 See my discussion in *Crowds and Party*, London: Verso, 2016, pp. 12-13.
49 Jodi Dean, *The Communist Horizon*, p. 138.
50 Charles Post, 'What is Left of Leninism? New European Left Parties in Historical Perspective', *The Socialist Register 2013: The Question of Strategy*, Leo Panitch, Greg Albo, and Vivek Chibber, eds., London: Merlin Press, 2012, pp. 174-197.
51 Hardt and Negri, *Commonwealth*, p. 334.
52 Hardt and Negri, *Commonwealth*, p. 333.
53 See my discussion in *Crowds and Party*, chapter 1.
54 As Lukács writes in 'Towards a Methodology of the Problem of Organization', 'the Communist Party as the revolutionary form of consciousness of the proletariat is a *process by nature*', (p. 316, italics in original); and 'the party exists in order to hasten the process by which these distinctions are smoothed out', (p. 326). The distinctions Lukács is referring to are stratifications within the class.
55 Hardt and Negri, *Commonwealth*, p. 363.
56 V. I. Lenin, 'The State and Revolution', *The Lenin Anthology*, Robert C. Tucker, ed., New York: Norton, pp. 311-98.
57 Hardt and Negri, *Commonwealth*, p. 354.
58 Hardt and Negri, *Commonwealth*, p. 360.
59 Hardt and Negri, *Commonwealth*, p. 382.
60 Hardt and Negri, *Commonwealth*, p. 383.
61 For a reading of Occupy as a political vanguard, see the last chapter of my *The Communist Horizon*.
62 Lukács insists that a communist organization 'can only be created through struggle', 'Towards a Methodology', p. 317.
63 Lukács, 'Towards a Methodology', p. 316.

RADICALIZING THE MOVEMENT-PARTY RELATION: FROM RALPH MILIBAND TO JEREMY CORBYN AND BEYOND

HILARY WAINWRIGHT

It is time to rethink the relationship between social movements and struggles and parliamentary institutions. Such relationships have a long history, but by the 1970s a common understanding was framed, at least among activists on the left in Europe, by the metaphor of 'voice'. A widely shared discourse referred to radical left parties, including Green parties, as 'the political voice of the social movements'. Or at least this was the aspiration. I want to challenge this framework and, in doing so, work towards a framework that enables us to understand better the complexities, contradictions and tensions in the relationships between parties and movements so as to radicalize those relations, with systemic transformation as our goal.

Parties and movements, even those that share similar values, exercise distinct sources of power that do not work in the same way and are not necessarily in harmony with each other. The notion that a left party is about standing for election on the basis of socialist policies in order to win national office and take control of the commanding heights of the economy is still at the back, if not the front, of the minds of many left activists. In this thinking, movements are understood, implicitly at least, as the foot soldiers for the election of a left government, in exchange for which the party voices their demands. I argue here that a radical left party whose power lies in its position of representation in the elective institutions of the state cannot simply through representation become a 'voice' for movements whose power lies in the creative capacities in society – as if these movements have no distinct, autonomous sources of power, which may possibly conflict with a left party in government – and also in the process of winning office.

Living in Britain, I have felt especially challenged to think through these tensions due to the most extraordinary political situation created when one of the most radical Labour MPs in Parliament, Jeremy Corbyn, who has always stood up for social movements and struggles – effectively acting as their advocate in the House of Commons – became leader of the Labour Party in September 2015. Corbyn was, in conventional terms, 'an outsider' who only just reached the required number of nominations from fellow MPs to get himself, reluctantly, onto the ballot paper for the leadership. Yet he not only won over 60 per cent of the party membership vote; he also mobilized tens of thousands from outside the traditional Labour Party supporters. During his leadership campaign, young people were attempting to climb in through the windows to hear him.[1] A reluctant leader with this kind of appeal stimulates us to rethink leadership.

One result of this enthusiasm was that around 300,000 new people took part as voters in the leadership election. This was the unintended result of a change in the rules of the party, originally designed to weaken the power of the unions. But it took no account of how angry individual union and Labour Party supporters had become. Allowing individual members a vote, far from producing a moderating influence on the choice of leader as had been expected, actually gave political expression to an otherwise disenfranchised and disaffected constituency. As in most parts of Europe, growing anger had developed among working or would-be working people in the UK, especially young people, about the inequalities produced by the unregulated market and the relentless imposition of austerity. This anger reflects a disaffection that has been accumulating beneath the political and mainstream media radar. A highly disproportionate electoral system and the increasing tendency of the main political parties to converge at the centre have meant that even the existence of this angry constituency hardly registered in mainstream politics. Indeed, a further factor stoking the anger has been this very distance and unresponsiveness of politicians, who come from a privileged class and are protected by an increasingly unrepresentative political system.

This anger created a political pressure cooker. Corbyn's campaign to be Labour leader opened the lid and the pressure lifted him to the leadership. But just as Syriza won office in January 2015 but not state power, so Corbyn's victory gave him the leader's office but not power over the party. Corbyn's main source of power vis-a-vis the Labour Party really was the democratic mandate of his overwhelming support and, potentially, of the disparate movement that emerged in the process of mobilizing this mandate. What is the nature of this power? And how is it to be realized to become a force? This is precisely what needs to be addressed. What Corbyn came to represent – as a magnet for disaffection, and more positively, as a hope for a new politics – should be seen, however, as only an initial moment in a process of activist engagement with the political process whose character and institutional form is yet to take shape.

On a *Socialist Register* panel in London shortly after Corbyn's election, Jon Lansman, the key organizer of Corbyn's leadership campaigns as well as of Momentum, the organization created to consolidate the disparate movement formed during the leadership campaign, summed up his view of the relationship between the new Corbyn-led party and the movement of new supporters with the remark: 'We will mobilize them.' This suggests there is still a certain old left mentality to overcome in the Corbyn camp. This mentality seems to imply: there are now lots of new people interested in politics, therefore lots of new voters, lots of new supporters; and our main aim must be to mobilize them behind the Labour party. From the standpoint of winning legislative power, this approach makes sense. My line of questioning starts from the recognition that the activists joining the campaign for Corbyn and then becoming part of Momentum and/or their local Labour Party should be seen as having a creative capacity and transformative power of their own, distinct from (not opposed to) electoral politics. Although, as indicated in their support for Corbyn's bid for the Labour leadership, they recognize the need for electoral engagement, this has to be on terms that acknowledge their autonomy and creativity.

We saw a similar, but more complicated, problem with this presumption of the predominance of electoral over transformative politics in the key period between Syriza's rapid rise to being a party of potential government in June 2013 to its final election in January 2015. During that period the emphasis became increasingly on how to turn Syriza's relationship with social movements from one in which it was previously seen to be part of those movements – actively contributing to their creative activities, especially in building networks of mutual solidarity in organizing the means of everyday survival – to one in which activists were instrumentalized by the party, mainly to be drawn into the process of getting Syriza elected. A similar process took place in Spain where in the preparation for the election of July 2016 Pablo Iglesias led Podemos into becoming 'an electoral machine' (in his own words) and closed local activist circles in the process.

I'm not concerned simply to dismiss these developments as 'electoralism', as if such a critique resolves anything. Rather, my argument is that when radical movements engage in electoral politics, this tendency for electoral pressures to swamp their autonomy as agents of transformation poses a dilemma. On the one hand, electoral success for a radical left party that has taken up the demands of the movements is likely to be favourable for social movements. After all, movements engage in electoral politics because they want changes that require government action, not least to end the rule of austerity economics. On the other, even those parties committed to radical left policies too often fail to take seriously enough, even if they 'talk the talk', the proven fact that electoral success is, on its own, an insufficient source of power – and practical knowledge – to achieve the social, economic and political transformation that both left parties and social movements desire.

Problems in the relations between parties and movements cannot, therefore, be resolved by plumping for electoral politics over autonomous social movement activity or vice versa. It cannot be one or the other. An adequate strategy involves understanding the possible dimensions of the relationship between the two, and designing institutions through which to achieve the most effective combination of their different sources of power. Rather than asking 'how will we mobilize them – the new members and supporters?', the really important questions therefore are what are the capacities of these new members and supporters, and what sources of power and transformation do they bring? Moreover, how can we as a party support these – perhaps new – sources of power? How do we open up our party to plural forces sharing common goals of social change? Any serious strategy for turning the long and widely pent up desire for radical political change into an effective force for radical change involves breaking the party's claim to a monopoly on transformative potential and recognizing the skills and capacities of civic movements. Rather than turning them into the foot soldiers of electoral politics, this involves working with them as knowledgeable and productive citizens on whose capacities a government committed to radical social change depends.

THE SIGNIFICANCE OF JEREMY CORBYN

All this is on the agenda for the British left today. The space and opportunity Jeremy Corbyn opened up, as he himself insisted, was not about him as a personality, though his modesty and sense of public responsibility suited him to the role. The uncertain, and undoubtedly destabilizing, space his election to Labour Party leadership opened in British politics could immediately be seen from the openly-expressed frustrations of most Labour MPs with his lack of deference to conventional parliamentary – and would-be Prime Ministerial – norms, from his dress style, to his attitude to the monarchy, to his channelling of ordinary people's questions to the Prime Minister in the House of Commons.

Corbyn's overwhelming victory in the leadership elections over the summer of 2015 had been a nightmare come true for the architects of New

Labour, who had no shortage of allies in the PLP. They still had sufficient hubris from their own earlier successes – not least in literally remaking the Parliamentary Party (PLP) to execute the project of New Labour, frequently imposing parliamentary candidates on local constituencies, especially in safe Labour seats[2] – to think that they could engineer Corbyn's downfall. Repeated rumors of a coup inside the PLP started to take more substantive shape in the run up to the first by-election after the May 2015 General Election, which took place in Oldham, a normally safe Labour seat in Greater Manchester. As John MacDonnell, Corbyn's close ally and his newly-appointed Shadow Chancellor of the Exchequer, subsequently said: 'We knew at that time, that for some time they were plotting to see if they could have a coup at some stage. Their first attempt was the Oldham by-election. If Jeremy had lost this, that might have been the opportunity for some form of coup or to start the first stages. But we won a resounding victory with a good local candidate and the enthusiasm of Corbyn supporters from across the country. So they backed off.' The rumours of a coup persisted, however, reaching a new crescendo with the approaching local government elections of May 2016. MacDonnell picks up the story: 'They said again "You can't win an election with Corbyn." We won every mayoral election we contested – every one. We won the seats in terms of local government, councils we were expected to lose, we won every one.'[3]

Then came the Brexit vote. The reality of Corbyn being in office but not being in power fully exploded a few days after the UK's EU Referendum of July 2016, when 51 per cent voted 'Leave' against 48 per cent for 'Remain'. Corbyn's position in the referendum campaign, in line with the Labour Party's official position, had been 'Remain but Reform'. His arguments (and indeed those of anyone arguing 'Stay in Europe to change Europe') were ignored by a media obsessed with the dramatic divisions within the Conservative Cabinet, but Corbyn had been around the country speaking at more meetings than any other Labour leader in favor of Remain, while a lacklustre official Party campaign relied on churning out dull leaflets and posters for party foot soldiers to deliver. But such details did not delay those who had been waiting for their moment to move against Corbyn. Beginning with a long-planned series of resignations from the shadow cabinet, this was the excuse for a determined revolt against the new Labour leader nine months after his overwhelming victory. One by one as if choreographed to cause maximum damage, Corbyn's critics resigned, in a perverse form of direct action aimed at destabilizing Corbyn and embarrassing him into resignation.

Corbyn stood firm, supported by only a small minority of MPs and the nascent movement of activist supporters from inside and outside the party, now rather more consolidated through Momentum. He appointed a new shadow cabinet, insisted on remaining true to his electoral mandate and declared himself willing to take on any challenger. A challenger was slow to emerge. The 'coupists' clearly lacked a strategy beyond ridding themselves of Corbyn – not understanding that his leadership victory was not about himself. But eventually, after much prevarication and farce, a challenger emerged in the form of Owen Smith, a relatively unknown MP from Wales, backed and frantically promoted by a well-financed and determined team.

It was a strange political moment: simultaneously superficial, hyperbolic and bad-tempered and yet seemingly of fundamental importance for the future of the Labour Party, trade unions, democracy and the lives of working or would-be working people, all facing a Tory government that has a renewed determination to carry through the authoritarian free market agenda of Mrs Thatcher. Media rhetoric alleged threatening behaviour towards MPs by revolutionary 'thugs'. The paltry substance of studio discussion was all about tactics, accusations of intimidation, party gossip and endless speculation: Will Labour split? Will Corbyn cave in? As MPs and Lords skipped lightly between studios tossing their inflammatory statements onto the bonfire of tittle-tattle, the hyperbole concerning yet another terminal crisis for Labour cruelly distorted the divisions between left and right that haunted the party's early years and have surfaced in many conflicts since.

CHANGING THE LABOUR PARTY: WAS RALPH MILIBAND WRONG?

In this frustrating political/intellectual context, it was a pleasure to turn to Ralph Miliband 's *Parliamentary Socialism*, as I had turned to it in 1986 when I wrote my own *Labour: A Tale of Two Parties*, not for predictions but for tools to identify tendencies underlying the febrile atmosphere of today's historic moment.[4] Miliband's great book provides exactly the historical perspective and structural analysis that is needed of the conditions that established and have sustained the Labour Party's monopoly hold over working-class political representation in Britain, and its persistent conservatism, including the seemingly permanent subordination of its left. Miliband enables us to understand how far today's conflicts indicate a breakdown of those conditions and the possible emergence of a new configuration of progressive political representation and with it a new relation between the Labour Party and the UK's diverse and diffuse social movements, including the labour movement.

What remains vital is Ralph Miliband's concept of 'parliamentarism', which means more than 'parliamentary' as understood in its normal usage

– as referring to parliamentary representation and through this, legislative change. Parliamentarism is, in Miliband's words the 'dogmatic devotion to the parliamentary system'. He explains: 'The leaders of the Labour Party have always rejected any kind of political action (such as industrial action for political purposes) beyond the framework and conventions of the parliamentary system. The Labour Party has not only been a parliamentary party; it has been a party deeply imbued by parliamentarism.' This has been reinforced on the one hand by a corporate and sectional trade unionism concerned with bargaining over work place issues, delegating wider political issues of welfare, taxation, industrial policy, macroeconomic policy and foreign policy to the parliamentary party. Here Miliband's concept of 'Labourism', complementary to 'parliamentarism', is important: the idea of the Labour Party as an instrument for a sectoral, corporate understanding of the interests of labour, reflecting 'the growing integration of the trade unions into the framework of modern capitalism'.[5]

Underlying Labour's devotion to the parliamentary system as a fixed point of reference and conditioning factor of their political mentality, Miliband also understood, is deference to the moral authority of the British state – the crown in Parliament. It is significant here, Miliband points out, that the party's founding manifesto, 'Labour and the New Social Order', contained virtually no commitment to constitutional reforms that would democratize the British state. Instead, it was fervent in its reassurance that the manifesto's policies of public ownership and redistribution would be carried out by means of parliamentary government, Westminster style. Here the role of the UK's unwritten constitution is most important and associated with this, the potent symbolism of the monarch as the entity to which MP's swear their allegiance – as distinct from the republican, and normal European, convention of an oath to the people. The significance of this oath to the crown is that in between elections moral authority lies within Parliament, and that means not simply in the laws it makes or agrees to, but in the process by which Parliament relates to the executive power of the state. To suggest authority lies anywhere else is in effect a challenge to the authority of the state. In this way, reselection of MPs, the non-parliamentary election of the leader, and party conference control over policy all confront the long British tradition of rule from above.

All this is crucial to understanding the non-cooperation that Corbyn faced from the PLP in spite of his overwhelming mandate from party members and supporters. The continuing hold of parliamentarism was evident in the statements of Corbyn's critics: 'He has great integrity. We share his values. But …', and here the speaker adopts a extra serious, almost reverential tone as if to emphasize its seriousness, '… the Labour Party is after all, a parliamentary party and a leader must have the confidence of the PLP.' What was so striking about the self-important dogmatism this expresses was the dismissal of Corbyn's overwhelming mandate. The hundreds of thousands of party members, plus those affiliated through the unions and those who signed up as supporters and most union leaders might as well not exist. Indeed most MPs – and Labour ones were joined by the Conservative 'honourable members' of the House of Commons in this – seemed genuinely puzzled and deeply irritated by Corbyn's insistence on sticking by this mandate. Hence their incomprehension as to why their rebellion did not, as intended, lead him to resign, as he might well have done had he been a lone and isolated MP instead of someone accountable to, and in effect created by, what has really become a movement.

In fact, as Miliband's *Parliamentary Socialism* showed, crisis has been endemic in the party's hybrid institutions – parliamentary and extra-parliamentary, and ideologies – socialist and social reformers. 'Like Hobbes and fear, crisis and the Labour Party have always been twins – Siamese twins', Miliband wrote.[6] The tense hybridity underlying this permanent state of crisis is also what sustains the legitimacy of the left; often referred to as part of 'the party as a broad church'. The party's organization developed in an ad hoc way that could be compared to buildings adapted to survive earthquakes. In the Labour Party, enthusiastic members and trade union militancy, for example, could unpredictably set off earthquakes. The formula at the heart of Labour had been until the mid-80s: trade union power plus the evangelical (but powerless) enthusiasm of constituency socialists equals Labour governments. Richard Crossman, a longtime leading Labour intellectual, described how this worked in practice: 'In order to maintain the enthusiasm of party militants to do the organizing work for which the Conservative Party pays a vast army of workers, a constitution was created which apparently created full party democracy while excluding these members from effective power.'[7] In other words, the formalities of the Labour Party's constitution, rather like the rituals of the UK's unwritten constitution as analysed by Bagehot, created a 'dignified' appearance that mystified the party's 'real' relations of power.

After the many compromises and disappointments of the 1964-70 Wilson Government, and as very much part of what Miliband called the 'state of desubordination' that marked the 1970s, the dignified appearance of Labour's constitution lost its awe, as party activists allying with increasingly well organized and politically conscious trade union militants pulled every formal or customary lever of democracy to its limits and demanded democracy for real. Jeremy Corbyn was part of this, and Jon Lansman cut his teeth in the party as an effective young organizer of the Campaign for Labour Party Democracy (CLPD). The left, led by Tony Benn, very nearly won control of the party, though not the leadership, through the long struggle over intra-party democracy as well as socialist policy that divided Labour right through the 1970s and into the early 1980s. The strength of the left proved too much for a group of right wing MPs who split from the party to form the Social Democratic Party, which subsequently merged with the Liberals (most of them have not been heard of since, except indirectly as a warning to would-be splitters that the future is bleak outside the party). But in the face of any further split in the party led from the right, first Michael Foot and then Neil Kinnock, like most left Labour MPs before them, took preserving the unity of the party on their shoulders, and were supported in this by the union leadership which had previously supported Benn and the CLPD.

It was precisely the endemic tendency to crisis inside the Labour Party that Tony Blair was determined to put an end to in taking the leadership in 1994. In a process begun by Kinnock, Blair and Peter Mandelson (then head of Communications at Labour HQ, later an MP, Minister, and a decisive power behind Blair's leadership) worked to change the party's constitution and establish institutions to effectively turn the party conference from an annual parliament of the labour movement, where a variety of resolutions from the grassroots of the movement were debated and where sometimes the leadership was defeated, to a leadership rally organized mainly for the media, with an adoring membership as scenery, also providing an opportunity for corporate networking with the politically influential. Furthermore, they weakened – effectively destroyed – the power of constituency parties to select parliamentary candidates.[8] An increasing number of candidates, especially in safe seats, were imposed centrally, sometimes against the wishes of the local party (this was the case with Angela Eagle, MP for Wallasey, who emerged as the leading critic of Corbyn). The significance of these reforms was that while the parliamentary party's independence from the rest of the party was strengthened, this only widened the gap between MPs and party members, many of whom left, while the independence of MPs led an increasingly disaffected youth, sharing the public's perception of politicians as a political caste feathering its own nest, to be repelled by party politics altogether.

They were joined in this by large numbers of angry workers and young would-be workers. Thatcher's attacks on the unions, epitomized most brutally by the defeat of the miners strike in 1984-85, laid the foundation for widespread disarray and demoralization in the labour movement, and a turn to the right among many working-class people. Yet it also left a new terrain of weakened organizations searching for the means of renewal, with many union activists ready to provide potential energy toward this end. In fact, Thatcher's class war against organized labour is central to understanding the present crisis of Labour. While the integration of the party into parliamentary politics was qualitatively strengthened during the Blair years, confirming Miliband's analysis, the integration of the trade unions into capitalism has been disrupted. Here the dual nature of trade unionism needs to be taken into account, which complicates the relations of trade unions to capitalism. Though trade union leaders often gain autonomy from their members and develop a vested interest in stability and preserving the strength of their union organization almost for its own sake, the membership, especially where it is part of a well-organized workplace with considerable bargaining power of its own, in practice often places limits on their leaders' autonomy. This in turn is liable to disrupt the kind of processes by which the unions are integrated into capitalism.

A sustained integration of the trade unions into capitalism of the kind that Miliband saw as a condition of the Labour Party's power structure, ensuring that the union leadership would accept the confines of parliamentarism and Labourism, requires a stable corporatist arrangement whereby the trade unions are acquiescent and integrated at the factory or company level along the lines of arrangements which may still have some viability in Germany. Such conditions do not hold in the UK, or indeed in most other capitalist counties today. Miliband could not foresee that this, together with new forms of 'popular insubordination', might lead to the breakdown of the PLP- trade union leadership alliance at the apex of Labour's power structure. Corbyn's victory in September 2015 owed a lot to the pent-up anger of trade union members, not only in the aftermath of Thatcherism but in response to Blair's continuation of many Thatcherite policies. Some trade union leaders, such as Len McCluskey, General Secretary of Unite, either shared this anger, or as with Dave Prentis at UNISON, the public service workers union, could not hold it back from influencing their own decision-making. Under Ed Miliband's regime as Party leader, the centralizing grip that Blair and Mandelson had imposed in their obsession with control was loosened, enabling local Constituency Labour Parties, including in safe seats, to choose their own candidates. Additionally, the rules of leadership elections were changed so that individual union members (rather than each union voting as a block) and party supporters could vote for the leader.

Ralph Miliband could not have predicted what happened with the unions in the aftermath of the Thatcherite counter-revolution's defeat of union militancy. The anger this produced eventually took a new political expression, as the economistic or syndicalist dynamics of trade unionism were blocked,[9] in support for Jeremy Corbyn in 2015, when almost 100,000 union members directly signed up to the Labour Party. It was their sense of the persistence of his commitment that led so many union leaders to support Corbyn against the coup mentality in the PLP right through the new leadership contest forced in the summer of 2016. This continuing commitment could also be seen in the remarkable action the organizers[10] of the Durham Miners Gala, an annual high point on the political agenda of the labour movement (both left and right), in declaring that none of the 127 MPs who turned against Corbyn would be welcome on the historic balcony of the County Hotel where Labour leaders and important figures have spoken and waved since the 1930s. Corbyn spoke to a record crowd of 150,000 labour movement activists and their families.

Neither could Ralph Miliband have predicted the extraordinary consequences of the equally pent-up anger of party members after decades of being treated with contempt, demonized and excluded from what they passionately considered their party. It was this that ensured that the Party's National Executive Committee would rule in July 2016 that Corbyn's name, even without the requisite number of MPs required for his standing again in the new leadership contest, would have to appear on the leadership ballot. Through the summer of 2016, Corbyn's rallies and very presence became like a spark that lit a prairie fire. The terrain was arid, desperate for water, for a source of political life that workers could trust. 'He's a decent man, with great integrity – but he's not a real leader' was the constant refrain from Corbyn's critics, questioning his electability. This was said at the same time that over half of the voting population had railed – in the Brexit vote – against the establishment, jam packed with would-be and retired leaders of the kind that critics want to put in Corbyn's place. Corbyn is not charismatic. He doesn't need to be. His record has been one of daily contradicting his oath to the crown in parliament and in practice, making and renewing an oath to the people. This explains his victory first time round, but it at the same time led him to come under ruthless and relentless fire from the British establishment and their media. Put simply, they will do everything to stop a socialist, who means what he says and has a popular base to support him, from becoming prime minister.

Corbyn could certainly never become Prime Minister through the traditional parliamentarist strategy of the past. The refusal of the PLP to follow the logic of Corbyn's practical – if as yet untheorized – rejection of parliamentarism is a wake-up call to the need for a different strategic vision beyond simply the personal example, rare and impressive as it is, of a principled, honest and courageous way of doing politics in practice. The next general election, whenever it comes, will not be taking place in a functioning political system with high turnout and strong levels of trust in the main political parties.[11] Rather, it will come after more than a decade of growing disengagement from mainstream politics, especially by the young and the poor and insecure, to the point where the present Conservative government was voted for by only 24 per cent of the eligible electorate, and when many constituency Labour parties struggled even to ensure a quorum at their meetings.

To be electable in today's mood of anti-establishment politics, any leader and party has to be able to reach out beyond the political system and give a voice to those who have no vested interest in that system. Corbyn showed himself able to reach out and demonstrate that he would open up spaces in politics for the disenfranchised, and ensure they had a voice. He has re-engaged hundreds of thousands of young people, whether or not they are union members. Typically, the young don't just engage with institutions as they are; they bring new ideas and they shake things up, producing new political configurations with the potential of attracting more of their generation. Hence Momentum, the organization created largely by these young 'Corbynistas', is not a recognizable organization by the stereotypes of the traditional left. It treats political education through football sessions with disaffected youth as important as left caucuses in the party, if not more so; it chooses initiatives like 'the people's PPE' (contrasting its popular education programme with the Oxford degree) over the stale, pale, male political rallies of the past. This is the generation whose culture, including political culture, has been shaped by using the tools of the new information and communication technology to share, collaborate and network, emancipating themselves daily from overbearing authority, hierarchy and other forms of centralized, commanding domination. A collaborative, facilitating kind of leadership and political organization is the only one with which they can engage.

In this way, they are building on the innovations of the class of '68, Corbyn's generation. For this reason, the gap between generations and classes shouldn't be exaggerated. Older working-class people of Corbyn's generation listened to Bob Dylan, and the women in their communities were influenced by and contributed to feminism. On the other hand, as the Brexit result demonstrates, there are distinct problems to be addressed among the white working class, where strong feelings of abandonment and powerlessness have led, with the aid of right-wing media and politicians, to a scapegoating of immigrants and the EU. Again, the Corbyn leadership, with its commitment to fight austerity, was well placed to reach out to those whose lives and communities have been all but destroyed by cuts, low pay (and no pay), privatization and casualization. Jeremy Corbyn can commit himself to putting money where his mouth is when he says that immigration is not the cause of people's social and economic desperation.

But the Brexit vote indicates that the problems are not simply economic. What has also surfaced is the problem of power and powerlessness. Here there is a confluence with the aspirations of the young to achieve some control over their future. But while the urban young use new technologies to create forms of daily collaborative control over their lives, people without easy resources for mobility and communication need other sources of control that they too can feel in their daily lives. Here the role of the unions is vital – but not so much in their conventional role as funders and foot soldiers for the party's election campaigns. Nor is it only about their ability to defend jobs or bargain for better wages. It is also about enabling their members and the wider workforce to obtain greater control over the organization and purpose of their work, especially in the public sector; an increasing emphasis on the organization of part-time and casual workers; and support for cooperatives and similar structures as a means by which precarious workers can develop collective strength. Already community branches created by Unite to organize and campaign beyond the workplace are illustrating new possibilities. Greater control of our working lives is limited, however, if our wider political environment is controlled by a remote, over-centralized political system through which there is little or no chance of having a voice in decisions about housing, the environment or the national and international matters of war and peace, trade and investment.

Following the defeats and brutal destruction of working class non-parliamentary sources of strength by Margaret Thatcher, consolidated by Tony Blair, the level of working-class industrial organization and associated community cohesion and solidarity is far too weak to sustain any insurrectionary strategy based on the revolutionary imaginary of a general strike leading to institutions of dual power built on by a left government as a midwife to a new economic and political order. This does not, I would argue, rule out the possibility of a strategy for anti-capitalist transformation based on the popular organization and assertion of transformative capacity. It would need to be supported by an elected government committed to systemic change through the exercise of multiple – and extra-parliamentary – sources of power and with a recognition of the popular capacity to create and exert power in social and economic life.

RETHINKING POWER AND KNOWLEDGE

To develop such a strategic vision, we need to distinguish between two kinds of power and explore how their combination for the purposes of radical social, economic and political change might underpin new institutions relating parties with social movements and radical initiatives in civil society. On the one hand, there is 'power over', which could also be described as 'power-as-domination', involving an asymmetry between those with power and those over whom power is exercised. On the other, there is 'power to', or 'power-as-transformative-capacity'. This is the power discovered by social movements, of students, radical workers and feminists as they move beyond protest to proposing practical, prefigurative solutions.

Historically, social democratic and communist parties have been built around at best a benevolent version of the understanding of power-as-domination. Their strategies have been based on winning the power to govern and then steering the state apparatus to meet what they identify as the needs of the people. It is a paternalistic political methodology.

The distinction between the two forms of power is central to the experimental search for appropriate forms of transformative democratic political organization in a context of extreme fragmentation, precarity and dispersal of working people. At a time when older forms of organization, such as the traditional mass workplace-based labour organizations, have either been defeated or are inadequate in today's changed circumstances, this distinction helps us to focus on the exact and distinct purposes that any new organizations have to be fit for. It is a search stimulated by the failures of the traditional parties of the left to bring about the changes in which their supporters had believed and for which they had originally built those organizations.

The notion of power-as-transformative-capacity emerged out of widespread frustration at the workings of power-as-domination exercised by political parties of the traditional left. The distinctive feature of the rebellions of the 1960s and 70s was that students, shop floor workers, radical women and others took power into their own hands, discovering through collective action that they had capacities of their own to bring about change. These were not simply pressure groups, demanding with extra militancy that the governing party do something on their behalf. Their approach was more directly transformative. For example, women took action directly to change their relations with men, with each other and with public services; workers took militant action in their workplaces not only to improve their working conditions but also to extend control over the purpose of their labour; and community groups squatted in empty buildings, occupied land against speculation and campaigned for alternative land-use policies for the wellbeing of their communities. They no longer focused primarily on the parliamentary politics of representation.

A common theme of these rebellions involved overturning conventional deference to authority and the forms of knowledge that those in authority deployed as a source of legitimacy. The other side of the movements' rejection of these forms of authority was a pervasive and self-confident assertion of their own practical and sometimes tacit knowledge, as well as their collaborative capacity, against the claims of those in authority to know 'what is best' or 'needs to be done'. Along with this self-confidence in their transformative abilities went inventiveness about the forms of organization that would build that capacity. While acknowledging the mixed and uneven legacy of the 1960s and 1970s,[12] I would argue that a distinctive feature of these radical movements was their tendency to emphasize the valuing and sharing of different kinds of knowledge, practical and experiential as well as theoretical and historical.

In their refusal to defer to authority, such movements broke the unspoken bond between knowledge and authority – the idea that those in power know what is best for the mass of people. The uncertain, experimental process of democratizing knowledge tends, in practice, to involve an emphasis on decentralized and networked organizations sharing and developing knowledge horizontally and breaking from models that presume an expert leadership and a more-or-less ignorant membership. The radically democratic approaches to knowledge pioneered in earlier decades (most notably by feminists but also networks of workplace and community organizations) laid the organizational and cultural foundations that have underpinned many civic movements ever since, from the alter-globalization movement of the late 1990s through to Occupy and the Indignados.

In many diverse locations, grassroots trade union and community alliances have been a driving force in the defence and improvement of public services or utilities in the face of privatization.[13] They have become a means of sharing knowledge and building transformative power, not only to defend public resources but also to advance projects of democratization. They have shown they can strengthen citizens' resilience in the face of policies that threaten their material security, offering a degree of autonomy and control that would not otherwise be available to them. And ultimately, by illustrating in daily practice that there are alternatives, realization of which lies in significant part with the people themselves, they have often become an important part of strategies for political hegemony. In this way, power-as-transformative-capacity has begun to produce an institutional infrastructure, which can be recognized as distinct from the institutions of representation, with the help of an understanding of its basis in a distinct source of power.

Yet what has also become very clear in developing new institutions through social and labour movements is that the autonomy of non-state sources of power tends to be precarious and difficult to sustain. This repeatedly has raised the question of how far, and under what conditions, power-as-domination (essentially, in this context, having control over state institutions, national and municipal) can be a resource for power-as-transformative-capacity. It is important to recognize that although there is a sharp distinction between these two types of power, they are not necessarily counter-posed. We therefore need to probe further into both concepts of power, and then into what new forms of institutions of representation could enable the two to best combine for purposes of transformation, perhaps revitalizing representation in the process. How, for example, could power-as-domination be a resource for power-as-transformative-capacity, as distinct from weakening or overwhelming forms of social power originally autonomous from the state? And what kinds of transformative capacity are strategically relevant to bring about change, with or without the resource of power-as-domination? Civic sources of power cannot automatically be assumed to be strategically significant. Under what conditions, if any, could institutions of representative democracy provide a framework or platform through which these two kinds of power could combine in a process of social transformation?

LESSONS FROM THE GREEK DEFEAT

The recent experience of Greece highlights the challenges involved in exploring the relationship between these two sources of power in the context of what is, formally at least, representative democracy. Following its electoral success in 2015 winning 36 per cent of the vote and leading a government with a small nationalist party, Syriza faced the problem of negotiating its rejection of the austerity Memoranda imposed by the EU and IMF and gaining both time and financial support to work with civil society to drive and support social and economic transformation in Greece, including radical reform of the corrupt and undemocratic Greek state. There was a widespread assumption, not only among the leadership of Syriza but also those sections of the left across Europe that shared Syriza's predominant political outlook, that the EU bureaucracy and its constituent government would, albeit reluctantly, respect its electoral mandate for ending the Memoranda – and negotiate on that basis.

The reality turned out to be rather different. 'I was astonished', reported Yanis Varoufakis, Greece's new finance minister and leading negotiator, 'to hear the German finance minister [Wolfgang Schäuble] say to me verbatim, that "elections cannot be allowed to change established economic policy".'[14] Varoufakis and his fellow Syriza negotiators were acting on the basis of a more or less radical variant of the left's understanding of democracy and its relationship to it, shared across post-war Europe. As Andreas Karitzis, then a member of the party's central committee, put it at the time: 'The assumption was that the elites were committed to accepting the democratically shaped mandate of an elected government.'[15] The response of the EU to the Greek government's refusal, on behalf of the overwhelming majority of Greek people, to accept the continued austerity regime imposed on previous Greek governments, was brutal. Not only did EU negotiators, led by Schäuble, treat Syriza's original electoral mandate with contempt, it also rebuffed the July 2015 referendum in which Greek voters again rejected the renewal of the austerity regime.

The consequences for the lives of ordinary Greeks have been disastrous. The experience has been such a terrible reversal of high hopes and expectations, on the part not only of the leaders of Syriza, but more significantly the majority of party and movement activists. Many are engaged in deep debate about what went wrong and what can be learnt for the future, including for the left across Europe and worldwide. Varoufakis resigned from the Syriza government and founded a movement, DiEM25, for the democratization of Europe. Others left Syriza to set up a new political party arguing for Greek exit from the eurozone. Some, like Karitzis, have left, not to found a new party but to experiment with a new strategy based on developing the capacity of organized citizens to take over basic social functions of daily life. In doing so, they have turned to the infrastructure of solidarity which was created after 2010 as a strategy of survival against the relentless austerity measures coming from the institutions of the EU and IMF, who are now also effectively controlling the Greek government. This network involves the self-management of basic social functions: health, the distribution of food, childcare, some aspects of education, and so on. It also increasingly involves links with agricultural production, as small and medium-size farmers who share the aims of the solidarity movement and have turned their farms into part of a solidarity food chain and into centres of education in eco-agriculture.

Some of these solidarity social organizations, especially the volunteer-run health centres, act as laboratories for new relations of social care at the same time as providing essential services. A volunteer psychologist described the contrast between his relationship with a patient in a conventional mainstream hospital and in the voluntary clinic where he worked. 'In the solidarity clinic', he said, 'I was able to treat him as an individual and with respect, talking to him, one to one; whereas in the hospital, the institution prescribed a relationship in which patients were more like a production line. In the clinic there is an egalitarian ethos. We are all volunteers self-managing the service; patients are fellow citizens with whom we are in solidarity.' If in the future there were the resources to reestablish public hospitals to take on such services, then he and his colleagues would introduce improvements they had learnt from the collaborative, egalitarian culture of the self-managed clinics, and transform the management and quality of service they provided.

Andreas Karitzis has explained very well what impelled him to turn to these networks as the foundation for a new way forward after the experience of Syriza in government:

> A strategy that wishes to be relevant to the new conditions must take on the duty of acquiring the necessary power to run basic social functions. It is the only way to acquire the necessary power to defy the elites' control over our societies ... We must modify the balance between representing people's beliefs and demands and coordinating, facilitating, connecting, supporting and nurturing people's actions. We must contribute heavily to the formation of a strong 'backbone' for resilient and dynamic networks of social economy and co-operative productive activities, democratically functioning digital communities, community control over functions such as infrastructure facilities, energy systems and distribution networks. These are ways of gaining the degree of autonomy necessary to defy the control of elites over the basic functions of our society.[16]

A NEW TYPE OF PARTY?

This reinforces the importance of radicalizing the relation between a radical political party and extra-parliamentary self-organization. Above all, it points to the importance of overcoming the separation of politics from economics inherited from the transition from feudalism to the capitalist market and representative democracy, and later reproduced in the separation between the industrial and political wings of the labour movement. This division between economics and politics, and the prohibition (often self-imposed) on unions becoming political, has weakened the potential for workers to exercise their collective transformative capacity. This is something that transformative party-union relations would have to change. Such a change would also involve a break from the still-lingering mentality that sees centralized state power as the key strategic objective for a party committed to change.

The notion of strategy and organization that flows from an understanding of the varied forms of knowledge – and hence of the individualized but also shared and collaborative nature of creativity – is one in which the party is a source of experimentation and capacity-building, rather than an organization focused exclusively on political representation. It acts more as a catalyst to building power as transformative capacity in the here and now than as an army bent on capturing the citadels of government in the future. We need therefore to envisage a party as a means of experimenting and prefiguring in the present, the relations we envisage in the future between politics and everyday material and cultural life, rather than letting the party's representative role predominate. Its work then becomes rooted in daily production and reproduction, and its task becomes to build and realize citizens' capacities for self-government and social and economic transformation. It would work with labour and community organizations for this purpose.

If power as transformative capacity is understood to include political economy and to recombine politics and economics in new ways, then a new kind of radical party would need to shift exclusive attention from both macro-economic flows (the supply of money, levels of taxation and the regulation of trade) and the purely national institutional framework of ownership towards questions of the content and social organization of production: Production for what purpose? With what technology? With what environmental and social consequences? And drawing on whose knowledge, with what relations to its workers and users? The planetary imperative towards a low carbon economy gives added impetus to create or at least illustrate transformed relations of production in the present (from which national policies for state support could be generated and popularized). The ICT revolution and the web have opened up potential opportunities (and potential problems) for a new socially – and ecologically – driven economy (and challenging the monopolies that now dominate the sector). The new party, in its policies and its practice, needs to be attentive and hence immersed in the development of these new possibilities. It could act as a political space for those engaged in the new production, overcoming the rift between politics, economics and society that has held thought and institutions in its vice since the early 19th century.[17]

This would imply a party membership that is self-educated and practically involved in the many social innovations that are emerging globally: open source software, co-operative platforms, collaborative consumption, new ways of growing and eating food, of producing and using energy, of light footed transport, of forms of trade and finance, of 'soft' care and health enabling systems, of cultural production and all those other aspects of a sufficient life. These would be the contemporary forms of knowledgeable citizen participation that would be the life of a pre-figurative, catalytic party.

Power-as-domination always implied that power is exercised most distinctively through government, which can turn aspects of state power into resources for power as transformative capacity. But state institutions, like all institutions, depend on social relations that people can reproduce or refuse and, under some conditions, take action to transform. I would call this 'revolutionary gradualism', distinct from the insurrectionary model implicit in the 'reform or revolution' model, but not under-estimating the resistance it will face and the likelihood of intense conflict and moments of radical rupture. An opportunity for a transformative party to support pre-figurative change in the present, as a way of preparing for more widespread systematic change when the party eventually won government power, would be at the level of municipal governments, which are increasingly under attack from national governments imposing austerity policies. It would be important for a transformative, catalytic party to use municipal government as both a site of experimentation and learning and a basis for educating members in the new culture of the party in sharing power between elected government and organized citizens. Cities especially tend to be both where citizens are regularly engaged in forms of formal and informal self-management and where the mechanisms are most easily invented for supporting them and acknowledging their capacity. City government can also be an institutional space where a radical party can consolidate its power and improve its ability to gain national governmental power. It is most important, therefore, for any radical party to campaign for the devolution of power to cities and regions.

All this might seem a long way from the Labour Party as we have known it, focused on elections, deferential towards state power, defensive about its trade union links. But in another sense it continues, in contemporary form, traditions embedded in the party's origins. Traditions which gave Clause 4, the party's famous commitment not only to common ownership but also 'popular administration and control of each industry and service' and to 'secure for the workers by hand or by brain the full fruits of their industry and the most equitable distribution thereof', its resonance. Note here the emphasis on 'workers by hand and by brain' and that it refers explicitly not to state or public administration and control but to 'popular administration and control'.

Surely an implication of this is that in the preparation for gaining power, the type of Labour Party leadership needed is one that not only prepares its shadow cabinet for managing the affairs of state, but also engages in a process of empowering education amongst its members and supporters, the labour movement and its social allies, for the process of 'popular administration and control of every industry and service'. Several of Corbyn's initiatives indicated how much his leadership is potentially open to this kind of process, as in various commitments: for Labour's Manifesto to be drawn up through a process of popular participation; for participatory processes for constitutional reform; for an 'Arms Conversion Agency' to involve workers in the defence sector in proposing alternative socially useful projects to which their skills could be put. Whatever the continuing opposition to such initiatives inside the PLP, there is no lack of resources and will outside parliament to make them viable.

There are already many initiatives that are not simply resisting austerity but also proposing and involving people in developing alternatives. Good examples include, for example, recent positive campaigns of the National Union of Teachers reaching out to parents and the wider community; also in the environmental movement around experiments in democratically organized renewable energy sources, and in the housing movement promoting ideas for social and co-operative housing, and for controlled rents. A younger generation of activists concerned with the future of our cities is retrieving and popularizing the history of radical municipal governments, like the Greater London Council in the early 1980s. Moreover, as far as political reform is concerned, the rise of the movement for Scottish independence (Radical Independence Campaign, RIC) in its grassroots form, autonomous from the Scottish National Party, has had repercussions across the border and lent urgency and possibility to the need for a democratic constitution. Furthermore, the separation of MPs from the people, and the crisis over Corbyn's leadership, makes the issue of democratizing the British state an urgent issue for the grassroots membership of the Labour Party as well as the broader left. What is needed is a fully participative process of creating a convincing alternative to Britain's unwritten constitution and the immense but opaque executive powers derived from it – from the extensive powers of patronage to the power to press the nuclear button, and in general the power to preserve the continuity of the British state. It is exactly this that the establishment fear most from the dynamics unleashed by Corbyn's leadership: that is, the democratic potential to realize a transformative politics beyond 'parliamentary socialism'.

NOTES

1 See Hilary Wainwright, 'The Making of Jeremy Corbyn', *Jacobin*, March 2016; Richard Seymour, *Corbyn: The Strange Rebirth of Radical Politics*, London: Verso, 2016.
2 For an excellent, thorough and well-informed study of New Labour's management of

the party see Lewis Minkin, *The Blair Supremacy. A Study in the Politics of Labour's Party Management*, Manchester: Manchester University Press, 2014. Chapter 12 examines the mangement of candidate selection.

3   John McDonnell, 'We're Standing Up for Democracy in the Party – For Members to Choose the Leader', *Red Pepper*, July 2016.
4   Ralph Miliband, *Parliamentary Socialism: A Study in the Politics of Labour*, London: Merlin Press, 1972 [1961]; Hilary Wainwright, *Labour A Tale of Two Parties*, London: Chatto and Windus, 1987. Also Leo Panitch and Colin Leys, *The End of Parliamentary Socialism*, London: Verso, 2001.
5   Miliband, *Parliamentary Socialism*, pp. 13-14.
6   Miliband, *Parliamentary Socialism*, p. 16.
7   Richard Crossman, 'Introduction' to Walter Bagehot, *The English Constitution*, London: Harper Collins, 1988.
8   Minkin, *The Blair Supremacy*, chapter 12.
9   Moreover with increasing proportions of trade union members being female and from the public sector, the industrial syndicalism of the 1960s and 1970s were less relevant.
10 Most notably Davey Hopper, General Secretary of the Durham Miners' Association, who sadly died just a few weeks later.
11 For an excellent analysis of the broader context, see Peter Mair, *Ruling the Void: The Hollowing of Western Democracy*, London: Verso, 2013.
12 This challenge to authority also had a reactionary aspect that we had not envisaged. It fed an individualism that denied the importance of social criteria for the administration of public resources and generated a culture of blame.
13 For detailed reports see H. Wainwright, *The Tragedy of the Private; the Potential of the Public*, Geneva: Public Service International and the Transnational Institute, 2014.
14 Yanis Varoufakis interviewed by Nick Buxton, 'We Need a New Movement for Democracy in Europe', *Red Pepper*, January 2016.
15 Andreas Karitzis, 'The 'Syriza Experience': Lessons and Adaptations', *OpenDemocracy*, 17 March 2016, available at www.opendemocracy.net.
16 Karitzis, 'The 'Syriza Experience'.
17 These arguments draw on an unpublished paper by Robin Murray for an online publication by the think and do tank Compass: Indra Adnan ed. '21C Party: Are You Being Served?, September 2016, www.compassonline.org.uk

THE HERITAGE OF EUROCOMMUNISM IN THE CONTEMPORARY RADICAL LEFT

FABIEN ESCALONA

If Euro-Communism, like Marxism itself, is in crisis, it is because we are in an experimental stage where parties are trying to work out this different type of strategy.

Nicos Poulantzas, 1979

Though the European radical left has not generally been of interest to mainstream political observers, it has nonetheless recently become the subject of significant media coverage. Such presentations have often fallen into two symmetrical pitfalls. On the one hand, left parties have sometimes been presented as completely new, with their historical development left unexamined. On the other hand, many editorialists and even academics have paid little attention to what is original about these organizations: some have seen them as a disagreeable avatar of the far left, others as a resurgent 'traditional' (and thus inoffensive) social democracy. In fact, the parties which have realized the most remarkable electoral gains certainly belong to a 'new' radical left,[1] though their theoretical orientations and the strategic challenges they face find an echo in a historical sequence which is today largely forgotten: that of Eurocommunism.

Several recent developments invite a revisiting of this episode, which stretched from the mid-1970s to the early 1980s. Firstly, we observe the same concentration in southern Europe of apparently resurgent left parties, raising high hopes among partisans of social transformation. Forty years ago, such people looked above all towards France, Italy and Spain, and to a lesser extent Portugal and Greece. Today, it is first and foremost Greece (with the coming to power of Syriza) and Spain (with the rise of Podemos) that command most attention, though Portugal is also significant given that the Bloco de Esquerda (Left Bloc) and the Coligação Democrática Unitária (an alliance between the Communist party and the Green party) support the government of Antonio Costa.

Secondly, in both periods, all these countries experienced both a structural crisis of capitalism and a political crisis. Stressing this backdrop, Fernando Claudin wrote in 1977 that what was at stake was 'the outcome to the global crisis of capitalism' as it was manifested 'in each of these weak links of developed capitalism'.[2] While the socio-political blocs supporting Italian Christian Democracy, French Gaullism and Spanish (post) Francoism eroded, the organizations of a socialist workers' movement grew. Similarly, the party systems of southern Europe are currently being shaken not only by the radical left but also by the decline of the traditional governing parties, which have supported austerity and whose reputations have been stained by numerous corruption scandals.[3] In Spain, the discourse of Podemos is even constructed around the diagnosis of a regime in crisis. The Constitution of 1978 – the fruit of a compromise between elites – rested on three pillars, which are either increasingly contested or in the process of collapsing: a parliamentary monarchy, a two-party system between centre-right and centre-left, and a territorial model characterized as 'asymmetric federalism'.

Thirdly, both periods raised the concerns about the international consequences and possible knock-on effects of the coming to power of parties to the left of social democracy. Forty years ago, it could have altered the confrontation between the Western and Soviet blocs, as well as stimulating and radicalizing social democracy in the West and dissident socialists in the East. Today, this takes the form of a potential challenge to the German 'ordoliberal' conception of the European Union (EU), as well as increased pressure on the parties of the centre-left to abandon their collusion with the conservative and neoliberal right.

Certainly, the differences are many and crucial. Despite the renewal of the radical left in the Iberian states and Greece, this is not the case in France and Italy. The former underwent both late democratization and integration into an economic and monetary zone dominated by stronger competitors without the organization of sufficient mechanisms of convergence. As a result, the southern periphery of the eurozone they comprised has been especially hard hit by the crisis, undermining the legitimacy of the compromises established during the transitions of the 1970s–80s. The latter have not been 'spared' solely because they belong to the core of the historic project of constructing a European community. After all, Italy, like Greece, has undergone a change of government at the will of the European authorities, who have pushed for the establishment of technocratic regimes to supervise policy. This, in turn, led in both cases to the rise of an oppositional party that destabilized the equilibrium of the party system.[4] Earlier however, the left had disintegrated after the choice of the Partito Comunista Italiano (PCI) to 'social democratize', thereby scuttling a good part of its intellectual and activist capital. As a result, no significant force was able to seize the window of opportunity opened by the crisis of 2008. France, on the other hand, showed enough resilience to avoid being swept away by the sovereign debt crisis, even if its relationship with Germany became clearly unbalanced in favour of the latter. The country has become 'the middle child in a dysfunctional family',[5] for now resigned to aligning itself with the most powerful actors so as to discipline the periphery without going as far as a definitive break.

This leads us to stress that the considerable advances of European integration constitute another major difference with the Eurocommunist phase, forming a hostile strategic terrain for anti-austerity parties with socialist objectives. If the crisis of the eurozone is only one aspect of the structural crisis of capitalism, it certainly creates a *specific* skein of difficulties. Also, the nature of the current global crisis is not identical to that of the 1970s. The latter was the result of the exhaustion of the Fordist-Keynesian configuration of capitalist accumulation, while the organizations of the workers' movement were perhaps at their apogee. This time, we have a neoliberal configuration that can no longer contain the disequilibria it has generated (between states, firms, social classes and so on). While no part of the globe is spared, the hypothesis of 'secular stagnation' and the threat of the development of even more predatory accumulation strategies is growing. Meanwhile, the 'infrastructures of dissent' capable of offering an alternative conception of civilization and human progress have been seriously weakened. Parallel to this, new forms of protest (like the occupation of public spaces) often reject conventional politics, which is increasingly unattractive to ordinary citizens as well as for those who wish to change the world.[6]

In spite of these differences, several strategic debates from the Eurocommunist sequence are still relevant today. They concern the capacity of the radical left to escape both marginality and normalization; in other words, to approach power without its desires for transformation being absorbed or liquidated by existing institutions. In fact, the Eurocommunist legacy is rich with inspiration (the search for a middle way between social democracy and the far left) and potential assets (in defining a strategy adapted to current European societies and the multiplicity of dominations which run through them), but also with unresolved problems (concerning in particular the relationship to the capitalist state).

WHAT EUROCOMMUNISM WAS

The historic genesis of the Eurocommunist phenomenon involves two dimensions. The first stems from the vicissitudes of international communism. Claudin described Eurocommunism as an 'Occidental schism' following the 'Oriental schism' previously brought about by the rupture with China.[7] According to his interpretation, it represented the terminal stage of the contradictions of the Communist 'world party', or in other words the claims of the Soviet Union to orchestrate the action of the communist parties (CPs). The legitimacy that this state had acquired in the eyes of communists, thanks to the (initially) emancipatory breadth of the October revolution, had for a long time blocked comprehension of a regime which had in fact generated a new dominant class and destroyed any authentically democratic space. During the two periods when the Soviet state had allied itself with the liberal democracies (1934-38 and 1941-47), it had allowed the CPs to participate in pluralist popular fronts. However, on each occasion it had reaffirmed its leading role in the world communist movement, and ruled out the hypothesis of 'national roads to socialism'. Above all, these periods of opening had fundamentally depended on strategic choices, which once reversed forced the fraternal parties to adopt the new line forged by the Kremlin, on the basis of its distinct interests.

In the Western countries, where Moscow disposed of less means of coercion than in the East, resistance to such subordination intensified, above all after 1956 (the crushing of the workers' councils in Budapest) and 1968 (the crushing of the Prague Spring). The imperialism of the USSR and its contempt for the popular will were too evident not to be noticed in societies where the rejection of democratic values had become a one-way ticket to political marginality. In addition, the explosion of plural revolts (workers' insubordination swamping trade union federations, student rebellion, feminist and ecological demands and so on), especially in France and Italy, also marked the upheaval of 1968. The broad mass of Western citizens had been won to the pluralism of representative regimes, while the increasing complexity of 'class positions' and the rise of hedonistic and anti-authoritarian values nurtured conflicts that could be thought through only with difficulty in the gnarled schemas of Marxism-Leninism. Consequently, the actions *and* the ideology of Soviet power proved increasingly to be a handicap in the competitive environment inhabited by the Western CPs. This situation increased the impetus to pursue an autonomous road to socialism. Gramsci's proposition according to which revolutionary strategy in Western Europe should consist of a 'war of position' rather than 'manoeuvre' seemed more valid than ever.

Several successive stages then led to the formation of a so-called 'Eurocommunist' orientation – a term adopted only with reticence by the parties concerned. In 1969, during the third world conference of CPs, several delegations (in particular the Italians and Spanish) criticized democratic centralism within the Communist family. While the following years were marked by denunciations of the Soviet state's attacks on liberties, the PCI signed two declarations with the Partido Comunista de España (PCE) and the Parti Communiste Français (PCF) (respectively in Livorno in July 1975 and in Rome in November 1975), which made official a shared conception of socialist transition that contradicted the path followed by the regimes in the East. The Rome Declaration included, for example, commitments to party pluralism, trade union independence, the development of democracy in the workplace, and the opening of state leadership to the working classes. In addition, the signatories specified that these resolutions arose from an 'analysis of the specific historical and material conditions of their respective countries', which was in effect a demand for autonomy.

Several striking declarations then followed, with Carillo (leader of the PCE) affirming that in 1976 'Moscow was no longer our Rome', while Berlinguer (leader of the PCI) reacted to the inauguration of martial law in Poland in December 1981 by stating that 'the propulsive force of the October revolution' and 'the capacity for renewal of the societies of Eastern Europe' were exhausted. Meanwhile, even if the PCF returned to very orthodox positions, the Eurocommunist theses had spread well beyond southern Europe, leading journalists and researchers to attribute the 'Eurocommunist' label to the British, Swedish, Swiss and even Belgian CPs. Bilateral relations were organized with socialist or social democratic leaders, while communists increasingly expressed support for the non-aligned movements of the Third World. All these ups and downs witnessed to the search for a 'third way' capable of transcending the historic defeats and fractures of the workers' movement.[8]

It is here that we observe the second dimension of the historic genesis of Eurocommunism, which concerns the contemporary radical left to a much greater degree. The Eurocommunist episode can be interpreted as one expression among others of a current of ideas and practices which has always been in a minority or defeated: a socialism which is anti-capitalist but liberal and pluralist, envisioning the transcendence of both the fetishes of the state and the commodity to allow human beings to democratically and consciously develop their social relations. In the past, social democracy had been the major expression of this current, which one can identify in the intellectual evolution of Jean Jaurès, in the Austro-Marxism of the inter war period, or in the guild socialism defined by certain contemporary Labour Party supporters.[9] Several themes, whose implementation remains tricky, have characterized this current: the rejection of an over-rigid separation between action in the state and action at the point of production; the will to democratize institutional apparatuses; and the conception of socialism as a source of moral, and not only material, progress. From this viewpoint, Eurocommunism tried to respond, in the circumstances of its time, to the eternal challenge of democratic socialism: to trace a strategic path between on the one hand, the simple reformist management of capitalism, and on the other hand a violent conquest of state power that would lead to the formation of a new oligarchy hostile to individual freedoms.

During the 1960s and 1970s, other political forces also faced this challenge, either through new independent formations (for example the small Parti Socialiste Unifié in France, which gathered revolutionary as well as reformist groups sharing anti-Gaullist, anti-colonial and anti-Stalinist views), or within the 'old' social democratic parties. Inside the Labour Party, for example, Tony Benn argued for a socialism that rested on workers' control, transparency of public decisions, methods of fighting bureaucracy, and the extension of political action beyond the parliamentary sphere. In the French Parti socialiste (PS) reborn in 1971 at Epinay, self-management was introduced among the objectives of an alternative to capitalism, alongside nationalization and democratic planning. Jean-Pierre Chevènement, then leader of the Centre d'études, de recherches et de réflexions socialistes (CERES, the main left-wing faction of the PS), affirmed that it was necessary to escape both the 'stomping of boots' of the barracks socialism of the East and the 'scraping of slippers' of Western social democracy. Another left-wing leader, Jean Poperen, had for a long time warned against the 'social-technocratic' illusion of those who claimed to transform society through skilled social engineering. In Sweden, the ideal of self-management was also taken up by a part of the social democratic and trade union left.[10] The projects of these factions suffered from certain limits, but they nonetheless contributed to legitimizing democratic demands to which the workers' movement had previously been too unreceptive.

One can say the same about Eurocommunism. The novelty of the Eurocommunist orientation resided in the will to integrate the emancipatory struggles that took place outside the sphere of strictly economic relations. This evolution remained timid at the level of political organizations (although somewhat less so in their left wings), but was developed further by intellectuals sensitive to such demands. For example, Christine Buci-Glucksman stressed the fact that socialism should deal with all forms of domination, whether of bureaucratic, sexual or technological origin. In her view, this 'transversal conflict' could only be expressed by a 'democratic historic bloc' which should think about politics *in relation* to the state and not only *in* the state'. The other major innovation of Eurocommunism resided in a new effort to think through the initiation of socialist transition in terms of a dialectic between a 'movement from above' (in the institutions) and a 'movement from below' (in society). Among intellectuals, Nicos Poulantzas showed best the point to which the state was structurally biased to the disadvantage of anti-capitalist movements, without however being a simple instrument in the hands of the dominant class – hence the promotion of a dual strategy engaging with the existing centres of power while creating autonomous and alternative spaces for the organization of social life.[11]

The Eurocommunist episode thus nourished a stock of ideas from which contemporary radical left formations can still draw. The parties that have now broken through in southern Europe have succeeded (at least initially) in accompanying the dynamic of the social movements without claiming a vanguard role, but by asserting the will to conquer power. They have also attracted new generations of voters by espousing a progressive agenda on questions of gender, ecology, human rights and territorial autonomy. Finally, they have benefited from their externality to the state apparatuses, which they promised to open to citizens and put at the service of the people. As Luke March had already noted before the crisis, the parties of the radical left holding the most potential for development are those which belong to the 'democratic-socialist' branch of this family, rather than those who have preserved at any price their Communist identity.[12] In a certain sense, the currently emergent radical left has taken up the torch of an alternative left which had attempted to break through from within the Communist tradition, and which one might have thought had been buried under the rubble of the latter. A discrete red thread certainly links the experiences of today and the Eurocommunist attempts of the 1970s (themselves close to other initiatives originating from social democracy).

REFLECTIONS ON THE FAILURE OF EUROCOMMUNISM

For all that, Eurocommunism failed to initiate any transition towards socialism, as did the left wings of social democracy that explored similar strategic and ideological paths. On a European scale, no common strategy or structure really emerged. At the national level, the parties which concentrated most hopes revealed the meagre potential for social transformation: the PCI was not able to participate in government even though it muddled its identity through compromise; the PCE collapsed in elections, then divided without having encouraged popular mobilizations; and the PCF opted for an identitarian turn without profiting from the PS's adaptation to neoliberalism. Other parties informed by the Eurocommunist theses found the resources to reconvert themselves after the fall of the Berlin Wall, but they remained minor actors in their party systems. The historic sequence that we are considering has then not bequeathed only inspiring elements to the contemporary radical left. It also appears as an *alert*. That is why it is important to consider the limits of Eurocommunism.

Some of these limits are located in the ambiguities of the relationship between Western CPs and the Soviet Union, as well as in the difficulty of going beyond an ideological and organizational matrix profoundly influenced by the past history of the workers' movement.[13] While sincerely wishing to free themselves of their subordination to Moscow, Eurocommunists for a long time nonetheless continued to characterize the Eastern regimes as 'socialist', contradicting the desire to identify socialism with effective democracy, or at least a more extended form of this than liberal representative democracy. But this contradiction is today a thing of the past. Of course, some adversaries have used the proximity of the contemporary parties of the radical left to some Latin American governments to challenge their democratic sincerity. However, most of the 'national-popular' (rather than strictly socialist) experiences in South America have not prevented the maintenance of pluralism and fundamental liberties. Moreover, no country or party in this region claims to be the centre of a world movement over which it holds power. The democratic commitment and national independence of the European radical left parties cannot be questioned with the same success as it was at the time of the Cold War.

Another problem, which finds more resonance today, concerns the organizational model of the Western CPs committed to Eurocommunism. By continuing to present themselves as the natural parties of the working class, they neglected the pluralism that they professed at the societal scale. Also, the internal structure of the CPs in fact left little room for a public and adversarial debate, the possibility of challenging the leadership, or the direct involvement of activists in the mechanisms of internal decisions. This inability to transcend the centralism falsely called 'democratic' undermined their attractiveness and the credibility of their discourse. The structures of contemporary radical left parties are more open, but there is nonetheless a risk that the famous 'iron law of oligarchy' will neutralize the activist rank and file and restrict ideological pluralism. The members of the left wing of Syriza have for example stressed how its transformation from a coalition to a single party served to strengthen the more moderate leaders.[14]

The institutionalization of Podemos has also generated tensions between partisans of a more vertical structure, and those who fear the marginalization of broader 'circles' and the excessive personalization of the organization.[15]

That said, it appears that contemporary radical left parties have greater room for manoeuvre than the CPs of the 1970s in adapting their structures to their message and their environment. The adoption of the Eurocommunist orientation in all its consequences meant challenging nearly all the basic principles of the CPs since their foundation. Accepting such an *aggiornamento*, meant endangering party unity, as illustrated by the splits in the PCE over 1983-85. Paradoxically, one could almost say that the disappearance of the USSR and the marginalization of the Soviet Communist reference point were crucial for the integration of the Eurocommunist orientation, or at least some of its basic principles, within the radical left.

Other limits of Eurocommunism can be found in the projects that were in competition in the Eurocommunist theoretical space. It is indeed impossible to speak of a comprehensive doctrine that would have unified the national trajectories regrouped under this label. Briefly stated, we could distinguish two opposite tendencies that polarized the Eurocommunist internal discussion. The first is what Christine Buci-Glucksmann and Göran Therborn have described as 'liberal-governmental'. According to them, this tendency only allowed for a kind of 'institutional rallying' of the CPs, while failing to thoroughly rethink the dialectical relationship between the party, social movements and democratic subjects. Instead of inventing a road beyond Leninism and social democracy, Eurocommunism in its liberal-governmental variety consecrated existing forms of politics, enclosing its strategy in a classic conception of the gradualist conquest of state power. It also misanalysed the crisis of capitalism, and its remedies remained prisoners of a productivist and *dirigiste* conception of the economy.[16] In the PCI, which was the party at the very forefront of the Eurocommunist phenomenon, Giorgio Amendola, leader of the party's right wing, incarnated this trend well. Amendola gave wholehearted support to the austerity practiced by the Christian Democrats (DC), a move he framed as a 'historic compromise' that could 'modernize' Italian capitalism (and thus speed up the development of the productive forces) and reduce the mistrust of the popular electoral base of the DC.[17] Concealed behind the liberal-governmental line was, in fact, the classic dilemma of young social democratic parties. The centrality of the electoral objective, perceived as the sole key for acquiring popular legitimacy and embarking on social transformation, tended to lead to the party's programmatic moderation, bureaucratization, and the absorption of its desires for change within the limits of the capitalist state.[18]

Today, it is obvious that Tspiras's choices as leader of Syriza, and then prime minister of Greece, can be criticized with the aid of this model. The last manifesto, sufficient to provoke a confrontation with Greece's creditors, was already the result of watering down the demands of the party. The government then found it difficult to act in connection with the social movements, which were in retreat, and did not seek support from the sectors remobilized by the referendum against a new austerity programme.[19] For its part, Podemos has also tended to moderate its economic proposals in the course of its short existence, to the point where they are now very close to a traditional social democratic agenda. A debate is also underway inside the party concerning the strategic balance between electoral politics on the one hand, and on the other the organization of a common political consciousness through longer-term militant and cultural action. The leadership of the party seems in any case to refuse the social movements significant autonomy, evidently viewing political legitimacy as the exclusive privilege of parliamentary representatives.[20]

It is useful to recall that there was, from the outset, a left Eurocommunism opposed to liberal-governmentalism. It was very attached to the struggle against 'generalized domination', leading to a much stronger proximity to the (new) social movements and the desire to combine representative democracy with other forms of citizen and worker self-government. Pietro Ingrao (who died in September 2015 at the age of 100) was the best representative of this tendency inside the PCI. For him, it was important to end the distinction between economic and political struggles, which divided the subaltern. The battles of the latter should take place across society as a whole, including both the state apparatuses and the places of production. However, it was not the time to invoke 'workers' councils', which were struggles liable to provoke divisions among the subaltern. Instead, Ingrao considered it necessary to integrate *all the people* within enlarged modes of representation, which represented a continuation of the unfinished work of the bourgeoisie. Poulantzas confided in one of his last interviews that he felt close to this Italian leader. According to the Greek thinker, the difference between the right and left wings of Eurocommunism turned on the importance given to direct democracy and on the conviction that any socialist transformation of state and economy would necessarily end in a 'moment of rupture'.[21]

Poulantzas remains the theorist of left Eurocommunism who posed with most rigour the following dilemma: a solely statist strategy reproduces the illusion of a neutral state (whereas it is generally 'strategically selective' in favour of the dominant classes); whereas a solely rank-and-file strategy conserves the illusion of escaping the grip of the state (which is in fact crucial to defining the terrain of struggle and the resources of the protagonists). However, despite many contentions as to how this contradiction is to be transcended, the question remains open. Indeed, left Eurocommunism has correctly been criticized for its strategic fuzziness, which could serve as the 'vestibule' to a liberal-governmental evolution. In particular, the most stimulating Trotskyist critics of Poulantzas, such as Colin Barker and Daniel Bensaïd, have reproached him for caricaturing the defeats of attempts to organize popular power, and inversely for having passed over too quickly the harmful implications of representative democracy (atomization of citizens, separation between their public life and their private activity).[22]

Unfortunately, the discussion is not at this level on the contemporary radical left, given the balance of forces after three decades of neoliberalism. That said, in the medium- to long-term, it seems certain that an exit from crisis on ecologically sustainable terms which would be favorable to the popular majority cannot take place on the basis of traditional Keynesian policies. On the contrary, this would demand a high level of social conflict, as the attack should be inflicted on capitalist logic, from the protection of 'natural' common goods, the extension of social ownership of financial and nonfinancial enterprises, the decarbonization of the global energy system, the contraction of the material production of the rich countries, a delinking of employment from profitability, a drastic levelling of wealth disparities, and so on.[23] As such, these strategic debates on the radical left remain very relevant indeed.

Finally, it needs to be said that the limits of Eurocommunism do not solely reside in the non-completion of the organizational transformation of the CPs, or in their difficulty thinking through the socialist transition. They also stem from an absence of coordination between parties sharing the same positions. Although their countries were afflicted by global crises, they defended distinct national roads to the construction of socialism. In other words, their fight for emancipation from Moscow prevented them from restructuring internationalist bonds among Eurocommunist parties, which would have strengthened the credibility of their anti-capitalist commitments.

The difficulty of acting at the supranational level according to a common agenda is far from having disappeared today. On the contrary, European integration renders this dimension of political engagement indispensable, but hardly suppresses the obstacles to its effective realization. Indeed, European integration encourages political groupings with common characteristics, but whose raison d'être is derived from conflicts expressed principally at the national level. The problem is that *identical* economic or cultural orientations can be combined with *different* positions on the EU, whether pro-, alternative- or anti-integration. The stance adopted by different parties on the question of the EU depends on the geopolitical situation of the country, the opportunities for broader alliances for the radical left, and the concrete analysis of the EU (roughly said: is there any point in opposing its policies without opposing its institutions?).[24]

Currently, the radical left party bloc is one of the least homogeneous groupings in the European political system, although we should not exaggerate the coherence of competing political forces. The weak institutionalization of the radical left family is visible in the fact that some crucial issues, like the democratization of the EU and the single currency, are currently debated in bodies other than GUE/NGL (that is the confederal Group of the United European Left/Nordic Green Left in the European Parliament) or the PEL (that is the transnational Party of the European Left recognized and funded by the EU). Such is the case with the newly founded movement Diem25, launched by Yanis Varoufakis (former Greek Finance minister under Tsipras), as well as the summits of Plan B organized in Paris and Madrid in early 2016.[25]

The multiplicity of multilateral forums can certainly be viewed as progress in comparison with the essentially bilateral relations maintained between the Eurocommunist parties during their heyday. This has probably improved mutual understanding among contemporary radical left organizations. However, such forums remain loosely structured and do not have the capacity to exert substantial political influence either at the national or European level, electorally or otherwise. Although this can be partly explained by the institutional structure of the EU, the main factor is the limited convergence among the interests of the respective member states within which these radical left parties are attempting to gain the support of the electorate. In particular, the size of a country, its mode of growth and the specific nature of its insertion within the eurozone and global economy produce a specific structure of opportunities and constraints. The crux of the matter is that the matrix of power in the EU maximizes the interdependences between member states without providing instruments through which their different patterns of development can coalesce, nor permitting the possibility of 'opting-out' from EU legislation where this poses a threat on the basis of specifically national concerns.[26] Consequently, common statements or proposals are necessarily vague and consensual.

RETHINKING THE EUROCOMMUNIST LEGACY IN 'NEW TIMES'

We have indicated that the major parties of the contemporary radical left have already acted in accordance with the best intuitions of Eurocommunism. They have avoided both workerist and vanguardist pretensions while appearing as the most credible vehicles for demands against austerity, corrupt elites and the dismantling of popular sovereignty. At the same time, the factors that resulted in the lack of coordination, coherence and attractive power of Eurocommunism again come into play for the contemporary radical left. Obviously, many characteristics of the Western CPs and the environment in which they operated have changed. However, certain tensions of the earlier period are present again today, because *they are those of democratic socialism confronted with the modern capitalist state*. Nonetheless, it is always necessary to be on guard against the temptation to draw conclusions too hastily. The contrast between the current situation and that of forty years ago is not completely summed up by the deterioration of the balance of class forces. The defeats suffered by the dominated classes are also reflected in an alteration of the strategic terrain on which the radical left operates. This means that the unresolved questions of Eurocommunism continue to be relevant, but in a context very different from the 1960s and 1970s in relation to the role and nature of the state.

Before his death, Poulantzas had already hypothesized a lasting evolution towards 'authoritarian statism', which would conserve the formal institutions of representative democracy while emptying them of their substance. Offe had anticipated at the time the 'cartelization' of the dominant political parties, i.e. their transformation into state agencies of government to the detriment of their role of representation of popular demands.[27] The degradation of representative structures in the advanced democracies cannot, however, be understood without accounting for supranational factors in the contemporary analyses of Eurocommunism. The state form typical of the post-Fordist phase of capitalist democracy is characterized not only by the reduction of pluralism internally, but also by the dispersion of state political authority, which it still manages despite no longer monopolizing. Indeed, state capacities to make and implement collectively binding decisions have been transferred to an unprecedented degree to international, transnational and private actors. In the same way that production chains have been fragmented at the global scale, so do nation states increasingly resemble internationalized complexes of authority, though the organization of democratic life remains confined within the same national spatial limits as before.[28]

The theorists of Eurocommunism had not (and probably could not have) anticipated such transformations. That is why Poulantzas's thinking on the bias and strategic selectiveness of the modern state remains useful, *providing it is updated*. One way to do so is to insist that we cannot understand the sovereign debt crisis and its results if one envisages the EU as a structure simply added to existing states. In fact, we have witnessed a transnational restructuring of state apparatuses in such a way that the EU constitutes a 'complex institutional matrix' that neutralizes popular intervention. The authoritarian statism anticipated by Poulantzas certainly corresponds to a less inclusive phase of capitalism, but it is concretely reflected by the strategic displacement of the tasks of government on several spatio-temporal scales. For example, during the sovereign debt crisis, 'national parliaments and the European Parliament have been increasingly bypassed and overrun by rapid decision-making processes between national executives made in the Council of the European Union and administrative bodies of the EU'.[29]

At the same time, this elitist supranational government contains but does not resolve the economic and monetary disequilibria internal to the zone: it undermines its own legitimacy in the eyes of citizens, whose tolerance threshold is unknown. In any event, this construction is unstable by nature, thus offering opportunities to alternative political forces. In Greece and in Spain, the unveiling of this complex mode of domination, and the denunciation of its anti-democratic character, have been at the heart of the arguments of the radical left. The way to overcome these issues poses many more problems.

Clearly, Syriza in office in Greece has faced the authoritarian statism – in defence of the euro and the EU – of an ultra-rigid economic and monetary order, locked down by treaties, institutions and dominant actors who are thoroughly determined to crush any pluralism threatening this 'new gold standard'. Indeed, it seems that the EMU has the means to thwart any political alternative, and one can hypothesize that it would explode in the improbable event that a majority of member states attempted to force Germany and its allies to delink the Euro from its ordoliberal constitution. As these lines are written, a whole section of the Greek radical left is witnessing a kind of 'normalization' of Syriza in power, while Brussels has given them no chance to construct an 'autonomous path' of exit from crisis – without even speaking of socialism. One can wonder if the party leaders, exhausted by incessant negotiations with creditors and leading a shattered state, still have the temporal or even theoretical resources to face the situation.

Podemos is less affiliated with the legacy of Eurocommunism than Syriza (the Greek party partially originates from a Communist split along this political line). Other political references have informed the Spanish party, like the work of Ernesto Laclau and Chantal Mouffe on populism, as well as the experiences of the Latin American left. That said, the reminiscences of Eurocommunist themes are quite clearly observable. For example, the party assumes the mobilization of citizens both by citizen participation on the ground and by electoral participation to send representatives to the institutions. The success of this 'strategic dualism', practiced through innovative use of media technology, distinguishes Podemos from other similar parties.[30] Also, Gramsci is a common reference for both Laclau and Mouffe and the Eurocommunist intellectuals of the 1970s. Even if the relationship of these theorists to Marxism is not the same, both wish to open the left to the multiplicity of democratic demands, and go beyond the dual impasse of Leninism and traditional social democracy.[31]

In late June, Podemos chose to contract an electoral alliance with Izquierda Unida (IU, the United Left), whose main driving force remains the former Eurocommunist PCE. Of course, strategic concerns were strong incentives for such an alliance: whereas the combined share of the vote among IU and Podemos overtook that of PSOE in 2015, the characteristics of the Spanish proportional voting system prevented them from overtaking the Socialists in terms of seats in Parliament. Common lists were supposed to be the recipe for becoming the main opposition force after the June rerun of December's inconclusive election, behind the right-wing Parti Popular but ahead of the PSOE. Eventually, the gamble was lost.[32] However, it confirmed that Podemos and IU belong to the same political space or even radical left family. On one hand, the majority of Podemos leadership has admitted that populism is only a 'thin ideology',[33] which needs to be anchored in a broader political culture that addresses a wider range of societal issues. On the other hand, the renewed leadership of IU has admitted that less traditional ways of mobilizing are needed to broaden the appeal of the radical left.[34] It remains to be seen whether the recent disappointing electoral results will hinder these evolutions in a Spanish radical left that has never been so powerful since the post-Francoist transition.

In any case, Podemos' strategy in relation to the EU does not appear to be qualitatively different from that of Syriza. A critique of existing European integration has been produced, but few lessons have been drawn. More exactly, the high level of strategic reflection of the leaders about conquering hegemony within society has no equivalent insofar as the analysis of the state form with which they will be confronted when they exercise power is concerned. The Portuguese Left Bloc, whose success is less striking, has worked more on the question of its relations with the EU, clearly affirming that limits exist to participation in the monetary union (and thus to its current support for the Socialist government of Antonio Costa). In France, the radical left candidate for the Presidency in 2012, Jean-Luc Mélenchon, makes a similar argument. More broadly, his will to 'federate the people' and give it the possibility to rewrite the Constitution rests on the conviction (nourished in his case by a radical Republican background) that the radical left must transform the strategic terrain to better promote (eco)socialist policies. Most of the other radical left parties in Northern or Central Europe (including Die Linke) seem to be less innovative.

What it is certain is that a reflection on the current complexity of state apparatuses will be unavoidable for the contemporary radical left if it wishes to democratize Europe at both the continental and national scale. In the weakest European countries – that is, where the left has the best electoral prospects – this work will be necessary even to obtain modest reforms. Today, as at the end of the 1970s, the difficulties experienced by the radical left in advanced capitalist countries are linked to an 'experimental stage' through which all attempts to end the austerity consensus necessarily will have to pass.

NOTES

1   Fabien Escalona and Mathieu Vieira, 'The Radical Left in Europe – Thoughts about the Emergence of a Family', Paris: Fondation Jean Jaurès, 19 November 2013.
2   Fernando Claudin, *L'eurocommunisme*, Paris: François Maspéro, 1977, p. 27.
3   Fabien Escalona, 'Au-delà de l'Espagne, la crise bouscule les systèmes partisans d'Europe du Sud', *The Conversation*, 23 December 2015.
4   Susannah Verney and Anna Bosco, 'Living Parallel Lives: Italy and Greece in an Age of Austerity', *South European Society and Politics*, 18(4), 2013, pp. 397-426.
5   Mark I. Vail, 'Europe's Middle Child: France, Statist Liberalism and the Conflicted Politics of the Euro', in M. Matthijs and M. Blyth, eds., *The Future of the Euro*, Oxford: Oxford University Press, 2015, pp. 136-60.
6   See (among others) Leo Panitch and Sam Gindin, 'Capitalist Crises and the Crisis This Time', in Leo Panitch, Greg Albo, and Vivek Chibber, eds., *Socialist Register 2011: The Crisis This Time*, 2010, pp. 1-20; Armin Schäfer and Wolfgang Streeck, eds., *Politics in the Age of Austerity*, Cambridge: Polity, 2013; Cédric Durand, *Le capital fictif*, Paris: Les Prairies ordinaires, 2014.
7   Fernando Claudin, *L'eurocommunisme*, p. 9.
8   Lilly Marcou, 'La seconde chance de l'eurocommunisme', *Le Monde diplomatique*, February 1989, p. 9.
9   Jean-Paul Scot, *Jaurès et le réformisme révolutionnaire*, Paris: Editions du Seuil, 2014; Norbert Leser, 'Austro-Marxism: A Reappraisal', *Journal of Contemporary History*, 11(2/3), 1976, pp. 133-48; Marc Stears, *Progressives, Pluralists, and the Problems of the State: Ideologies of Reform in the United States and Britain, 1906-1926*, Oxford: Oxford University Press, 2002.
10 Anthony W. Benn, 'The New Politics: A Socialist Reconnaissance', Fabian Tract 402, London: The Fabian Society, 1970; Jacques Mandrin, *Socialisme ou social-médiocratie*, Paris: Seuil, 1969; Jean Poperen, 'Unification socialiste ou technocratie autoritaire',

Cahiers du Centre d'Etudes socialistes, Paris: Editions Maspéro, 1963; Bo Bernhardsson and Jan Kolk, *Det nödvändiga uppbrottet. En debattbok om 80-talets socialdemokratiska politik*, Stockholm: Rabén & Sjögrens, 1980.

11   Nicos Poulantzas, *State, Power, Socialism*, London: Verso, 2014; Christine Buci-Glucksmann, 'De la crise de l'Etat keynésien au nouveau socialisme? La politique au-delà de l'Etat', in C. Buci-Glucksmann, ed., *La gauche, le pouvoir, le socialisme. Hommage à Nicos Poulantzas*, Paris: PUF, 1983.

12   Luke March, *Radical Left Parties in Europe*, London and New York: Routledge, 2011.

13   Fernando Claudin, *L'eurocommunisme*, pp. 101-150.

14   Stathis Kouvélakis, 'Greece: Phase One', *Jacobin*, 22 January 2015.

15   Jeanne Moisand, 'Espagne: de l'indignation à l'organisation', *La Vie des idées*, 20 March 2015.

16   Christine Buci-Glucksmann and Göran Therborn, *Le défi social-démocrate*, Paris: François Maspéro, 1981, pp. 39-76.

17   Amendola, like Ingrao cited later, was interviewed by Henri Weber in *Le Parti communiste italien: aux sources de l'eurocommunisme*, Paris: François Maspéro, 1977. Weber, who was then a leader of the Trotskyist *Ligue communiste révolutionnaire*, very much opposed to the Amendola line and sceptical on the Ingrao line, ironically became a leader of the French PS and one of the most fervent supporters of the politics practiced by François Hollande.

18   These processes were the subject of an early literature, notably in the work of Rosa Luxemburg and Robert Michels, but even Max Weber. These three authors are evoked in Claus Offe, *Contradictions of the Welfare State*, London: Hutchinson, 1984, pp. 183-8, where the latter writes: 'no competitive party system so far has ever yielded a distribution of political power that would have been able to alter the logic of capital and the pattern of socio-economic power *it* generates. [We could] postulate the emergence of political parties capable of … leading to a challenge to class power through politically constituted power. I do not think that there are many promising indications of such a development, in spite of Euro-communist doctrines and strategies that have emerged in the Latin-European countries in the mid-1970s' (pp. 187-188). We should cite also Fred Block, 'Beyond Relative Autonomy: State Managers as Historical Subjects', in Ralph Miliband and John Saville, eds., *The Socialist Register 1980*, London: Merlin Press, 1980, pp. 227-41.

19   According to Paul Blackledge, in 'Left reformism, the State and the Problem of Socialist Politics Today', *International Socialism*, 130, 2013: 'In Syriza's case, there is a tension between the very positive and highly welcome political critique of austerity and their orientation towards capturing the existing state machine through parliamentary elections. It is their parliamentary statism, however mediated, that tends to trap left reformist parties like Syriza within capitalist relations in ways that pressure them to come into conflict with and, unless successfully challenged from the left, eventually undermine the radicalism of their own base.'

20   Iñigo Errejón, 'Podemos a mitad de camino', *CTXT*, 23 April 2016; Emmanuel Rodríguez and Brais Fernández, 'Todavía no somos suficientes populistas. En respuesta a Íñigo Errejón', *CTXT*, 26 April 2016.

21   Nicolas Poulantzas, Interview in *Marxism Today*, July 1979, pp. 194-201.

22   Colin Barker, 'A "New" Reformism? – A Critique of the Political Theory of Nicos Poulantzas', *International Socialism*, 4, 1979; Daniel Bensaïd, 'Eurocommunisme, austromarxisme et bolchevisme', *Critique communiste*, 18-19, 1977.

23   Michael Roberts, 'The Global Crawl Continues', *International Socialism*, 147, London, 2015; Daniel Tanuro, *L'impossible capitalisme vert*, Paris: La Découverte, 2012.

24   Michael Holmes and Knut Roder, eds., *The Left and the European Constitution*, Manchester: Manchester University Press, 2012.

25 Gaël Brustier, Corinne Deloy, Fabien Escalona, 'Political families in the European elections May 2014: an assessment', Brussels: Fondation Robert Schuman, 2014; Fabien Escalona, 'Sur l'Europe, gauches radicales et droites nationalistes n'ont pas grand-chose en commun', *Slate*, 9 March 2016.
26 Fritz Scharpf, 'After the Crash: A Perspective on Multilevel European Democracy', MPIfG Discussion Paper 14/21, Cologne: Max Planck Institute for the Study of Societies, 2014.
27 Claus Offe, *Contradictions*, p. 191; Richard Katz and Peter Mair, 'Changing Models of Party Organization and Party Democracy: The Emergence of the Cartel Party', *Party Politics*, 1(1), 1995, pp. 5-28.
28 Stephan Leibfried, Evelyne Huber, Matthew Lange, Frank Nullmeier, Jonah D. Levy, eds., *The Oxford Handbook of Transformations of the State*, Oxford: Oxford University Press, 2015.
29 Sune Sandbeck and Etienne Schneider, 'From the Sovereign Debt Crisis to Authoritarian Statism: Contradictions of the European State Project', *New Political Economy*, 19(6), 2014, p. 866.
30 Alexandros Kioupkiolis, 'Podemos: the Ambiguous Promises of Left-Wing Populism in Contemporary Spain', *Journal of Political Ideologies*, 21(2), 2016, pp. 99-120.
31 Ernesto Laclau and Chantal Mouffe [1985], *Hegemony and Socialist Strategy: Towards a Radical Democratic Politics*, London: Verso, 2013.
32 Miguel-Anxo Murado, 'What Happened to the Podemos Fairy Tale?', *The Guardian*, 23 June 2016.
33 Ben Stanley, 'The Thin Ideology of Populism', *Journal of Political Ideologies*, 13(1), 2008, pp. 95-110.
34 Fabien Escalona, 'Unidos Podemos: la véritable "belle alliance" de la gauche?', *Slate*, 9 June 2016.

REVOLUTION IN A WARMING WORLD: LESSONS FROM THE RUSSIAN TO THE SYRIAN REVOLUTIONS

ANDREAS MALM

It doesn't take much imagination to associate climate change with revolution. If the planetary order upon which all societies are built starts breaking down, how can they possibly remain stable? Various more or less horrifying scenarios of upheaval have long been extrapolated from soaring temperatures. In his novel *The Drowned World* from 1962, today often considered the first prophetic work of climate fiction, J. G. Ballard conjured up melting icecaps, an English capital submerged under tropical marshes and populations fleeing the unbearable heat towards polar redoubts. The UN directorate seeking to manage the migration flows assumed that 'within the new perimeters described by the Arctic and Antarctic Circles life would continue much as before, with the same social and domestic relationships, by and large the same ambitions and satisfactions' – but that assumption 'was obviously fallacious'.[1] A drowned world would be nothing like the one hitherto known.

In more recent years, the American military establishment has dominated this subgenre of climate projection. Extreme weather events, the Senate learned from the 2013 edition of the 'worldwide threat assessment' compiled by the US intelligence community, will put food markets under serious strain, 'triggering riots, civil disobedience, and vandalism'.[2] If the armed forces are firefighters tasked with suppressing outbreaks of rebellion, their workload will increase in a warming world. Pursuing its consistent and candid interest in the issue, in such stark contrast to the denialism of the American right, the Pentagon submitted a report to Congress in July 2015 detailing how all combatant commands are now integrating climate change into their planning. The 'threat multiplier' is already at work, undermining fragile governments, turning populations against rulers unable to meet their needs: and it will only get worse.[3] Most of it will play out in overcrowded littorals. In *Out of the Mountains: The Coming Age of the Urban Guerilla*, David Kilcullen, perhaps the most astute mandarin of the military wing of the empire, predicts a near future of megacities in the Global South filled to the brim with restless masses, mostly on low-lying coastal land; not only cutting into their food and water supplies, climate change will threaten to directly drown those masses. How can they not pick up whatever arms they have and start marching? Mixing lessons from the second intifada, Central Asian jihads, the Arab Spring and the Occupy movement, Kilcullen envisions a century of permanent counterinsurgency in hot slums sliding into the sea.[4]

So far, the sworn enemies of revolution have dominated this frenzy of speculation. Little input has come from the other side: from the partisans of the idea that the present order needs to be overthrown or else things will turn out very badly. But if the strategic environment of counterinsurgency is shifting, so is – by definition – that of revolutionaries, who then have just as compelling a reason to analyze what lies in store. The imbalance in the amount of preparation is glaring. Those who pledge allegiance to the revolutionary tradition – in whose collective mind the experience of 1917 will probably always loom large – should dare to use their imagination as productively as any writer of intelligence reports or works of fiction. One might begin by distinguishing between four possible configurations of revolution and heat.

REVOLUTION AS SYMPTOM

How can rising temperatures translate into social turbulence? In a pair of papers which have caused a stir in the research community, Solomon M. Hsiang and his colleagues collect some fifty data sets covering 10,000 years of world history, feed numbers into their computer models and distil a straight link from heat to various forms of confrontation. On all scales and in all cultures, anomalously hot weather induces hostile honking, police brutality, baseball pitchers hitting batters, urban riots and, at the end of the spectrum, 'the forcible removal of rulers'. Somehow exceptional warmth incites more contentious behaviour in individuals, and the effect is three times larger for 'intergroup conflict', the box in which the spectre of revolution appears.[5] Claiming robust quantitative proof of causation, Hsiang et al. proceed to conclude that if the past is anything to go by, a hotter twenty-first century will see all manner of strife – 'the future holds nothing else but confrontation', they could have quoted the opening lines of Public Enemy's *Apocalypse 91*.

Naturally, critics have taken aim at the deceptive simplicity of this thesis. By placing all other variables within brackets – a prerequisite for isolating the climate factor – Hsiang and his colleagues effectively invent a unilinear, monocausal mechanism: bad weather—conflict.[6] That criticism could be taken one step further. If there is any link between climate change and the kind of unrest that may issue in a full-fledged revolution, it *cannot possibly be immediate*. No matter how hot it gets, no one will ever go on strike or attack a police station just for feeling over-heated. There has to be a pre-existing score to settle, some sort of simmering rage brought towards a boiling-point, for otherwise the aggression would be completely random, and so unable to feed into collective action of any significance (hostile honking here excluded). The statistical methodology of Hsiang et al., in which everything but climate is relegated to the dead category of *ceteris paribus*, should be inverted: if the aim is to understand how global warming may set off discord, it must not be posited as acting on its own.[7]

That criticism, however, also curves back on some of the critics of the thesis. Laying all emphasis on the variables omitted by Hsiang et al., one team of researchers argues that 'it is probably more critical to understand "the nature of the state" than the "state of nature"'.[8] Given that climate never operates in isolation – this is the logic of the argument – it cannot really be that important. But that is to jump to the mirror error. That the violent repercussions of global warming must have travelled along social pathways does not make the process any less powerful. Unmediated, exclusive causation cannot be posited as a criterion for the efficacy of climate change in calling forth something like a revolution, for that would presuppose an empty planet, the non-existence of human societies on earth. Since there are societies – in whose absence we would not have had fossil fuel combustion in the first place, nor contentious politics in streets or squares – any climatic spark will *always* burn through relations between people on its way to an explosion. Even societies crumbling under four degrees of warming will be shot through with inequalities of power. The critical state of nature is mediated – in no way negated – by the nature of the state. Or, in short, it is a matter of *articulation*. That is what needs to be understood and acted upon.

This academic debate now has a testing ground where the stakes count in millions of human lives: Syria. In the years leading up to the outbreak of the 2011 revolution, that country reeled under an epochal drought. Sustaining the agriculture of the Mediterranean basin since time immemorial, a relatively stable regime of rainfall coming in from the sea between November and April abruptly gave way, in the 1970s, to a trend of ever more fickle precipitation and persistent drying.[9] The worst effected corner was the Levant, particularly the area known as the Fertile Crescent, and particularly the part of it located in Syria. 1998 marked another shift towards semi-permanent Syrian drought, the severity of which, tree rings reveal, has no equivalent in the past 900 years.¹⁰ Not only have the winter rains failed, but the higher temperatures have also sped up evaporation in summertime, depleting groundwater and streams and parching the soil.¹¹ There is no natural explanation for the trend. It can only be ascribed to the emissions of greenhouse gases.

The Syrian drought reached its highest peak of intensity so far in the years 2006–10, when the sky stayed blue for longer than anyone could remember. The breadbasket of the northeastern provinces collapsed. Wheat and barley crops more than halved; by February 2010, nearly all livestock herds had been obliterated. In October of that year, the calamity reached the pages of the *New York Times*, whose reporter described how 'hundreds of villages have been abandoned as farmlands turn to cracked desert and grazing animals die off. Sandstorms have become far more common, and vast tent cities of dispossessed farmers and their families have risen up around the larger towns and cities of Syria.'¹² Estimates range between one and two million displaced farmers and herders. Fleeing the wastelands, they hunkered down on the outskirts of Damascus, Aleppo, Homs, Hama, joining the ranks of proletarians seeking to find a living from construction work, taxi-driving, or any other, mostly unavailable, job. But they were not alone in feeling the heat. Due to the drought, the marketplaces of the country exhibited one of the central vectors of climatic influence on popular livelihoods: doubling, tripling, uncontrollably spiking food prices.¹³

What did the regime of Bashar al-Assad do when the people ate dust? The onset of the peak drought coincided almost exactly with a concerted push to renovate the foundation of the Syrian ruling class. After years of sclerosis, Assad and his closest accomplices resolved to nurture a fresh clique of private businessmen, encourage them to seize hold of large swathes of the economy and task them with launching a bonanza of accumulation. While the crops withered, real estate markets underwent fabulous booms, free trade zones opened up, investments poured in from the Gulf and Iran, luxury boutiques and fancy cafes sprang up in the centres of Damascus and Aleppo, a first car factory was constructed, plans were tabled for rebuilding the entire centre of Homs into a model of Dubai complete with golf courses and residential towers. One individual, Rami Makhlouf, owner of mobile phone operator SyriaTel and king of the crony capitalists, reputedly extended his tentacles into 60 per cent of the economy.¹⁴ In the countryside, the regime matched the dustbowl with a new law allowing landowners to expel their tenants. Subsidies on fuel and food were slashed. State farmlands ended up in the pockets of private entrepreneurs, water in the thirsty cotton plantations and other vain agribusiness projects.¹⁵ In *Burning Country: Syrians in Revolution and War*, Robin Yassin-Kassab and Leila al-Shami capture the scene after four years of extreme drought: 'water shortages plagued the cities too – during the hot summer months the taps sometimes only flowed once a week in poorer areas, while the lawns of the rich remained lush and green.'[16]

And then Syria exploded. Starting in Dera'a – a town in the southern outpost of the agricultural heartland, nearly as heavily impacted by the drought as the northeast – the Syrian revolution stood out in the Arab Spring for having its basis outside the main city centres.[17] The people who first dared to march, chanting against Assad and smashing the windows of SyriaTel, lived either in rural regions or in neighbourhoods on the peripheries of the cities, where large numbers of migrants had taken up residence. When the demonstrations morphed into civil war in 2012, the armed rebels streaming into the cities from their liberated villages found the most avid support precisely in those neighbourhoods, in a geographical pattern that has persisted ever since (witness eastern Ghouta or northern and eastern Aleppo). Looking back on one year of revolution in *Jadaliyya*, Suzanne Saleeby summed up the lingering effects of the drought: 'In these recent months, Syrian cities have served as junctures where the grievances of displaced rural migrants and disenfranchised urban residents meet and come to question the very nature and distribution of power.'[18] Combined with a host of other sparks, climate change, it seems, had ignited the fuse.

But to some activists and scholars, that thought is obnoxious. Francesca De Châtel has argued against ascribing any role in the Syrian crisis to the climate. To make her case, she must first brush aside all the signs that the pre-revolution drought was unprecedented and anthropogenic. Instead, she claims, it was but a routine episode in a country accustomed to dry weather, with no demonstrated ties to rising temperatures.[19] Global warming poses no serious threat to Syria's water resources – any scarcity is the regime's own doing. Blaming fossil fuel combustion is to chime in with the Assad propaganda. The 'role of climate change in this chain of events is not only irrelevant; it is also an unhelpful distraction', lending credence to the efforts of the regime to 'blame external factors for its own failings'.[20] It remains to be investigated how revolutionaries on the ground perceive the situation, but it is not inconceivable that many of them would agree. We are fighting Assad and Makhlouf, not ExxonMobil or Chinese coal!

And yet De Châtel's argument is flawed in several respects. Firstly, it is premised on a sort of local climate denialism that cannot stand up against the overwhelming scientific evidence. Secondly, if we were to follow the principle that global warming should not be attributed any responsibility for miseries to which provincial exploiters and oppressors have also made contributions, then that planetary fire – and more precisely, the people who have lit it, maintained it, and pour fuel on it on a daily basis – would be very successfully exonerated. Thirdly, and most importantly, the marks of climate change on Syria's fate by no means wipes Assad's slate clean. Had the country been a perfect democracy, in which households shared resources equally and made sure to distribute water and food to those who suffered losses, the drought might still have caused stress and even widespread hunger, *but it could not possibly have contributed to a revolution.* That could only happen because the climatic impact was articulated through the social formation over which Assad presided – or more simply put, the drought could only push people towards rebellion because some lawns were perversely lush and green. Climate change does not take away any of the iniquities of the regime: it is constituted as a destabilizing force *in relation to them.*[21]

The Levant has seen a similar logic play out before. In *The Climate of Rebellion in the Early Modern Ottoman Empire*, Sam White tells the story of how that empire came close to falling apart in the early seventeenth century when a series of extraordinarily severe droughts crippled what is today eastern Turkey and Syria.[22] The droughts were the result not of global warming, but of global cooling caused by the natural drop in solar radiation known as the Little Ice Age. Freezing dry winters killed off the crops and cattle of Anatolian and Levantine peasants – and how did the sultan respond? By levying heavier taxes on those peasants, forcing them to deliver greater quantities of grain, sheep and other provisions to the imperial capital and its armies. Just as famine spread on the plains, the centre moved to squeeze them ever harder, and it was this additional curse, White stresses, that tipped the hungry peasants into open revolt. Starting around the turn of the century, they attacked tax collectors, raided stores and set up military units, coalescing into the great armies of the Celali rebellion, whose territories at one point stretched from Ankara to Aleppo. The sultan eventually defeated the Celalis, but a cycle of drought—higher taxes—rebellion—greater deficits in provisioning—even higher taxes continued to roll through the Empire in the seventeenth century. In 1648, the sultan and his detested grand vizier were killed in a rare uprising in the heart of Istanbul, whose chronic problems of food supply, public health and low wages had been exacerbated by the massive influx of refugees from the desolated countryside: 'when the people saw that the sultan's favorites still had water while the mosques and fountains went dry, they rose up and forced out the grand vizier'.[23]

We can thus propose a first hypothesis for a Marxist theory of climate-induced social confrontation. 'The specific economic form', Marx writes in the third volume of *Capital*, 'in which unpaid surplus labour is pumped out of the direct producers determines the relationship of domination and servitude.'[24] Now if the direct producers experience a climatic shock that reduces their capacity to reproduce themselves, and if the pump continues to operate or even accelerates, sending ever more resources towards the top, chances are that the former will rise up. If they cannot command the clouds to open, at least they can break the pump that takes away what little they have left. These are the relations of domination and servitude through which the impact of climate change is fundamentally articulated. In the case of the Ottoman Empire, they ran along the axis of taxes pumped out of peasants and into the imperial capital, and the shock was of an entirely natural character. What can we expect in a capitalist world rapidly heating up because of fossil fuel combustion? Now the central pump would seem to be the extraction of surplus-value from productive labour. Is the shock felt at the bottom here, too?

There are indications that a new bone of contention between classes is being formed. In the report *Climate Change and Labour: Impacts of Heat in the Workplace*, several union federations and UN branches draw attention to what might be the most universal *and* the most widely ignored experience of global warming: it's getting hotter at work.[25] Physical labour makes the body warm. If it takes place under the sun or inside facilities without advanced air-conditioning systems, excessively high temperatures will make the sweat flow more profusely and the bodily powers sag, until the worker suffers heat exhaustion or worse. This will not be an ordeal for the average software developer or financial adviser. But for people who pick vegetables, build skyscrapers, pave roads, drive buses, sew clothes in poorly ventilated factories or mend cars in slum workshops, it already is; and the bulk of exceptionally hot working days are now anthropogenic in nature. With every little rise in average temperatures on Earth, thermal conditions in millions of workplaces around the world shift further, primarily in the tropical and subtropical regions where the majority of the working population – some four billion people – live their days. For every degree, a greater chunk of output will be lost, estimated to reach more than a third of total production after four degrees: in this heat, workers simply cannot keep up the same pace. Or can they? Here is a source of any number of clashes, since workers will have to slow down and take long breaks, while capitalists and their representatives – if their entire past is anything to go by – will demand that production be maintained (and preferably sped up). In a hotter capitalist world, the pump can only extract the same amount of surplus-value by squeezing the last drop of sweat out of workers, but on the other side of some locally determined tipping point, that might not be sustainable.

A workers' revolution to win rest in the shade? Probably not. If the conflict between the victims of drought and the insatiable sultan of the Ottoman Empire was straightforward enough, the equivalents in the twenty-first century look set to be rather more complex. Extraction of surplus-value may still be the central pump, but the most explosive impacts of climate change will scarcely be transmitted in any straight line along its axis. If there is one overarching logic of the capitalist mode of production through which rising temperatures will be articulated, it is probably rather that of uneven and combined development.[26] Capital expands by pulling other relations into its orbit; as it continues to accumulate, people stuck in those external-but-internalized relations – think of herders in north-eastern Syria – will enjoy few if any of the benefits, and might not even come close to the threshold of wage-labour. Some amass resources, while others, outside the pump but inside the orbit, struggle to get a chance to produce them. If a catastrophe descends on such a society – deeply divided *and* deeply integrated – chances are that it starts breaking apart along some of the cracks. The Syrian revolution might indeed be a template in this regard.

Incidentally, uneven and combined development plus catastrophe was also the equation that touched off the Russian revolution. The catastrophe in question was, of course, the First World War, which caused the entire food supply system of Tsarist Russia to crash. To make matters worse, heavy floods in the spring of 1917 washed away roads and railway lines and blocked further procurements.[27] On 8 March – the story is well known, but now casts a new light on the future – the women workers of Petrograd went on strike and marched through the streets, demanding bread from a duma incapable of delivering it. Soon they called for the fall of the Tsar. The crisis took a new plunge in August 1917, when grain prices suddenly doubled and Petrograd faced the challenge of surviving without any flour. 'Famine, genuine famine', one government official described the situation, 'has seized a series of towns and provinces – famines vividly expressed by an absolute insufficiency of objects of nutrition already leading to death.'[28] It was at this moment that Lenin penned what is arguably his key text from 1917, 'The Impending Catastrophe and How to Combat It', in which he made the case for a second revolution as the only way to avert total nationwide famine. In his internal and external agitation, this was his stock argument for striking the October blow:

> There is no escaping the famine, and *there can be none* except by an uprising of the peasants against the landowners in the countryside, and by a victory of the workers over the capitalists in the cities. ... 'In insurrection delay is fatal' – this is our answer to those having the sad 'courage' to look at the

growing economic ruin, at the approaching famine, and still *dissuade* the workers from the uprising.[29]

The Pentagon refers to climate change as a 'threat multiplier'. Lenin spoke of the catastrophe of his time as a 'mighty accelerator' bringing all contradictions to a head, 'engendering world-wide crises of unparalleled intensity', driving nations 'to the brink of doom'.[30] His wager was, of course, to seize the unique opportunity thereby opened up. That did not diminish his hostility to the war – it had no more implacable enemies than the Bolsheviks – but he saw in all its miseries the most compelling reasons to take power, and nothing worked as effectively to rally the workers behind him. Climate change is likely to be the accelerator of the twenty-first century, speeding up the contradictions of late capitalism – above all the growing chasm between the evergreen lawns of the rich and the precariousness of propertyless existence – and expedite one local catastrophe after another. What should revolutionaries do when it hits their turf? Seize the opportunity to depose any exploiters and oppressors they can get their hands on. But there is, needless to say, no guarantee of a happy outcome.

COUNTER-REVOLUTION AND CHAOS AS SYMPTOMS

Acute shortages of food and water are poised to become some of the most tangible effects of global warming. In the run-up to the Tunisian and Egyptian revolutions, rising food prices partly caused by extreme weather intensified the latent tensions, and the Middle East – so far the revolutionary cauldron of the century – can expect more to come. No region is as prone to water scarcity, and none as vulnerable to 'tele-connected food supply shocks', or harvest failures in distant breadbaskets driving up prices of the imports on which the population depends.[31] In revolutionary Russia, the supply shock originally stemmed from the blockades and demands of the First World War and then multiplied across the vast territory; for the Bolsheviks, it was as much a curse as a blessing. In his remarkable study, *Bread and Authority in Russia, 1914–1921*, Lars T. Lih shows how the dearth of food not only propelled them to power, but prompted them to develop the authoritarian tendencies that would later devour them.

Moreover, those tendencies were in full swing already before October. The Tsarist state itself took the first steps towards a 'food-supply dictatorship', in which the state applies coercion to enforce the delivery of food to starving citizens. 'The food-supply question has swallowed up all other questions', one government employee observed in the autumn of 1916, and 'as economic anarchy has spread, all the deeper is the process of penetration of the state principle into all aspects of the economic existence of the country.'[32] The Provisional Government continued on the same track – all political currents save the anarchists agreed on the necessity of strict centralised control to bring forth the grain – but proved utterly unequal to the task. The Bolsheviks turned out to be the sole party disciplined and hard-hitting enough to reconstitute the centre and reign in the centrifugal forces. But to succeed in their efforts, they had to ditch any ideological doubts about the state and make maximum use of the remaining scaffoldings of the Tsarist bureaucracy. The problem was that they had promised 'all power to the Soviets'. According to a logic Lih reconstructs in painful detail, genuinely self-governing soviets (and communes and factory committees) had the interests of their own constituencies closest to heart: in the countryside, they held back grain from the cities; in the cities, they sent volunteers to the countryside to collect whatever could be found and distribute it to their members. The experiment in direct democracy the Bolsheviks had done so much to encourage merely deepened the chaos in the food system – the one plague they had vowed to eradicate. Locked into this contradiction, they opted for subjugating the soviets to the party, shooting suspected hoarders, stationing agents in the villages to surveil the peasants, setting the whole train of bureaucratic control in motion.

But the choice – this is Lih's main point – was forced upon the Bolsheviks by the situation. Exacerbated by first civil war and then drought, the scarcities seemed to allow for no other general course of action than a food-supply dictatorship, to which the vast majority of Russians eventually resigned themselves, preferring some stability and food on the table to the endless deprivation and uncertainty of the revolutionary years. Here the seeds of Stalinist counter-revolution were sown. Paradoxically, in Lih's analysis, they sprang from a remarkable feat: precisely because they were so ruthless and consistent in their centralisation of the food system, the Bolsheviks *did* avert total breakdown. In a formulation now pregnant with meaning, Lih sums up his view of their young state: 'a Noah hastily constructing a small ark against imminent disaster'.[33]

Now if very many more disasters are imminent, and if they will trigger revolutions, will they also trigger *counter*-revolutions in the shape of rough beasts and bloated bureaucracies (claiming to be) indispensable for containing the hardships? It is too early to tell, of course. One hint at such a scenario, however, may be abstracted from the military coup that ended the Egyptian revolution. In the final days of the Morsi regime, the 'deep state' orchestrated massive shortages of fuel and food and rolling blackouts, sapping the support for the democratically elected president and prodding millions to take to the streets against him.[34] After the coup of 3 July 2013, those deficiencies miraculously disappeared overnight; the Sisi junta took full credit and won stomachs and minds across the country. This episode obviously has no link to any impacts of climate change, but it points to a political logic that might conceivably reappear when they bite deeper: a strong leader poses as the sole guarantor of a minimum of stable supplies and monopolizes power. That would not necessarily have to wait for a revolution to materialise; it could be stimulated by the scarcities as such.

The broader danger lurking here might be labelled ecological fascism. It has few adherents so far, but they do exist: in *The Climate Challenge and the Failure of Democracy*, Australian scholars David Shearman and Joseph Wayne Smith reject the Marxist contention that capitalism is the source of global warming and assigns all the blame to democracy. Now is the time to realise that 'freedom is not the most fundamental value and is merely one value among others. Survival strikes us as a much more basic value.'[35] As climate change puts the survival of the human species in question, it has to rediscover its true nature: rigid hierarchy. 'The human brain is hard-wired for authoritarianism, for dominance, and submission' (just look at the apes).[36] More precisely, Shearman and Smith advocate a fusion of feudalism and the one-party state – but without any planned economy – headed by 'an altruistic, able, authoritarian leader, versed in science and personal skills', backed up by a class of 'philosopher kings or ecoelites' trained since childhood – 'as in Sparta' – to steer the world through the heat.[37] (We also learn that female brains are geared towards children, that 'black rap songs' expressing 'desires to murder white people' should be banned, and that Islam is demographically torpedoing the Western world.)[38] Such lunacy has not yet found much of an audience. But when survival *really* starts hanging in the balance, one cannot exclude the scenario that it gains traction; indeed, climate change has already brought some lunatic ideas of once-despised mavericks to the fore (notably geoengineering).

If ecological fascism could be an explicit ideological trend for a very warm future, another possibility is nihilistic, opportunistic, even racist violence: in the drying Ottoman Empire, Sam White records, the Celalis professed no particular political or religious conviction. They merely plundered their way through the ruined landscape. A particular stronghold of theirs was the city of Raqqa: epicentre of the recent drought, capital of the faux caliphate of Daesh. White reports that the droughts fanned the flames of fundamentalist revivals among the various sects of the Empire.[39] In the endless bread queues of revolutionary Russia, rumours of Jews stockpiling and speculating on grain spread like wildfire; the step from the closed bakery to the pogrom remained short.⁴⁰ In 1917, Lenin measured the 'mood of despair among the broad masses' and prophesized that 'the hungry will "smash everything, destroy everything, even anarchically"', *if* the Bolsheviks are not able to lead them in a decisive battle'.⁴¹ The anti-Semitic Black Hundreds waited for the Russians to swing behind them, and Lenin saw objective tendencies working in their favour. 'Can one imagine a capitalist society on the eve of collapse in which the oppressed masses are *not* desperate? Is there any doubt that the desperation of the masses, a large part of whom are still ignorant, *will* express itself in the increased consumption of all sorts of poison?'⁴²

Celalis, Daesh, Black Hundreds: Christian Parenti has offered a similar prognosis in his *Tropic of Chaos: Climate Change and the New Geography of Violence*. 'Damaged societies, like damaged people, often respond to new crisis in ways that are irrational, shortsighted, and self-destructive', and the societies of this world – particularly those ravaged by colonialism, Cold War counterinsurgency, wars against terror, neoliberal restructuring – are nothing if not damaged.⁴³ We can anticipate a 'slide toward entropy and chaos', 'intercommunal strife, brigandry', the undoing of the modern state – which might, of course, flip over into its opposite and resurrect some green-brown Sparta. What about those who can insulate themselves against the heat with any amount of air conditioning? As the most likely protection of their material interests, Parenti foresees a 'politics of the armed lifeboat' or 'climate fascism', by which the ruling classes continue on their present course and mercilessly keep their victims at bay with walls, drones and detention centres.⁴⁴ One genocide scholar has recently gone one step further and warned that the expected flows of climate refugees towards the North will revive 'the genocidal impulse', a scenario possibly gaining some plausibility from the circumstance that one of the greatest flows will likely consist of people from Muslim-majority countries heading towards a European continent thoroughly infected with Islamophobia.⁴⁵ That could be another form of articulation. As such, however, it would be the outcome of relations shaped in struggle. Revolutionaries in a warmer world would then have to be as much vigilant and militant anti-fascists. We might be living not right after, but at the very dawn of the age of extremes.

REVOLUTION FOR TREATING THE SYMPTOMS

So far we have two configurations, then, although the line between them may be difficult to draw: revolution and/or counter-revolution/chaos as *symptoms* of climate change. One might take a leaf from meteorology to conceptualise this symptomaticity. Climate scientists often speak of how rising temperatures 'load the dice' in favour of extreme weather events:

a superstorm could have happened in the eighteenth century, but all the carbon dioxide accumulated in the atmosphere since then has filled the weather systems with material, such as hot and high sea surfaces, that works like an extra weight at number six, making a deadly hurricane dramatically more likely. The type of extreme *social* events on which we have speculated here can evidently also happen without anthropogenic climate change, but that novel mega-weight inside all planetary systems now seem to push things in such directions. If all of this sounds surreally extreme, consult state-of-the-art climate science. The shattering of the material foundations on which human existence stands *really will be* fatal if global warming rolls on, it tells us, and it reports on a monthly basis on how much faster the process unfolds than first predicted.

In January 2016, the average temperature on Earth was 1.15°C higher than for the period 1951–80. It was a record jump instantly beaten by February, which reached 1.35°C.[46] By then the planet stood right on the threshold to a 1.5°C warming above pre-industrial levels, identified by world leaders congregating in Paris for COP21 in December 2015 as the limit that should not be crossed (although a more common marker for the shift from already dangerous to extremely dangerous climate change is still 2°C).[47] When might that be attained? Fresh results suggest it could happen sooner rather than later: in clouds, for instance, ice crystals reflect more sunlight back to space than do liquid droplets, but climate models have vastly underestimated the share of the latter, missing a considerable extra warming effect already in the pipelines.[48] Others have revised the estimate of how much temperatures would increase if all proven fossil fuel reserves were burnt. Using conservative figures, excluding any future discoveries and deposits made available by new technologies, Katarzyna Takorska and her colleagues place the effect in the ballpark of 8°C – hitting 17°C in the Arctic – rather than the previously believed 5°C. Converted into actual conditions for life on Earth, those average eight degrees would, of course, spell the end of all stories.[49] This will not happen tomorrow, but it now marks *the general direction of late capitalist history*. Anyone who wishes to dispute the forecast that the ensuing dislocations will usher in an age of political extremes would need to build a case for the astounding stoicism of the human species, or for its utter detachment from what happens inside ecosystems. However that case might look, it would certainly not be materialist.

But there is the possibility for cushioning against some impacts. Consider the case of Syria. Most agriculture in that country still relies on flood irrigation – peasants opening channels and flushing water through their fields – which might have been an adequate method in the days of old, but not in this dry era.⁵⁰ Shifting to drip irrigation is imperative, so as to save or make optimal use of every valuable drop of water. A state attuned to the needs of poor farmers and willing to provide them with the basic productive forces could make it happen, but the Assad regime has instituted water policies sucking the land dry. In Egypt, the rising Mediterranean pushes saltwater ever deeper into the clayey soil of the Nile Delta. To save their crops from being killed, farmers try to 'elevate' fields by applying enormous amounts of sand and fertilisers, but only the richest farmers can afford such measures of adaptation.⁵¹ Along the coastlines, storm surges are growing in frequency and strength, but sea walls and other buffer systems are primarily built in front of resort towns, while communities of fisherfolk and farmers are left unprotected.⁵² The Egyptian revolution represented an opportunity to fill such cracks in the armour and move towards comprehensive, popular adaptation to climate change. It would be an understatement to say that it was missed.

Here, then, can be discerned the contours of a third hypothetical configuration: revolution to *treat* the symptoms of global warming. The Syrian and Egyptian cases are no outliers. Surveys have found that the day-to-day processes of capital accumulation – enclosures, commodification, planning for real estate, centralisation of resources – heavily distort most adaptation projects around the world, leaving precisely the most vulnerable people without cushions.⁵³ But 'in revolutionary times the limits of what is possible expand a thousandfold', recalling Lenin.⁵⁴ If social relations block the way to effective pro-poor adaptation, they ought to be overhauled. Here is one more reason to seize every opportunity catastrophes open up. Unlike the two previous configurations, this one would presuppose revolutionaries who *consciously* act against the impacts of climate change on the terrain over which they can wield influence. But that influence will by nature be constrained.

REVOLUTION AGAINST THE CAUSES

Adaptation to three, four, not to speak of eight degrees is bound to be a futile endeavour. No matter how advanced the sprinklers Syrian farmers install, irrigation requires water. No walls can save the Nile Delta from the underground infiltration of the sea. No one can perform any kind of physical labour when temperatures settle above a certain level, and so on. But the proven fossil fuel reserves can be kept in the ground. Emissions can be slashed to zero. 'Everybody says this. Everybody admits this. Everybody has decided it is so. Yet nothing is being done,' and this is the rationale for the most exigent type of revolution, the one that, in full consciousness of the roots of the problem, wages a full-scale onslaught on fossil capital, just as the Bolsheviks set themselves the task of putting 'an immediate end to the war', insisting that 'it is clear to everybody that in order to end this war, which is closely bound up with the present capitalist system, capital itself must be fought.'[55] *This* is the moment to read the Lenin of 1917 anew and salvage the kernel of the Bolshevik project:

> We can draw, perhaps, the most striking comparison of all between reactionary-bureaucratic methods of combating a catastrophe, which are confined to minimum reforms, and revolutionary-democratic methods, which, to justify their name, must directly aim at a violent rupture with the old, obsolete system and at the achievement of the speediest possible progress …[56]

– speed here being the critical dimension. The dawdling bourgeoisie, meanwhile, 'as always, are guided by the rule: "*Après nous le deluge*".'[57] Policies that would save millions or even billions of lives could be put in place, if only the obstructing interests were removed. 'The ways of combating catastrophe and famine are available, the measures required to combat them are quite clear, simple, perfectly feasible, and fully within reach of the people's forces.' We could begin by updating the *Communist Manifesto* and list ten:[58]

1. Enforce a complete moratorium on all new facilities for extracting coal, oil or natural gas.
2. Close down all power-plants running on such fuels.
3. Draw 100 per cent of electricity from non-fossil sources, primarily wind and solar.
4. Terminate the expansion of air, sea and road travel; convert road and sea travel to electricity and wind; ration remaining air travel to ensure a fair distribution until it can be completely replaced with other means of transport.
5. Expand mass transit systems on all scales, from subways to intercontinental high-speed trains.
6. Limit the shipping and flying of food and systematically promote local supplies.
7. End the burning of tropical forests and initiate massive programmes for reforestation.
8. Refurbish old buildings with insulation and require all new ones to generate their own zero-carbon power.
9. Dismantle the meat industry and move human protein requirements towards vegetable sources.

10. Pour public investment into the development and diffusion of the most efficient and sustainable renewable energy technologies, as well as technologies for carbon dioxide removal.[59]

That would be a start – nothing more – yet it would probably amount to a revolution, not only in the forces of production but also in the social relations in which they are so deeply enmeshed. Just how thoroughly the phenomenon of CO_2 emissions is bound up with class society has recently been highlighted by two striking reports. One tenth of the human species accounts for half of all present emissions from consumption, half of the species for one tenth. The richest 1 per cent have a carbon footprint some 175 times that of the poorest 10 per cent; the emissions of the richest 1 per cent of Americans, Luxembourgians and Saudi Arabians are two thousand times larger than those of the poorest Hondurans, Mozambicans or Rwandans. Shares of the CO_2 accumulated since 1820 are similarly skewed.[60] Some ecological class hatred is certainly warranted, and then we have not even mentioned the hard inner core of fossil capital, the Rex Tillersons of this world, the billionaires who swim in money from pulling fossil fuels out of the ground and selling the fuel for the fires.[61] Make no mistake: this revolution would have its fair share of enemies.

Who shall execute it? Who are the Petrograd metalworkers and the Kronstadt sailors of the climate revolution? Look at the country that tops a survey of the populations most worried about global warming: Burkina Faso, currently devastated by declining rains and magnified sandstorms, topping the list of African nations suffering from excessively hot working days.[62] Can a farmer from Burkina Faso storm the Winter Palaces of fossil capital – can she even catch sight of them in her lifetime, or are the headquarters of ExxonMobil in Texas and the glittering towers of Dubai so distant as to be utterly beyond her reach, let alone her and her peers' capacity for effective revolutionary action? It would probably be as easy to gain mass support for the above programme in Burkina Faso as it would be hard to implement it from there.

Precisely the abysmal divides within the species – belying the talk of the 'Anthropocene', of humanity in general as responsible, of 'us all' as the enemy – may prove the greatest obstacle to attacking the causes of catastrophe: the victims of the systematic violence known as fossil fuel combustion may simply be *too far away* from the perpetrators to topple them. 'Revolutions-as-symptoms' target exploiters and oppressors in the immediate vicinity and so are not hard to imagine when some lives become unbearable, but 'revolutions-against-the-causes' must, if they are to be launched by the classes most concerned, travel across the globe. Uprisings then seem likely to continue targeting nearby Makhloufs rather than faraway Tillersons. Put differently, the spontaneous formation of trade-union consciousness in a warming world – a basic prerequisite for any kind of October thrust – looks like a very uncertain prospect. It is otherwise with, for instance, oil exploration – when a corporation intrudes on a people's ancestral homeland to drill for the fuel, the antagonism is in your face and resistance comes naturally – but global warming *as such* can slaughter millions from within a castle never seen and, alas, hard to raid.

This appears to be the fundamental strategic conundrum for the struggle against climate change. The most promising vision for breaking out of it has been formulated (although not in such terms) by Naomi Klein in *This Changes Everything: Capitalism vs. the Climate*. Short-circuiting the distance problem, she argues that, since present-day capitalism is so saturated with fossil energy, more or less everyone involved in some social movement under its rule is objectively fighting global warming, whether or not she or he cares about it or suffers its consequences. Brazilians protesting fare hikes and demanding free public transit all but raise the banner of the fifth measure in the list above, while the Ogoni people kicking out Shell are busy working on the first.[63] Similarly, European auto-workers fighting for their jobs, in accordance with the kind of trade-union consciousness they have always possessed, have an interest in converting their factories to the production of technologies required for the transition away from fossil fuels – wind turbines, buses – rather than seeing them disappear to some low-wage destination.[64] *All* struggles are struggles against fossil capital: the subjects only need to be made aware of it. In Klein's words, 'the environmental crisis – if conceived sufficiently broadly – neither trumps nor distracts from our most pressing political and economic causes: it supercharges each one of them with existential urgency'.[65] This formula has the added appeal of making the broadest possible alliance conceivable. Clearly, nothing less will be needed in this struggle.

It remains to be seen if this is a solution that can substitute for the absence of immediately victimized strike forces. So far in a warming world, the position analogous to the Palestinians fighting Zionist occupation or to factory workers striking against speed-ups has been vacant – not in-itself (the expelled and sweated are there) but for-itself (they are not actively combatting their enemies) – and so far, that absence has stifled the outbreak of explicit climatic unrest on a scale commensurate to the problem. What we do have is a fledgling climate movement. In any alliance drawing in the full spectrum of social movements to take down fossil capital, this one will have to be the linchpin. It has some compelling arguments to make, along the lines of the slogan 'there are no jobs on a dead planet': whatever *else* you are clamouring for presupposes a reasonably stable climate, and even if the desert sands do not encroach on your doorstep in this particular moment, be sure some impact or other is on its way. If the German worker shrugs his shoulder at the condition of the farmer in Burkina Faso, or in optimist fashion comforts himself with the thought than in Germany things are not nearly so bad, the climate movement can tell him: '*De te fabula narratur*'. This movement collects and crystallizes the insights that Syria cannot survive the disappearance of the Fertile Crescent, or Egypt a three metre sea level rise, or Burkina Faso four degrees of warming; it articulates the interests of their most vulnerable masses even if only *on behalf* of them. Yes, there is here, for structural reasons yet to be overcome, a component of what classical Marxists would have called substitutionism and voluntarism.

This movement has scored a number of noteworthy victories of late. The shelving of the Keystone XL pipeline, the retreat of Shell from the Arctic, the spiralling divestment campaign, the cancellation of coal projects from Oregon to Orissa have been added in rapid succession to its vita. The movement further raised its profile with the 'Break Free' campaign in May 2016, the largest coordinated wave of direct action against fossil fuel extraction so far, stretching from the Philippines to Wales, New Zealand to Ecuador.[66] The centrepiece of the campaign was the camp known as Ende Gelände, erected a stone's throw from Schwarze Pumpe, 'the black pump', a power-plant in the German region of Lusatia running on lignite coal – dirtiest of all fossil fuels – extracted from an adjacent mega-mine, and one of the largest point-sources of CO_2 emissions in Europe. The various quarters of the sprawling tent camp were named after distant low-lying island nations: Kiribati, Tuvalu, the Maldives. On Friday 13 May 2016, the multi-pronged offensive against Schwarze Pumpe was set off when some one thousand activists – the camp would attract nearly four thousand – descended into the mine, seized the gargantuan digging machines and settled in for the weekend. On Saturday morning, there were even more occupying the railway lines that bring the coal to the black pump. A brief incursion into the compound of the power plant itself provoked the outnumbered police to hit back indiscriminately with pepper spray, baton wielding and arrests, but the blockades held until on Sunday morning the owners declared that climate activists had forced them to suspend all electricity production.[67] That had never before happened in central Europe.

The background to the action is instructive. In the parliamentary elections in Sweden in 2014, Gustav Fridolin, leader of the Green Party, kept a piece of coal in his pocket. Wherever he went, in every speech and televised debate, he waved that piece of coal and promised, stern determination in his voice, to take the hands of the Swedish state off the fuel. Deep inside the pits of eastern Germany, those hands have long sullied the self-image of Sweden as a *föregångsland* or 'pioneering country' in climate politics, since the state-owned corporation Vattenfall owns and operates Schwarze Pumpe and four other lignite complexes of the same volcanic size. By the time of the election, the Swedish state produced CO2 emissions from these assets equal to all emissions from its own territory plus a third. Now, Fridolin declared, was the time to liquidate them and put a lid on the coal in the ground. If the Greens entered the government, the single most important promise of their election campaign would be to make sure that Vattenfall closed its German mines and plants. Two years later, they were no longer in Swedish hands. They had been *sold* to a consortium of capitalists from the Czech republic – including its richest man – craving more resources for the lignite renaissance currently sweeping out from their corner of the continent. The Greens, in other words, resolved to throw some of the greatest lignite riches straight into the mouth of fossil capital. That decision contributed to the worst crisis in the history of the party – probably the most influential of its kind in the world – and hence one of the worst in the history of reformist parliamentary environmentalism. To cap the debasement, Fridolin, on behalf of the Swedish government, denounced the Ende Gelände action as 'illegal'.[68]

In any science-based reality, Ende Gelände is the type of action that should be repeated and scaled up a thousandfold. Inside the advanced capitalist countries and the most developed zones of the rest, there is no shortage of appropriate targets: just look around for the closest coal-fired power plant, pipeline, SUV, expanding airport, growing suburban shopping mall, and so many others. That is the terrain on which a revolutionary climate movement should trespass in one great accelerating surge. Obviously, it is still very far from such size and capacity. Perhaps some extreme weather event of truly traumatic proportions could catalyze a leap. Even then, however, as the Vattenfall story makes clear, direct action in itself would solve nothing: there have to be decisions and decrees from the state – or, in other words, the state must be wrested from all the Tillersons and Fridolins of this world for any transitional programme like the one sketched above to be realized. In the post-1989 ideological hangover that still affects the activist milieus making up the climate movement in the North, however, there lingers a fetishization of horizontal direct action as a self-sufficient tactic and a reluctance to consider Lenin's lesson: 'The key question of every revolution is undoubtedly the question of state power.'[69] Rarely if ever has it been more important to heed that lesson than now.

Can the climate movement grow by several orders of magnitude, gather progressive forces around it *and* develop some viable strategy for projecting its aims through the state – all within a relevant time frame in this rapidly warming world? It is a tall order, to say the least. But in the words of Daniel Bensaïd, perhaps the most brilliant theorist of revolutionary strategy in the late twentieth century, 'any doubt bears on the possibility of succeeding, not on the necessity of trying'.[70]

NOTES

1   J. G. Ballard, *The Drowned World*, New York: Liveright, 2012 [1962], p. 58.
2   'US Intelligence Community Worldwide Threat Assessment, Statement for the Record March 12, 2013', in *United States Central Intelligence Agency (CIA) Handbook: Strategic Information, Activities and Regulations*, Washington, DC: International Business Publications, 2013, p. 40.
3   Department of Defense, 'National Security Implications of Climate-Related Risks and a Changing Climate', report submitted to Congress 23 July 2015, available from archive. defense.gov. The spectre of escalating conflict in a warming world is not the only one to haunt the Pentagon: a wide range of military installations face the risk of inundation, including the Norfolk naval base in Virginia, the largest of its kind in the world. See e.g. Peter Engelke and Daniel Chiu, *Climate Change and US National Security: Past, Present, Future*, The Transatlantic Partnership for the Global Future, Brent Scowcroft Center and the Ministry for Foreign Affairs of the Government of Sweden, 2016.
4   David Kilcullen, *Out of the Mountains: The Coming Age of the Urban Guerrilla*, London: C. Hurst & Co., 2013.
5   Solomon M. Hsiang, Marshall Burke, and Edward Miguel, 'Quantifying the Influence of Climate on Human Conflict', *Science* (2013), 341, p. 4. Cf. Solomon M. Hsiang and Marshall Burke, 'Climate, Conflict, and Social Stability: What does the Evidence Say?', *Climatic Change* (2014), 123: 39–55.
6   Clionadh Raleigh, Andrew Linke and John O'Loughlin, 'Extreme Temperatures and Violence', *Nature Climate Change*, 4, 2014, pp. 76–7. See further John Bohannon, 'Study Links Climate Change and Violence, Battle Ensues', *Science*, 341, 2013, pp. 444–5; Mark A. Cane et al., 'Temperature and Violence', *Nature Climate Change*, 4, 2014, pp. 234–5; H. Buhaug et al., 'One Effect to Rule them All? A Comment on Climate and Conflict', *Climatic Change*, 127, 2014, pp. 391–7.
7   Hsiang et al. would perhaps retort that to study the interaction between climate and other factors, one first has to know that the former *is* a factor in its own right, and that is what their research demonstrates. There is some merit to that argument. The state of this science seems to be precisely that of having identified climate as driver of social conflict, but without a clear idea of how that driving works. Cf. Idean Salahyan, 'Climate Change and Conflict: Making Sense of Disparate Findings', *Political Geography*, 43, 2014, pp. 1–5.
8   Raleigh et al., 'Extreme temperatures', p. 77.
9   Martin Hoerling, Jon Fischeid, Judith Perlwitz et al., 'On the Increased Frequency of Mediterranean Drought', *Journal of Climate*, 25, 2012, pp. 2146–61.
10 Benjamin Cook, Kevin J. Anchukaitis, Ramzi Touchan et al., 'Spatiotemporal Drought Variability in the Mediterranean over the Last 900 Years', *Journal of Geophysical Research: Atmospheres*, 121, 2016, pp. 2060–74.
11 Colin P. Kelley, Shahrzad Mohtadi, Mark A. Cane et al., 'Climate Change in the

Fertile Crescent and Implications of the Recent Syrian Drought', *PNAS*, 112, 2015, pp. 3241–6.

12   Robert F. Worth, 'Earth is Parched Where Syrian Farms Thrived', *New York Times*, 13 October 2010. See further W. Erian, B. Katlan and B. Ouldbdey, 'Drought Vulnerability in the Arab Region: Special Case Study: Syria', *2011 Global Assessment Report on Disaster Risk Reduction*, United Nations; OCHA (United Nations Office for the Coordination of Humanitarian Affairs), *Syria Drought Response Plan, 2009–2010: Mid-Term Review*; Francesco Femia and Caitlin Werrell, 'Climate Change Before and After the Arab Awakening: The Cases of Syria and Libya', in Caitlin Werrell and Francesco Femia, eds., *The Arab Spring and Climate Change*, Center for American Progress, Stimson, and The Center for Climate and Security, 2013, pp. 23–32; Peter H. Gleich, 'Water, Drought, Climate Change, and Conflict in Syria', *Weather, Climate & Society*, 6, 2014, pp. 331–40; Myriam Ababsa, 'The End of a World: Drought and Agrarian Transformation in Northeast Syria (2007–2010)', in R. Hinnebusch and T. Zintl, eds., *Syria from Reform to Revolt, Vol. 1: Political Economy and International Relations*, Syracuse: Syracuse University Press, 2015, 199–222.

13   See e.g. Kelley et al., 'Climate Change'.

14   Bassam Haddad, *Business Networks in Syria: The Political Economy of Authoritarian Resilience*, Stanford: Stanford University Press, 2012, p. 104; Shamel Azmeh, 'The Uprising of the Marginalized: A Socio-Economic Perspective of the Syrian Uprising', LSE Middle East Centre Paper Series, no. 6, 2014; Robin Yassin-Kassab and Leila Al-Shami, *Burning Country: Syrians in Revolution and War*, London: Pluto, 29–33.

15   Ababsa, 'The End of a World', pp. 210–17.

16   Yassin-Kassab and Al-Shami, *Burning Country*, p. 33.

17   On the drought in Dera'a, see e.g. Caitlin E. Werrell, Francesco Femia and Troy Sternberg, 'Did We See it Coming?: State Fragility, Climate Vulnerability, and the Uprisings in Syria and Egypt', *SAIS Review of International Affairs*, 35, 2015, p. 31.

18   Suzanne Saleeby, 'Sowing the Seeds of Dissent: Economic Grievances and the Syrian Social Contract's Unraveling', *Jadaliyya*, 16 February 2012.

19   Francescva De Châtel, 'The Role of Drought and Climate Change in the Syrian Uprising: Untangling the Triggers of the Revolution', *Middle Eastern Studies*, 50, 2014, pp. 521–34.

20   De Chatel, 'The Role of Drought', p. 532.

21   Another attempt to downplay the drought is made in Christiane J. Frölich, 'Climate Migrants as Protestors? Dispelling Misconceptions about Global Environmental Change in Pre-Revolutionary Syria', *Contemporary Levant*, 1, 2016, pp. 38–50. She has interviewed people from Dera'a who say that the refugees from the countryside living in camps around the town did not orchestrate the early phase of the uprising; moreover, she claims they lacked the social networks required for such an adventurous undertaking and could not possibly have led the charge against the regime. This supposed disproof of the link rests on an extremely narrow testing procedure. It is concerned only with Dera'a, and only with directly revolutionary activities of the migrants sheltering there, ignoring the wider effects of the drought – including food price hikes and water shortages – as well as plenty of evidence that the revolutionary process as a whole took off primarily in the areas where such effects were most strongly felt (which is not necessarily to say that climate refugees organised the revolution: few if any have made that claim).

22   Sam White, *The Climate of Rebellion in the Early Modern Ottoman Empire*, Cambridge: Cambridge University Press, 2011. For a world-encompassing narrative (whose treatment of the Ottoman crisis is, naturally, superficial compared to White's), see Geoffrey Parker, *Global Crisis: War, Climate Change and Catastrophe in the Seventeenth*

Century, New Haven: Yale University Press, 2013.
23 White, *Climate of Rebellion*, p. 242. In this particular incident, an earthquake had aggravated the water shortages in the capital.
24 Karl Marx, *Capital: Volume III*, London: Penguin, 1991, p. 927.
25 Matthew McKinnon, Elise Buckle, Kamal Gueye et al., *Climate Change and Labour: Impacts of Heat in the Workplace*, UNDP, ILO, WTO, UNI, ITYUC and others, 29 April 2016, available from e.g. www.ilo.org.
26 For an attempt to further conceptualise the articulation of climate change through uneven and combined development, see Andreas Malm, 'Tahrir Submerged? Five Theses on Revolution in the Era of Climate Change', *Capitalism Nature Socialism*, 25, 2014, pp. 28–44.
27 Lars T. Lih, *Bread and Authority in Russia, 1914–1921*, Berkeley: University of California Press, 1990, pp. 65–7.
28 N. Dolinsky quoted in Lih, *Bread and Authority*, p. 111.
29 V. I. Lenin, *Revolution at the Gates: Selected Writings of Lenin from 1917*, edited and introduced by Slavoj Žižek, London: Verso, 2004, p. 155.
30 Lenin, *Revolution at the Gates*, pp. 17, 46.
31 Cristopher Bren d'Amour, Leonie Wenz, Matthias Kalkul et al., 'Teleconnected Food Supply Shocks', *Environmental Research Letters*, 11, 2016, 035007. On the role of food in the Egyptian revolution, see Malm, 'Tahrir Submerged?' and references therein.
32 Anonymous employee quoted in Lih, *Bread and Authority*, p. 32.
33 Lih, *Bread and Authority*, p. 266.
34 See e.g. Ben Hubbard and David D. Kirkpatrick, 'Sudden Improvements in Egypt Suggest a Campaign to Undermine Morsi', *New York Times*, 10 July 2013.
35 David Shearman and Joseph Wayne Smith, *The Climate Change Challenge and the Failure of Democracy*, Westport: Praeger, 2007, p. 133.
36 Shearman et al., *The Climate Change Challenge*, p. 130.
37 Quotations from Shearman et al., *The Climate Change Challenge*, pp. 13, 141, 134.
38 Quotation from Shearman et al., *The Climate Change Challenge*, p. 111.
39 On the Celalis and other rebels in Raqqa, see White, *Climate of Rebellion*, e.g. pp. 179, 234, 237, 244; on fundamentalism see p. 215.
40 Lih, *Bread and Authority*, pp. 37, 75, 98, 169.
41 Lenin, *Revolution at the Gates*, p. 157. Emphasis in original.
42 Lenin, *Revolution at the Gates*, p. 159. Emphases in original.
43 Christian Parenti, *Tropic of Chaos: Climate Change and the New Geography of Violence*, New York: Nation Books, 2011, p. 8.
44 Parenti, *Tropic of Chaos*, p. 11; cf. e.g. pp. 20, 183, 209, 214–15.
45 Alex Alvarez, 'Borderlands, Climate Change, and the Genocidal Impulse', *Genocide Studies International*, 10, 2016, p. 30. Cf. e.g. Rafael Reuveny, 'Climate Change-Induced Migration and Violent Conflict', *Political Geography*, 26, 2007, pp. 656–73.
46 Damian Carrington and Michael Slezak, 'February Breaks Global Temperature by "Shocking" Amount', *The Guardian*, 14 March 2016.
47 For our position on this threshold see: Joeri Rogelj, Gunnar Luderer, Robert C. Pietzcker et al., 'Energy System Transformations for Limiting End-of-Century Warming to Below 1.5°C', *Nature Climate Change*, 5, 2015, pp. 519–27.
48 Ivy Tan, Trude Storelvmo and Mark D. Zelinka, 'Observational Constraints on Mixed-Phase Clouds Imply Higher Climate Sensitivity', *Science*, 352, 2016, pp. 224–7. For just one more, all-too-typical recent identification of underestimated effects, see Robert M. DeConto and David Pollard, 'Contribution of Antarctica to Past and Future Sea-Level Rise', *Nature*, 531, 2016, pp. 591–7.
49 Katarzyna B. Tokarska, Nathan P. Gillett, Andrew J. Weaver et al., 'The Climate

Response to Five Trillion Tonnes of Carbon', *Nature Climate Change*, 2016, online May 23.
50 Glick, 'Water, Drought', p. 334.
51 Andreas Malm and Shora Esmailian, 'Ways In and Out of Vulnerability to Climate Change: Abandoning the Mubarak Project in the Northern Nile Delta, Egypt', *Antipode*, 45, 2013, pp. 474–92.
52 Andreas Malm and Shora Esmailian, 'Doubly Dispossessed by Accumulation: Egyptian Fishing Communities between Enclosed Lakes and a Rising Sea', *Review of African Political Economy*, 39, 2012, pp. 408–26; Andreas Malm, 'Sea Wall Politics: Uneven and Combined Protection of the Nile Delta Coastline in the Face of Sea Level Rise', *Critical Sociology*, 39, 2013, pp. 803–32.
53 Benjamin K. Sovacool, Björn-Ola Linnér and Michael E. Goodsite, 'The Political Economy of Climate Adaptation', *Nature Climate Change*, 5, 2015, pp. 616–18.
54 Lenin, *Revolution at the Gates*, p. 40.
55 Lenin, *Revolution at the Gates*, pp. 69, 163.
56 Lenin, *Revolution at the Gates*, pp. 88-9.
57 Lenin, *Revolution at the Gates*, p. 97.
58 Lenin, *Revolution at the Gates*, p. 70.
59 This list is inspired by an email sent by Michael Northcott, professor of theology and ethics at the University of Edinburgh, to the geoengineering list serve on 17 April 2016.
60 Lucas Chancel and Thomas Piketty, *Carbon and Inequality: From Kyoto to Paris*, Paris School of Economics, 3 November 2015; Oxfam, 'Extreme Carbon Inequality', Oxfam Media Briefing, 2 December 2015.
61 For more on the category of fossil capital, see Andreas Malm, *Fossil Capital: The Rise of Steam Power and the Roots of Global Warming*, London: Verso, 2016.
62 Ami Sedghi, 'Climate Change Seen as Greatest Threat by Global Population', *The Guardian*, 17 July 2015; Laetitia van Eeckhout, 'Winds of Climate Change Blast Farmers' Hopes of Sustaining A Livelihood in Burkina Faso', *The Guardian*, 7 July 2015.
63 Naomi Klein, *This Changes Everything*, London: Penguin, 2014.
64 See particularly the work of Lars Henriksson: at bilpolitik.wordpress.com; 'Cars, Crisis, Climate Change and Class Struggle', in Nora Rathzel and David Uzzel, eds., *Trade Unions in the Green Economy: Working for the Environment*, Abingdon: Routledge, 2013, pp. 78–86; 'Can Autoworkers Save the Climate?', *Jacobin*, 2 October 2015.
65 Klein, *This Changes Everything*, p. 153.
66 See breakfree2016.org.
67 Marit Sundberg, 'Miljöaktivister har stoppat Vattenfalls elproduktion', SVT Nyheter, 15 Maj 2016. For a fuller report on the action, see Andreas Malm, 'The End of the Road', *Salvage*, salvage.zone, 16 May 2016.
68 TT, 'Fridolin tar avstånd från kolprotest', *Sydsvenska Dagbladet*, 16 May 2016.
69 Lenin, *Revolution at the Gates*, p. 106.
70 Daniel Bensaïd, *An Impatient Life: A Memoir*, London: Verso, 2013, p. 312.

BEYOND ECO-CATASTROPHISM: THE CONDITIONS FOR SOLAR COMMUNISM

DAVID SCHWARTZMAN

In a vivid, much-cited and much-abused passage, Karl Marx put forward one of his boldest formulations:

> The bourgeois mode of production is the last antagonistic form of the social process of production — antagonistic not in the sense of individual antagonism but of an antagonism that emanates from the individuals' social conditions of existence — but the productive forces developing within bourgeois society create also the material conditions for a solution of this antagonism. The prehistory of human society accordingly closes with this social formation.[1]

Indeed the reproduction of capital, utilizing productive forces powered by fossil fuels, created the material conditions leading to both this bifurcation *and* its potential resolution, which we now face in the twenty-first century: either the abyss of climate catastrophe driven by carbon emissions, or an ever-diminishing chance of what would appear to be a miraculous escape from this abyss powered by renewable energy technologies. This is the potential negation of the negation (to use the dialectical metaphor) of pre-industrial low-efficiency solar power (animal and biomass), through energy derived from fossil fuels, to the high efficiency collection of solar radiation using technologies of wind turbines, photovoltaics, and concentrated solar power in deserts. Fossil fuels, coal and petroleum, simply contain potential chemical energy derived from ancient solar energy, buried in sedimentary rocks.

In fossil fuels, the time of photosynthesis hundreds of millions of years old is compressed so that living labour can be condensed, their timelessness the material prop for a tyranny of the abstract. The perpetual circulation of capital, its fluid move from one circuit to the next, is made possible – a logical paradox – by absolutely *inert*, noncyclical, non-flowing strata of concentrated energy. In this dimension no less than in space, abstraction has its substratum firmly placed within the earth's crust: capital can fly high above all qualitative determinants only by digging and drilling into it.[2]

Abstract time and space were the necessary social creations for capital reproduction.

While eco-catastrophe is not inevitable, its potential is growing and we already witness ever-stronger signals.[3] This is truth-telling: acknowledging the best evidence available from climate science and biogeochemical research. It is a rejection of elitist politics that allegedly protects the masses from disempowering evidence. Rather, socialists and climate activists need to share these assessments, coupled with a vision of why it is still possible to avert such a catastrophe. I take this as a rejection of apocalyptic politics.[4]

Humanity and existing biodiversity are now facing a huge challenge: shall civilization emerge in a new mode with the end of what Marx called our prehistory, the rule of capital over our planet, or shall we plunge into a deep abyss of climate catastrophe – for the few who survive? Prehistory would be left behind should the world pass through an eco-socialist transition to solar communism in the twenty-first century, only three hundred years since the Industrial Revolution. This is the global revolutionary challenge of the twenty-first century. Post-capitalism will either mean a return to a pre-capitalism of the abyss or the creation of a much more hopeful future. This is the imminent bifurcation facing humanity, and the outcome is not possible to predict. There are actually two major threats to human civilization. The first is that of nuclear war, which would be deadly even if localized because of the resulting climatic impact on agriculture. The second threat is catastrophic climate change, a likelihood if carbon emissions are not rapidly and radically reduced, and if the already unsafe atmospheric level of carbon dioxide is not reduced by sequestration technologies. Only transnational class struggle on a scale not witnessed in human history has any chance of preventing catastrophic climate change.[5] Paradoxically, however, we are also privileged to confront this challenge, since the process of removing these threats raises the possibility of ending the rule of capital on our planet.

THE (SOLAR) COMMUNIST HORIZON

Marx and Engels' critique of the utopian socialists centred on their construction of a future society, often elaborated in great detail, without a scientific analysis of capitalism and its contradictions. They wrote little about communism, aside from arguing that increases in labour productivity under capitalism would be among the necessary conditions for its realization. We now see such necessary conditions in the existing and potential technologies of information, renewable energy, and organic agriculture based on the science of agroecology. I define socialism as the first phase (stage) of communist society, hence well along in the transition from capitalism to communism.[6]

Communism was an inspiring vision to millions in the twentieth century, with well-known failures in its realization as 'really existing socialism,' or what some Marxists prefer to call 'state capitalism'. The construction of socialist societies in the twentieth century occurred in a very unfavorable context, under continuous attack by capitalist powers – starting with initial intervention soon after the Russian revolution, followed by the Second World War and the cold war. Socialist societies of the twentieth century had both real internal achievements and well-documented state-sanctioned mass suffering and death, in parallel with immense positive impacts on global politics, including the defeat of fascism, the post-Second World War end of colonial oppression, and the development of social-welfare programmes by capitalist states challenged by the benefits for working classes in socialist countries (e.g., West Germany and the German Democratic Republic). Of course there were negative environmental impacts of rapid industrialization in the Soviet Union before the Second World War, but what some have called 'eocide'[7] came as a result of nuclear weapons development in the postwar era, in particular radioactive contamination in the Urals preceding the Chernobyl disaster.[8] As a result, a robust ecological movement challenging government policy emerged, along with valuable Soviet theoretical studies on nature/society relations.[9]

Really-existing twentieth-century 'socialism' (and its survivals into the twenty-first century) combined characteristics of communism, capitalism and state capitalism. But this is no surprise, given the impurity and complexity of a real transition from capitalism, potentially into communism.[10]

Why *solar* communism? Solar is by far the most abundant source of energy and the technologies to harness it are already in use. And, given a robust social management process during its lifecycle, solar also has very low negative health and ecological impacts. Moreover, a global transition to solar is actually achievable within the time frame necessary to avoid catastrophic climate change. Under 'really existing capitalism', solar is also the energy source most compatible with decentralized, democratic management and control, relatively free of the dictates of the Military Industrial Complex

(MIC), compared to fossil fuels and nuclear power. Finally, a solar 'clean energy' transition is a critical component of the Global Green New Deal, and an ecosocialist path out of capitalism.[11] But this vision has nothing in common with the stereotype of one-party dictatorships; if realized it will be the product of bottom-up struggles, a profoundly democratic process.

Jodi Dean reasserts the vision of radical materialist utopia that has been buried, reburied, yet never extinguished.[12] But to her invocation of a communist horizon in the twenty-first century one must add that this will be solar communist. An ecosocialist horizon is imperative to prevent and prefigure activity embodied in multidimensional class struggle in our world dominated by the rule of capital; to prevent catastrophic climate change and along the way demilitarize, solarize, and transform agriculture with agroecologies; to prefigure the future in the present by expanding the commons, virtual and material; and to move toward the ecosocialist horizon, reaching it and moving toward the solar communist horizon.

To simply say capitalism must be replaced by socialism is a conclusion, not a strategy; and to claim that capitalism must be immediately replaced by socialism to prevent catastrophic climate change is a cowardly rejection of responsibility to living and future generations. However, simply relying on green capitalism to implement a prevention programme using the usual market-driven mechanisms is a recipe for disaster. Global greenhouse emissions continue at all-too-high levels because fossil fuel consumption continues while market-led renewable energy growth is too slow to replace fossil fuels in the short window of time remaining. Further, fierce corporate resistance continues to block the replacement of industrial/GMO agriculture by agroecologies.

Solar communism is defined as a global civilization realizing Marx's aphoristic definition of communism for the twenty-first century: 'from each according to her ability, to each according to her needs,' referring to both humans and ecosystems.[13] Critical to this conception is the relevance of thermodynamics, with its concept of entropy, for comprehending the energetic and material basis of a new global civilization. Here, the Earth as an open system to energy transfers is a critical consideration.[14] The concept of entropy captures the ability to do work: the increase of entropy is equivalent to the diminished ability of an isolated system to do work, resulting from the degradation of low entropy energy into waste heat. An isolated system is defined as being closed to both energy and matter transfers in or out, while a closed system is only closed to matter transfers. The Earth is an open system, but essentially closed with respect to our considerations of matter transfers. Fossil fuels supply useful work to civilization, but will become unavailable because of the ever-increasing impacts of climate change rather than being exhausted because of their finite reserves in the crust. On the other hand, global wind and solar power will be available for millions of years into the future. The energy base of the global physical economy is critical: global wind/solar power will pay its 'entropic debt' to space as non-incremental waste heat, unlike its unsustainable alternatives.

An historical materialist account of an ecosocialist transition to a future global society should include a full conceptualization of the technological basis of this transition; a vision of this future global society should encompass its full materiality, in both the technological and social senses of that term.[15] Socialist or Marxist political economy is necessary but not sufficient in itself to advance a vision of twenty-first century socialism. This vision must fully engage the natural, physical and informational sciences in particular – climatology, ecology, biogeochemistry, and thermodynamics. These sciences will inform the technologies of renewable energy, green production, and agroecologies, whose infrastructure are to replace the present unsustainable forms. The cutting edge knowledge of climate science must inform an ecosocialist agenda, above all in giving humanity a clear signal of how much time is left to reach the political tipping points for preventing catastrophic climate change before irreversible change has occurred. Likewise the sciences of ecology, (bio)geochemistry, and thermodynamics must provide the basis for an effective catastrophic climate change prevention programme, in particular the most efficient processes of carbon sequestration from the atmosphere, bringing the atmospheric carbon dioxide level below 350 ppm (the most often cited planetary boundary for carbon emissions).

ECOSOCIALIST STRATEGY VERSUS THE MILITARY-INDUSTRIAL COMPLEX

Nearly seventy years after President Eisenhower first identified it as a threat, the Military Industrial Complex (MIC) has become a critical block to achieving global cooperation for rapidly curbing global greenhouse gas emissions, and a full transition to wind and solar power. Though the Pentagon is going 'green' with respect to energy conservation and use of renewables, it is simply 'greenwashing' its imperial role. The Pentagon's recognition of the growing security threat from climate change reinforces US imperialism and global militarism. This is the critical obstacle posed by the MIC, not the sizable, but widely exaggerated, greenhouse gas emissions entailed by US military operations.[16] Of course there are real contradictions within capital regarding energy policy, and the Green New Deal strategy must capture the 'solar' faction of capital into a multi-class alliance to force demilitarization and termination of the perpetual war dynamic to have any hope of implementing a catastrophic climate change prevention programme in time. Does any socialist believe that this prevention programme can be realized as long as the state terror apparatus is locked in a vicious cycle of violence with its useful enemy, its terrorist antagonist? This strategy remains very relevant: build a transnational movement for a Global Green New Deal (GGND). This is not a strategy relying on the capitalist market driving 'green' capitalist investment, rather one opening up a path for a catastrophic climate change prevention programme, and a more favorable terrain for global ecosocialist class struggle.[17] And this struggle requires contesting state power, on all scales from the local to the transnational. Paul Mason and Andreas Malm both emphasize that the state must play a critical role in curbing carbon emissions, replacing the capitalist market as the mechanism for doing so. But neither author discusses how the level of class struggle necessary for a postcapitalist transition would manifest itself.[18]

The MIC is likely the biggest single obstacle to preventing catastrophic climate change because it is central to global capital reproduction with its colossal waste of energy and material resources. What is also critical here is the longstanding role of the nuclear industry in the MIC. While it is true that the construction of new nuclear power plants in the United States has been put on hold, this is not yet the case globally. The nuclear power industry is transnational with technology being commonly shared. The fossil fuel/nuclear industry is integrated in the MIC, through their role in the defence industries and energy supply chains for the military, and the threat of nuclear attack is a long-standing instrument of imperial policy.[19] The Pentagon is the 'global oil-protection service'[20] as well as for strategic metals necessary for the US imperial agenda, indeed for the transnational capitalist class itself.[21] Since the MIC has a prominent role in setting the domestic/foreign policy agenda, not only of the United States in particular, but of all the big capitalist powers, the imperial nature of American foreign policy blocks the global cooperation and equity required to prevent catastrophic climate change.

A global solar transition replacing the present unsustainable energy supplies must be parasitic on these supplies, just as the industrial fossil fuel revolution was parasitic on biomass energy (so-called 'plant power') until it replaced the former supply with sufficient capacity. Each stage of history has been energy-parasitic on the previous: pre-industrial (low efficiency solar, i.e., photosynthesis), then industrial (fossil fuels, nuclear fission), and now in the twenty-first century we face the challenge of transition to post-industrial high efficiency solar while parasitizing the remaining reserves of fossil fuel energy, particularly conventional liquid oil (the preferable choice for limiting carbon dioxide in emissions). To have any chance of avoiding the worst impacts of climate change, the goal must be to use the minimum amount of conventional oil necessary to create a global wind/solar energy infrastructure. While Bill McKibben, leader of 350.org, does not explicitly recognize this point, it is implicit in his argument to keep most of the fossil fuels in the ground.[22] Humanity now confronts a potential transition from entropy-limited capitalism through ecosocialism to energy-abundant solar communism.[23]

Mainly because of its lower carbon emission footprint compared to coal, the preferred fossil fuel to make a solar transition is conventional petroleum,[24] but excluding tar sands, natural gas (because of methane leakage directly to the atmosphere), and dangerous drilling on deep water continental shelves. Oil-rich countries in the Middle East and South America (e.g., Venezuela) will be valuable partners in this solar transition, assuming it materializes, by providing the needed petroleum.[25] But a global regime of equity and cooperation is required. And only a check on imperial hegemony will make this global regime possible.

Real climate security requires radical reduction of the MIC in its broadest definition, including demilitarization of foreign policy, closure of military bases, drastic reduction of military expenditures, and the dissolution of the 'surveillance complex', along with the rapid phase-out of fossil fuels and nuclear power. Without this, we can anticipate at best all-too-weak curbs on carbon emissions (as with the recent Paris Agreement, which is insufficient to avoid catastrophic climate change),[27] combined with expanded military enforcement of the conditions for transnational capital reproduction. But the growth of solar power capacity and energy efficiency undermines at least some of the rationale and popular support for the MIC. And the struggle against the imperial agenda promotes a more peaceful and cooperative world, thereby freeing up both resources and labour for the creation of a global solar energy infrastructure. Likewise, a path for global ecosocialist transition is opened up. While individual capitalist countries may go far in solarizing their energy supplies, global 'solar capitalism' is an unlikely outcome for the twenty-first century, given the legacy and political economy of really-existing capitalism and the level of transnational class struggle necessary to avoid catastrophe.[28] The latter, combined with the ever-increasing potential of information technologies making value obsolete, should push global political economy towards an ecosocialist transition.

PREFIGURING A SOLAR COMMUNIST TRANSITION

The concept of prefiguration in existing capitalist societies is critical to the emergence of a global subject with the capacity to end the rule of capital.[29] Two examples of prefiguration are considered here: expanding the commons and the Universal Declaration of Human Rights.

To return to the metaphor 'the negation of the negation', a commonly cited example: we begin with the first negation of primitive communism into class-stratified societies, and then pass to the second, the final negation into communism, from prehistory to history. I submit that the growth of movements around our globe to 'defend, extend, and deepen the commons'[30] is the beginning of the second negation within the womb of capitalism itself. The ancient commons of humanity, the oceans, forests, grazing lands, are now joined by 'open source' in cyberspace, a contested terrain in the struggle to decommodify information.[31] Social management of communally-owned land is of course found even in capitalist countries in the form of national parks, biosphere reserves, and recognition in international law of the common heritage of humanity – such as Antarctica, the oceans, the atmosphere, and the Moon. This social management will be vastly expanded in an ecosocialist transition to solar communism.

Besides waging defensive battles against austerity, social-service cuts, and the privatization of public resources, expanding the ecosocialist horizon entails going on the offensive for social governance of production and consumption including the following objectives:

1) Creation of decentralized solar power, food, energy and farming cooperatives and worker-owned factories: a 'solidarity economy';[32]
2) Publicly owned and accountable banks;
3) Municipalization of electric and water supplies;
4) Nationalization of the energy, rail, and telecommunications industries; and
5) Compulsory licensing of state-of-the science wind/solar and information technologies, making them freely available globally, following the precedent of the US Clean Air Act.

The Universal Declaration of Human Rights is a prefiguration of potential alternate social rights and relations. The adoption of the Universal Declaration of Human Rights (UDHR) on 10 December 1948 by the General Assembly of the United Nations was a vision inspired by the victory over fascism in the Second World War. The critical role of the Soviet Union in making this victory possible forced the inclusion of economic, social and cultural human rights language into this historic document, although Western governments succeeded in splitting off these rights in legally binding covenants starting in 1951 and have continued to resist implementation.[33] Nevertheless, human rights discourse has emerged as a powerful asset in this struggle, even within the United States.

Life expectancy statistics demonstrate that the vision of the UDHR and conventions that followed remains unfulfilled in this world of continuing great disparities dominated by the reproduction of capital. As Bill Bowring put it: '… neither the concept of human rights nor that of social justice can have content, meaning and significance except through their complete reinvention and reintegration in the real activity of women and men in the always turbulent and dangerous world into which they are thrown.'[34]

A critical complement to universal human rights is the right of future generations to continue to enjoy the existing biodiversity of our planet, and even the partial restoration of what has been largely eliminated (e.g., prairies). The historic Convention on Biological Diversity entered into force on 29 December 1993. The convention has been ratified by 196 countries, but not by the United States, a fact that greatly weakens its implementation.[35] The protection of biodiversity is closely tied to the imperative of replacing present unsustainable energy sources with wind and solar, the conversion of agricultural systems to agroecologies, and of course implementing an effective prevention programme to avoid catastrophic climate change. James O'Connor, founding editor of *Capitalism Nature Socialism*, argued:

> In ecological Marxist theory, the struggle over production conditions has redefined the class struggle beyond any self-recognition as such, at least until now. This means that the capitalist threats to the reproduction of production conditions are not only threats to profits and accumulation, but also to the viability of the social and 'natural' environment as a means of life.[36]

Thus, global class struggle to protect ecological sustainability must be a central objective of twenty-first-century ecosocialism.

It is clear that the divisions in the global working class and potentially allied strata, derived from the exploitation of differences in nationality, ethnicity and race, gender, sexual preference, etc., must be significantly overcome if there is to be any hope of creating a countervailing force to national and transnational ruling classes in the global struggle for power. Of course, these divisions have a long history of utility to ruling classes. Overcoming them can ignite a force of unprecedented dimensions for ending the rule of capital. A transnational ecosocialist movement must emerge as a component for the success of this struggle, in the course of which traditional forms of organization will be superseded through the immense creativity of those involved in the global peace and climate justice movement, especially youth.[37] We see these forms emerging in embryo in the networking and inventions of solidarity in the World Social Forum and Occupy movements, and in particular, in the women's and indigenous peoples' struggle.

Transnational labour at the core of global peace and justice movements must by necessity emerge as the central countervailing force to transnational capital, which increasingly contests nation-centric forms of capitalist accumulation.[38] The goal of the overall movement: first constrain, then do away with the global rule of capital. The reformability of really existing capitalism must be tested by actual class struggle, in other words, by defending and expanding democracy in the social, political and economic spheres.

It is precisely now, as global capitalism faces the converging economic, social and climate crises, that struggles for a Global Green New Deal (GGND) should emerge as the focus for an ecosocialist movement. Unlike the New Deal, because demilitarization must be a component, the GGND will not end with a reinforcement of militarized capital, as was the case in the Second World War and the cold war aftermath. Rather, the GGND has real potential for opening up a path out of capitalism into ecosocialism.[39] Meeting this challenge will require raising class struggle to a pitch not yet witnessed. The struggle must be waged at every level, from the workplace and the classroom to the globe (transnational), and at every intersection of the oppressed and the exploited (race, gender, sexual orientation, ethnicity, citizenship status, (a)religion, age, degree of able-bodiedness). But intersectionality should be unpacked with Marxist analysis, as done with great clarity by Victor Wallis, who emphasizes that class domination is its cement or binding agent.[40]

In particular, the centrality of women's oppression must be recognized for its revolutionary potential.[41] The range of women's struggles in recent years is astonishing, from protection of the forest commons and of the Niger Delta, to the revolt against unwaged housework. The latter has directly confronted the valorization of labour power. David Laibman stresses the critical role of class struggle in determining this valorization: 'Labor power is, always and necessarily, a special commodity, never subject to full valorization like other commodities. Its value is always the outcome of the balance of class forces ('balance' here in the sense of 'relationship' or 'correlation,' with no implication of 'equilibrium' or any sort of inherent equality or consistency)'.[42]

Peter Frase conceptualizes class struggle in relation to the workplace, arguing that 'the strengthening of the working class both inside and outside the workplace becomes the force that pushes us toward the utopian ideal of a post-scarcity society and the abolition of wage labor'.[43] Drawing from the analysis of Marx's 'Fragment on Machines,' Paul Mason, too, argues that postcapitalism is inevitable because of the elimination of scarcity driven by the ever-growing power of the 'general intellect'. Information technology expands its reach into every aspect of life. 'The class struggle becomes the struggle to be human and educated during one's free time.'[44] Mason sees the ongoing increase in productivity growing out of both high efficiency renewable energy and information technologies as a serious potential basis for the system beyond capitalism.[45] But only global class struggle has the capacity to realize this potential for all of humanity and not simply a privileged elite living in gated communities.

However, Nick Dyer-Witheford finds the impact of the 'general intellect' under really-existing capitalism contradictory, with a 'moving contradiction' between 'the encompassing of the global population by networked supply chains and agile production systems, making labour available to capital on a planetary scale, and on the other, as a drive towards the development of adept automata and algorithmic software that render such labour redundant'.[46] And several prominent Marxist scholars disagree with Marx's formulation in the 'Fragment on Machines'. For example, Michael Heinrich argues that Marx confused immediate labour-time with abstract labour, which embodies the substance of value, and this confusion was gone in *Capital*.[47] Nevertheless, the discovery of the 'Fragment on Machines' in the 1960s and 1970s has in the twenty-first century ignited a vision of the end of the rule of capital on our planet utilizing the cutting edge of science and technology.[48]

A critical material prerequisite of the end of value is the availability of virtually free abundant energy derived from a global infrastructure of high-efficiency capture of solar energy. This infrastructure will create the supply and quality of energy necessary to radically reduce negative environmental impacts, indeed to also restore and repair both the technosphere and ecosphere,[49] though irreversible damage has already occurred (e.g. biodiversity loss). In contrast, continued reliance on the present unsustainable energy supply not only contributes to well-known negative environmental, ecological and health impacts, but also thereby reduces labor productivity while externalizing the costs of these negative impacts. Meanwhile the capitalist state subsidizes fossil fuels and nuclear power while cutting budgets for health and environmental protection. The huge subsidies going to fossil fuels, estimated in a recent IMF study at $5 trillion a year, also contain indirect costs including health impacts from air pollution (with 3-7 million estimated to die every year from this source).[50]

What is the ultimate limit to global energy consumption? Presently the global anthropogenic energy flux is equal to 0.03 per cent of solar flux to land; hence tapping the solar flux has huge potential as the energy basis of solar communism, with much smaller impacts on global ecology than now.[51] For example, global appropriation of wind power on order of the present energy consumption level equivalent to 18 trillion watts (terawatts) is far from being limited by geophysically-imposed constraints.[52] We may now be near revolutionary breakthroughs in high efficiency thin-film photovoltaics, or hydrogen generation by water-splitting driven by solar energy, with the potential to deliver very low cost and abundant energy to all of humanity. The emergence of such technologies and their appropriation by the global commons may yet detonate a transnational movement that does away with the MIC, thereby opening up an ecosocialist transition for the future of all humankind.[53]

The global North should transition to a simpler lifestyle – with examples such as mass transit, bicycle transport in place of cars, smaller homes, and a great reduction in the consumption of obsolescent gadgets – that break with the endless creation of manufactured desire driven by the reproduction of capital. If the transformation of agriculture to fossil fuel-free agroecologies situated closer to population centres is included, this degrowth translates into lower energy consumption in the global North, resulting in a higher quality of life with a more healthful environment: cleaner air, water, and organic food free of the chemicals and genetic contamination now inherent in industrial/GMO agriculture.

But the world needs more, not less, energy consumption than now, with most of humanity living in the global South requiring a significant increase to reach the rough minimum of 3.5 kilowatt/person. Note that reaching this minimum is necessary but not sufficient for acquiring the highest life expectancy, as several petroleum-exporting countries in the Middle East as well as Russia now fall well below that goal. Life expectancy for the United States is likewise below most industrial countries of the global North. Income inequality is robustly correlated with bad health, and must be reduced to achieve the world standard life expectancy and quality of life. Supplying the minimum 3.5 kilowatt/person for the present world population of 7 billion people requires a delivery equivalent to 25 trillion watts, with the present delivery equal to 18 trillion watts. Even with a complete transition to a global wind and solar power infrastructure by 2050, including its roughly 30 per cent gain in efficiency, at least 22 trillion watts will be required to guarantee the minimum energy per person necessary for a state-of-the-science quality of life (3.5 kilowatt/person x 0.7 x 9 billion people, with the latest United Nations projection for 2050 is 9.7 billion people).[54] Additional capacity will be necessary especially for ongoing carbon-sequestration from the atmosphere and climatic adaptation, with the total required likely approaching 25 to 30 trillion watts.[55] This approach is imperative because these applications will require extra capacity to be created as early as possible because of the physics of greenhouse gases.[56]

Given the global North's historic responsibility for the threat of C3, transfer of wind and solar capacity to the global South from the global North is imperative. With 1 to 2 per cent of current annual consumption of energy (85 per cent derived from fossil fuels) being used for wind and solar power creation per year, a global-scale transition can be achieved in no more than thirty years, with the complete elimination of anthropogenic carbon emissions derived from energy consumption to the atmosphere and the provision of the minimum per capita energy consumption level required for state-of-the-science life expectancy level for all.[57] Further, if this transition commences in the near future it would maximize the probability of achieving a less than 2 degree Celsius increase over the pre-industrial level, with a potential 1.5 degree Celsius limit by 2100.[58]

It is increasingly clear that only with a radical shift to a global regime of peace and cooperation will it be possible to implement an effective prevention programme to avoid catastrophic climate change. The threats of catastrophic climate change and nuclear war pose an unprecedented opportunity to end the rule of capital, because the main obstacle to elimination of these threats is the MIC at the core of really existing capitalism.[59] Thus, the challenge to dissolve the MIC puts an ecosocialist transition on the agenda for humanity – an ecosocialist transition out of prehistory and into a new global civilization, solar communism in the twenty-first century.

COMMITTED SCIENCE AND COMMUNITIES OF STRUGGLE

Solar communism will entail the final end of capital reproduction and thus of value. This passage from Jim Davis is illuminating:

> New technologies express the fulfillment of Marx's writings in his 'Fragment on Machines' – a production system without human labor, where the productivity of technology so overwhelms the production process that 'labor time ceases to be the measure' of wealth and 'production based upon exchange value collapses'... I argue that as a historical category, Value has at least a theoretical end ...The new technological climate does not in itself destroy the Value system, or capitalism, but it does create the conditions for Capital's destruction and the construction of a communist society. The end of Value is not automatic, but a conscious act by class forces born out of the new conditions.[60]

Davis ends his essay, 'This is how Value will end – as a political act, the exercise of class power'. The goal of the class struggle that will lead to this is nothing less than this: every child born on earth has the right to a full life of creative fulfillment, to an environment free of hatred and pollution, and to a world with what is left of our planet's biodiversity intact. This will require the termination of the present global regime prioritizing capital reproduction over human needs as well as those of nature. Reloading Lenin now in our political practice is essential; first to recognize the potentiality of the moment and act, else we lose the chance to change the future; and second, to utilize every division in the ruling class to gain the necessary political momentum to prevent catastrophic climate change. But the vision itself and its realization can only come about as a product informed by the dialogue between a committed scientific/technological intelligentsia and communities of struggle, as embryos of the future are created within the womb of globalized capitalism, and as global class struggle unfolds to achieve its full reality.

NOTES

1. Karl Marx, *A Contribution to the Critique of Political Economy*, New York: International Publishers, [1859] 1970, pp. 21–22.
2. Andreas Malm, *Fossil Capital,* London: Verso, 2016, p. 307.
3. James Hansen et al., 'Assessing 'Dangerous Climate Change: Required Reduction of Carbon Emissions to Protect Young People, Future Generations and Nature', *PLOS ONE,* 8 (12), 2013; John Bellamy Foster, 'The Great Capitalist Climateric', *Monthly Review,* 67 (6), 2015, pp. 1-18; Sybren Drijfhout et al., 'Catalogue of abrupt shifts in Intergovernmental Panel on Climate Change climate models', *Proc. Natl. Acad. Sci. U.S.A.,* 112 (43) E5777-E5786, 2015; T. Gasser et al., 'Negative emissions physically needed to keep global warming below 2 °C', *Nature Communications,* 6, 7958, 2015; Michael Slezak, 'Global warming taking place at an 'alarming rate', UN climate body warns', *The Guardian,* 21 March 2016; James Hansen, et al., 'Ice melt, sea level rise and superstorms: evidence from paleoclimate data, climate modeling, and modern observations that 2 °C global warming could be dangerous', *Atmos. Chem. Phys.,* 16, 2016, pp. 3761-3812.
4. Agreeing here with Sasha Lilley, David McNally, Eddie Yuen, and James Davis, *Catastrophism*, Oakland: PM Press, 2012.
5. See my following essays: 'A Critique of Degrowth and Its Politics', *Capitalism Nature Socialism,* 23 (1), 2012, pp. 119–25; 'The Great Bifurcation and Prospects for Solar Communism in the Twenty-First Century', *International Critical Thought,* 3 (4), 2013, pp. 480-95; 'Ted Trainer and the Simpler Way: A Somewhat Less Sympathetic Critique', *Capitalism Nature Socialism,* 25 (2), 2014, pp. 112-17; 'My Response to Trainer', *Capitalism Nature Socialism,* 25 (4), 2014, pp. 109-15; 'Is Zero Economic Growth Necessary to Prevent Climate Catastrophe?', *Science & Society,* 78 (2), 2014, pp. 235-40.
6. Karl Marx, *Critique of the Gotha Program,* New York: International Publishers, [1875] 1938.

7   Murray Feshbach and Alfred Friendly Jr., *Ecocide in the USSR*, New York: Basic Books, 1992.
8   Zhores A. Medvedev, *Nuclear Disaster in the Urals*, New York: W.W. Norton, 1980.
9   John Bellamy Foster, 'The Planetary Crisis & Late Soviet Ecology', *Monthly Review*, 67 (2), 2015, pp. 1-20. I discussed several of the Soviet books mentioned by Foster in 'What's New in the Noosphere?', *Environmental Action*, 14 (6), 1983, pp. 25-27.
10   Thus I take exception to Paul Mason's view that the Soviet Union was worse than capitalism (Paul Mason, *Postcapitalism: A Guide to Our Future*, London: Allen Lane, 2015, p.145), and likewise to Slavoj Zizek's common reduction of this whole experience to a huge disaster, triangulating between the left and neoliberals while posturing as a communist (of course I cannot deny I am highly entertained by Zizek's jokes and media analysis). However, it is important to note Zizek's recognition of the political genius of Lenin (e.g., in Sebastian Budgen, Stathis Kouvelakis and Slavoj Zizek, eds., *Lenin Reloaded*, Durham and London: Duke University Press, 2007) and likewise the extremely difficult context for the development of Soviet socialism.
11   David Schwartzman, 'Green New Deal: An Ecosocialist Perspective', *Capitalism Nature Socialism*, 22 (3), 2011, pp. 49-56.
12   Jodi Dean, *The Communist Horizon*, London: Verso, 2012.
13   David Schwartzman, 'To Each According to Her Needs', *Dialogue & Initiative*, no. 4, 1992, pp. 16–19; David Schwartzman, 'Solar Communism', *Science & Society*, 60 (3), 1996, pp. 307–31.
14   Schwartzman, 'Solar Communism', pp. 307–31; Schwartzman, 'The Limits to Entropy: Continuing Misuse of Thermodynamics in Environmental and Marxist Theory', *Science & Society*, 72 (1), 2008, pp. 43–62. Here I again addressed the concept of entropy, as even some Marxists did not get it right.
15   David Schwartzman, 'Ecosocialism or Ecocatastrophe?', *Capitalism Nature Socialism*, 20 (1), 2009, pp. 6–33.
16   David Schwartzman, 'COP21: Achievements and challenges to the climate justice movement', CNS WEB, 29 December 2015..
17   David Schwartzman, 'Green New Deal: An Ecosocialist Perspective', *Capitalism Nature Socialism*, 22 (3), 2011, pp. 49-56.
18   Malm, *Fossil Capital*; Paul Mason, *Postcapitalism*.
19   Joseph Gerson, *Empire and the Bomb*, London: Pluto Press, 2007. The possibility of a nuclear war continues, with nuclear weapons now being possessed by nine nations, including notable hotspots (e.g. India/Pakistan and Israel/Iran.) Israel is believed to possess several hundred deliverable nuclear weapons; the US refusing to consider a nuclear-free Middle East, even though Iran has given up the capacity to develop nuclear weapons. These remain important, if indirect, parts of the calculations of energy markets.
20   Michael Klare, 'The Pentagon v. Peak Oil', *Synthesis/Regeneration*, 45 (Winter), 2008.
21   William I. Robinson, *A Theory of Global Capitalism*, Baltimore: Johns Hopkins University Press, 2004; Jerry Harris, 'To Be or Not To Be: The Nation-Centric World Order Under Globalization', *Science & Society*, 69 (3), 2005, pp. 329–40.
22   Bill McKibben, 'Why We Need to Keep 80 Percent of Fossil Fuels in the Ground', *Yes! Magazine*, 15 February 2016.
23   Schwartzman, 'Solar Communism', pp. 307–31; Schwartzman, 'The Limits to Entropy', pp. 43–62; Robert Biel, *The Entropy of Capitalism*, Chicago: Haymarket, 2013.
24   Vaclav Smil, *Energy at Crossroads*, Cambridge: MIT Press, 2003; Robert W. Howarth, 'A Bridge to Nowhere: Methane Emissions and the Greenhouse Gas Footprint of Natural Gas', *Energy Science & Engineering*, doi: 10.1002/ese3.35, 2014.
25   David Schwartzman and Quincy Saul, 'An Ecosocialist Horizon for Venezuela: A Solar

Communist Horizon for the World', *Capitalism Nature Socialism,* 26 (3), 2015, pp. 14-30.

26 David Schwartzman, 'The Path to Climate Security Passes Through Gaza: A Prologue to Rethinking Strategy', *Greenwashing Apartheid: The Jewish National Fund's Environmental Cover-Up,* 2011, pp. 38–41.

27 D. Schwartzman, 'COP21: Achievements and challenges.

28 Schwartzman, 'Ecosocialism or Ecocatastrophe?', pp. 6–33. But what about the BRICS (Brazil, Russia, China and South Africa)? The BRICS nations are emerging as a potential economic and military counterforce to the Imperial Axis of US/NATO, but with very contradictory aspects (Patrick Bond and Ana Garcia, eds., *BRICS: An Anti-Capitalist Critique,* Chicago: Haymarket, 2015). The BRICS global infrastructure program is in some respects even worse than that of its competitor (Nancy Alexander, ed., *Infrastructure: For People or For Profit?,* Heinrich Boll Foundation and Latindadd, 2014), particularly in its energy sector with its climatic impacts (note e.g., China's plan to build more nuclear power plants and its role in helping to finance Hinkley Point in Somerset UK). As in the industrial revolution, capitalist growth in China was driven by the consumption of several billion tons of coal, and as a result China now has the highest carbon emissions in the world (Malm, *Fossil Capital,* pp. 327-66). But China is also the biggest investor in wind/solar technologies. Could China actually emerge as the leader of an ecosocialist path for the rest of the world? Could this be the outcome of class struggle of sufficient power growing out of both the huge negative impacts of its industrial infrastructure on its population, and the paradox of its capitalist development under the banner of 'communist' ideology, with remnants of twenty-first-century socialism still in place?

29 Joel Kovel, *The Enemy of Nature: The End of Capitalism or the End of the World?,* New York: Zed Books, 2002. Prefiguration captures the vision of 'eroding' capitalism, while reforms such as nationalization of the energy industry are close to the category of 'taming' capitalism (Erik Olin Wright, 'Why Class Matters', *Jacobin,* 23 December 2015; and 'How to Think About (And Win) Socialism', *Jacobin,* 27 April 2016).

30 Derek Wall, *Babylon and Beyond,* London: Pluto Press, 2005, p. 184.

31 Jim Davis, Thomas Hirschl and Michael Stack, eds., *Cutting Edge,* London: Verso, 1997; Nick Dyer-Witheford, *Cyber-Marx, Cycles and Circuits of Struggle in High Technology Capitalism,* Urbana and Chicago: University of Illinois Press, 1999; Nick Dyer-Witheford, *Cyber-Proletariat,* London: Pluto Press, 2015.

32 Gar Alperovitz, 'Socialism in America is Closer Than You Think', *The Nation,* 11 February 2016; Gar Alperovitz, *What Then Must We Do?,* White River Junction, Vermont: Chelsea Green Publishing, 2013. But see: Sam Gindin, 'Chasing Utopia, Worker Ownership and Cooperatives Will Not Succeed by Competing on Capitalism's Terms', *Jacobin,* 10 March 2016.

33 A. Belden Fields, *Rethinking Human Rights for the New Millennium,* New York: Palgrave MacMillan, 2003.

34 Bill Bowring, *The Degradation of the International Legal Order?,* New York: Routledge, 2008, p. 166.

35 Convention on Biological Diversity, List of Parties. Available at: https://www.cbd.int/information/parties.shtml.

36 James O'Connor, 'Capitalism, Nature, Socialism: A Theoretical Introduction', *Capitalism Nature Socialism,* 1(1), 1988, p. 34.

37 W. Warren Wagar, *A Short History of the Future,* 2nd ed. Chicago: University of Chicago Press, 1992; David Schwartzman, 'To Each According to Her Needs', *Dialogue & Initiative,* no. 4, 1992, pp. 16–19; David Schwartzman, 'A World Party, Vehicle of Global Green Left', *Ecosocialist Review,* Spring, 1992, pp. 4–5; Kovel, *The Enemy of*

Nature?; Dyer-Witheford, *Cyber-Proletariat*, pp. 202-3.
38   William I. Robinson, *A Theory of Global Capitalism*, Baltimore: Johns Hopkins University Press, 2004; Jerry Harris, 'To Be or Not To Be: The Nation-Centric World Order Under Globalization', *Science & Society*, 69 (3), 2005, pp. 329–40.
39   See my: 'Green New Deal, pp. 49–56; 'Is Zero Economic Growth Necessary to Prevent Climate Catastrophe?', pp. 235- 40.
40   Victor Wallis, 'Intersectionality's Binding Agent', *New Political Science*, 37 (4), 2015, pp. 604-619.
41   Ariel Salleh, ed., *Eco-Sufficiency & Global Justice*, London: Pluto Press, 2014; Silvia Federici, *Revolution at Point Zero: Housework, Reproduction, and Feminist Struggle*, Oakland, California: PM Press, 2012; Selma James, *Sex, Race, and Class*, Oakland, California: PM Press, 2012.
42   David Laibman, 'Editorial Perspectives: Whither the Occupy Movement: Models and Proposals', *Science & Society*, 76 (3), 2012, pp. 283–88.
43   Peter Frase, 'Ours to Master', *Jacobin*, 17, Spring 2015.
44   Paul Mason, *Postcapitalism*, pp. 136-137. Also see Nick Srnicek and Alex Williams, *Investing the Future*, London: Verso, 2015.
45   Jeremy Rifkin has also recently argued that high efficiency renewable energy and information technologies are posing an alternative beyond capitalism. See his: *The Zero Marginal Cost Society*, New York: Palgrave MacMillan, 2014.
46   Dyer-Witheford, *Cyber-Proletariat*, p. 14.
47   Michael Heinrich, 'The "Fragment on Machines" in the *Grundrisse* and its Overcoming in *Capital*', in Riccardo Bellofiore, Guido Starosta and Peter D. Thomas, eds., *In Marx's Laboratory*, Chicago: Haymarket, 2013, pp. 197-212.
48   See George Caffentzis, 'From the *Grundrisse* to *Capital* and Beyond: Then and Now', in Bellofiore, Starosta and Thomas, eds., *In Marx's Laboratory*, pp. 265-81.
49   Barry Commoner, *Making Peace with the Planet*, New York: Pantheon, 1990.
50   David Coady, Ian Parry, Louis Sears and Baoping Shang, 'How Large Are Global Energy Subsidies?', *IMF Working Paper*, Fiscal Affairs Department, 2015; UNEP, *Year Book 2014 emerging issues update. Air Pollution. World's Worst Environmental Health Risk*, 2014.
51   Schwartzman, 'Solar Communism', pp. 307–31.
52   Kate Marvel, Ben Kravitz, and Ken Caldeira, 'Geophysical limits to global wind power', *Nature Climate Change*, 3, 2013, pp. 118-21.
53   See scenario 2 in David Schwartzman, '4 Scenarios for 2050', *Capitalism Nature Socialism*, 23 (1), 2013, pp. 49-53. An alternative scenario for a transition might emerge as an outcome of a future global economic slump that reprises the crisis of 2008-10. Such a crisis would not only result in a plunge in carbon emissions, but also could be a conjuncture in which a transnational movement forms to push for a GGND that has the potential of preventing catastrophic climate change.
54   United Nations, *World Population Prospects The 2015 Revision*, New York, 2015.
55   David Schwartzman, 'How much and what kind of energy does humanity need?', *Socialism and Democracy*, forthcoming; David Schwartzman, 'Should we reject Negative Emissions Technologies, except for organic agriculture?', *CNS WEB*, 5 February 2016.
56   H.D. Matthews and Ken Caldeira, 'Stabilizing climate requires near-zero emissions', *Geophysical Research Letters*, 35, L04705, doi:10.1029/2007GL032388, 2008.
57   Peter Schwartzman and David Schwartzman, '*A Solar Transition is Possible*', published online at: http://solarUtopia.org, 2011; David Schwartzman and Peter Schwartzman, 'A Rapid Solar Transition Is Not Only Possible, It Is Imperative!', *African Journal of Science, Technology, Innovation and Development*, 5 (4), 2013, pp. 297–302. Updates, corrections available at: http://www.solarutopia.org.

58 Peter D. Schwartzman, David W. Schwartzman, Xiaochun Zhang, 'Climatic implications of a rapid wind/solar transition', *Arxiv.org*, March 22, 2016, pp. 1-17.
59 Schwartzman, 'Ecosocialism or Ecocatastrophe?', pp. 6–33.
60 Jim Davis, 'The End of Value' Marxism 2000 Conference, Amherst, MA, September, published online at: http://www.gocatgo.com/texts/eov.html, 2000.

SOUTH AFRICA'S NEXT REVOLT: ECO-SOCIALIST OPPORTUNITIES

PATRICK BOND

The political ecology of South Africa reflects extreme uneven and combined development. As one crucial aspect of this condition, environmental degradation extends deep into the households and workplaces populated mainly by the country's black majority. The regroupment of the socialist movement will, in the coming months and years, have to embrace the environmental challenge just as profoundly as it will need to reindustrialize the economy under worker and social control, while also redistributing wealth and restructuring the reproduction of labour power in a humane, rational manner to spread what is now women's caregiving responsibilities properly. As these overlapping processes unfold, there are opportunities to 'red-green' several aspirational strategies now being articulated by leading eco-socialist currents: renewable energy generation, manufacturing localization, minerals beneficiation, land reform, urban repurposing and desuburbanization, the cessation of migrant labour relations, shifts from private to public transport and other overdue geographical restructurings. These objectives are supported, at least in principle, by all social forces aside from the most dogmatic neoliberals.

But under ever more intense domination of the South African state by capital and its agents (e.g. international credit ratings agencies Fitch, Moody's and Standard & Poor's), it is likely that these strategies will be tokenistic. They will be underfunded, will fall prey to 'Green Economy' eco-capitalist manoeuvres, and will eviscerate any potential eco-socialist orientation. In the municipal site of Durban, for example, greenwashing has been extremely aggressive even under the reign of an ostensibly communist mayor and city manager since 2002. Hence the challenge is to wrench power from corporations and their allied politicians and state officials, by developing a programmatic approach that internalizes as many 'red-green' values as possible, notwithstanding all the countervailing pressure. To gain space to do so will also necessarily mean coming to grips with the extreme international vulnerabilities associated with post-1994 neoliberalism. These include South Africa's exposure to world commodity overproduction, its financial vulnerabilities, its economy's contradiction-ridden sub-imperial positioning within Africa, and most explicitly today, the failure of the BRICS project: the mistaken idea that alliances with Brazil, Russia, India and China would generate radically new global governance power relations that would successfully address economic, social, geopolitical and ecological crises from the top down.

In contrast, several bottom-up victories since the end of apartheid in 1994 offer examples of the decommodification, destratification and deglobalization approaches that can be emulated so as to move forward the eco-socialist agenda: access to free HIV/AIDS medicines, the partial decommodification of municipal water and electricity services, and workplace health and safety class-action lawsuits (especially over silicosis). These are instances of struggle that bring home – to the scale of the body itself – some of the socio-ecological processes most damaged by capitalism, where revolt has been most portentous. There are also some isolated but important cases of environmental justice victories over polluters that contribute to broader eco-socialist conceptions and movement-building. And a few institutions and visionary leaders have begun to emerge to carry forward the eco-socialist agenda across South Africa's rocky terrain. Finally, a new generation of activists is emerging from university struggles (#FeesMustFall), which in 2015 were partially successful in gaining not only a freeze on student payments (partially offset by increased state funding), but also linking with casualized 'outsourced' campus workers who the students assisted in winning in-sourcing and a living wage.

Still, the most vital missing element in 2017 is a political party that reflects and regenerates eco-socialist campaigns and ideology deep within the society. All other ideologies currently in the mainstream of political discourse – especially nationalism, neoliberalism, petit-bourgeois radicalism, Black Consciousness and an ossified 'Marxist-Leninism' promoted by the official Communist Party, as well as half-hearted mainstream environmentalism – have failed to achieve the potential that a red-green political process offers. Even the best prospect for an eco-socialist ideology – the National Union of Metalworkers of South Africa (NUMSA) in alliance with the Association of Mineworkers and Construction Union (AMCU) and a slow-maturing 'United Front' with social movements – has a great distance to travel before the merits of radical environmentalism are evident to leaders and lay members alike.

The narratives required to make this case will be diverse but must somehow fuse the economic, environmental, social, political, gendered and even spiritual critiques of the status quo: something akin to the (much-abused) vernacular 'Ubuntu' framing in which the philosophy that 'we are who we are through others' also requires future application to society-nature relations. If not, too many silo-specific narratives will continue to compete with each other and the progressive forces in South Africa will never generate the kind of overarching anti-capitalist ideology, programme and network that they did during the 1980s in the final push to defeat apartheid. But those deficiencies may soon be addressed as a socialist party emerges from the independent left's numerous fragments of struggle.

To assess this potential with the optimism of the will and pessimism of the intellect required now more than ever demands that we review, first, the characteristics of capitalist crises felt so acutely in economic, socio-ecological and gendered respects following two decades of neoliberal-nationalist politics; second, the now-shifting political alliances from above, and from below the fragmented red and green political forces that have, albeit haltingly, finally begun a regroupment process; third, inspirational moments when indicative victories were won in spheres of social reproduction; which in turn, fourth, may inform a series of struggles that lie ahead.

The crisis-ridden conditions of accumulation and the uneven state of class struggle may collide in a way that compels the working class to decisively address the forces and relations of production – especially devaluation of overaccumulated capital – such that through leaps and bounds, reversals and maturations, a South African version of eco-socialism begins to make common sense to the society. The fabled 'second stage' of socialist struggle was forever delayed by the historic forces of liberation, especially the African National Congress (ANC) led by Nelson Mandela (ANC president from 1991-97), Thabo Mbeki (1997-2007) and Jacob Zuma (2007-present). New forces are pregnant, but how deeply they generate red-green philosophy, analysis, strategies, tactics and alliances remains to be seen.

NEOLIBERAL FRAGMENTATION
AND ACCUMULATION CRISES

The fragmentation of red and green political potentials is not unusual in the contemporary world, but few if any sites are subject to the extremes of South Africa, not least because of increasingly adverse conditions for capital accumulation. Neoliberalism has dug itself deep into social and environmental management since 1994. On the one hand, that year's achievement of the liberation movements' hard-fought 'one person, one vote in a unitary state' demand, and the cessation of the formal legal and geographic framework of apartheid, can never be discounted. On the other, the costs of political victory – i.e., concessions demanded by white South Africans and their international capitalist allies – were high. The disastrous socio-economic and environmental results of an 'elite transition' imposed upon the majority are well known.[1] They include much more severe unemployment, poverty and inequality than even under apartheid, plus extreme damage to the country's natural assets. The liberation movement itself became distorted, following the classic route Fanon described as 'pitfalls of national consciousness'.[2]

The elite transition's neoliberal culture spread deep into the society. The working class is both ripe for a new, overarching left political initiative, while contradictorily, corporate advertising and consumerist culture have made this class ever more committed to standard modernization processes in the reproduction of daily life. South Africans are prone to celebrate even those features of Western eco-social abuse which are rapidly coming into question in the rest of the world: suburbanization, individual auto use, diets based on meat and sugar, genetically-modified crops, and consumer credit binging associated with over-consumptive (and import-intensive) tastes. The hedonistic values of pre-1994 South Africa – in which the country's wealthiest 5 million white residents (9 per cent of the population) plus a smattering of Indian, 'coloured' and African middle-class consumers lived an advanced Western materialist lifestyle – were deracialized after liberation. Mass marketing, post-racial advertising and liberalized credit meant the conditions for consumption overwhelmed residual attempts at transformation.

There are limits, however, including the ceiling to credit expansion and the broader macro-economic crisis. The former ceiling was hit in 2008 when half of the country's 20 million credit-active consumers (out of 53 million residents) were given 'impaired credit' ratings by the National Credit Regulator as non-performing loans (i.e. defaults) soared, a ratio that has remained steady since. Although a 2005 National Credit Act had anticipated these problems, instead of sharing liability between creditor and debtor, the law invoked a role for debt counsellors to assist banks with repayments. The contradictions proved overwhelming, and African Bank, the major lender catering aggressively to the most desperate sections of the working class, lost 54 per cent of its stock market value during a mid-2013 investor panic and went bust the following year. As formal financial institutions' appetite for working-class lending waned, credit became even more exploitative within the smaller-scale microfinance markets. To illustrate, the name 'mashonisa' refers to the ubiquitous usurer in black South African townships; the isiZulu word means 'to impoverish' (or 'to sink').[3]

The deeper micro-economic dilemma was something that the ANC's Economic Transformation Committee had become aware of a decade earlier: 'The commercial micro-lending sector has rapidly reached the limit of its expansion. The nature of its business model is such that it can only extend financial services to the salaried workforce.' One of the country's main advocates of microfinance, Ted Baumann, conceded that poor people were unable to generate surpluses sufficient to make loan repayments, especially in rural areas: 'Unlike peasantries elsewhere in Africa, South Africa's rural poor lack access to basic means of production, such as land, because of unresolved issues of comprehensive settler dispossession. They live in crowded rural villages squeezed between commercial farmland (no longer exclusively white) and tourist-oriented game reserves.' Likewise for urban residents, income-generating activity is 'constrained by South Africa's manufacturing and retail sectors, the most advanced in Africa, which relegate small-scale trading and manufacturing to the margins'.[4] Displacing capitalism's crises into the credit sphere simply enhanced the contradictions over time.

Indeed South African capitalism bumped up against the latter ceiling – macro-economic in character – around 2011, partly because of forces beyond local managerial control: world capitalist crisis dynamics. Since 1994, there were three periods in which integration into the global economy adversely affected South Africa, and one period in which terms of trade and global interest rates were relatively more benign. From 1994-2002, the economy was liberalized and with deindustrialization and the import of capital-intensive machinery, society suffered a doubling of unemployment and worse poverty and inequality than before 1994. Repeated currency crises reduced the Rand's value by more than 20 per cent within a few weeks, in 1996, 1998 and 2001. The R3.6/$ level in 1994 was untenable under the pressure, and a low was reached in 2001 of R11.9/$ before bouncing back strongly over the subsequent decade. The result of these crashes was a spike in interest rates – at worst by 7 per cent in two weeks during mid-1998 – that made local manufacturing investment yet more expensive.

The only positive experience from greater global economic integration came from the 2002-11 commodity price 'super-cycle', in which South Africa's four main mineral exports of coal, gold, platinum and iron ore soared in price and output. But the negative features of integration returned during the 2008-2009 world recession, with South Africa's budget deficit rising to more than 7 per cent of GDP as 2010 soccer World Cup related infrastructure spending helped the economy to survive the world crash. Although China's vast Keynesian investment boom from 2008-2011 raised global commodity prices in a last gasp for the extractive industries from 2009-2011, the subsequent period has been disastrous for an economy that had grown so reliant upon minerals exports. It is true that the local Rand price of those minerals fell faster than the global commodity index – the peak currency was R6.3/$ in 2011 and it fell to a low of R18/$ in early 2016, whereas the prices of four main minerals fell 50 per cent. But that also created a temptation for mining houses to increase output, thus exacerbating the global gluts, in search of profits, rather than reduce supply.

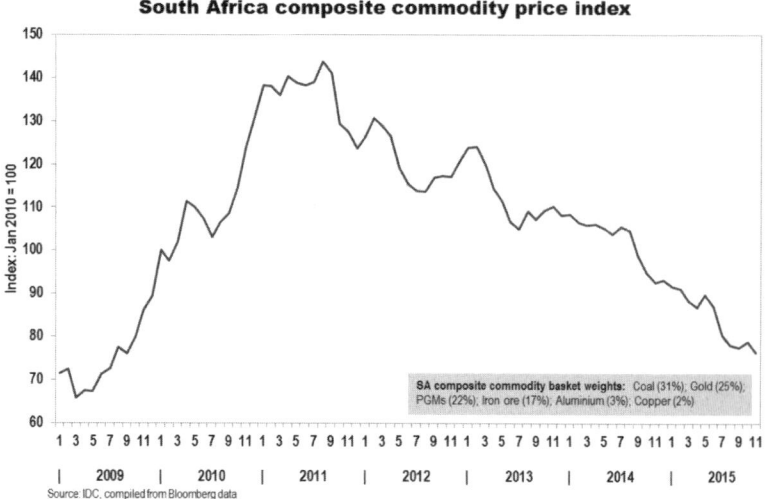

As a result, by mid-2016 South Africa's current account deficit had fallen to a critical -5 per cent of GDP because the balance of payments (mainly profit outflows) suffered rapid decay. The other component of the current account, the trade deficit – i.e., imports minus exports – is trivial in comparison. Most disastrously for the macro-economic balancing act, the net outflow of corporate dividends paid to owners of foreign capital reached $11 billion in the first quarter of 2016 (measured on an annualized basis), 30 per cent higher than the equivalent 2015 level (and in comparison, that quarter's trade deficit was just $2.5 billion). At the time, only one other country among the 60 largest economies, Colombia, had a higher current account deficit. Because repatriating profits must be done with hard currency, South Africa's external debt had by then soared to 39 per cent of GDP, $125 billion, from a level less than 16 per cent of GDP ($25 billion) in 1994.[5]

This pressure to raise hard currency for foreign shareholders, in turn, quickened the metabolism of extraction in which capital, labour and nature interact. The mass of profits (in hard currency) that mining corporations require to please owners and to service debt must be kept at a satisfactory level. If commodity prices drop, one way to address the problem is to increase the volume of output, hoping that costs of production in a specific site are far enough below competitors to drive them out of business. This appeared to be a strategy adopted in South Africa, for as the minerals slump began in 2011, many of the global mining and smelting corporations squeezed harder, for they too faced attack by investors. Anglo American and Glencore lost three quarters of their share value in 2015 alone, and Lonmin was down 99 per cent in value from its 2011 peak to 2015 trough.[6] Desperate, such firms took to exporting profits ever more rapidly, in comparison with the overseas-generated profits that South African corporations paid to local shareholders.[7]

In turn, that outflow was the result of a policy choice during the 1990s, remarked upon by ANC Secretary General Gwede Mantashe in 2015: 'At the time when neoliberalism was on the ascendancy as an ideology, it became fashionable to allow companies to migrate and list in the stock exchanges of developed economies.'[8] Exchange control liberalization had begun in 1995 with the dual exchange rate's abolition and sped up when in 1999 permission was granted by Finance Minister Trevor Manuel and Reserve Bank Governor Tito Mboweni to allow the country's largest firms to delist from the Johannesburg Stock Exchange and shift dividend flows abroad. (Manuel and Mboweni received accolades from world financiers and by 2014 were employees of Rothschild's and Goldman Sachs, respectively.) Exchange controls were relaxed on dozens more occasions. The 2015 concessions, for example, allowed the wealthy to take $650,000 offshore annually, 2.5 times more than prior years. As a *Moneyweb* reporter explained, this 'effectively ended [individual] controls for all but the most wealthy South Africans'.[9] Meanwhile, institutional investors – representing the savings, pension funds and insurance accounts of the mass of small investors – are compelled to keep 75 per cent of their assets in local investments. By all accounts, such controls prevented the 2008 world crisis from melting South Africa's finances.[10] But the big institutions have avoided reinvestment in fixed capital; instead, they keep price levels on the Johannesburg Stock Exchange and real estate at the world's most over-valued levels.[11]

The rapid haemorrhaging of corporate profit outflows is all the more frustrating because, according to the Reserve Bank, corporate fixed investment shrank nearly 7 per cent in early 2016, while government investment also fell 12 per cent.[12] The only major new South African fixed investment came from parastatals: the electricity company Eskom's over-priced and ecologically destructive Medupi and Kusile coal-fired power generation plants (running at $10 billion each). Even more destructive projects by the

Transnet rail and port agency lie ahead, costing more than $20 billion each: the planned export of 18 billion tonnes of coal via a new rail line, and the eight-fold increase in the South Durban port-petrochemical capacity. These are the top two of Pretoria's National Development Plan infrastructure priorities, both mainly located in Zuma's home province. Notwithstanding such subsidies, South Africa's investment-wary corporations claim they act rationally, leaving local profits as idle cash especially in the wake of the Reserve Bank's four interest rate hikes in 2015-16. By mid-2016, South Africa's medium-term interest rates had risen to fourth highest amongst the world's major countries surveyed by *The Economist*. As for the price of debt, only governments in Brazil, Venezuela and Turkey pay a higher interest rate, and only companies in these countries plus Argentina, Ukraine, Egypt and Russia pay more when borrowing.[13]

Even more frustrating, the same firms – mostly in the extractive industries – removed an additional $21 billion offshore *annually* as 'illicit financial flows' through tax-dodging techniques from 2004-13, according to the Washington NGO Global Financial Integrity.[14] These outflows exceed $80 billion annually across the continent, reported Thabo Mbeki's African Union commission, throwing into question the merits of Foreign Direct Investment.[15] Several spectacular local cases were documented: tax avoidance by the biggest platinum companies, especially Lonmin with its Bermuda 'marketing' arm, at a time when 9 per cent of the London firm was owned by the former mineworker leader and main author of the country's 1996 constitution, Cyril Ramaphosa (who became Zuma's Deputy President in 2014 and so disinvested); De Beers with its $2.8 billion in diamonds mis-invoicing over seven years; and profit diversions from several African countries to the hot money centre of Mauritius by the continent's largest cell phone company, MTN (under then chairman of the board Ramaphosa). In 2016, the 'Panama Papers' revealed how infamous corporate cowboys set up profit hideouts in Mauritius and similar sites, including the president's nephew Khulubuse Zuma and 1700 other South Africans.[16]

Such 'economic crime' is common, laments the Johannesburg NGO Corruption Watch: 'Two years ago PricewaterhouseCoopers revealed in their 2014 Global Economic Crime Survey that 69 per cent of [SA] respondents indicate they had experienced some form of economic crime in the 24 months preceding the survey.' In its 2016 Survey, PwC once again recorded a world-leading 69 per cent corporate corruption rate for South Africa, compared to a global average for economic crime of 36 per cent. According to the firm's forensic services chief Louis Strydom, 'We are faced with the stark reality that economic crime is at a pandemic level in South

Africa'.[17] The authorities' inability to uncover such crime, prosecute it and put criminals into jail is no secret. More than two thirds of PwC's 232 South African respondents believe Pretoria lacks the regulatory will or capacity to halt the top financial criminals.

Extraordinary profits are outsourced from mining but even starker damage to the society and environment is being done by the smelting industry, most obviously in the aluminium factories run by BHP Billiton. The firm was once a South African operation, Gencor (whose roots are in Harry Oppenheimer's Anglo empire but whose ownership he shifted to Afrikaners during the mid-1960s so as to ensure the Pretoria regime had an interest in mining industry profitability). Gencor was given special permission by the finance minister (who later resumed his career as chief executive of the same firm) to externalize a vast share of its capital in 1993 so as to purchase Shell Oil's Billiton minerals division, which merged with Broken Hill Properties in Melbourne to become the world's largest mining house by the early 2000s. Its South Africa profits were artificially augmented by deals its leadership made with Eskom and the Treasury to supply electricity – sometimes as much as 8 per cent of the grid – at \$0.01/kWh, the world's cheapest for most of the 1990s-2000s. Yet BHP Billiton faced overproduction of aluminium and a 50 per cent price collapse from 2011-16. Instead of increasing South African production (as were other, more desperate mining houses), it rationalized its structure and cut output. In 2013, it spun off the South African operations as part of a new firm, South32. BHP Billiton appears to be in a position to buy up much of the world's devalued mining industry and emerge from the present crisis stronger than ever.

The steel industry is also suffering extreme overproduction tendencies, also emanating from South Africa's BRICS 'partner', China. In spite of an early 2016 commitment to cut back capacity, Chinese capitalists were overproducing steel at an unprecedented rate: more than a billion tonnes/year at a time when world overcapacity was already 550 million tonnes in 2016.[18] The three South African victims were also BRICS country investors: Lakshmi Mittal (the Indian owner of Arecelor Mittal), Tata Steel (from India), and Roman Abramovich (the Russian owner of Evraz Highveld). These firms simply ran the South African capital stock into the ground with very little reinvestment (even basic maintenance), as even Trade and Industry Minister Rob Davies (an SA Communist Party member) complained.[19] They priced their local output far higher than the steel they exported (as they desired a higher share of hard currency in their revenue stream). With thousands of jobs at stake, by 2015 there were more insistent calls by NUMSA for the renationalization and then protection of the steel industry. Evraz Highveld and Tata Steel went into formal bankruptcy but Abromovich repeatedly sabotaged rescue efforts, as his accountants found it more profitable to liquidate the firm. Arcelor Mittal closed the majority of its foundries, while Tata's local subsidiary desperately sought new owners in a 2016 court battle. The only relief was a 10 per cent import duty imposed in 2015 by Davies, but it was too little, too late.

The essence of the situation facing steel and other exposed capitalists is who will suffer the costs of devaluation during the shakeout of producers, financiers and other asset holders made vulnerable by overaccumulation, not to mention labourers, communities and ecologies. One of the first deep Marxist probes of the overaccumulation process, including devaluation, was by Heinrich Grossman in his (well-timed) March 1929 *Law of Accumulation and Breakdown of the Capitalist System:* 'However much devaluation of capital may devastate the individual capitalist in periods of crisis, they are a safety valve for the capitalist class as a whole. For the system devaluation of capital is a means of prolonging its life span, of defusing the dangers that threaten to explode the entire mechanism.'[20]

Resistance to devaluation is a necessity for anyone in the South African economy disadvantaged when the currency swings from R6.3/$ to R17.99/$ in just 54 months, but especially workers (and their families) who face sustained unemployment as a result of plant and mine shutdowns, nearby communities and those defending the environment that is often left degraded by failure to pay for restoration. The social potential for combining these red-green agendas through higher-scale narratives is enormous, for in 2015 the Pew Research Center's biannual survey of world opinion found that South Africans (like the world's citizens) prioritized climate change (47 per cent) and global economic instability (33 per cent) as the top two problems about which they are 'very concerned' (the world rates were 46 and 42 per cent, respectively).

Success in fusing the environmental and economic struggles would have an extraordinary teaching impact, and unify poor and working people in a manner that shakes off the traditional South African reliance upon mining and energy for employment. As a first step, waging defensive battles against devaluation successfully is a logical prerequisite for gaining the momentum and direction that would turn existing ideologies towards eco-socialism. We turn to those potential alliances next, because tensions between nationalist politicians, corporatist trade unions, confused Communists and corrupt corporations reflect the limits of the 1994 elite transition to neoliberal 'democracy'.

CORPORATE-POLITICAL ALLIANCES AND MOVEMENT MOBILIZATIONS

In any analysis of power dynamics in South Africa, it is clear that transnational corporations still determine the character of overproduction and devaluation. Aside from those moments when their own share values are demolished (most of the mining houses in 2015), these corporations are generally willing and able to transfer these costs to workers, communities, women and the environment. The state is complicit, for the largest industries and financiers have also corrupted the political integrity of a once-proud liberation movement whose main manifesto – the 1955 Freedom Charter – had called for mines, banks and monopoly capital to be nationalized. The current state's occupants are the beneficiaries of largesse from these companies, and vice versa. From the internal mass movement, the main personality who capital pursued – providing at least a billion dollars' worth of Black Economic Empowerment deals – was Ramaphosa, after he shifted from being National Union of Mineworkers leader to ANC Secretary General in 1991. Ramaphosa lost a 1994 power struggle with Mbeki to be Mandela's Deputy President, but then led the Constitution-writing exercise in 1996. That document confirmed the overarching power of property rights.[21] The ANC (and most of the SACP) leadership were willing allies for the legitimation of the largest post-apartheid corporations, illustrated by the warm tribute they paid to Harry Oppenheimer upon his death in 2000, and by the 2003 remark by Mandela upon launching the Mandela-Rhodes Foundation in Cape Town: 'I am sure that Cecil John Rhodes would have given his approval to this effort to make the South African economy of the early twenty-first century appropriate and fit for its time.'[22]

The largest firms on the Johannesburg Stock Exchange relentlessly pursued the objectives of internal sectoral restructuring and internationalization with ANC assistance. Their role as all-encompassing corporate conglomerates quickly evolved, for in the mid-1990s the big mining houses and financial institutions shed most non-core businesses so as to attract foreign investment. Indeed their denationalization was completed by the early 2000s, as the largest apartheid-era firms – Anglo, De Beers, BHP Billiton, the Old Mutual and Liberty Life insurers, SA Breweries, Didata IT, Investec Bank, Mondi Paper and others – shifted their primary stock market listing to London and Melbourne. The ongoing importance of racial power relations within the largest corporations was illustrated tragically in August 2012 when the Lonmin mining firm's co-owner Ramaphosa sent emails to the minister of police demanding a 'pointed response' to a wildcat platinum mineworker strike at the Marikana mine, resulting in a massacre of 34 workers the following day.[23]

After the commodity super-cycle peaked in 2011, the subsequent crash left major investments in mining exposed not only to declining Chinese demand and the financial whims of London stockbrokers, but to workers who began to win higher wages as well as expensive class action lawsuits for long-suppressed occupational health and safety (e.g. a huge silicosis settlement in 2015). The corporations' extreme contributions to ecological degradation also became more expensive to remediate, for acid mine drainage caused by mining-related pollution began to be understood as a profound threat to Johannesburg's water table. A new set of corporate liabilities emerged to raise state funds for pumping and cleaning the water. Polluted air was another source of protests, law suits and legislation that threatened corporate profits. Community activism against polluters was becoming much more evident in high-profile sites such as the South Durban petrochemical complex, the Vaal River's steel complex, the Wild Coast's Xolobeni titanium mining zone (site of a high-profile community leader's assassination in March 2016), the Somkhele/Fuleni coal mining and conservation area of KwaZulu-Natal, and a half-dozen other mining sites.

Yet simultaneously, the state has made environmental protection a much lower regulatory priority. The Infrastructure Development Act of 2014 downgrades Environmental Impact Assessments so as to fast-track megaprojects. In 2015, new Minimal Emissions Standards began to apply to 119 firms – including the toxic operations of Eskom, Sasol, AngloPlats, PPC cement, Shell, Chevron and Engen oil refinery – whose more than 1,000 pollution point sources are subject to the Air Quality Act. One of these (Sasol in Secunda, which squeezes oil from coal and gas) is the single largest point source of CO_2 emissions on earth. A decade before, as the air quality legislation was prepared, these firms should have begun the process of lowering emissions. Just as the law was about to take effect, Environment Minister Edna Molewa let 37 of them (mostly the largest) off the hook for another five years by granting exemptions at just the point the state could have benefited from fines for the purpose of raising clean-up funds and reparations payments.

Moreover, the continual heightening of the most extreme forms of extractivism amplified many of the highest-profile workplace conflicts. As platinum prices fell precipitously in 2014, for example, AMCU called a massive strike of most of the sector's workers: 80,000 were out for five months, followed immediately by NUMSA's five-week strike in the metals sector. Both strikes were judged successful thanks to the power of these institutions to withstand pressure from capital and the state, even if their lost wages will not be readily recovered notwithstanding the substantial wage percentage increases won. In 2015-16, precedent-setting silicosis-damage victories by labour lawyers against Anglo and other mining houses had a similar impact on profits, at a time international investors no longer had any appetite for the extractive industries. Hence Lonmin's 2015 efforts to fund a $400 million capital injection were barely successful, and only because the South African state's pension fund guaranteed the purchase of the largest share of the firm's offering: once again, a form of devaluation, this one born by older working-class civil servants.

The need to oppose this degree of brazen corporate-state interlocking power, by linking activists across various sectors of struggle, became clear once Eskom began to regularly cut its supply mainly to consumers and small firms. Starting in late 2014, Eskom threatened near-daily 'load-shedding' (i.e., black-outs generally lasting two hours), predicting the situation would prevail for years to come due to insufficient power generation capacity (only 30,000 MegaWatts when 43,000 are technically available, due to constant maintenance crises). But at the time, the mining corporations retained their access to electricity, symbolized in 2014 when Mike Rossouw, a former executive of the world's largest commodity trading firm, GlencoreXstrata, was seconded into Eskom to represent mining interests. For many years Rossouw served as chair of the Energy Intensive Users' Group (EIUG), the lobby group of the nearly three dozen largest mining and smelting firms which together consume 44 per cent of the country's electricity supply.[24]

South Africa's load-shedding phenomenon had begun in earnest in 2006 and could mainly be blamed on excess demand from EIUG mining and smelting firms at the height of the commodity super-cycle. This is not an unusual configuration in 'resource-cursed' Africa, where vast amounts of electricity are delivered via high-tension cables to multinational corporate mining houses for the sake of extraction and capital-intensive smelting. Meanwhile, below those wires, most African women slave over fires to cook and heat households: their main energy source is a fragile woodlot, their transmission system is their back, and their energy consumption is often done while coughing thanks to dense particulates in the air. The transition from HIV-positive status to full-blown AIDS is just one opportunistic respiratory infection away, again with gendered implications for care-giving.[25]

The South African low-income household's fight for electricity access will require confronting the EIUG's prodigious power, as witnessed in the November 2014 load-shed crisis caused by the collapse of a coal silo at Eskom's Majuba operation, a Stage 1 System Emergency. At that point, 'National Load Shedding was implemented affecting municipal customers and Eskom residential customers,' according to the EIUG, *but not its own members*. It was 10 days later that, finally, EIUG arranged electricity-demand 'curtailment from Key Industrial Customers to assist Eskom in meeting demand requirements over the peak'.[26] Likewise in February 2008, as an early round of load-shedding crippled the economy, the chair of Standard Bank, Derek Cooper, suggested offhandedly to Mbeki at a private crisis meeting that BHP Billiton's Richard Bay smelter supply be temporarily cut since it provided just 1,500 jobs and less than 0.5 per cent of GDP, but Mbeki did not muster the courage to take his advice.[27]

In this context of such terribly adverse power relations, it is vital for every opponent of corporate privilege to link their issues and present a united front. For example, a Cape Town-based 'Million Climate Jobs' campaign already suggests how turning off the vast flow of electricity to South Africa's smelters and mines would, in turn, help redirect employment there to more constructive, post-carbon activities: jobs in renewable energy, public transport, insulation retrofitting, digging biogas digesters and many others. As for communities, a class/race analysis of electricity access is expressed readily when some of the more advanced groups show visitors their own dirty household energy (paraffin, wood or coal), often in the immediate vicinity of a massive mine, smelter or power-plant.[28]

The terrain for connecting dots between the environment-labour-community-feminist sites of struggle has been fertile, especially in the provinces – Limpopo, Mpumalanga and KwaZulu-Natal – attracting the most militant and sophisticated attacks on Big Coal anywhere in Africa. They are carried out by a myriad of community and environmental groups, including Mining Affected Communities United in Action, the Green Revolutionary Council, Bench Marks Foundation (a progressive church-based research/advocacy network), radical NGOs groundWork and Earthlife (the latter hosts a branch of the International Coal Campaign), the Centre for Environmental Rights and Legal Resources Centre when lawyers are needed, the local ActionAid branch (also providing funding assistance), and women's resistance organizations (supported by Women in Mining, WoMin).

What precedents of struggle can they turn to, what principles of 'commoning' resources apply, and what experience do activists have in jumping from body-scale politics – where so much environmental racism is directly visited upon the working class – to national policy? How will these serve as the building blocks for a more widespread eco-socialist practice? And finally, in what ways are discussions now underway about a forthcoming Workers Party conducive to fusing these fragments of eco-social resistance, given the predominance of 'Marxist-Leninist' philosophy and Third Internationalist ('two stage') strategies born by NUMSA and other key unions? The final two sections of this essay consider a few case studies and the broader ideological problems on the horizon.

CONTINGENCIES AND CASES OF ECOLOGICAL ANTI-CAPITALISM

Naomi Klein's *This Changes Everything* names capital as the major threat to future human existence because of its relatively unhindered rush to emit greenhouse gases.[29] Klein asks whether, because capitalism profits from climate change, *if we want to solve the latter, must we not also transcend the former?* Although she may be insufficiently explicit about the socialist alternative, her answer is in the affirmative. A South African parallel is instructive, for a great many left scholars and revolutionary activists made a well-meaning mistake with a similar framing of capitalist's extra-economic functional needs during the 1960s-80s, the last period in which explicitly (neo-)Marxist political economic analysis really flourished. Because capitalism profited from apartheid, they asked: if we want to rid the state and society of legally structured racism, *must we also end capitalism*? The independent left answered affirmatively, in part because scholars and activists alike were impressed by the rapid emergence of trade unionists after the Durban dock strikes of 1973 followed by many other manifestations of radical anti-apartheid opposition, often with socialist phraseology.[30]

It thus surprised many when in 1985 the leading bloc within white English-speaking big business began shedding the apartheid shell, paving the way to the replacement of race discrimination with more intensive class exploitation after 1994. In other words, what had seemed to be a theoretically-informed *necessity* of political economy in South Africa was in reality a contingency of politics, one strongly mediated by the class alliances described above. Some leading Marxists reacted to this change by replacing the terms 'apartheid capitalism' with 'racial Fordism,' attempting in the process to introduce 'progressive competitivism' and other post-Fordist visions of reintegrating successfully into the world economy. The distinction between necessity and contingency is, thus, the critical problem for analysts of extra-economic features of capitalism, especially in such a resource-extractive site of accumulation. It represents the danger in positing an inexorable logic of eco-socialism as the next stage of the South African revolt.

But eco-socialist potentials in South Africa need not rely upon overtly functionalist readings of contemporary political ecology. There are much more nuanced ways of contemplating a trajectory towards eco-socialism, starting with real-world experiences that include activist mobilizations for free AIDS medicines, struggles over water decommodification and labour's compensation for workplace environmental injustices. These cases offer indicators of the sensibilities needed to continue advancing the next set of South African revolts, and direct them into eco-socialist opportunities associated with the devaluation of over-accumulated mining and smelting capital.

In the first instance, the 1998 establishment of the Treatment Action Campaign (TAC) by several ex-Trotskyists, notably Zackie Achmat, gave five million HIV-positive South Africans – then a tenth of the population – able representation, even if TAC activists numbered only a few thousand at peak. TAC soon allied with the US group ACT-UP (AIDS Coalition to Unleash Power) to pressure the Bill Clinton administration to drop the so-called 'full-court press' that the US State Department had put on South African Minister of Health Nkosazana Dlamini-Zuma to withdraw the 1997 Medicines Act. That law allowed generic medicines to replace expensive branded imports, at a time when the cost of Anti-Retroviral (ARV) treatment was $15,000/year, far beyond the reach of low-income Africans.[31]

TAC increased pressure on Mbeki – in the streets and courts – by targeting the Pretoria administration's 'AIDS-denialist' tendencies, and in 2001 won a Constitutional Court case judgment forcing the provision of ARVs to pregnant women so as to halt the disease's transmission to infants. By 2004, TAC's advocacy work – including hundreds of daily arrests during one push – forced the ANC leadership to renounce Mbeki's AIDS policies, which were regularly termed 'genocidal' by that stage. Generic ARV production began soon thereafter. By 2016, more than 3.8 million South Africans were getting free ARV treatment, and the country's life expectancy had soared from 52 in 2004 to 62 a decade later. By 2016, activist control of the ARV decommodification process was by no means complete and satisfactory, as shortages and uneven treatment at clinics remained sources of conflict between TAC and the state. But TAC moved into a more collaborative relationship with the state – albeit a partnership suffused with regular protest – in order to watchdog policy, provide administrative support in AIDS treatment and maintain lobbying power. One exceptional step that resulted from the victory was the transformation of society's stigmatization of AIDS into social solidarity with TAC activists, even against Mbeki (indeed, AIDS denialism was probably one of main delegitimizing forces that led to Mbeki's 2007-2008 political downfall). The biopolitics that destratified, decommodified and 'commoned' AIDS medicines proved to South Africans that the struggle for post-apartheid liberation would entail a battle with the outmoded forces within transnational corporate capital and its allies, within the South African state, and within social consciousness.[32]

Water and electricity also offer prefigurative examples of eco-socialist potentials, at least in providing lessons for community organizing, decommodification, community control and the limits to constitutional 'socio-economic rights'. During the 1990s, sustained efforts were made by neoliberal South African state and parastatal water administrators (both apartheid and post-apartheid) together with the main French and British water privatizers (especially Veolia, Suez and Thames) to establish public-private partnerships in major cities, including Johannesburg. The continent's main industrial hub was an especially difficult site for water commodification because Johannesburg's new bulk water supply – several Lesotho mega-dams – were being built at a cost five times (per unit of water delivered) higher than prior bulk water supplies.[33]

The soaring water cost was one of the factors that spurred the resentment that led to community organizing in various Johannesburg-area townships (as well as in many other South African locales), eventually leading to the 2000 launch of the regional Anti-Privatization Forum (APF) of leftist civic groups. Boasting a constitution committing the APF to promoting socialism, the group's protests intensified against 'service delivery' shortcomings. As these became more intense in the run-up to the country's December 2000 municipal elections, Water Minister Ronnie Kasrils (a committed Communist who eventually left the ANC due to its 'Faustian pacts' with big capital) insisted that state policy should include a 'Free Basic Water' component, as had been mandated in the first democratic election campaign six years earlier. However, Johannesburg municipal water management contracts with Suez were signed before this took effect. As prepayment meters and price hikes were imposed in Soweto, activists – mainly in the Soweto Electricity Crisis Committee led by Trevor Ngwane – began to politicize the illegal reconnection of water and electricity, with their rapidly-trained plumbers and electricians serving the cause for free. They also hired lawyers to oppose pre-payment water meters and they demanded a doubling of Kasrils' free service of 25 litres per person per day.[34]

The Sowetans' street battles included scores of protests and an 'arms race' in terms of the technology of metering (e.g. Eskom replacing plastic meter boxes with tight-welded metal so as to add the element of electrocution risk). They also embarked on a legal strategy that finally appeared successful when in 2008 both the High Court and Supreme Court ruled in favour of the activists against the Johannesburg City Council. But in 2009, on appeal the Constitutional Court rejected these rulings and authorized the city to continue with existing policies; those advocating the Constitution's rights to water and to a clean environment had hit the ceiling of what a capitalist state would permit. The unintended consequence was even greater activist recourse to illegal connections; Eskom has conceded that 80 per cent of its Soweto electricity customers are not paying.[35] Ubiquitous advertisements proclaim that community activists are 'inzinyoka' (snakes) but this had little impact in the communities which mainly viewed redistribution of electricity and water as a form of commoning, As articulated in a NUMSA-hosted national electricity strategy meeting in 2015, commoning entailed both redistributive and community control objectives. By 2016, the widespread theft of services was celebrated by the Economic Freedom Fighters leader Julius Malema in his municipal election campaign.[36]

Activists called disconnected meter boxes 'statues', simply for show. To be sure, electrocutions when children stumbled on live wires and the degradation of water systems resulted from the illegal connections in many parts of the country, but the Sowetans in Ngwane's network were given training on insulation, laying electrical wires safely and rejoining water piping.[37] But from this case, a clear eco-socialist lesson is that once a form of dual power is won in communities, it behoves a movement to jump scale and consider how to achieve metropolitan-wide (and national) redistribution. That could entail higher-level service standards and a larger free lifeline tariff amount, and could allow environmentally sound and socially humane management of resources at both bulk supply and household consumption level. For example, imposing much higher prices not on poor households (the neoliberal approach) but instead on destructive, extractive corporations – which are the main consumers of electricity and water in many locales – as well as on rich people, could limit overconsumption. That in turn would slow the construction of further environmentally destructive dams as well as coal-fired electricity generators. The difference between the eco-socialist perspective and one that instead celebrates autonomist-style commoning without wielding state power is evident here, and in practice was one of the activist splits that Ngwane attributes to the APF's eventual demise, since his allies' eco-socialist visions were not universal.[38]

The third case of interest made headlines in 2016: the struggle against occupational hazards, specifically silicosis from asbestos, which has been suffered by hundreds of thousands of mineworkers since the late nineteenth century. The legal victory in gaining class-action tort rights was hard-won, reflected courageous lawyering, and is hence less explicitly eco-socialist in potential. But like AIDS medicines, it also explicitly highlights the personal biopolitical interests of workers against capital, as mainly black mineworkers bore on their bodies the ecological harm of gold mining, just as the areas they worked and lived in were despoiled by water, air and land pollution.

State regulators have been in the mining houses' pockets, before and after 1994, yet it took until 2012, after new class-actions were opened within hostile courtrooms, for 17,000 living mineworkers to be put in a position to obtain an out-of-court settlement that could yield tens of millions of dollars in compensation. As the workers' primary lawyer, Richard Spoor, put it as victory emerged in mid-2016, 'Corporations are soulless entities that do what is in the best interest of their shareholders. To appeal to them to do the right thing is futile.'[39] The case is a reflection of the ineffectiveness of the main mining unions, as well as the limits of the Corporate Social Responsibility paradigm – which relies upon voluntary compliance – that had appealed to so many South African trade unions, NGOs, environmentalists and communities in high-pollution sites. With South Africa's state mining and environmental agencies showing all the symptoms of the classic 'captive regulator', the use of the courts, in at least this instance, highlights the need to consider all options to prevent free externalities, such as the dreadful death by suffocation of so many mineworkers who gave the ruling class so much of its wealth. The same principle goes for the environmental liabilities these firms seek to avoid, for example by renaming and reregistering mining firms in different jurisdictions, and selling near-exhausted mines to Black Economic Empowerment elites (like Ramaphosa) who then use their political clout to avoid paying for ecological damage.

What all this shows is the potential for undermining South African capitalist political ecology through social organizing, starting with some important local victories, but which had national-scale impact. As Greg Albo explained in a powerful critique of eco-localism, 'the "liberated" ecological and political spaces can only be defended to the extent that the scale and scope of capitalist market activities are reduced and the scale and scope of democracy is extended'.[40] Is there an ideological orientation that can take these insights from the case studies forward to a higher structural scale?

PREFIGURATIVE ECO-SOCIALISM

Eco-socialist allies of the social, community and labour movements have expressed both hopes and reservations about the translation of examples such as these – and myriad other environmental justice struggles – into a full-fledged eco-socialist ideology. The 2008 launch of the Democratic Left Front (DLF) was one opportunity to link independents under the rubric of eco-socialism, and led many of its activists into the anti-extractivism that Latin Americans were establishing as part of the 'Buen Vivir' framework. The DLF ultimately faded in importance as its cadres were integrated into the United Front, a larger progressive network convened by NUMSA, in 2014. Although NUMSA did not provide sufficient resources to sustain the work, and although its own rank-and-file were mainly absent from building the Front, the union's current advancement of a 'Movement for Socialism' relies on the idea that promoting grassroots campaigning is the sine qua non to establish the terrain which its (self-described) 'Marxist-Leninist' vanguard can operate within.[41] This is directly connected with NUMSA's break in the last year from the SACP's Third-Internationalist-era communist-nationalist traditions by taking on the ANC from the left; NUMSA's leaders often claim that they alone maintain the integrity of those traditions, given how far the official Communist Party has slipped into defending nationalism.[42]

Unlike many earlier-generation socialist activists who located themselves deep in the trade union movement, today's generation finds different campaigns attractive. Alternative Information and Development Centre political economist Dick Forslund suggests eco-socialist potential in organizing to support 'subsistence farming in many areas that are now contested by the mining corporations, unleashing many struggles for the land'. He points to one such area of intense contestation (Xolobeni on the Wild Coast of the Eastern Cape where a local anti-mining leader Bazooka Rhadebe was assassinated in 2016), arguing that, given the collectivized land ownership and pre-capitalist social relations in such sites, politics should emerge 'in the way the land users want it, taking the parts of "modernity" that are not destructive and unsustainable into "the communal mode of production". Eco-socialism can put food security at its centre.'[43] Indeed, an independent-left food sovereignty campaign emerged (with strong residual influence by DLF cadres) in part because of the difficult conditions in the ex-homelands, as well as food price inflation. One of the main intellectual influences in this movement is Vishwas Satgar, formerly the secretary of the SA Communist Party in greater Johannesburg, prior to a purge that left traditionalists in charge, and also a professor of international political economy at Johannesburg's main university. According to Satgar, 'The ANC state has surrendered to market-centred green neoliberalism and the logic of ecocide ... It has shown itself incapable of leading transformative just transition. Instead, this has to be led from below by forces such as the United Front, the emerging Food Sovereignty Alliance, the Solidarity Economy Movement, community-mining networks and rural movements.'[44]

Satgar's colleague, Jacklyn Cock, has been most persuasive in repeatedly showing how 'new coalitions and forms of co-operation between both labour and environmental activists contain the promise of a new kind of socialism that is ethical, ecological and democratic'. For Cock that would entail,

... collective, democratic control of production for social needs, rather than profit; the mass roll out of socially-owned renewable energy could mean decentralized energy with much greater potential for community control; the localisation of food production in the shift from carbon-intensive industrial agriculture to food sovereignty; new relations between men and women and the sharing of resources in more collective social forms.[45]

An example of the ideological innovations emerging to this end within social movements is the Womin eco-feminist network's critique of the Paris climate summit in late 2015, amongst the loudest critics amidst the protestors of the pro-corporate, Washington-designed deal. In their statement, they were not exaggerating in claiming a privileged space for feminist mutual aid systems in the struggle against corporate capitalism, because these are the same tasks in social reproduction they carried out more than a century before apartheid fell, as migrant labour systems became generalized:

African women, alongside our working-class, indigenous, peasant and black sisters in other parts of the world, offer the most revolutionary alternatives to this deeply destructive model of development. These alternatives are found in the ways African women produce food, conserve and steward natural resources, and take care of our families and communities. Ours are the *living* alternatives to be recognised, built on and supported.[46]

Together, these ideological and practical prefigurations represent a reflection of how South Africans are tackling what Albo observes to be 'the most immediate and daunting challenge for renewing eco-socialist alliances and political organization'. On the one hand, 'Class and ecological struggles against capitalism depend upon campaigns won in families, workplaces, neighbourhoods and communities, all of which are located within particular environments'. On the other, the organizers must ensure that 'everyday acts of resistance in daily life connect with one another through time, so that they can become the building blocks in the process of collectively helping to envisage and build an organizational alternative. This is most basic element of socialist and ecological renewal.'[47]

In South Africa it is already evident that the process of left organizational regroupment will rely upon local resistances to the daily indignities and life-threatening attacks by capital, such as those noted above at the scales of the health-impaired body and the household needing basic water and electricity supplies. But jumping scale to the national level, the period immediately ahead is also vital for South African workers – who are judged by the World Economic Forum as the world's most militant from 2012-16 – to transcend defensive measures when warding off extreme devaluation of overaccumulated capital (such as in the mining and smelting sectors). The left-Keynesian macroeconomic arguments noted above offer one framing that can help jump scale to national policy. But as socialists, the main advocates of a different macroeconomic approach are the NUMSA militants who implicitly understand the 'non-reformist reforms' of Andre Gorz. That means ensuring that small victories won today (e.g. a 10 per cent import tariff on Chinese steel in 2015 demanded and won by NUMSA) can build working-class confidence and work against the logic of the existing system. Those reforms may appear protectionist or based on outmoded loose-money theory when considered in surface appearance, but they are not the endpoint of the macroeconomic debate.

Tomorrow's opportunities can be grasped only through the ever-closer interaction of environmental and social justice activists with a soon-to-be-formed radical labour federation (announced in May 2016 with NUMSA and AMCU as the leading forces, and the well-known socialist Zwelinzima Vavi as the likely general secretary). It is only through broader-ranging fronts and coalitions that an *anti-capitalist* 'just transition' will be envisaged and implemented. And that transition will only occur if there is a massive shift in state subsidies towards major public works – community-oriented, worker self-managed, socially-controlled – aimed at the kinds of changes to 'everything' required: energy, transport, rural land use, urbanization, production, consumption and disposal. Invoking climate change as a link issue will be critical for an eco-socialist transition, in part because in the period leading up to the current left regroupment, many activists suffered from a tendency towards localism. They celebrated momentary insurgencies, sometimes as 'the uprising of the poor' – although these were often, more soberly, 'popcorn protests' which while briefly up in the air could be blown by right-wing winds into dangerously xenophobic territory. Another scourge was single-issue civil society campaigning – which even TAC was accused of, at least until the 2008 xenophobia attacks when the group broadened its mandate. These problems will continue to beggar left politics long into the future, so long as activists do not develop unifying campaigns, much less a unifying ideology.

Perhaps the activists will determine that the only route through to such campaigning and ideological clarity is what has been termed eco-socialism (although in South Africa it is just as likely to benefit from different, organic phraseology). As the metabolism of capital-labour-society-environment becomes more exploitative, as overaccumulated mining and smelting capital continues to devalue in ever more destructive ways, and as climate change implications become ever more obvious, the main question is whether the route forward will be blocked by the narrowness of ideology-free localist and sectoral-based activism. Or whether, in considering prior working-class victories that empowered their very bodies, the next generation of radicals turns to the eco-socialist themes so essential to our broader prospects for survival.

NOTES

1 The book-length political economy literature includes Patrick Bond, *Elite Transition: From Apartheid to Neoliberalism in South Africa*, London: Pluto Press, 2014; William Gumede, *Thabo Mbeki and the Battle for the Soul of the ANC*, London: Zed Books, 2005; Gillian Hart, *Rethinking the South African Crisis*, Pietermaritzburg: University of KwaZulu-Natal Press, 2013; Hein Marais, *South Africa: Limits to Change*, London: Zed Books, 1998; and Sampie Terreblanche, *Lost in Transformation*, Johannesburg: KMM Review Publishing, 2012.
2 Frantz Fanon, *The Wretched of the Earth*, Boston: Grove Press, 1963.
3 Patrick Bond, 'Debt, Uneven Development and Capitalist Crisis in South Africa: From Moody's Macroeconomic Monitoring to Marikana Microfinance Mashonisas', *Third World Quarterly*, 34(4), 2013.
4 Cited in Patrick Bond, 'Contradictions in Consumer Credit: Innovations in South African Super-Exploitation', *Critical Arts*, 29(2), 2015.
5 South African Reserve Bank, *Quarterly Bulletin*, Pretoria, June 2016.
6 Rob Rose and Marc Hasenfuss, 'Hot Stocks 2016', *Financial Mail*, 14 January 2016; Thomas Biesheuvel and Kevin Crowley, 'Anglo beats Glencore in Bad Performance', *Business Report*, 10 December 2015.
7 The ratio is about two to one, in the same range of 20 to 50 per cent of local profit retention characterising the other BRICS countries: Brazil, Russia, India and China. South African Reserve Bank, *Quarterly Bulletin*, Pretoria, September 2015.
8 Gwede Mantashe, 'Rising Inequailty May Destroy Us', *The Star*, 7 August 2015.
9 Patrick Cairns, 'How to Invest in Funds Offshore', *Moneyweb*, 17 July 2015.
10 Anton Rupert, 'We All Have A Job To Do To Make SA Work', *Leader*, 31 October 2008.
11 FTSE, FTSE/JSE All-Share Index, London, 30 June 2016.
12 South African Reserve Bank, *Quarterly Bulletin*, Pretoria, June 2016. This trend isn't peculiar to South Africa, for according to the United Nations, in 2011 $224 billion in Foreign Direct Investments were sunk in the extractive industries, and in 2015 just $66 billion. United Nations Conference on Trade and Development, *World Investment Report*, Geneva, 2016.
13 *The Economist*, Financial Indicators, 30 June 2016.
14 Dev Kar and Joseph Spanjers, *Illicit Financial Flows from Developing Countries: 2004-2013*, Washington, DC: Global Financial Integrity, December 2015.
15 Lee Mwiti, '$80 billion, not $50 billion: loss of African funds even worse than thought – Mbeki', *Mail & Guardian*, 27 April 2016.
16 African News Agency, 'Call for Action Against Khulubuse Zuma After #PanamaLeaks Revelation', *Mail & Guardian*, 4 April 2016; Alternative Information and Development Centre, 'Lonmin, the Marikana Massacre and the Bermuda Connection', Cape Town,

2 June 2014; Sarah Bracking and Khadija Sharife, 'Rough and Polished', Manchester: Manchester University Leverhulme Centre for the Study of Value Working Paper, 15 May 2015; Moyagabo Maake and Karl Gernetzky, 'Panama Papers Cast Spotlight on Missing Fidentia Money', *Business Day*, 5 April 2016; Craig McKune and George Turner, 'Ramaphosa and MTN's Offshore Stash', *Mail & Guardian*, 2 October 2015; Greg Nicolson, 'Platinum Strikes: The Battle Intensifies', *Daily Maverick*, 2 June 2014.

17   PricewaterhouseCoopers, *Global Economic Crime Survey 2016: Adjusting the Lens on Economic Crime*, Johannesburg, 2016.

18   Mark O'Hara, 'Will Global Overcapacity Weigh Heavy on Steel Prices?', *Market Realist*, 4 March 2016; Lingling Wei, Bob Davis and Jon Hilsenrath, 'Glut of Chinese Goods Pinches Global Economy', *Wall Street Journal*, 1 June 2015.

19   Rob Davies, 'Steel Industry Strategic for SA's Growth', *Business Report*, 31 August 2015.

20   Henryk Grossman, *The Law of Accumulation and Breakdown of the Capitalist System*, London: Pluto Press, 1992.

21   John Saul, 'On Taming a Revolution: The South African Case', in Leo Panitch, Greg Albo and Vivek Chibber, eds., *Socialist Register 2013: The Question of Strategy*, London: Merlin Press, 2012; Patrick Bond, 'Constitutionalism as a Barrier to the Resolution of Widespread Community Rebellions in South Africa', *Politikon*, 41(3), 2014.

22   South African Press Association, 'Mandela Criticises Apartheid Lawsuits', *Financial Times*, 25 August 2003.

23   John Saul and Patrick Bond, *South Africa – The Present as History*, Oxford: James Currey, 2014.

24   Patrick Bond, 'Challenges for the Climate Justice Movement: Connecting Dots, Linking Blockadia and Jumping Scale', in L. Temper and T. Gilbertson, eds., *Refocusing Resistance for Climate Justice*, Barcelona: Universitat Autònoma de Barcelona, 2015.

25   David McDonald, ed., *Electric Capitalism: Recolonising Africa on the Power Grid*, Pretoria: HSRC Press, 2008.

26   Patrick Bond, 'South Africa in the Dark', *Counterpunch*, 9 February 2015.

27   Barry Sergeant, 'A Career Limiting Move?', *MoneyWeb*, 28 March 2008.

28   Patrick Bond and Faith ka-Manzi, 'Women from KwaZulu-Natal's Mining War Zone Stand Their Ground against Big Coal', in L. Temper and T. Gilbertson, eds., *Refocusing Resistance for Climate Justice*, Barcelona: Universitat Autònoma de Barcelona, 2015. The 'Big Debate' television show regularly covers these contradictions from the activists' standpoint, e.g. in 2014, www.youtube.com/watch?v=OUNHCO-zf24

29   Naomi Klein, *This Changes Everything*, New York: Simon & Schuster, 2014.

30   Scholars did not serve the movement well in broad strategic terms of identifying what in the race-class relation was theoretically necessary and what was merely contingent. Intellectually, the country's New Left was armed first with the 'articulations of modes of production' critique provided by Harold Wolpe, spelling out the apartheid Bantustans' race-gender-ecological intersections with high-profit capital accumulation. Between then and the early 1990s, other socialists added theoretical components to a (university-based) political economy that included Poulantzasian fractions-of-capital analysis of how the apartheid state emerged, a Gramscian understanding of the organic crisis then rising, a Thompsonian social history of particularist experiences under apartheid domination, and the notion of 'racial Fordism' (and post-Fordist fantasies) inspired by French Regulation Theory. Later, 'Minerals Energy Complex' studies led to a specification of South Africa's financialization and extreme 'uneven and combined development'. For the seminal texts in these traditions, see, respectively, Harold Wolpe, 'Capitalism and Cheap Labour Power', *Economy and Society*, 1, 1972; Rob Davies, David Kaplan, Michael Morris and Dan O'Meara, 'Class Struggle and the Periodisation of the State in South Africa', *Review of African Political Economy*, 7, 1976; and for a critique see

Simon Clarke, 'Capital, Fractions of Capital and the State: "Neo-Marxist" Analysis of the South African State', *Capital & Class*, 5, 1978; John Saul and Stephen Gelb, *The Crisis in South Africa*, New York: Monthly Review Press, 1981; Charles van Onselen, *The Seed is Mine: The Life of Kas Maine, A South African Sharecroper, 1894-1985*, Cape Town: David Philip, 1996; Stephen Gelb, ed., *South Africa's Economic Crisis*, Cape Town: David Philip, 1991; Ben Fine and Zav Rustomjee, *The Political Economy of South Africa*, London: Christopher Hurst, 1996; Samantha Ashman, Ben Fine and Susan Newman, 'The Crisis in South Africa: Neoliberalism, Financialization and Uneven and Combined Development', in Leo Panitch, Greg Albo and Vivek Chibber, eds., *Socialist Register 2011: The Crisis This Time*, London: Merlin Press, 2010.

31 Offering TAC solidarity, ACT-UP's disruptive tactics against presidential candidate Al Gore defeated Big Pharma's insistence on Washington's strong-arming of Dlamini-Zuma during his mid-1999 campaigning. Activists haranguing Gore raised the nuisance costs beyond the $2.3 million that Big Pharma had donated to the Democratic Party that year, forcing Gore into a U-turn on AIDS medicines. In late 2001, the George W. Bush administration suffered a similar defeat at Doha when the World Trade Organization approved an exemption to intellectual property rights for essential medicines during pandemics. Patrick Bond, *Against Global Apartheid*, London: Zed Books, 2003.

32 Mandisa Mbali, *South African Aids Activism and Global Health Politics*, London: Palgrave Macmillan, 2013.

33 Patrick Bond, *Unsustainable South Africa*, London: Merlin Press, 2002; Trevor Ngwane, 'Sparks in the Township', *New Left Review*, 22, 2003.

34 Patrick Bond, 'Water, Health and the Commodification Debate', *Review of Radical Political Economics*, 42(3), 2010.

35 Matthew le Cordeur, 'Eskom to Waive Soweto Users' Debt – On Condition', *Fin24*, 25 May 2016.

36 National Union of Metalworkers, 'Civil Society Statement on Electricity Crisis', Johannesburg, 1 June 2015.

37 Patrick Bond, 'South Africa's Bubble Meets Boiling Urban Social Protest', *Monthly Review*, 62(?), 2010.

38 Patrick Bond, Ashwin Desai and Trevor Ngwane, 'Uneven and Combined Marxism Within South Africa's Urban Social Movements', in C. Barker, L. Cox, J. Krinsky and A. Nilsen, eds., *Marxism and Social Movements*, London: Routledge, 2013.

39 Chris Barron, 'Scales of Justice Will Weigh Gold Against Cost to Health', *Sunday Times*, 22 May 2016.

40 Greg Albo, 'The Limits Of Eco-Localism: Scale, Strategy, Socialism', in Leo Panitch and Colin Leys, eds., *Socialist Register 2007: Coming to Terms with Nature*, London: Merlin Press, 2007, p. 16.

41 Vishwas Satgar, 'Where to for South Africa's Left?', *Review of African Political Economy*, Radical Agendas #6, 27 January 2016.

42 Samantha Ashman and Nicolas Pons-Vignon, 'NUMSA, the Working Class and Socialist Politics in South Africa', in Leo Panitch, Greg Albo and Vivek Chibber, *Socialist Register 2014: Registering Class*, London: Merlin Press, 2013.

43 Dick Forslund, email communication to Patrick Bond, 15 June 2016.

44 Vishwas Satgar, 'The Climate is Ripe for Social Change', *Mail & Guardian*, 17 December 2014.

45 Jacklyn Cock, 'An Eco-Socialist Order in South Africa', *Review of African Political Economy*, Radical Agendas #5, 18 January 2016.

46 Women in Mining, 'An African Ecofeminist Perspective on the Paris Climate Negotiations', Johannesburg, 2015.

47 Albo, 'The Limits Of Eco-Localism', p. 22.

TURNING THE TIDE: REVOLUTIONARY POTENTIAL AND THE LIMITS OF BOLIVIA'S 'PROCESS OF CHANGE'

ROBERT CAVOORIS

Revolutionary energy in Latin America today seems to be at a lull. During the last 20 years, leftist heads of state Hugo Chávez, Evo Morales, and Rafael Correa have made radical-sounding pronouncements denouncing capitalism, standing up to imperialism, and capturing the imagination of the international Left with a bit of panache. But it appears that the time of such leaders is coming to a close; Cristina Fernandez Kirchner's chosen successor in Argentina, already a moderate choice, was defeated at the presidential polls at the end of 2015 by the notoriously corrupt right-wing politician Mauricio Macri, and shortly thereafter Venezuela's *Chavistas* lost their parliamentary majority while that country's economic crisis deepened. Do these electoral losses signal the end of the region's revolutionary potential?

Even before these losses, left-leaning state functionaries were reducing expectations for the region's pink tide. In 2009, Bolivian Vice President Álvaro García Linera suggested that conditions were ill-suited for any sort of socialist revolution, and that the immediate goal in Bolivia was a post-neoliberal, Andean-Amazonian capitalism 'focusing on the conquest of equality, the redistribution of wealth, and the expansion of rights'.[1] Bolivia, along with Venezuela, Ecuador, Argentina, and Brazil, can now trumpet some achievements along these lines, though whether these regimes are truly post-neoliberal is a point of debate. But have these gains come at the cost of all revolutionary vigor? And are they sustainable in light of the Left's recent electoral routs?

To answer this, we might look beyond the state, to movements, margins, and social practices offering alternatives to capitalism. Raquel Gutiérrez, participant alongside García Linera in the Bolivian group *Comuna*, a onetime forum for theoretical work on and among Bolivian social movements, approaches the issue from an angle opposite her former collaborator. She cites 'an exclusive epistemic disjunction between State-centered politics and autonomous politics'.[2] In this view, the revolutionary potential of Latin America was never encapsulated by states or charismatic leaders, and still less by their rhetoric. The possibilities for an alternative to capitalism have always been strongest at the grassroots. This distinction, says Gutiérrez, presents itself as an irreducible political choice: on the one hand, to '"occupy" public posts in order to "consolidate" what has been won' and 'change some of the most oppressive social relations', or on the other, 'to develop and expand the range of autonomy in everyday life as to propel struggles and impose limits on the capitalist devastation of life in general'.[3] She places herself squarely in the latter camp. Her formulation, however, likewise suggests reduced expectations. To enter the state and seek reform, or to seek reform at the level of everyday life? The shared moderation between two otherwise divergent figures casts doubt on the prospects for revolution. Where, if anywhere, are the possibilities for a further political and economic rupture? Have the achievements of the various left-leaning states set stage for further revolutionary breaks with the current order, or have they reached a dead end?

In the following, I examine the Bolivian case more closely in order to address these questions. Bolivia is arguably the most successful example among the Latin American countries that have made a left turn, facing neither economic crisis nor national right-wing political opposition. But even there the ruling *Movimiento al Socialismo* (MAS) faced a recent defeat when their attempts to alter the constitution and permit Morales to run for a fourth term were upset in a referendum. A deeper exploration of recent Bolivian history that outlines its objective political obstacles, as well as subjective failures and missed opportunities, will permit some observations on the issue of revolutionary viability in Latin America today, as well as the meaning and strategies of revolution more generally.

THE INHERITED CONSTRAINTS OF THE BOLIVIAN LEFT

In examining the shortcomings of the MAS government in Bolivia, we cannot be satisfied with explanations that attribute, for better or worse, the vicissitudes of the Bolivian political process to the class status, class origin, or ethnicity of state functionaries.[4] The structure of the capitalist state exceeds the subjectivity of those who work within it, and subjectivities in any case are not easily reducible to social status on an individual basis. Nor however can we be satisfied with criticisms that view the state as a rigid functionality existing independently of social relations of power within a social formation.[5] While this latter set of critics, including Gutiérrez, have raised the essential issue of autonomous movements and alternative communal practices, these social constituents must be analyzed in relation to the contingencies of a given state.

How do we understand these contingencies, then, and their relation to society? The state, in capitalism, is relatively autonomous. At a minimum, a capitalist state must create positive conditions for some stable model of accumulation; however, a state's means of doing this, and the configuration of class fractions it includes, are contingent. This autonomy, which is neither voluntarism, nor a position of uninterested mediation between classes, can only be understood vis-à-vis relationships of social power in which a state's role is articulated. Relative autonomy is not freedom, but a way of conceptualizing the contingency by which the state reproduces the stable conditions of capitalist production. This contingency lends itself, in certain moments, to the intervention and gains of popular classes.[6]

Yet the goals of the capitalist state are difficult to achieve, a fact which both conditions the positive possibilities for workers, peasants, and revolutionaries, and also places them on the edge of a void. A protest movement may spawn a left government, as in Bolivia, but the government's duration is predicated on its success at mending the gaps in the social formation that are its own conditions: economic crisis, the fear of a military coup or foreign intervention, popular insurrection, claims of secession. The government finds itself pushed toward a policy of stabilization, constrained by the balance of power on a world, regional, or local scale, as well as by the political and ideological structures in place during the period of its ascension. As Marx writes in *The Eighteenth Brumaire*, 'Men make their own history, but they do not make it as they please'. The question that presents itself, in such a case, is whether that government can create more possibilities for making history, more opportunities for popular intervention, to push beyond the limitations it has inherited.

A domestic political breakdown during 2000–2005 opened the door for the MAS's election to the executive in 2006. The epoch of insurrectionary protest arose in response to the sweeping neoliberalization of the Bolivian economy in which all major political parties had participated.[7] They had collaborated since 1985 to implement austerity policies, demobilize the working class, and privatize the country's main sources of wealth: mineral mining and hydrocarbon extraction.[8] When popular protests deposed neoliberal architect Gonzalo Sanchez de Lozada in October 2003, the political elite suffered a devastating blow – though less devastating, of course, than the 67 deaths for which his repressive reaction was responsible in the two months before his resignation.[9] Then, when even his technocratic successor,

Carlos Mesa, could not appease the masses, it became clear that only an outsider could hold the executive, and only on condition of a promise to nationalize the country's extensive gas reserves.[10] This pattern echoed a rejection of neoliberalism elsewhere in the region: in each case, the crisis of neoliberalism was a *political* crisis, the resolution of which required new parties and politicians. Be it a once-jailed military officer with a nationalist reputation like Chávez, a little-known governor like Néstor Kirchner, or even a US-educated economist like Rafael Correa, the legitimacy of these new regimes depended on their distance from the established circles of political elites. Among this wave of outsiders, the MAS had the special credibility of having actually been created by popular movements.[11]

Morales and his team faced considerable constraints once they took office. On the international level, despite a positive outlook for regional political and economic solidarity opportunities,[12] the era of privatizations had created a massive foothold for international capital in all of Bolivia's key sectors. The state-owned *Corporación Minera de Bolivia* (COMIBOL) had been all but dismantled, and the mining fraction of Bolivian capital had partnered up with transnational firms to increase foreign investment, bolstered by new laws attacking worker protections, guaranteeing international investments, and expanding foreign access to the emerging hydrocarbons sector. Alongside these privatizations were loans from the IMF and the World Bank, bearing all of the terms that one would expect.[13] Moreover, the international pressures were not only economic: no left-leaning government in Latin America can discount the possibility of a US-supported coup, as was attempted in Venezuela in 2002 and achieved in Honduras in 2009. Thus as the MAS took power, the constraints from the international arena were pitted against the political will of the movements which, over the course of five years, had decisively rejected the entire neoliberal model of accumulation and were demanding a nationalization of key industries.

The MAS, in addition to being subject to the conflict between popular power and the power of capital, faced liberal institutional and discursive confines. The introduction of political liberalism after democratization in 1982 contrasted with the extra-parliamentary pendulum of coups and street politics that prevailed from 1952 until the mid-1980s, when the defeat of the mining unions destroyed the traditional lever of working-class power.[14] The 1990s, in turn, saw a hodgepodge of seemingly isolated political actions, but there were two decisive trends: a decentralization of the electoral structure on the one hand, and the growth of an indigenous politics of recognition, heavily media- and NGO-focused, on the other. The institutional decentralization was part of the neoliberal strategy to devolve state welfare responsibilities to so-called civil society and dilute opposition to the new policies, while the state's discursive turn toward multiculturalism was an attempt to co-opt both indigenous political leaders and leftist intellectuals.[15]

This decentralization set the stage, however unintentionally, for an increase in popular organization. In particular, rural indigenous organizations flourished. The MAS itself was born as a 'political instrument' of the coca growers' unions in their movement against US-sponsored coca eradication, establishing local hegemony in the Chapare region before catapulting into the national political arena in 2002. Thus, from its inception, the MAS has been a mechanism for translating popular struggles into the electoral sphere, even as its roots harken back to Bolivia's syndicalist past. The 1990s also saw the immense growth of a number of other indigenous organizations: the *Confederación de Pueblos Indígenas de Bolivia* (CIDOB), the *Confederación Sindical Única de Trabajadores Campesinos de Bolivia* (CSUTCB), and the *Consejo Nacional de Ayllus y Markas del Qullasuyu* (CONAMAQ) each represented thousands of insurgent agricultural workers and small peasant producers. These organizations, along with the MAS, were central to the strength of the mobilization during 2000–2005, but they were not alone; urban neighborhood associations, unions, students, civic organizations, and resource collectives all played a role.[16]

The local anchoring of many of these smaller organizations, however, made a nation-wide movement difficult.[17] The MAS's decisive electoral turn, which involved a reorganization of the party in 2004, therefore resolved the key strategic issue of movement unity, but the solution carried the constraints of liberalism; it dulled the edges of indigenous struggle, which in the best of cases had brought capitalism itself into question, to focus on a more general claim to indigenous recognition, increasingly bound up with a kind of nationalism.[18] The point here is less to condemn the MAS for its electoral politics than to understand that while their electoral efforts resolved the issue of movement unification, they did so in a particular way, conditioned by the liberal political context.

POLITICS AND ECONOMICS AFTER 2006

Given these constraints, how have revolutionary hopes fared since Morales took office? Today, Bolivia's economic model centres on the extraction and export of raw materials. With definite variation, this is the trend among most of Latin America's left-leaning states. Some have sought to characterize this as a continuation, or reconstitution, of the neoliberal economic model that these governments were elected to oppose.[19] Yet while resource extraction has long defined Latin America's role in the international division of labour, the specific means by which these states now secure the conditions for accumulation are distinct from those of the neoliberal period.

Whereas neoliberal models in the 1990s relied on a more diverse set of exports – in tandem with attacks on the working class to keep wages low – Latin America today actually faces a 'reprimarization'. That is, export diversity, which increased in some instances under neoliberalism, has been reduced in favour of primary commodity exports. At the same time, while there have been only limited wage increases,[20] in certain cases exacerbated by inflation, all of the pink tide states in Latin America have institutionalized popular welfare programmes and worker subsidies – a significant departure from the austerity underpinning the investment attraction strategies of the 1990s. The expansion of healthcare, education, and direct cash transfers speaks to this redistribution in Bolivia.[21] In Argentina, conservative president Mauricio Macri has refrained from dismantling popular transfers introduced by Fernandez de Kirchner, even expanding some, indicating a right-wing hesitation to return entirely to the neoliberal status quo ante.[22] The central feature of the neo-extractive model is that these welfare programmes are directly funded by the rents on exported primary commodities, and are thus a key mechanism whereby subaltern classes are brought into the ruling coalition. In Bolivia, this has been achieved by 'nationalizing' the hydrocarbon industries, which in practice meant becoming the majority shareholder in shared production partnerships with the same foreign companies that previously dominated the sector. Thus, critics correctly highlight the continued presence of transnational capital in Bolivia's extractive industries; the state has arguably *increased* the country's economic dependence on resource extraction in partnership with these foreign companies, but has responded to its popular mandate by gaining a greater stake in the extractive surplus.[23]

At the same time, neoliberal or not, the demands of an extractive economy have created new political contradictions. As a result, the state has resorted to strategies of both repression and division – and its targets have not just been the resurgent right, but the very social movement organizations that brought the MAS to power. The famous conflict over the TIPNIS highway illustrates both of these approaches. The highway in question would be built through the *Territorio Indígena Parque Nacional Isiboro Sécure*, which is both a protected natural reserve and a legally recognized indigenous territory. In opposition to this thoroughfare, which residents argued would be environmentally and socially disruptive, some indigenous organizations led by the CIDOB began a march in August of 2011 from the city of Trinidad to the government seat of La Paz. On 25 September, the 800 marchers were intercepted in the town of San Lorenzo de Chaparina by 500 police officers, attacked with tear gas and batons, and leaders of the march were detained. Planes from the Bolivian Air Force attempted to land in Chaparina to remove the arrested. The detained were saved by the solidarity of locals who blocked the runway and prevented the planes from touching down, then freed the marchers from the buses where they were held. When the marchers finally arrived in La Paz, the increased attention had consolidated their numbers, making them 500,000 strong.[24]

This first attempt to stop the highway illustrated that while the extractive model created a contradiction between the state's developmental plans and the autonomy of indigenous peasants and workers, the latter could still depend on solidarities established during years of insurrection. Thus, when repression didn't work, the state developed a new strategy: division. Within the TIPNIS, there are both lowland indigenous groups with long histories in the area as well as more recently settled Aymara coca producers. The former often have mixed economies of subsistence agriculture, communal farming, and some market-oriented activities, while the latter are principally dependent on the coca leaf market.[25] After the government appeared to concede to the mostly lowland highway protesters in October 2011, a similar march organized by the *Consejo Indígena del Sur* (CONISUR), the main coca growers association in the TIPNIS, arrived in La Paz in order to demand, conversely, that the government build the road. On this basis, the state organized a 'consultation' of the residents of the TIPNIS, where they claimed to have found that 80 per cent of the communities consulted were in favour of the construction. In fact, according to some independent monitoring groups who sought to corroborate this claim, many communities that the government claimed to have consulted were never contacted, and of those who were, only 17 per cent came out in favour of the highway.[26] But the announcement of these 'results' was enough to sow the seeds of division among the various communities in the TIPNIS. One group of anti-highway protesters defined the MAS strategy as such: 'The interference of the government in the organic structures of indigenous peoples [serves] to divide us, using extortion, intimidation and criminalization of leaders and representative indigenous organizations.'[27]

As it stands, the highway is set to be built, but its commencement has been delayed. Whether it is ultimately constructed will be an index of the political and organizational capacity of those who oppose it. As Salazar Lohman writes: 'The consultation proposed by the government was simply a state attempt at disarticulation and disruption of regional communitarian structures and of their historic struggle, and although in this sense this was achieved by the state, the fact that until now ... the highway has not been built demonstrates that there exists a popular force that has been able to delay its construction.'[28] That is, the delay indicates that popular movements can still serve as a potential political limit to the neo-extractive orientation of the state.

The extra-parliamentary organizations, however, face increasing challenges. The Bolivian state continues to demobilize the groups that helped bring the MAS to power. The *Pacto de Unidad*, in which all the major indigenous organizations pooled their power during the 2006 Constituent Assembly, fell apart in response to the TIPNIS conflict, and MASistas in both the CIDOB and CONAMAQ have managed to split the organizations into *oficialista* factions, who support the government and receive resources from it, and *orgánica* factions who oppose the MAS's interference.[29] These splits have undermined the political potential built by these organizations during 2000–2005; rather than serving as a force to advance the struggle, they have had to continually defend their autonomy against the initiatives of the state and private enterprise, designed to attract more extractive capital. It is this political decomposition, owing in part to state strategies to rout popular opposition, that is the most demoralizing feature of the current conjuncture.

OPPORTUNITIES LOST

Comparing the MAS to the *Movimiento Nacionalista Revolucionario* (MNR), which came to power in the Bolivian national revolution of 1952, we find a paradox. As Webber suggests, the MNR went quite a bit further with its promised reforms than the MAS, yet the rhetoric of the MAS is much more radical, steeped in the language of social movements, indigenous rebellion, and popular power.[30] While the MNR had a left flank, its main line spoke mainly the language of moderate nationalism, even as it sought US cooperation. So how does a party with less revolutionary will become the more revolutionary party? It is a question of the social relations of power: the MNR depended upon armed, self-organized workers to defeat reactionary elements of the military when it took power, and until it supplanted those popular militias by resurrecting the discredited armed forces, it could ignore workers at its own peril. The military, that repressive arm of the capitalist state, was on the verge of permanent ruin – though once the MNR revived them, the armed forces quickly destroyed their reanimator. By contrast, while the insurrectionary power of 2000–2005 was organized and effective, the state power achieved through the MAS, even with extra-parliamentary backing, was only a small foothold from which to contend with a robust set of defences against any sort of break with capitalism.

Taking the rhetorical radicalism of the MAS at face value, this presents us with another problem: what might the MAS have done, once in power, to invigorate the political process, to radicalize its base, to open up an alternative path forward, outside the confines of an extraction-based welfare state? In other words, even granting all of the factors – all of the history weighing on the Bolivian situation as of 2006, and all of the international and national constraints of capital and the state – what were the possibilities for tipping the balance of power in favour of the masses? Looking back, we see a watershed involving a choice between two distinct approaches, two possible relationships between the state and the society, between constituted and constituent power.[31] The MAS could either create opportunities for mass political intervention to push the process into uncharted waters, or it could ensure its own position by seeking out new allies and building a merely ideological set of mechanisms to activate its base.

The Constituent Assembly of 2006 was a defining moment for the question of what kind of relationship the state would have with society in the post-insurrectionary period. The demand for the Assembly went back to the 1990 March for Territory and Dignity, and with the second Gas War and the abdication of Carlos Mesa in 2005, its realization was a condition for the MAS's rule. Owing perhaps to a recognition of its own insecurity with regard to the overall social relations of power, as well as to legislative opposition from other parties, the MAS accepted an assembly framework with limited opportunities for popular political participation. Even as the social movements, and in particular the indigenous social movements which formed the *Pacto de Unidad*, pledged to critically support the process, they were not actually permitted into the assembly as such – they had to stand as individuals and affiliate with a political party. And the proportional voting system, which the social movements decried, allowed an outsize minority representation for the discredited elites. Once the Assembly was in session, the movements in the *Pacto de Unidad* proposed their own set of amendments on key issues, but were effectively rebuffed by the MAS leadership.[32]

What was missed in the Constituent Assembly was a chance to open the Bolivian state to new democratic political practices, to displace the domination of liberal politics that the MAS inherited, and to create new formulas of constituted and constituent power. Indigenous communities, for instance, hoped to use their own methods of selection in order to choose their representative delegations to the legislature – that is, to participate in alternative forms of community deliberation, beyond a simple vote. They proposed a series of democratic mechanisms that may have allowed popular participation to counterbalance the weight of reaction, including immediate recall of legislators, communal assemblies, and citizen legislative initiatives. They sought to create a fourth branch of government, the 'Social Plurinational Power', which would be composed of representatives of indigenous nations and community organizations.[33] At stake in these proposals was a step toward a proletarian state. Just as Marx drew his own vision of such a state based on the practical developments of the Paris Commune, here was a set of new, if uneven, mechanisms whereby the labouring classes could secure for themselves a weapon against their enemies.

Yet these ideas were largely excised from the final constitutional proposal. Alternative forms of delegation, though recognized in the abstract by Article 11 of the constitution, were not instituted as a means for any actual elections. The idea of special Legislative Assembly representatives for indigenous territories was deferred for future parliamentary debate, and worker, peasant, and community organizations failed to achieve institutionalized representation. The masses had offered an imaginative set of democratic possibilities that would have reshaped the entire social arena. An alliance of rural and urban indigenous groups was one pole of a social antagonism manifest at the level of the state, shaping the possibilities for the MAS as it faced increasing pressure from the right in its first term; only by marshalling that popular support could the conditions have been created for a further rupture with the old order. But the MAS chose a different route.

STRATEGIC POPULISM AND THE IDEOLOGY OF DIVISION

In describing the pink tide, one is tempted to use the term *populism*, understood, following Ernesto Laclau, as the suturing together of various demands into a single identity, the 'people', that produces a concomitant reduction of the social field into two opposing camps.[34] Yet to leave things there would permit simple excuses for the democratic failures of Latin America's left-leaning states; if the social field were so simplified, we might concede that the battle for hegemony against the right is more important than the political content of the left.[35] But the real communal and popular struggles against the state belie the suggestion of both a dualistic contest, and of a subject, the 'people', capacious enough to encompass dissent from the left. Indeed, by creating the appearance of such a populist reduction, of a simplification of politics into a Manichean clash, the pink tide governments have strategically displaced political antagonisms arising from the neo-extractive model. Veronica Gago explains the relationship between economics, politics, and ideology that underlies the populist garb:

> The relationship that the *progresista* governments of the region have with their populations and with natural resources is politically complex: the equation is that the primary *commodities* are the source of financing social subsidies. The exploitation by … transnationals is thus legitimized owing to a discursive state mediation that emphasizes the function of social integration achieved on the basis of the capture of these extraordinary rents. Faced with this, the attempts from below to politicize resistance against these businesses are repeatedly infantilized, or treated as irrelevant for those outside of them who hope to disqualify their critical force. … Indeed, what is blocked in this state refusal of legitimacy for the demands arising from the mode of accumulation is exactly the dynamic of recognition that would characterize a democracy mapping its constituent practices onto the points of antagonism.[36]

In other words, the contradictions generated by the model of extractivism, wherein specific groups of workers and indigenous communities bear its negative effects, are subsumed by another apparent conflict between the state and various right-wing enemies. The state can ignore one set of political antagonisms by emphasizing another, even as it seeks out 'partnerships' with the latter set of supposed antagonists, including transnational companies and politicians from the old neoliberal parties.[37] Thus Morales and García Linera denounce all critics, left or right, as anti-Bolivian, or as imperialists, because they oppose the supposedly national-popular consensus of resource extraction and surplus redistribution – but the object of the critics is precisely the influence of the national and international right in the 'process of change'.[38] A populist political logic is certainly at play here, but it is a shock absorber for a more complex set of political conflicts. Real social antagonisms run up against rhetorical oppositions.

To ground this strategic populism, the MAS skillfully wields liberal mechanisms and plays on their limitations in order to reduce political choices and transfer them to terrain where they can win. Nancy Postero highlights a tension between liberalism and what she calls a 'post-liberal' emphasis on constituent power in the governing style of the MAS. According to her, the MAS's strategy is 'the latest attempt to make liberalism overcome its limitations, by deepening the promise of democratic participation'.[39] But today this generous interpretation cannot be sustained.

In fact, the approach of the MAS is as much about limiting constituent power as about invoking it. The entire strategy is reflected in the tactic of the popular referendum pioneered by Hugo Chávez, and employed skillfully by Correa and Morales. In 2008 Morales proposed a recall referendum when the MAS was feuding with the right-wing landholding class over the finalization of the new constitution. Morales handily won his recall, and several of the opposition's governors were ousted. Salazar points out that the effect of this was to give Morales the support necessary for completing the new constitution without bringing the masses into the street again, except in order to vote, since the indigenous organizations would likely have mobilized to demand their own constitutional proposals if they had been called to defend the Assembly.[40] Through the referendum, the choice was reframed: either the MAS-supported constitution, or the intransigence of the right. Such tactics bolster liberal democratic legitimacy while also alluding to constituent power; but indeed it is only an allusion, providing no space for autonomous popular activity. The continuous electoral consolidation of the MAS – though it has recently suffered its first defeat in a vote on abolishing presidential term limits – is therefore neither an unproblematic reflection of the general will, nor, conversely, a case of some supposed false consciousness. The 'people' have not been duped, as an elitist trope would have it; but we must recall that the 'people' is always the reductive representation of a heterogeneous multitude, brandished in this case against those on the left as well as those on the right.[41]

Another feature of the MAS strategy of consolidation is nationalism. This theme did not originate with the MAS, of course. Even in the original insurrections of the early 2000s, nationalism played a central role. The Gas Wars were stoked by the idea that Bolivian gas would be going through Chile, an old rival according to some popular narratives of Bolivian history, and going to the US, the object of nationalist ire throughout Latin America for obvious reasons. For the MAS, this nationalist element of the insurrection has not been a problem so much as a solution – a solution for those whose task, as soon as the executive was taken, was to make Bolivia governable again. The MAS, in order to survive, needed to overcome the challenges I have already mentioned: a fragmented elite with bastions of power in regional governments, economic dependence on foreign-dominated extractive industries, a set of neoliberal cultural policies, and, of course, an organized popular insurrection from whence the MAS came. In such a context, nationalism has provided a specific way of configuring state power to overcome concrete issues presented by continuing class conflict. As Étienne Balibar argues, the nation form itself is always an ongoing 'process of reproduction, of permanent *re-establishment* of the nation':

> In order completely to identify the reasons for the relative stability of the national formation, it is not sufficient, then, merely to refer to the

initial threshold of its emergence. We must also ask how the problems of unequal development of town and countryside, colonization and decolonization, wars and the revolutions which they have sometimes sparked off, the constitution of supranational blocs and so on have in practice been surmounted, since these are all events and processes which involved at least a risk of class conflicts drifting beyond the limits within which they had more or less easily confined by the 'consensus' of the nation state.

The state effort toward building the nation, through policy and discourse, is ever renewed to address instability in processes of capital accumulation. The irony in this case is that the MAS is itself a manifestation of class struggle from below that challenged the white-mestizo conception of the Bolivian nation, posing itself as an alternative 'dominated nationalism', but now calling on nationalism to confine class struggle through a new consensus.[42]

As Kohl and Farthing argue, the articulation of nationalist and anti-imperialist sentiments with demands around natural resources in Bolivia has been a powerful basis for social mobilization since 1952.[43] The specific innovation of the MAS has been to employ what Silvia Rivera calls 'strategic ethnicity' claims to refigure Bolivian nationalism in accordance with resurgent indigenous politics. The MAS's claim to what she calls an 'authoritarian and idealist conception of the Nation ... that would be in the process of consolidating itself as a primordial identity' stands in contrast to ambiguous language of 'plurinationalism' which is enshrined in the constitution, yet the MAS has been able to invoke both ideas. Rivera argues that this is possible because of the prominence of 1990s neoliberal identitarian politics: 'The state has made use of that strategic ethnicity precisely because the latter was constructed in the cultural sphere of neoliberal reforms.' For instance, Morales's electoral slogan '*Soberanía y dignidad*', combines a classic watchword of the nationalist movement, sovereignty, with one of the 1990s indigenous movement, dignity. With an appeal to indigeneity as identity, or as a set of values, instead of as a concrete set of political and social circumstances, the government can recognize the many indigenous communities as part of the Bolivian nation, disregarding the real conflicts that some of these communities have with state-supported national development projects. The underlying strategy here, which manifests itself likewise at the grassroots level of political discourse, is that of 'marking indigeneity as national and the Bolivian nation as indigenous'.[44]

Naturally, invocations of the indigenized Bolivian nation were important for fending off the secessionist challenge from the right in 2008. But they have likewise been used against those who protest the TIPNIS highway, against independent research organizations, against social media, against MAS dissidents, and against anyone else who opposes the plans of the state from the left.

STATE, REVOLUTION, TRANSFORMATION

If the right appears resurgent today throughout Latin America, this is in part because of the ambivalent positions of the state-centered left. Moderate leftism in the global periphery, balancing between popular pressure and acquiescence to international capital, tends to wear itself out; capital has little use for an ambivalent ally, and revolutionary energies wane in the face of halting political contradiction.[45] While this conflict has not yet reached its denouement in Bolivia, things are coming to a head elsewhere: Venezuela is in the midst of a full economic crisis, and Brazil a political one. Notwithstanding important differences, the popular support that has carried these governments through difficult times in the past has made only a tepid appearance. And with Argentina's Macri in office, the regional solidarity that has bolstered the centre-left in times of crisis is also in question. Bolivia too is facing a growing set of corruption-related scandals, leading the MAS to lose its bid for a constitutional amendment permitting Morales and García Linera to compete for a fourth term. This loss, however, can only be good for the chances of the Bolivian process.[46] In its wake, extra-parliamentary movements and perhaps the MAS grassroots will have to consciously develop their organizational strength and reconsider their trajectory.

But what is the revolutionary path forward? Indeed, what can we learn from the pink tide about revolution and state power more generally? There is the temptation to reject the relevance of capitalist state power altogether, to lump the pink tide in with the entire history of social democratic failures and betrayals with which all Marxists are familiar, to retreat to the bitter position that the only thing the state has ever been good for is smashing. But can we afford to be so cynical? The re-emergence of parliamentary socialism in the US and the UK, the recent experience of Syriza in Greece, and the ongoing prospects of Podemos in Spain suggest that the issue of the revolutionary left's relationship to the capitalist state and to electoral politics demands further elaboration.

Among other Marxist contributions on this point, we might look to the work of Nicos Poulantzas, which points to the double necessity of both seizing positions of state power and also changing the balance of class forces at a social level, maintaining independent political organizations outside the state, and working toward a transformation of the state's institutional materiality. The key insight of Poulantzas is that the state is not a monolith; class conflict is rather 'inscribed into the institutional structure of the state' because of its own internal horizontal divisions – between branches, departments, offices, military commands, etc. – as well as its vertical ones – between officers and rank-and-file soldiers, for example, or university administrators and staff. These divisions allow, in some moments, echoes of popular will to find their way into the state apparatus, intentionally or otherwise, as 'the establishment of the State's policy must be seen as the result of class contradictions inscribed in the very structure of the State'.[47] Through the interaction of the various departments and branches affected in different ways by class relationships, the state takes on a number of potentially conflictive projects, whose resolution constitutes its autonomy as it resolves them to reshape the means by which capital accumulation is made possible.

This conception of the state suggests possibilities for its capture as part of a revolutionary strategy that surpasses social democracy. The state is not figured here as a site for the gradual transition to socialism, and even a piecemeal acquisition of the state apparatus cannot achieve this end. As Poulantzas says in a 1976 interview by Henri Weber, 'I do not believe that the masses can hold positions of autonomous power – even subordinate ones – within the capitalist state'. Instead, 'they act as a means of resistance, elements of corrosion, accentuating the internal contradictions of the state'.[48]

The other side of a revolutionary strategy involving positions of state power, then, must be to shift the balance of class forces outside the state. What the Bolivian case further illustrates on this point is the need for a certain directionality, a constant movement by which the state is forced into a sharper articulation of class struggle on a social level. As I have argued, what has been missed in the case of Bolivia 'is the necessity of radical transformation' in the *institutional materiality* of the state – in the means and circuits through which relations of power are crystallized in a determinate social formation, and by which the state is linked to the reproduction of capitalist relations of production.[49] The transformations themselves would not constitute a transition to socialism, but by creating the mass basis for a political intervention, they could permit an accelerating process tending toward an actual rupture with capitalism, 'a *stage of real breaks*, the climax of which – and there has to be one – is reached when the relationship of forces on the strategic terrain of the State swings over to the side of the popular masses'.[50] Such was the wager of Poulantzas in any case, though in his own conjuncture Communist Parties carrying out the Eurocommunist strategy in the 1970s proved both too rigid and too opportunistic to serve as an organizational basis for these changes.[51] Still, the observation that a movement toward socialism could only be founded on a transformation in the *political* relations between state and society itself, between constituted and constituent power – a process which must be differentiated from even major welfare-oriented policy shifts in response to popular demands – presents a resonant corrective *avant la lettre* of the pink tide's current trajectory.

Of course, the distance between the institutionalized Communist Parties in Italy, France, and Spain in the 1970s on the one hand, and the emergent MAS in the context of organized, society-wide insurrection on the other, means that the underlying issues of the former cannot be transposed onto the latter – not to mention the particular challenges of building a socialist organization *ex nihlio* in the US, or of transforming Labour in Britain. The obstacles in each case are unique. But the distinction between a revolutionary transformation of the state and a doomed reformism cuts across all of them.

In the context of high neoliberalism that characterized the origins of the pink tide, the left in the state apparatus may have fallen prey to misconceptions about what is at stake. As Gago points out, if neoliberalism is thought abstractly as the dominance of the market over the state, then the presumed solution would be the wielding of state power to restore a balance. This seems to be the practical ideology at work among those leftists in power throughout the region. But if neoliberalism consisted, in its ascent, not of a weakening of the state, but of 'the creation of a political world (regimen of governmentality) that arises as a "projection" of the rules and requirements of the competitive market', then the challenge is not merely the instrumental use of state power, but an intervention in the relationship between state and society, and in the multiple ways in which power is articulated across and within the divisions implied by this relationship.[52]

Here, we must also emphasize that the state is, among other things, an instance of the broader social division of labour within capitalism that separates the manual from the intellectual.[53] As the specific set of institutions charged with social organization, the fullest expression of the capitalist state's intellectual function is the power of the technocracy, deepened under neoliberalism in accordance with creditor demands and at the expense of democracy. The social democratic approach to the state does not challenge this arrangement. Even when working to redistribute wealth, to regulate capital, or to bolster its organizational role in certain industries by nationalizing them, the centre-left elements in state power have tended toward technical solutions. In contrast, a revolutionary perspective on this point would have to refigure this divide: if the science of governance is an intellectual project of capital, then the science of revolution must be an intellectual project of the masses: 'Without political and social vanguards who have the credibility to pose an alternative social project, who lack even the capacity to elaborate such an alternative, it will fall to the mobilized sectors of society ... to reflect on whether we must be subject to definitions of reality elaborated from the spaces whose political power and control over the existing social order are currently in dispute.'[54]

The hope for revolution, then, resides in the possibility of distinct knowledges – and let us conceive of knowledge here in terms of material practice – functioning in tandem with the strategic corrosion of state power, and the organized, popular mobilization against the existing state of affairs. As I have argued here, the pink tide has not seen revolutionary transformation considered in these terms.

Those positions of state power are now being lost. And at the level of organization, extra-parliamentary movements, most powerful in the case of Bolivia, have proven susceptible to cooptation. Leaders who left organic organizations to become bureaucrats will find it hard to return to the grassroots, and movements depending on state resources will find themselves starved if the right continues its electoral gains.[55] Important autonomies, developed in the heat of struggle, have been lost. This decomposition would seem to suggest that that the time for action has passed.

Yet if struggles that began the present cycle are any indication, sparks can fly even at the darkest hour. For if we examine what Raquel Gutiérrez calls the 'internal horizon' of recent struggles throughout the region, we find continuing possibilities grounded in autonomous and communal practices, concrete knowledges whose exclusion has been the tragic – or perhaps farcical – flaw of the recent cycle.[56] The potential power of a collective challenge to capital remains rooted there, in 'an extremely heterogeneous, dense, and rich web of everyday social practices, in which thousands of men and women carry out the material reproduction of their lives'.[57] That is, there remains the possibility of emergent subjectivities organized on the basis of 'communal-popular' economic, social, and political practices. Desires for autonomy, and communal practices like the Andean *ayni*, an informal system of reciprocal expectation, and *pasanaku*, a mode of sharing common resources on a rotative basis, continue to flourish, transform, and travel throughout the Latin American subcontinent.[58] Such tendencies toward 'the production of the common in an everyday form' hold open the possibility for political alternatives.[59]

Yet on their own, disperse subjectivities and practices, with often localist limitations in their practical reach, cannot substitute for a positive political project. An organized push from below, not merely in defence of stagnating governments, but in the spirit that exploded the dour consensus that 'There is no alternative' over the last two decades, is the only way to reset political coordinates, to unite the various strands of the anti-extractivist movement, and to displace the populist myth that there is only *one* alternative, centred on welfare distribution and the exclusion of popular power. This means that movements must make positive demands for political space: more power to the communes in Venezuela,[60] more land for the landless movements in Brazil, more space for the self-management of unions and *ayllus* in Bolivia, and for the 'taken' factories in Argentina. All of these fragments of autonomous potential can, if organized in yet-to-be discovered ways, form a coherent counter-power to the right, and prove that the only hope to protect and deepen the social gains of the pink tide is a pivot in their direction. For now, the right is taking the initiative. The revolutionary hopes of Latin America today rely on the left doing the same.

NOTES

1   Álvaro García Linera, *Las vías de la emancipación: Conversaciones con Álvaro García Linera*, Pablo Stefanoni, Franklin Ramírez and Maristella Svampa, eds., México D.F.:Ocean Sur, 2009, pp. 74-88. Excerpt available at http://www.contextolatinoamericano.com/documentos/el-descubrimiento-del-estado/#.

2   Raquel Gutiérrez, 'Los ritmos del Pachakuti: Cómo conocemos las luchas de emancipación y su relación con la política de la autonomía', *Desacatos*, 37(September-December) 2011, p. 28.

3   Gutiérrez, 'Los ritmos', p. 28.

4   Jeffery R. Webber, *From Rebellion to Reform in Bolivia: Class Struggle, Indigenous Liberation and the Politics of Evo Morales*, Chicago: Haymarket, 2011, pp 3, 63-4. Álvaro García Linera, 'El Estado en transición. Bloque de poder y punto de bifurcación', *La potencia plebeya: acción colectiva e identidades indígenas, obreras y populares en Bolivia*, Pablo Stefanoni, ed., Buenos Aires: CLACSO/Prometeo, 2008, pp. 397-9.

5   Raquel Gutiérrez, *Horizonte comunitario-popular: Antagonismo y producción de lo común en América Latina*, Cochabamba, SOCEE/Autodeterminación, 2015; Huáscar Salazar Lohman, *Se han adueñado del proceso de lucha: Horizontes comunitario-populares en tension y la reconstitución de la dominación en la Bolivia del MAS*, Cochabamba: SOCEE/Autodeterminación, 2015.

6   Nicos Poulantzas, *State, Power, Socialism*, Translated by Patrick Camiller, London: Verso, 2014; For more on my own interpretation of Poulantzas' arguments in that text and their relationship the Latin American conjuncture today, in addition to what follows in the present essay, see Robert Cavooris, 'From Subaltern to State: Toward a Left Critique of the Pink Tide', *Viewpoint Magazine*, 3, 2014.

7   See chapter 3 of Benjamin Kohl and Linda Farthing, *Impasse in Bolivia: Neoliberal Hegemony and Popular Resistance*, London: Zed Books, 2006. These privatizations were carried out under the auspices of economic necessity in order to pay off the debts of the various military dictatorships that reigned from 1971 until the early 1980s. Political figures cycled and recycled through the various governments during this epoch, culminating at its most farcical in the election of Hugo Banzer, the military dictator who had been overthrown in 1978 and whose economic policies had been partially responsible for the massive indebtedness of the Bolivian economy in the first place.

8   Raquel Gutiérrez Aguilar and Álvaro García Linera, 'El ciclo estatal neoliberal y sus crisis', in *Democratizaciones plebeyas*, La Paz: Muela del diablo, 2002, pp. 12-16.
9   Jefferey R. Webber, *Red October: Left-indigenous Struggles in Modern Bolivia*, Chicago: Haymarket, 2011, p. 267.
10 Webber, *Red October*, p. 245.
11 Íñigo Errejón and Juan Guijarro, 'Post-Neoliberalism's Difficult Hegemonic Consolidation: A Comparative Analysis of the Ecuadorean and Bolivian Processes', *Latin American Perspectives* 43(1), 2016, pp. 34–52.
12 Webber, *From Rebellion to Reform*, p. 15; Fander Falconí and Julio Oleas-Montalvo, 'Citizens' Revolution and International Integration Obstacles and Opportunities in World Trade', *Latin American Perspectives*, 43(1), pp. 137-8.
13 Brent Z. Kaup, *Market Justice: Political Economic Struggle in Bolivia*, New York: Cambridge University Press, 2013, pp. 61-2, 71-89; Webber, *From Rebellion to Reform*, pp. 33-5.
14 Álvaro García Linera 'La muerte de la condición obrera del siglo XX: La marcha minera por la vida', in *El retorno de la Bolivia plebeya*, La Paz: Muela del diablo, pp. 23-60. For a strong account of Bolivia's pre-democracy history in English, see James Dunkerley, *Rebellion in the Veins: Political Struggle in Bolivia 1952-1982*, London: Verso, 1984.
15 Kohl and Farthing, *Impasse*, pp. 131, 136-7; Kaup, *Market Justice*, p. 86; Nancy Postero, 'The Struggle to Create a Radical Democracy in Bolivia', *Latin American Research Review*, 45(4) 2010, pp. 61-2; Silvia Rivera Cusicanqui, *Mito y desarrollo en Bolivia: El giro colonial del gobierno del MAS*, La Paz: Piedra Rota/Plural, 2015, pp. 32-4.
16 Kohl and Farthing, *Impasse*, pp. 132–3, 145; Forrest Hylton and Sinclair Thomson, *Revolutionary Horizons: Past and Present in Bolivian Politics*, London: Verso, 2007, p. 104.
17 Raúl Prada, 'Multitud y contrapoder. Estudios del presente: Movimientos sociales contemporáneos', in *Democratizaciones plebeyas*, La Paz: Muela del diablo, 2002, p. 107.
18 Sven Harten, 'Towards a "Traditional Party"? Internal Organisation and Change in the MAS in Bolivia', in *Evo Morales and the Movimiento al Socialismo in Bolivia: The First Term in Context*, Adrian J. Pearce, ed., London: Institute for Study of the Americas, pp. 84-7; Rivera Cusicanqui, *Mito y desarrollo*, pp. 25-8.
19 Maristella Svampa, 'Commodities Consensus: Neoextractivism and Enclosure of the Commons in Latin America', *South Atlantic Quarterly*, 114(1) 2015, p. 65; Webber, *From Rebellion to Reform*; Salazar Lohman, *Se han adueñado*.
20 Falconi and Oleas-Montalvo, 'Citizens' Revolution', p. 127; Webber, *From Rebellion to Reform*, pp. 217-22.
21 Linda C. Farthing and Benjamin H. Kohl, *Evo's Bolivia*, Austin: University of Texas, 2014, pp. 98-113.
22 'Asignación universal por Hijo pasó de 837 persos a 966 pesos', *La Nación* (Argentina), 11 February 2106; 'Mauricio Macri anunció un aporte de $ 400 para los beneficiarios de la Asignación Universal por Hijo y las jubilaciones mínimas', *La Nación* (Argentina), 21 December 2015.
23 Webber, *From Rebellion to Reform*, p. 82; Kaup, *Market Justice*, pp. 28, 129-34.
24 Rivera Cusicanqui, *Mito y desarrollo*, pp. 33, 44-5, 48; Salazar Lohmann, *Se han adueñado*, p. 283; Farthing and Kohl, *Evo's Bolivia*, p. 53; Carlos Gonçalves, *Encrucijada latinoamericana en Bolivia: el conflict del TIPNIS y sus implicaciones civilizatorias*, La Paz: Autodeterminación, 2013, p. 83.
25 In Bolivian social discourse, Andean Aymara and Quechua rural producers who have moved to different parts of the country are often called, not necessarily pejoratively, *colonizadores*. The other 34 indigenous groups recognized by the constitution are primarily smaller, lowland communities. It is worth noting, in this sense, that these social divisions did not originate with the Morales government, but rather have been underlying, in some form, the political process in Bolivia for a long time. The recent

26 Salazar Lohmann, *Se han adueñado*, p. 288.
27 'Manifiesto Público de la IX Marcha Indígena Originaria', in *Antología del pensamiento crítico boliviano contemporáneo*, Silvia Rivera and Virginia Aillón Soria, Buenos Aires: CLACSO, p. 366.
28 Salazar Lohmann, *Se han adueñado*, p. 289.
29 Beatriz Layme, 'CIDOB dividida por el Gobierno de Morales', *Pagina Siete* (Bolivia), 25 September 2013; Nancy Vacaflor, 'Dirigentes denuncian que el MAS busca injerencia en el Conamaq', *Pagina Siete* (Bolivia), 17 September 2013.
30 Webber, *From Rebellion to Reform*, p. 101.
31 For a discussion of these concepts in the Latin American context, see Jon Beasley-Murray, *Posthegemony: Political Theory and Latin America*, Minneapolis: University of Minnesota, 2010.
32 Emir Sader, *The New Mole*, Translated by Ian Bruce, London: Verso, 2011, pp. 139-40; Salvador Schavelzon, *El nacimiento del estado plurinacional de Bolivia: etnografía de una Asamblea Constituyente*, Buenos Aires: CLACSO, 2012, pp. 143-7; Webber, *From Rebellion to Reform*, p. 86; Salazar Lohman, *Se han adueñado*, pp. 191-206.
33 Lucía Linsalata, *Cuando manda la asamblea: lo comunitario-popular en Bolivia*, La Paz: SOCEE/Autodeterminación, 2015, p. 260; Asamblea nacional de organizaciones indígenas, originarias, campesinas, y de colonizadores de Bolivia, 'Propuesta para la nueva constitución política del estado', in Raul Prada, *Horizontes de la Asamblea Constituyente*, La Paz: Ediciones Yachaywasi, 2006, pp. 176, 179.
34 Ernesto Laclau, *On Populist Reason*, London: Verso, 2005.
35 See for example Marta Harnecker, *A World to Build: New Paths Toward Twenty-First Century Socialism*, Translated by Federico Fuentes, New York: Monthly Review Press, 2015.
36 Verónica Gago, *La razón neoliberal: Economías barrocas y pragmática popular*, Madrid: Traficantes de suenos, 2015, p. 245.
37 Webber, *From Rebellion to Reform*, p. 82; Harten, 'Towards a "Traditional Party"', pp. 78-9.
38 Fernando Molina, 'El gobierno boliviano amenaza con expulsar a cuatro ONG críticas', *El País*, 18 August 2015; See also, for example, Álvaro García Linera, *Geopolítica de la Amazonía*, La Paz: Vicepresidencía del Estado, 2012.
39 Postero, 'The Struggle to Create', p. 75.
40 Salazar Lohman, *Se han adueñado*, pp. 209.
41 This topic in political philosophy dates to Hobbes and Spinoza. The basic conceptual distinction is that the *people* comes into existence by and in relation to a state, whereas the multitude pre-exists, or exceeds it. Contemporarily, thinkers like Antonio Negri and Enrique Dussel have debated the merits of these concepts. See Beasley-Murray, *Posthegemony*, for a discussion of these concepts in relation to Latin American populism. For an alternate perspective see Donald Kingsbury, 'Between Multitude and Pueblo: Venezuela's Bolivarian Revolution and the Government of Un-Governability', *New Political Science*, 35(4) 2013, pp. 567-85.
42 Étienne Balibar, *Politics and the Other Scene*, London: Verso, 2002, pp. 60, 64-5; Étienne Balibar, 'The Nation Form: History and Ideology', in E. Balibar and I. Wallerstein, *Race, Nation, Class: Ambiguous Identities*, London: Verso, 1991, p. 93.
43 Benjamin Kohl and Linda Farthing, 'Material Constraints to Popular Imaginaries: The Extractive Economy and Resource Nationalism in Bolivia,' *Political Geography*, 31(4) 2012, p. 225.

44 The reference to 'dignity' evokes the 'March for Territory and Dignity', which set the agenda for the lowland indigenous movements throughout the 1990s. Rivera Cusicanqui, *Mito y desarrollo*, pp. 25, 40-41, 54; Tom Perreault and Barbara Green, 'Reworking the Spaces of Indigeneity: The Bolivia Ayllu and Lowland Autonomy Movements Compared', *Environment and Planning D: Society and Space*, 31(1) 2013, p. 51.

45 The contradictions of this position have many precedents in Latin America, owing primarily to the constant presence of foreign capital and imperialist political pressure. In Bolivia, for example, both the MNR after 1952 and the brief period of 'military socialism' from 1969-71 collapsed on the basis of similar contradictions. Claudio Katz, 'Is South America's "Progressive Cycle" at an End?', Translated by Richard Fidler, posted 3 February 2016, available at: http://lifeonleft.blogspot.ca/2016/02/is-south-americas-progressive-cycle-at.html.

46 Angus McNelly, 'The Latest Turn of Bolivia's Political Merry-Go-Round: The Constitutional Referendum', *Viewpoint Magazine*, posted 18 February 2016, https://viewpointmag.com.

47 Poulantzas, *State, Power, Socialism*, pp. 125, 131, 133.

48 Nicos Poulantzas, 'The State and the Transition to Socialism', in James Martin, ed., *The Poulantzas Reader: Marxism, Law, and the State*, London: Verso, 2008, p. 337.

49 Nicos Poulantzas, 'Interview with Stuart Hall and Alan Hunt', *Marxism Today*, July 1979, p. 196; Poulantzas, *State, Power, Socialism*, p. 44.

50 Poulantzas, *State, Power, Socialism*, pp. 258-59.

51 Asad Haider, 'Bernstein in Seattle: Representative Democracy and the Revolutionary Subject (Part 2)', *Viewpoint Magazine*, posted 23 May 2016, https://viewpointmag.com.

52 Gago, *La razón neoliberal*, p. 219.

53 Poulantzas, *State, Power, Socialism*, pp. 55-6.

54 Decio Machado, 'Ecuador y el ocasio de los dioses', *Contra/Tiempos*, posted 20 May 2016, available at: https://contratiemposec.wordpress.com/2016/05/20/ecuador-y-el-ocaso-de-los-dioses/.

55 Linsalata, *Cuando manda la asamblea*, p. 261.

56 Gutiérrez Aguilar, *Horizonte*, p. 22.

57 Veronica Gago and Sandro Mezzadra. 'Actualidad de la revuelta plebeya: Por una nueva política de autonomía', *Lobo suelto!*, posted 1 July 2015, available at: http://anarquiacoronada.blogspot.com/2015/07/actualidad-de-la-revuelta-plebeya-por.html?q=mezzadra.

58 Gago, *La razón neoliberal*, pp. 298-9.

59 Gutiérrez Aguilar, *Horizonte*, p. 119.

60 See George Cicariello-Maher, 'Building the Commune: Insurgent Government, Communal State', *South Atlantic Quarterly*, 113(4) 2014.

SOMETHING LEFT IN LATIN AMERICA: VENEZUELA AND THE STRUGGLE FOR TWENTY-FIRST CENTURY SOCIALISM

STEVE STRIFFLER

The Latin American left at the start of the 1990s looked a lot like its counterparts throughout much of the world. It was a fragment of its former self. Military regimes had wiped out much of the left in South America during the 1970s and 1980s, and counterinsurgency had finished the job in Central America by 1990. Nor was there much reason for hope. Structural adjustment reigned supreme. Labour was on the defensive, unable to mount much of a challenge to neoliberal policies that were decimating the working class and its capacity to fight. The countryside was eerily quiet. Peasants had been neutralized and demobilized by a combination of repression and government policies that made both organizing and daily life increasingly difficult. The Soviet Union had disintegrated, Cuba was isolated and on the brink of collapse, and the Sandinistas – once a beacon of hope – had been soundly defeated.

In short, although it took a peculiar path to get there, Latin America was firmly in step with global political trends. Its body politic, from NGOs and academics to political parties and labour unions, had moved decisively to the right during the 1980s, as the Washington Consensus enveloped the region. Talk of revolution and socialism seemed out of place. The left was reeling. Neoliberalism had become the only alternative, and was being implemented by nominally democratic governments that used varying degrees of repression to impose policies that destroyed left institutions, undermined the capacity of popular groups to forge solidarity, and redistributed wealth upwards.

It is all the more remarkable, then, that only a quarter century later there is no better place to think about revolution and revolutionary agency than Latin America. For a range of reasons, not least of which were the devastating consequences wrought by neoliberalism and US imperialism, a reconstituted left put together a broad-based anti-neoliberal bloc with the political capacity to remove neoliberal governments from power. The left named neoliberalism, subjected it to debate, and dismantled the neoliberal rudder that had united and guided Latin American elites for two plus decades. In so doing, popular-left forces made anti-neoliberalism reputable, if not hegemonic, regained a potent street presence, and built considerable political power both within and outside the state.

More than this, these forces have implicitly or explicitly embodied understandings and practices of revolution, revolutionary agency, and socialism that differ substantially from the (stereotypical) model that is often associated with 'October 1917'. Unlike Russia, China, Cuba, and Nicaragua, as well as numerous left-led insurrections that failed to capture state power in the twentieth century, twenty-first century socialism in Latin America has not involved armed insurgencies or protracted wars. No colonial power or brutal dictator served to unify the people. In this respect, they share more with Chile than Cuba or Nicaragua.

At the same time, the distinctive nature of recent revolutionary initiatives should not be all that surprising. Latin American revolutions, from Mexico and Cuba to Chile and Nicaragua, have never followed Marxist orthodoxies with any precision. Revolution today, much like Latin American revolution in the twentieth century, has not been initiated or led by political parties or a particular sector of the working class (i.e. industrial workers or peasants). Rather, social movements comprised of indigenous peoples, workers, students, street vendors, peasants, neighborhood organizations, the landless, and others who had been politically excluded and economically discarded took to the streets, ousted neoliberal governments, and then captured some degree of (formal) power through the messy realm of electoral politics.

Not surprisingly, these elections did not sweep away old regimes with the speed and decisiveness of armed revolution. Once elected, leftist governments, as had been ominously the case in Chile almost fifty years earlier, found themselves in charge of countries where the opposition still controlled most of the media, the economy, the church, and significant sectors of the state. New governments had to contend with powerful and energized, if divided, oppositions while managing competing interests and ideologies within their own coalitions. They came to power after decades of increasing corporate influence, reduced state capacity, and ever-widening income inequality. The struggle has been more about reversing neoliberalism – and convincing people that politics and governments are potentially positive forces – than waging a full assault on capitalism or implementing socialism. It has also meant that the left's hold on power has been quite fragile, requiring a never-ending war of position upon deeply polarized political landscapes.

Nevertheless, the parameters of debate in Latin America moved to the left as neoliberalism lost its hegemony. This was a hard-earned, if partial, victory. The shift has not always translated into dramatic policy changes, and powerful sectors continue to push for a reconstituted form of neoliberal capitalism. Yet, debate has more frequently drifted between two poles: one that envisions a post-neoliberal world defined by a more humane version of capitalism and another that seeks to build socialism in the twenty-first century. This paradigm shift is important, but constantly under threat and deeply contradictory.

On the one hand, it means that the concept of socialism, which had seemed thoroughly discredited, was revived. In Venezuela and Bolivia, discussions about socialism became not only open and central to public debate, but have actually informed policy. In other countries, such as Brazil, Argentina, and Chile, where the balance of forces was less favourable, such debate was less prominent but nonetheless partially shaped discussion about the role of popular movements and the state's place in the economy. On the other hand, the concept of socialism has often become exceedingly vague, at times meaning little more than a slightly more equitable version of capitalism.

To be sure, opening up the concept of socialism to (re)interrogation has produced some healthy consequences. Sectarianism is less prevalent, the privileged place of a particular revolutionary agent is no longer assumed, and long-held principles – around state ownership of the means of production or the dissolution of the market economy – are points of departure rather than absolute mandates. Yet at the same time, if the old guideposts no longer apply, and new ones remain overly vague, there is also the danger that the demands, goals, visions, and institutions we develop will simply not be up to the task of transcending neoliberalism, let alone capitalism. There is something left in Latin America. It is just not entirely clear what.

THE LEFT TURN

If the prospects for revolutionary transformation seemed as bleak in Latin America as elsewhere at the start of the 1990s, the ideological foundation upon which neoliberalism rested was more fragile than it appeared. Part of this underlying instability stemmed from the intensity with which structural adjustment policies had been implemented throughout the region. Latin American political elites embraced neoliberalism, sold it as the only alternative, and imposed a draconian form that was repressive in implementation and devastating in practice. In some countries, like Chile, Colombia, Guatemala, and El Salvador, its implementation required intense repression, while in others it was more successfully sold as a way to reduce inefficient/corrupt governments and grow the economy. Regardless, neoliberalism did not simply decimate labour unions and working-class power. It bestowed a 'lost decade' upon the region in which overall productivity stagnated while wealth flowed upward.

What this meant was that organized labour, along with much of the urban middle class, found themselves in increasingly precarious situations. The poor, in turn, not only saw their capacity to subsist severely undermined by policies that drastically shrank the safety net, but growing numbers became altogether irrelevant to the economy. This was true in both rural and urban areas. As more people found themselves politically excluded, economically marginalized, and simply unworthy of exploitation, more traditional struggles over wages and job security morphed into battles over basic survival that challenged the legitimacy of the political system itself.

By the early 1990s this struggle, or rather the success that elites had in implementing a particularly vicious strand of neoliberalism, began to produce a political backlash that served to undermine both neoliberal ideology and the political class itself. Although the 1989 Caracazo in Venezuela can be seen as one of the earlier and more explosive expressions of this popular discontent, it was peasant and indigenous groups who would first animate and sustain the challenge to neoliberalism in the early and mid-1990s. These rural efforts were quickly followed and complemented by the emergence of urban-based irruptions, so that by the late 1990s and early 2000s it seemed as though rebellion was once again sweeping the region.

Initially, it was unclear where this cycle of insurrection was headed. The daily struggle to survive, combined with a broader alienation from all things political, meant that rebellious moments were often local, or at least defensive in nature, focusing on subsistence needs and stressing democratic self-rule at the level of neighbourhoods, communities, and workplaces. In a context where even 'progressive' candidates quickly embraced neoliberalism once in office, strategies to bypass state corruption by carving out semi-autonomous spheres at the local level became attractive. Groups could experiment with more democratic and participatory forms of self-rule as they struggled to survive. The Zapatistas were an early and emblematic expression of this tendency, but were hardly alone. On a larger level, the global justice movement which coalesced in the late 1990s reinforced this inclination to seek change without taking state power.

It would not take long however before some of these popular insurrections – most of which had anti-systemic leanings – would coalesce into national-level anti-neoliberal blocs. This was partly due to the fact that political elites refused to ease off on neoliberalism even as its contradictions deepened. In fact they doubled down, ensuring that the 'political class' would forever be associated with the neoliberal nightmare. The modest economic upturn of the mid-1990s bought neoliberal regimes some time, but this was followed by five years of stagnation (1997-2002) and then a commodities boom that enriched Latin American elites, delivered few benefits to working people, and further devastated indigenous territories located on mining and oil concessions.[1]

This explosion of political activity, diverse in both its demands and composition, led more Latin Americans to realize that although ecological and economic devastation was manifested and experienced quite differently across the region, most of these varied symptoms could nonetheless be pinned on neoliberal policies; and they demonstrated that although the traditional agents of progressive change such as political parties, labor unions, and peasant coalitions had been greatly weakened or discredited by two decades of neoliberalism, anti-systemic and even anti-capitalist projects were not completely off the table. The renewal of this possibility, and the growing realization that alternative social actors and projects were viable, encouraged a broader re-thinking of what progressive change might look like and who might be its central protagonists.

The most dramatic and cohesive expression of this emerging anti-neoliberal bloc came in the form of very large anti-systemic movements that removed democratically-elected neoliberal governments from office, in some cases more than once. Ecuadorians occupied public spaces on massive scales during the late 1990s and early 2000s, effectively impeaching three governments in less than ten years (1997-2005) while dealing a significant blow to neoliberalism and a corrupt political class. Although Rafael Correa was largely disconnected from the social movements that drove these popular insurgencies, his election in 2006 was premised on the promise to dismantle neoliberalism, usher in a new political system, and re-take control of natural resources from multinationals. Bolivia experienced its own cycle of mobilization in the early 2000s that saw massive protests against neoliberalism, most conspicuously in the form of large-scale opposition to water privatization and foreign control over natural resources. The protests enjoyed considerable success in that they led to the removal of a neoliberal president and initiated an uneven reversal of neoliberal policies. Venezuelans in some sense started the large-scale backlash against neoliberalism in the streets of Caracas in 1989, even if subsequent expressions were driven as much from 'above' as 'below' – in part because social movements in Venezuela tended to be more fragmented and lack the organizational infrastructure of counterparts in Bolivia or Ecuador.

Nevertheless, if popular sectors were able to say no to neoliberalism and oust its strongest proponents from presidential palaces, they would find it difficult to develop the political capacity to win elections, and even more challenging to inhabit, transform, and capture state power once in office. Indeed, the transition from popular insurrection to political power proved difficult in at least two senses.

First, despite massive protests that removed neoliberal governments, many of the centre-left coalitions that emerged out of these revolutionary moments, and sought political power through electoral means, produced governments that would share much with their neoliberal predecessors. The left lacked the capacity to push these coalitions in more radical directions. Argentina is an oft-cited example, in that few expected Kirchner to be even remotely revolutionary, but Chile and Brazil clearly fall into this camp as well. Although these moderate shifts to the left were important, both politically and for working people who saw modest benefits, they were nonetheless disappointing given the power of the revolutionary expressions and hopes that preceded them. Such shortcomings ultimately reflected the weakness of left-revolutionary institutions, the level of public consciousness, and the fact that the opposition did not simply give up once people took to the streets. Indeed, it is worth remembering that even the Chávez government was relatively moderate when first elected (i.e. the 'Third Way'). The electoral coalition that brought him to power in 1998 could not have supported a rapid radicalization regardless of the government's ideological orientation.

Second, if electing a decently progressive government proved difficult, the political landscape would not get easier once in office. If anything, the fiercest battles began after the votes were counted, as the left in Venezuela, Bolivia, Ecuador, and elsewhere learned the important distinctions between getting into office, actually wielding power, and then ruling effectively while trying to deepen reforms. Once elected, heterogeneous social movements and political coalitions had to be constantly mobilized and sufficiently unified to effectively confront the opposition and remain in power. And this had to be done while attempting to implement policy that would break from the prevailing political and economic model. In Ecuador, Bolivia, and (to a lesser extent) Venezuela for example, there have been intense debates and divisions within the left over whether to expand natural resource extraction in order to increase social spending, or whether to scale back on mining in order to protect the environment and local populations. Managing such tensions within the left while trying to keep the opposition in check and the government functioning has not been an easy task, and partially explains why many progressive governments pursued relatively moderate reforms and/or lost political ground.

This speaks to a broader challenge and contradiction facing revolution in the twenty-first century. On the one hand, despite the state violence and gross levels of inequality associated with neoliberalism, armed revolution (by the left) has nonetheless become an illegitimate means for pursuing social transformation. This broader discrediting of violent revolution is due at least in part to the institutionalization of liberal democratic norms and human rights practices within Latin America during the last three decades. On the other hand, if we assume that armed revolution is off the table; that socialism has to be advanced (partially and significantly) through the electoral system; and that it will be implemented within a contradictory and unfavorable context of representative democracy, constitutions, legal systems, and property regimes that (in the short to medium term) support capitalism, we begin to realize how difficult it is to push forward revolutionary projects within bourgeois democracy. It requires constantly winning and moving the public debate, persuading, organizing, and mobilizing popular sectors to not only forge viable coalitions to win elections, but to occupy and transform the state while both confronting capitalism directly and creating new sources of popular political and economic power.

As the varied cases of Cárdenas in Mexico, Allende in Chile, and Arbenz in Guatemala all attest, this struggle to carry forth revolution within constitutional boundaries is hardly new, but became salient once again as the left returned to power throughout much of Latin America. And it is worth remembering, as Venezuela amply demonstrates, how incredibly conflictual this process is in practice. Attempting to change the structure, operation, and even personnel of the state while simultaneously confronting capital and putting key sectors of industry, finance, and commerce under social control/ownership produces the fiercest opposition. This is precisely why, as both Chávez and Morales recognized, the process must be accompanied by the creation of alternative organs, institutions, and spaces of working-class power. Collectively, this is an exhausting, difficult to sustain, and yet absolutely necessary series of struggles.

The left governments that came to power in Latin America during the past two decades did not do so through armed revolution, did not seize control of the means of production (on any large scale), and have not been defined by a revolutionary party that controls the political system. Rather, they pushed forth the 'revolutionary' process, challenging capital while building alternative economic forms, through a system defined by liberal democratic norms, the electoral process, and a multi-party system – even if their commitment to these norms has at times been both shaky and shaken. This experimental, open, and flexible approach to social transformation, and the constant interrogation of Marxist orthodoxies and understandings of socialism, is hardly unique to twenty-first century socialism. Yet the rapid emergence of left leaning governments through electoral processes across much of Latin America has not only put socialism back on the public radar, but has also demonstrated how difficult it is to build the kind of working-class power necessary for advancing and sustaining significant challenges to capitalism while working within liberal democracy. What is the process by which left governments transcend or transform a system of rule – bourgeois democracy – that represents both the path forward and a profound obstacle to systemic change? How does one transcend bourgeois capitalist democracy through the norms, practices, and institutions of bourgeois capitalist democracy? Is the incrementalist path, by which reform in a highly charged and polarized here-and-now eventually leads to deeper transformation, actually possible?

The fact that consolidating power while deepening the revolution is no easy task does not make it any less essential. Revolutionary transformation may be a process, perhaps even a never-ending one, but if it proceeds too slowly, and loses momentum, it becomes ever more vulnerable to attack. The power of capital must be broken or the bourgeoisie will eventually destroy the revolution. The difficulty is that even in Venezuela, the Latin American country where conditions were the most favorable and where the reforms have been the deepest and most sustained, every effort to challenge capital, strengthen socialism, and re-constitute the state has been met by incredibly stiff opposition on the part of the oligarchy.

VENEZUELA

Although one could engage in a long debate about which Latin American country got hit worst by neoliberalism during the 1980s and 1990s, there is certainly a case to be made for Venezuela. Due in part to declining oil revenues, Venezuela's GDP declined at a faster rate – by over 25 per cent – than any other country in the region during this period. Poverty went from under 20 per cent in 1980 to over 60 per cent by the mid-1990s, and the country's total debt rose from less than 10 per cent of the gross national product to over 50 per cent between 1970 and 1994. By the end of the 1980s, economic decline and crisis had become permanent features of Venezuelan life.[2]

The situation came to a head with the election of Carlos Andrés Pérez in 1988. Pérez, who had previously been president during the oil boom of the 1970s, campaigned against neoliberalism but then quickly implemented an IMF-stamped structural adjustment programme upon taking office. The public backlash was immediate, particularly among the poor who took to the streets in February of 1989. Hundreds died at the hands of police in what came to be known as the Caracazo, which dealt a blow to neoliberal hegemony and foreshadowed the intense class polarization that would define Venezuela in the coming decades. The stage was set.

Chávez's coup attempt in 1992 emerged in the aftermath of the Caracazo and within the context of neoliberal disaster. The failed coup turned him into a national, even heroic figure and paved the way for his successful presidential campaign in 1998 and the next decade-plus of Chavismo. The Bolivarian Revolution, which has promoted something of an alternative political and economic model, emerged within a complex and constantly changing terrain of class struggle. The uneven transformations advanced were themselves the product of (1) a differentiated popular base whose interests, contradictions, and internal currents were only partially shaped by the Chávez government, but always challenged, limited, and stimulated the process and pace of change; and (2) an opposition that was heterogeneous and contradictory in composition and deed, but whose reactionary aggression had the somewhat ironic consequence of leading the Chávez government to radicalize the revolution.

The first two years of Chávez rule (1999-2000) were defined by moderation. The immediate focus was on political reforms, with the government leading a critical and broad-based discussion about the existing political system. This debate ultimately produced a new constitution that enshrined the notion of participatory democracy within the body politic and led to modest economic reforms. Subsequent years saw a more direct confrontation with neoliberalism, a process that alienated a portion of Chávez's middle-class and moderate supporters, many of whom joined the opposition and took to the streets, in effect facilitating the coup in April 2002, the oil industry lock out, and the attempted recall of Chávez in 2004.[3]

In short, the first years of the new millennium were characterized by intensifying class polarization. The opposition's hardening stance forced open confrontation and created a situation in which the government could either face defeat or push the revolution forward. With remarkable consistency, the opposition's aggression led the Chávez government, supported by a mobilized but fragmented base, to push the revolution down more radical paths through a series of electoral victories. It was not simply that the government was able to repel the coup, resist economic sabotage, or defeat the presidential referendum, but that these disruptions created opportunities for the Chávez government to further weaken its opponents and deepen the process of change.[4] To a certain extent the government had little choice, and it is quite possible that the ongoing conflict pushed Chávez in more radical directions than he initially envisioned.

This somewhat chaotic method of constantly consolidating power while driving forward transformational processes was remarkably successful. Looking back, one can – as many Venezuelan leftists did at the time – wonder whether the level of popular support might have allowed the Chávez government to push reforms even further and faster, and more deeply cripple an opposition that refused to compromise and whose primary goal was regime change. This decision about how fast and how far to push change is an inherently difficult one and hardly unique to Venezuela. The Allende government in Chile and the Sandinistas in Nicaragua, both of whom started with clearer visions about the transition to socialism, wrestled with this as well.

Although by 2005 Chávez could openly advocate for socialism, was in firm control of congress, and faced a divided and weakened opposition, it was always a balancing act. One of the government's main initiatives during this period, starting in 2003, was the creation of targeted social programmes under the rubric of 'missions', often emanating from the presidential palace, designed to meet people's basic needs and reduce poverty. The missions were immensely successful, both in terms of improving lives and gaining support for the government, but were dependent on state funding that was itself a function of high oil prices. Indeed, the missions only became possible after Chávez got control of the PDVSA and oil revenue in 2002-2003. By lifting a significant portion of the population out of poverty, these social programmes put people in a better position to engage politically, but they did not change the state apparatus, serve as vehicles for mobilizing working-class power, or provide people with self-sustaining forms of livelihood. When oil prices later collapsed it would prove difficult for the government to sustain this level of social spending. The inherent limitations of the missions as engines for driving the revolution forward are no doubt why the Chávez government pursued other paths – experimenting with workers cooperatives, increasing expropriations, bolstering worker presence on state company boards, and eventually spearheading the much larger scale effort to create thousands of communal councils, not to mention, as we shall see below, the creation of a new socialist party.[5]

As Steve Ellner points out, the development of the Bolivarian Revolution during Chávez's rule came to be defined by a pattern that consisted of 'conflict, the exit of moderates, the consolidation of power, and the radicalization of goals'.[6] Though broadly successful, this process was also problematic on a number of levels. On the one hand, the process was remarkable in that although Venezuela did not become 'socialist', the country nonetheless initiated a process whereby a left-wing government not only managed to acquire and retain (a large degree of) state power over a significant period of time, but actually became more radical over time. As the right hardened its stance, Chávez was effectively forced to push the revolution further, a process that required, drove, and was fuelled by the constant reconfiguration and mobilization of the popular classes (who were internally divided and only partially took their cues from the Chávez government). In short, a certain amount of polarization created opportunities to push the revolution forward.

On the other hand, a number of factors called into question the long-term sustainability of what has been an imperfect, uneven, and somewhat chaotic process characterized by ever-deepening polarization. To begin, as the level of polarization intensified and the opposition dug in, the survival and advancement of the revolution came to require the near-permanent mobilization of mass support, something that is impossible to maintain even with a more unified base. In part because such a high level of mobilization is unsustainable, the Chávez government was often forced to (or at least did) make various concessions to either win over or temporarily appease sectors of the business class. Such compromises, including unholy alliances with a corrupt business class, some of whom enriched themselves through connections with the Chávez-Maduro governments (i.e. the 'boli-bourgeoisie'), had real costs for the revolution. Nonetheless, these concessions were seen as necessary to ensure a basic level of political and economic stability.[7] The opposition, though divided, still possessed the capacity to seriously disrupt the economy, generate political instability, and undermine support for the government. Indeed, this conflict – and the need to deal with powerful reactions by elites – is inherent in any gradual transition to socialism that takes place within liberal democracy.

There is perhaps no better expression of this than the periodic efforts by the business class to create a scarcity of consumer goods by reducing production, selling products in alternative markets, limiting imports, or simply hoarding supplies, in effect promoting economic turmoil in order to foment political instability. Indeed, for years, Venezuelans 'have acknowledged that scarcity of basic consumer goods spikes around important elections, as businesses seek to pressure voters' into turning against the government.[8] The government's response to these shortages has been to put price and exchange rate controls in place (starting in 2003) and increase the number of protected products. Such action was to ensure that Venezuelans, especially the poor, had access to affordable goods while also encouraging domestic-oriented industry. The private sector responded by in effect deepening the cycle, further reducing production and/or limiting imports to the domestic market which in turn created more scarcity, hardship, and instability. The government then expropriated companies to ensure continued production and encourage/intimidate other companies to maintain production.[9] By making US dollars available at artificially low prices to some sectors in order to sustain imports, increase internal production, and maintain a steady flow of affordable goods, the government also formally expanded the (already unsustainable) system of currency exchange.

To the extent that government expropriations gave the state more control over the economy they could be said to advance socialism. Likewise, the expanded currency exchange system ensured, at least in the short term, that basic goods would remain available at affordable prices. These policies and initiatives did not, however, represent a coherent, planned, or extensive process, so much as a response to a reactionary opposition – a response that simultaneously weakened and fed the opposition. More than this, it has proved hard to get off this downward spiral of politically-driven shortages, difficult-to-sustain government price/exchange controls, disruptive black markets, out of control inflation, capital flight, and all the long lines, corruption, unholy alliances, uncertainty, and turmoil that goes along with it. This contributed to an ever-deepening process of polarization and the perception that the government was incapable of creating a basic level of stability and security.

It is important to remember that although this deepening crisis could be partly attributed to government missteps, the situation itself – and the tough decisions the government faced – were a byproduct of class conflict characterized by open warfare on the part of the business class. Elites defended their interests, the government responded in kind, and the conflict deepened.[10] This level of polarization, which both sides fomented, served to mobilize supporters and opponents alike, and at times generated opportunities for the revolution. It also, however, made it difficult to govern, let alone sustain the long-term transformational process that revolution requires.

Recognizing the need to blunt the opposition and limit its ability to destabilize the political system, the Chávez government redoubled efforts to strengthen popular power. This came most forcefully through two initiatives – the creation of communal councils and the formation of the *Partido Socialista Unido de Venezuela* (PSUV) – starting in 2006 at a particularly opportune moment. Chávez had just been re-elected by a wide margin, was in control of the National Assembly, faced a deeply debilitated opposition, and enjoyed high oil prices.

By the end of 2006, or just months after the initiative had been announced, over 10,000 councils had formed and were receiving a massive infusion of state resources. Tens of thousands more would be created in the following years, eventually reaching over 40,000. The basic idea was that legally-constituted communal councils, representing relatively small communities, would be the building blocks of a more democratic, people-controlled, parallel state. Socialism would emerge out of these local structures, eventually developing on regional (i.e. communes) and national levels, in effect replacing the bourgeois state with a communal state. Unlike the existing state, which was so perverted by capitalism that it had to be transcended, the communal councils would foster the capacity of working-class people, ultimately making the communal state a legitimate expression of working-class power and democracy.[11]

In practice, councils were eligible for funding directly from the federal government in order to carry out community projects ranging from constructing roads, housing, and community centres to improving health, education, and agriculture – addressing needs as defined by communities. With more than 40,000 councils, this initiative has directly involved millions of people in the organization, planning, and development of their own communities. They created something of a parallel state, allowing the federal government to bypass local governments and put financial resources directly in the hands of 'the people'. In so doing, they increased popular participation with(in) the Venezuelan state on an unprecedented scale. Not surprisingly, however, there was wide variation in terms of how these councils were run, how well they functioned, how their purpose was understood, how they related to the state – and the extent to which they advanced socialist goals. The council programme, heavily dependent on revenue from oil production, was certainly vulnerable to clientelism and created additional points of contention and bureaucracy between Venezuelans and the state, even apart from problems associated with small-scale development initiatives in general.[12]

Since 2010, the councils have not only continued to expand in number, but have increasingly become oriented towards the creation of alternative sources of livelihood (i.e. they have branched out beyond supporting state-funded community projects). They have also been organized at higher levels through the establishment of over one thousand communes, which coordinate the efforts of local councils to create socially-controlled production units and increase popular political power at larger scales. Many of these have become focused on limiting the crisis connected to collapsing oil prices, with the idea of providing Venezuelans access to affordable goods through the creation of farms and non-profit food shops. The establishment of tens of thousands of cooperatives has also been part of this broader effort, which in tandem with the councils/communes have bolstered social production through the creation of alternative forms of economy that provide both basic goods and a means of livelihood for thousands of Venezuelans. These initiatives have expanded into virtually every conceivable area of the economy, including not only food-related enterprises but transportation, communications, housing, health, banking, etc.[13]

And yet, although they have received billions of dollars, the councils have not been able to transform a state that still controls the vast majority of the government's resources and makes most of the important, national-level, decisions. Even at the local level, municipal governments retained considerable power. Likewise, the attempt to create a more socially-controlled economy through (a) the creation of alternative economic forms such as councils/cooperatives and (b) a fairly limited effort to nationalize, develop, or appropriate various industries and companies has thus far not produced a more mixed economy. Private capital still controls roughly the same amount of the economy as when Chávez first came to office in 1999. In short, the councils did not replace the bourgeois state, create sufficiently powerful alternative economies, or seriously challenge capital. To a large extent, rather than serving as the incubators of a socialist economy, they were dependent on a state flush with oil revenue. This became more apparent as the political crisis deepened, oil prices declined, and funding for the councils became more difficult to sustain.

The local and developing nature of the communal councils is partly why Chávez announced – following his landslide electoral victory in 2006 – the formation of the PSUV, a consolidated political party that was to unite all of the various parties and social forces of the left in support of the Bolivarian Revolution. Chávez urged all parties on the left to dissolve into the PSUV, insisting that it would be run from the bottom-up and become the most democratic party in the history of Latin America. It was a vehicle through which socialism would be energized and advanced, avoiding the one-party pitfalls of bureaucratization and authoritarianism. Ideally, a collective leadership, semi-independent of Chávez and the state, would be elected through democratic channels and facilitate the revolutionary break from capitalist institutions.[14]

As with the communal councils, the need for a robust and unified party was and is both sound and apparent. It was, however, controversial in theory and complicated in practice. To begin with, there were the practical difficulties of incorporating a wide range of political views and pre-existing bureaucratic structures and personal investments into a single entity. A number of parties and trade unions valued their autonomy and feared not only being subsumed by the PSUV, but by the government and Chávez himself. Issues around internal democracy have been complicated by a level of bureaucratization, corruption, and disorganization.[15]

The broader issue, however, is that although the emphasis on political participation, internal democracy, and competing within a multi-party system is part of what has made the PSUV attractive (and allows it to avoid charges of trying to develop a single-party political system controlled by a socialist state), it has also meant that the PSUV was trying to get off the ground at the same time as it was fighting struggles on virtually all fronts. Creating a new party within a crowded political landscape, with a functioning infrastructure, that has healthy internal debates and elections, and incorporates diverse organizations and millions of members, is not an easy task under any circumstances. Doing so within the context of constant 'life or death' political campaigns, a particularly vicious opposition that foments political instability at every turn, and a deteriorating economic situation that undermines popular enthusiasm for the government has proven more than the party is capable of handling. More than this, because this is not a form of socialism where party functionaries effectively control all levels of the state, the creation of a strong socialist party under liberal democracy does not automatically translate into socialist control of the state by a revolutionary government.

Indeed, well before the death of Chávez, the ambitious aspirations that animated the PSUV's formation were severely circumscribed. The PSUV began to look more and more like a traditional bureaucratic party that was narrowly focused on the electoral realm, not particularly democratic, and too closely tied to the apparatus of the state; parts of its leadership had become a political caste that negotiated with other party leaders and state officials while promoting their own interests. It lost much of its popular-participatory character, its connection to the mass base deteriorated, and instead of being a semi-independent force that would help democratize the state it became a top-down institution largely controlled by upper echelons of the Chávez-Maduro governments. These shortcomings were partly expressed through, and at times exacerbated by, increasing divisions and departures within/from the party itself – fractures that became even wider and more open after the death of Chávez in March of 2013.[16] The importance of these flaws was revealed as the crisis deepened and exposed the need for a more democratic and vigorous political party.

Many of the Bolivarian Revolution's most conspicuous gains – in poverty reduction, education, healthcare – were direct byproducts of very large public spending increases made possible by the election of a government with decent priorities and a commodity boom that sent oil prices skyrocketing. The Chávez government did not simply pour money into the missions, which lifted people out of poverty and strengthened the Chavista base. It also channelled resources towards the support and creation of popular organizations, such as the councils and communes, which were to provide an alternative base of power. Ideally, these institutions would allow for the transformation of the political and economic system – a force that would theroetically remain at least partially independent of any particular government.

Oil money made these efforts possible, but also obscured some of the limitations associated with them. As long as the state had sufficient revenue to lift people out of poverty, finance popular organizations, and support the (unsustainable) system of currency exchange, the Chávez government was able to keep a handle on the economy and retain sufficient support among its base of working poor. This allowed the government to ignore or not deal aggressively enough with a whole host of problems that simmered beneath the surface (and which have plagued other left governments throughout the region), including: the ongoing erosion of middle-class support, which was somewhat tolerable as long as the working-class base could be sufficiently mobilized to keep the opposition in check and deliver votes in a never-ending string of electoral contests; the ongoing problems of corruption, clientelism, and patronage, all of which not only fed the opposition's moralizing rhetoric but produced a popular support that could be thin in places and dependent on the continued flow of government largesse; the limitations of missions/councils as vehicles for creating alternative bases of political and economic power; the failure to build state-controlled domestic industries, or other forms of economic activity that could diversify the economy and generate resources without being so heavily dependent on exports; and the broader inability to wrest control of key sectors of the economy from the business class.[17]

The crash of commodity prices exposed these underlying issues, as government revenue dried up. To be fair, because virtually no one predicted that the price of oil would tumble so fast and so far, assuming prices would remain high indefinitely, there was little sense that the window of opportunity was so small. There was, or seemed to be, time to build the kind of political and economic power that was needed to seriously challenge capital and advance socialism.

What this meant was that as commodity prices collapsed – not long after Chávez died – it became clear that what the Bolivarian Revolution had been able to create in political, economic, and cultural terms was not sufficiently strong to sustain sectors of the working class whose lives and organizations were dependent on government spending, an economy that was under constant attack by the opposition, and a political base that was both fragile and absolutely necessary come election time. These (and other) vulnerabilities became exposed, eroding popular support for the government while re-energizing the right. The partial reversal of neoliberalism clearly improved people's lives while generating increased support for the Chávez government. Yet although increased spending on social programmes bought the Chávez government some time to develop the working-class power needed to transform the state, challenge capital, and build alternative economic forms, this is not the same as actually doing so. More than this, the window for advancing a deeper challenge to capitalism that this increase in social spending created could not remain open forever, especially as commodity prices began to plunge. Most of the gains with respect to poverty reduction, for example, happened prior to the 2008-09 global recession and the first drop in oil prices. Capacity had to be rapidly built and deployed in such a way that fundamentally altered the developmental model and undermined the oligarchy's control over the economy.

As the six-year plan (2013-2019) for the Bolivarian Revolution suggests, this point was hardly lost on Chávez:

> We shouldn't let ourselves be deceived: the social and economic system that still prevails in Venezuela is a capitalist and rentier system. This is precisely a program to strengthen and consolidate socialism, looking for a radical suppression of the logic of capital ... it is necessary to completely pulverize the bourgeois State that we have inherited.[18]

This did not happen, and the opposition was able to regain its footing after Chavez's death partly because his absence created a void; partly because opposition efforts to destabilize the government intensified under the presidency of Chávez's successor, Nicolas Maduro; partly because the inflation and scarcity associated with the system of currency exchange continued to spiral out of control; and partly because oil prices, which had dropped during the recession of 2008-2009 but then rebounded, began to drop quickly in the second half of 2014. Not many governments could have weathered this storm. Even during the collapse of oil prices and state revenue, the Maduro government emphasized the continued importance of the councils to the Bolivarian Revolution and increased the flow of financial aid to the communes.

Inflation, however, which had been increasing at the end of Chávez's rule, reached triple digits by this time. This was tied to the rising price of imported food due to the shortage of dollars. The exchange rate made dollars artificially cheap, creating an ever-greater demand for dollars, which increased the black market price and drove up the cost of imports and rate of inflation.[19] A policy that had been designed to keep the import of basic goods flowing, and even encourage business to invest more in domestic production, ultimately had the opposite effect. As Gregory Wilpert explained right before the fateful December 2015 elections:

> A vicious cycle thus began in early 2014, where an ever-widening gap between the official and unofficial exchange rates created ever-greater incentives to profit from that gap, thereby further widening that same gap. The black market exchange rate thus began to increase exponentially in the course of 2014 and 2015 … creating a 125:1 ratio between the black market and the official exchange rates. Massive profits of up to 12,500 per cent were thus possible. As a result, more and more people became involved in efforts to acquire dollars at the official rate, mostly by purchasing subsidized goods in Venezuela and (re-)exporting them across the border for enormous profit.[20]

Much of what Venezuela imported was simply being exported again, creating a greater scarcity of goods and fuelling inflation. Worst yet, the opportunities for speculation and corruption became incredibly tempting as one of the only secure ways to make money, which further undermined confidence in the government and economy. For a time, the Maduro government was able to keep a lid on this downward spiral by stabilizing the black market rate for dollars, but that became increasingly difficult to do as the collapse of oil prices drained government reserves. In other words, as long as the government had dollars that it could give away at a fraction of their value to encourage businesses to import goods, it was at least barely able to keep the problem under control in the short term, even as inflation and an overall reduction in imports caused uncertainty, hardship, and chaos for virtually all sectors (and especially the poor who had limited access to dollars).[21] But such policies were not only financially unsustainable, especially as oil prices dropped, they also left control over imports in the hands of the private sector, in effect giving the opposition the power to create a scarcity of basic goods. This broader situation proved impossible to sustain, and in the end Maduro had to choose between further radicalizing the revolution or working with sectors of the business class. Because the government needed to consolidate power in order both to survive and to prevent the opposition from completely reversing the revolution's gains, Maduro largely chose the latter as the crisis worsened after 2013: cutting taxes and implementing more business-friendly policies, appointing representatives of the business class to key government offices, reducing certain social programmes, expanding mining, and aggressively paying down the national debt. The economic and political crises effectively fed one another, leaving Maduro with few good options.[22]

In terms of what lies ahead, although neither the communal councils nor the PSUV were able to transform the bourgeois state, create a parallel state, or ensure political stability, much depends on whether they can yet become critical vehicles for driving the revolution forward. Large sections of the state remain hostile to communal power, both as a political force and as productive alternatives. But the councils remain a crucial base of support for Maduro, who has pushed forward the communal process by encouraging the creation of communes and the National Assembly of Communes. Equally important, the councils/communes are the most important expression of popular power that exists independently of the government. For its part the PSUV, although hardly the revolutionary force that Chávez and others envisioned, remains the most significant party in Venezuela. Given the precariousness of the present, and the difficult position of the Maduro government, the path forward absolutely requires building popular power from below through a variety of working-class organizations. How the councils and the PSUV respond to this challenge will be the key to the survival of the Bolivarian Revolution.

CONCLUSION

The Latin American left has had a rough couple of years. Lula-Rousseff faced indictment, impeachment, and a de facto political coup over a two-year period starting in 2014, Kirchner-Fernandez was defeated in Argentina in 2015, Chávez-Maduro lost a critical legislative election at the end of 2015, and Morales experienced defeat on a 2016 constitutional amendment that would have allowed him to run for a third term. While US imperialism played some role in all of this, the fact is that most of these governments have suffered defeats in the very same way that they came to power in the first place – through the ballot box and institutions of representative democracy.

More than this, the road to ruin, or at least setback, was broadly similar across the region and not all that different from the path to success a decade earlier. The commodity boom delivered, but so too did the bust.[23] Left governments came to power in the late 1990s and 2000s through popular insurgencies of varying intensity and composition. Once in office, they focused on consolidating political power both via legalistic measures, most notably through the creation of progressive constitutions, and by continuing to build and mobilize the diverse constituencies that brought them to power in the first place. This process alone was significant. It mobilized people, invested larger numbers in the political process, and in some cases produced important advances for indigenous and Afro-descendant populations. This political process did not, however, necessarily create the basis for radically restructuring the political economy or pose a significant threat to property relations.

In fact at least initially, and in some cases permanently, these newly elected governments pursued a path of development that shared much with the models that preceded them. Dependence on agricultural and mineral exports continued and in many cases even increased as high commodity prices allowed governments to invest in infrastructure, public sector employment, and a range of social programmes. This, too, was significant. By unevenly reversing neoliberalism, increased public spending helped alleviate poverty and improved people's lives. It also restored, at least partially, faith in the potential role of the state and put 'socialism' back on the public radar. And it antagonized elites, who after decades of neoliberalism had come to assume that they would be the primary, if not the only, beneficiaries of state policy.

Yet although the willingness of the new governments to increase social spending produced significant results and was 'radical' in relation to the low bar set by two-plus decades of neoliberalism, such spending did not represent the arrival of a new economic model. It was not simply that increased public spending was heavily dependent on high commodity prices, and tended to come with increased patronage, clientelism, and consumerism, all of which served to erode transformative processes and lend credence to the right's discourse of corruption and inefficiency. It was that this increased spending did not in itself represent a fundamental shift in economic relations, or necessarily provide the basis for pushing forward structural transformation. For the centre-left governments that emerged in Brazil, Argentina, and Chile this appears to have represented the boundaries of change. Social spending was increased, but the basic structure of the economy remained largely untouched.

The governments of Venezuela, Bolivia, and (to a much lesser extent) Ecuador, however, all took steps to deepen the process of change. Flush with oil money, Venezuela went the furthest. But as commodity prices plunged, economies contracted, and inequality once again increased, people protested against attacks on the social-public goods they had won over the past two decades. Popular frustration was now directed at left governments that had come to power on an anti-neoliberal wave, promising to rule on behalf of the nation.

Such setbacks are, however, to be expected in deeply contested class struggles for systemic change within bourgeois democracy. Although the specifics differ, the contentious and polarizing nature of these struggles, the loss of middle-class support, and the difficulty of advancing and sustaining left projects in such circumstances is clearly part of the explanation as to why the left has experienced setbacks in not only Venezuela, but Argentina, Brazil, Nicaragua, and Bolivia. How the Latin American left responds remains to be seen, but the simple fact is that it has become an important force on the political landscape. During the past twenty years in Latin America, progressive forces have discredited neoliberalism and rescued socialism from the sectarian margins, transforming it into a sufficiently broad platform from which a revitalized left has organized around a series of reforms that, if not clearly anti-capitalist, have put an important claim back on the public agenda: The state and political system are important and necessary terrains of collective struggle that working people must (and can) capture if we are to live in a world where social needs are prioritized over market forces. It took decades of neoliberalism, an intense political backlash, and years of sustained organizing to get to the point where something is left. It will take decades more to nurture and channel this public consciousness while building the political forms and institutions capable of consistently and effectively advancing socialism.

NOTES

1   I would like to thank George Ciccariello-Maher, Aviva Chomsky, Steve Ellner, Lesley Gill, and Adolph Reed for commenting on an early draft of this paper.
    For capital's ever-deeper expansion into indigenous territories and the place of indigenous movements and environmental concerns in the emergence of the Latin American left see: Aviva Chomsky and Steve Striffler, 'Labor Environmentalism in Colombia and Latin America', *Working USA: The Journal of Labor and Society*, 17(December), 2014, p. 491-508.
2   Gregory Wilpert, 'Venezuela: An Electoral Road to Twenty-First-Century Socialism', in Jeffrey R. Webber and Barry Carr, eds., *The New Latin American Left: Cracks in the Empire*, New York: Roman and Littlefield Publishers, 2013, p. 192-3.
3   Steve Ellner, 'Social and Political Diversity and the Democratic Road to Change in Venezuela', in Steve Ellner, ed., *Latin America's Radical Left: Challenges and Complexities of Political Power in the Twenty-First Century*, New York: Roman and Littlefield, 2014, p. 79-102. See also Gregory Wilpert, 'Venezuela: Participatory Democracy or Government as Usual', *Socialism and Democracy* (online), 31 March 2011, available at: sdonline.org; Wilpert, 'Venezuela: An Electoral Road'; George Ciccariello-Maher, 'Constituent Moments, Constitutional Processes: Social Movements and the New

Latin American Left', in Steve Ellner, ed., *Latin America's Radical Left*; and Steve Ellner, *Rethinking Venezuelan Politics: Class, Conflict, and the Chávez Phenomenon*, New York: Lynne Reiner Publishers, 2007; Jeffrey R. Webber, 'Where is Venezuela Going', *Solidarity*, January-February, 2010, available at: www.solidarity-us.org.

4   Steve Ellner, 'Social and Political Diversity'; Steve Ellner, 'Setting the Record Straight on Venezuela', *Jacobin*, 4 December 2015.

5   Ellner, 'Social Policy and Diversity'; Wilpert, 'Venezuela: Participatory Democracy'; Roger Burbach and Camila Piñeiro Harnecker, 'Venezuela's Participatory Socialism', *Socialism and Democracy*, 21(3), 2007.

6   Ellner, *Rethinking Venezuelan Politics*, p. 139.

7   For a good discussion of the Boli-bourgeoisie, including the opposition's efforts to reduce all of Venezuela's problems to 'corrupt socialism', see Steve Ellner, 'Beyond the Boliburguesía Thesis', *NACLA*, June 9, 2016. Available at: nacla.org.

8   Ryan Mallett-Outtrim, 'How Bad is Venezuela's Economic Situation', *venezuelanalysis. com*, 25 January 2016. See also: Peter Bolton, 'The Other Explanation for Venezuela's Economic Crisis', Council on Hemispheric Affairs, 24 March 2016, available at: www.coha.org.

9   Ellner, 'Setting the Record Straight'; Steve Ellner, 'After Chávez: The Maduro Government and the "Economic War" in Venezuela', *New Left Project*, 24 December 2014, available at: www.newleftproject.org.

10 Ellner, 'Social Policy and Diversity'; Ellner, 'Setting the Record Straight'.

11 Burbach and Piñeiro Harnecker, 'Venezuela's Participatory Socialism'; Ellner, 'Social and Political Diversity'; Wilpert, 'Venezuela: Participatory Democracy'.

12 Burbach and Piñeiro Harnecker, 'Venezuela's Participatory Socialism'; Ellner, 'Social and Political Diversity'; Wilpert, 'Venezuela: Participatory Democracy'; Dario Azzellini, 'The Communal State: Communal Councils, Communes, and Workplace Democracy', *NACLA*, 30 June 2013.

13 Andrew Kennis, 'The Quiet Revolution: Venezuelans Experiment with Participatory Democracy', *In These Times*, 10 August 2010; John Bellamy Foster, 'Chávez and the Communal State: On the Transition to Socialism in Venezuela', *Monthly Review*, 66(11), 2015; George Ciccariello-Maher, 'Venezuela: Comuna o Nada!', 22 March 2016, *Roar Magazine*, roarmag.org; Frederick B. Mills, 'Chavista Theory of Transition Towards the Communal State', *Open Democracy*, 8 August 2015.

14 Burbach and Piñeiro Harnecker, 'Venezuela's Participatory Socialism'; Ryne Maloney-Risner, 'Development of the United Socialist Party of Venezuela', *venezuelanalaysis.com*. 12 November 2009.

15 Burbach and Piñeiro Harnecker, 'Venezuela's Participatory Socialism'; Maloney-Risner, 'Development of the United Socialist Party'.

16 On recent issues within the PSUV see: Eva Maria and César Romero, 'Chavismo From Below', *Jacobin*, 15 April 2016; Ewan Robertson, 'Venezuela's PSUV Accused of Expelling *Marea Socialista* Dissidents', venezuelanalysis.com, 24 November 2014; Patrick Guillaudat and Pierre Mouterde, 'Venezuela: Behind the Defeat of December 6, 2015', *Life on the Left*, 18 January 2016.

17 For example, about two-thirds of the Venezuelan GDP is currently controlled by the private sector, or roughly the same proportion as in 1998 when Chávez was first elected. Guillaudat and Mouterde, 'Venezuela: Behind the Defeat'.

18 'Venezuela: Hugo Chávez's Six-Year Plan for Venezuela', *Links: International Journal of Socialist Renewal*, http://links.org.au/node/3079.

19 Mark Weisbrot, 'How to Fix Venezuela's Troubled Exchange Rate', *Fortune*, 2 August 2014.

20 Gregory Wilpert, 'The Roots of the Current Situation in Venezuela', *Telesur*, 22 November 2015.

21 On crisis also see: Victor Alvarez, 'What is at stake is not the stability of a government but the viability of a nation', *Venezuela analysis,* 23 March 2016, venezuelanalysis.com; Ryan Mallet-Outtrim, 'Does Venezuela's Crisis Prove Socialism Doesn't Work', *Counterpunch*, 25 May 2016, available at: www.counterpunch.org.
22 Eva Maria and César Romero, 'Chavismo From Below'; Steve Ellner, 'Las expectativas falsas de la estrategia negociadora en Venezuela', *Aporrea.org*, 5 March 2016.
23 For a good discussion on the region's continued dependence on export-oriented extractivism see: Claudio Katz, 'Is South America's "Progressive Cycle" at an End: Neo-Developmentalist Attempts and Socialist Projects', *The Bullet,* 4 March 2016, available at: www.socialistproject.ca.

IN SEARCH OF THE 'MODERN PRINCE': THE NEW QUÉBEC REBELLION

PIERRE BEAUDET

Since the beginning of the millennium, there have been many experiences of mass struggles and even popular insurrections in various regions of the world. The most far-reaching have occurred in South America, where some neoliberal governments have been forced to retreat by popular pressure, leaving the space for new left governments. Unprecedented mass mobilizations have shaken other parts of the capitalist 'periphery' – the Arab Spring in North Africa and the Middle East, the popular uprisings in Nepal, Thailand, Burkina Faso, Guadeloupe, etc. On a lesser scale, there have been the mobilizations of the Indignados in southern Europe, Occupy in the United States and Canada. The internationalization of social struggles and movements has now become obvious. Political and cultural boundaries are overcome through a vast web of circulating experiences. Even words and designations have acquired an international dimension and are adopted across cultural and linguistic barriers: 'intifada', 'Tahrir', 'Pachamama', 'Indignados'.

The winds of change initiated in South America are faltering on the issues of governance, corruption, incapacity to come out of a subaltern resource-dependent economy, etc. The Arab Spring has destabilized the elites, but has been unable to eradicate their dense networks, so closely allied with global imperialism. The left in Europe is also in a difficult moment, especially after the failure of Syriza. In the Anglo-American milieu, the system has successfully resisted Occupy and other mass movements while it remains unclear whether the enthusiasm sparked by the rise of Jeremy Corbyn and Bernie Sanders will shift the orientations of social movements and centre-left parties toward transformative projects.

Yet amidst the ups and downs of the past decade of struggles, the process still goes on, refuelling a worldwide debate about reform/revolution, class/state, organization/spontaneity, as well as the key question of 'agency'.

Considering that in Marx's view, history is not predetermined but is informed by a host of 'objective' and 'subjective' factors, change has to be 'driven' by a specific project, organized around a specific 'process' involving specific organizational structures. Whose project is it? What indeed is the 'project'? What is the process (how to get there)? And what are the structures (how are we going to organize the struggle)?

These questions cannot be answered abstractly. This essay will address them specifically in relation to the 'Carrés rouges' in Québec, the leading site of rebellion in North America in recent years. As this popular movement created a new space for itself as part and parcel of a larger process, it also richly revealed the dialectics between the 'local' and the 'international'. Indeed, the Québec militant ascendency can be associated with an unprecedented international mobilization around a complex and prolonged battle to challenge US and Canadian-led globalization processes (in particular the 'Free Trade Area of the Americas'). In the late 1990s, a wide coalition involving trade unions and many grass-roots groups was created to move into action (beyond organizing conferences and lobbying governments), in conjunction with the emerging South American opposition. This coalesced into the People's Summit of the Americas in 2001,[1] an event organized by the Réseau Québécois sur l'intégration des Amériques in conjunction with networks in English Canada, the US, Mexico, Brazil, Chile and Argentina. The Summit not only brought more than 50,000 people to Québec City, it also seeded a deeper 'community of resistance' in a process that, unpredictably, was part of the creation from below of what an essay in the *Socialist Register* called a new 'transnational subject'.[2]

More or less during the same period, the World Social Forum (WSF) was first convened in 2001 by Brazilian organizations. This international meeting became more than an event, but also a complex and multi-scaled process of exchanges and debates. As the WSF expanded its course from 2002 onwards, it met with tremendous interest within the Québécois militant milieu. Thousands of people from different popular movements actually went to Porto Alegre and later other cities where the WSF was held. This Québec participation was more than 'left tourism', as organizations used these moments to really engage on strategic issues that were important to the subsequent mobilizations. They decided collectively which of the myriad of workshops to attend. Daily briefings allowed delegates to reflect, take critical distance and start a discussion on how to go further. Extensive debriefings were held after returning home, within the confines of the participating organizations and through public debates. This accelerated political matchmaking, breaking small boundaries and creating an atmosphere of convergence. The Social Forum process in Québec, in that sense, became an organizational and intellectual process, functioning year-round before, during and after the Forums, allowing innovative local/international encounters and explorations.[3]

It was these international foundations that gave popular movements in Québec a particular impetus from the 1990s onwards. There was on the one hand a learning experience where the gains and successes of movements worldwide became much more accessible, and integrated into local dynamics. There was, on the other hand, a boost of self-confidence because Québec popular movements, in comparing themselves to many other situations, actually discovered that they had more organizational and political skills and assets than they had previously thought.

All this came together in the consistent efforts by popular movements and the left to build a counter-hegemonic project in Québec over the past decade, a period in which mass movements and struggles intensified, from student strikes to major confrontations led by community organizations (such as the powerful housing coalition FRAPRU[4]) and trade unions. At the same time, a battle of ideas continued unabated in publications and journals and think tanks.[5] In these experiments, the transformative project was organized and reinforced through inquiries and studies built on an active and constant dialogue between practice and theory, and rendered to social movements as learning and organizational tools. Notably, largely outside the universities, social movements have created their own think tanks within their own structures or in conjunction with like-minded independent collectives. In the tradition of Gramsci and Bourdieu, we can recognize here the establishment, through the prolonged and complex engagement of a 'popular bloc', of a counter-hegemonic power inside and outside the multiple structures of the state, fighting on multiple fronts in the economic, political and cultural domains. This reformulates, in our time, the Gramscian idea of the 'modern prince' as 'a dynamic process, which aims at nothing less than a totalizing expansion across the entire social formation, as a new organization of social and political relations'.[6]

THE REBELLION IN HISTORICAL PERSPECTIVE

The popular republican uprising known as the 1837-38 rebellion represented the unique mix in the cauldron of Quebec, alone in the Anglo-American 'new world', of the French revolutionary spirit with the spirit of national liberation that had engulfed the new, and first, post-colonial state formations in Latin America and the Caribbean. The terrible defeat of the rebellion resulted in the repression of any and all mass movements with the support of an ultra-reactionary political and economic elite, which deeply marked Quebec right up to the mid-twentieth century. During that dark period, no socialist, communist or even trade-unionist networks of significant scope were able to shake the edifice of power.

After the Second World War, however, the old ruling bloc (mostly the Anglo-American bourgeoisie, local elites, and the Catholic hierarchy) was destabilized. A 'new', largely Francophone, bourgeoisie, along with an educated layer of professionals primarily in the booming public sector, emerged around a paradigm of Keynesian economic, social and political restructuring. It was commonly termed a 'Quiet Revolution' through which society was changed from the top down in the name of 'modernization', which meant becoming more aligned with what was happening elsewhere in the capitalist world, particularly in North America. But this 'quiet' process progressively became not so 'quiet'. Trade unions were re-activated by independent activists, mostly from left Catholic circles, while substantial layers of workers, especially in the expanding public sector, got organized.

The new generation, which mobilized under the impetus of a massive secularization and expansion of public education through the 1960s, came together for a Québécois version of May 1968, heavily influenced by the ideologies of Third World national liberation, Sartrean Marxism and Camusian liberalism.[7] By the end of the decade, Québec was in flames, with spectacular confrontations involving workers, communities, and students.[8] All of this created a radical milieu based on social movements and a mixed 'soup' of ideologies ranging from Fanon to Che Guevara and Gramsci via the Black Panthers, the Chinese revolution and Italian *operaismo*. This creative confusion was partly based on the fact that the traditional organized left, whether communist or social democratic, remained very weak in Québec (although it had left traces in trade-union organizations). What many radical activists saw as a weakness was probably, viewed retroactively, a blessing in disguise.

The 'blind spot' of that movement was nonetheless a certain ambiguity concerning the link between social and national emancipation. As in other capitalist countries with internal national questions, radical mass movements in Québec could not escape the fact that the political order built by the colonial-capitalist state had to be confronted, and that no broad popular coalition against the Canadian bourgeois state could be built without incorporating the struggle against national oppression as an integral part of the 'socialist project'. However, reconciling the two terms, 'national' and 'social', was a tough challenge.[9] For a while in the 1970s the 'national' came to dominate, as many radical social movements tended to support the centrist-bourgeois Parti Québécois (PQ), which aspired to create an independent state well within the confines of North American capitalism.[10] Some left intellectuals theorized that this phase of supporting a bourgeois-nationalist project was a necessary 'first stage' on the road to emancipation.

This proved to be disastrous, firstly because the PQ leadership had no real intention of responding to the other (social) term of the equation, and secondly, because it was totally unable to confront the Canadian ruling bloc. Popular movements were sidelined in the PQ project apart from vague promises, and slowly but surely once it was in the government the PQ distanced itself from its original reformist outlook while postponing to an indefinite future the fight for independence. This was even more the case after 1980, when the first referendum on 'sovereignty' called by the PQ was roundly defeated.[11]

The disorientation of social movements allowed the resurgence of an 'old-new' left current that reconnected with the tradition of the socialist circles of the past, such as the Communist Party, arguing that national independence was essentially a conspiracy to 'divide the working classes'. In addition to their total theoretical incompetence, these born-again 'Marxist-Leninists' adopted a Stalinist version of the 'vanguard party', trying literally to 'take over' popular movements, in their eyes desperately seeking the 'science' of revolution through centralized and authoritarian processes.[12] By the early 1980s, the sectarian 'M-Lers' were largely overcome by the developing dynamic of social movements, especially the feminist movement, and by their inability to relate to the powerful grassroots mobilizations that developed around the 1980 referendum (even though it was ultimately defeated). The *coup de grâce* of course was the far left's inability to overcome the PQ's turn to austerity following the referendum, and the defeat of the labour movement that ensued.

Later into the decade, social movements slowly rebuilt their capacities. The influence of small but significant networks (like the Mouvement socialiste led by trade unionists or the Regroupement pour le socialisme, a mix of left-Christians and Gramscian communists) grew. However, it was within mass movements that the spirit of rebellion was redefined. Unlike in many other capitalist countries, this milieu was not confined to the university. It coalesced with many popular movements and progressive think tanks, where 'organic intellectuals', working with and within movements, produced an interesting landscape of sociological, political and economic initiatives in the language of the people, directly related to people's struggles.

The first important idea was to dispel illusions about the PQ and put forward the need to create a new 'social bloc' that could advance both social and national emancipation. Resistance against the Québec state (including when it was governed by the PQ) strengthened with the expansion of newly proletarianized social sectors composed of downgraded skilled workers and professionals working in health, education, media and the public sector in general. Empowering social movements as the drivers of the struggle was the main methodology, in contrast with the vanguardism and substitutionism of the 'Marxist-Leninist' remnants that had long been criticized by socialist and communist critical thinkers.

In a parallel process, the feminist impulse had an enormous influence on the society at large, and the movements in particular. Feminists were able to directly attack capitalism and patriarchy and integrate issues of inequality and gender within social struggles, not only against the 'system' but also in relation to the contradictions within movements. They built mass movements and led mass struggles for the 'right to choose', for childcare and equality in the work place. They created feminist movements, circles, committees, and activities within mainstream social movements.[13]

By the mid-1990s, it appeared that a relatively subtle red line was about to be crossed. Open confrontation with the PQ was on the agenda, eventually materialized in the form of a vast social movement led by the formidable Fédération des femmes du Québec (FFQ) in the 1995 March of Women Against Violence and Poverty, involving many thousands of people across the province's cities and villages. Similarly, trade unions were gearing up for massive battles against the state, for example, blockading important facilities like ports and bringing tens of thousands of people onto the streets to defend public education and childcare. When a Liberal government was elected in 2003, confrontations erupted in opposition to its right-wing agenda. A few months earlier, following a worldwide call issued at the World Social Forum in Porto Alegre, hundreds of thousands of citizens and activists joined together to oppose the war against Iraq in the streets of Montréal, Québec City and most other towns throughout the province. It was the biggest anti-war demonstration in North America. And indeed, the battle of ideas was won on that issue. The massive hostility in Québec to the war forced the Canadian government to officially renounce joining the US-led coalition.

This cycle of mobilization continued through 2005, when college and university students came out again in an enormous strike. They set up a new student federation, the Association pour une solidarité syndicale et étudiante (ASSÉ). The movement had a long-term programme, but at the same time it was very aware of the necessity to build a mass movement, and was wary of ending up as just another radical sect. The first strike was organized against government plans to cut back on loans and bursaries, and in the end forced the right-wing government to backtrack on student fees.

At the same time, new discussions were held on how to intervene on the political scene. They arose simultaneously from social movements and left circles that had survived beyond the myths of the 'vanguard party': left nationalists still operating within the paradigm of 'national liberation', Marxists and socialists of different varieties, but more importantly grassroots activists who thought that, to reinforce the social strength they had acquired, it was necessary to build another piece of the puzzle. As that process coalesced, it led in 2006 to the creation of an unusual kind of left party called Québec Solidaire (QS) out of the merger of '*Option citoyenne*', a political network created by feminists, and small socialist and '*independentist*' parties with informal networks of leftists within trade unions and community and student organizations. This went beyond the traditional left boundaries (in the vein of the experiments in 'broad left' parties elsewhere), refusing to adhere to precise platforms and ideologies and including a very wide range of outlooks, from left-leaning social-democrats to Marxists, left nationalists and even '*libertaires*' activists.

Without defining itself as 'anti-capitalist', QS's general outlook was about exploring 'plural economy' alternatives to capitalism. A large majority of delegates at the 2011 party convention went so far as to endorse a statement calling for 'an eventual socialization of economic activities, based on a strengthened public economy (state-owned companies and nationalization of major enterprises in some strategic sectors), a greater role for the 'social economy' (cooperatives, community-owned firms), and a controlled private sector, with much greater emphasis on promoting small and medium enterprises (SMEs)'. All-in-all, QS packaged a programme that combined: a strategic framework of striving for the independence of Québec; a focus on feminism both programmatically and organizationally (as in male-female parity in party structures); pluralism via inclusion of all who agreed to support and work to implement the party's 'values' and general orientations; and respect for minority opinions including the right of members with particular perspectives to organize within the party in support of their views; and internationalism – placing anti-imperialism, solidarity and global justice at the core of the new party's politics'.[14]

From the outset the idea was that QS was not going to be the 'leader', rather it was to be a part of the popular movement. On the other hand, although the idea was to run for office in provincial elections and challenge the right-wing parties, including the PQ, the initial idea was that 'winning elections' was not the only or even the main goal.

Entering the political scene was one path, not the only path, towards liberation. In fact, QS was initially conceived as a modest project, basically to project the voice of the movements within the confines of the political scene, taking its inspiration from new political experiments like the MAS (Movimiento al Socialismo) in Bolivia while foreshadowing the development of parties like Podemos in Spain.

CARRÈS ROUGES

But the major steps towards the creation a new 'modern prince' in Québec were taken at the beginning of this decade, as new social movements emerged to confront the state through huge coalitions involving large contingents of organizations newly engaged in politicizing social struggles. Like all social struggles, a social movement is never 'spontaneous': 'Beneath the surface, social forces are constantly interacting and reconfiguring life'.[15] While social protests may appear as an almost automatic response to specific economic or political events, they are in fact the result of 'self-conscious self-activity on the one hand, and a return of repressed collective trauma in a moment of collective struggle, on the other'.[16] This best captures how to appreciate what has happened in Québec since 2010, from the large 'Mains rouges' anti-austerity events and demonstrations to the broad 'eco-territorial' networks south of the St. Lawrence River, which effectively paralyzed an emerging shale-gas industry, and finally to the student-led Printemps érable (Maple Spring) uprising of 2012.

It took a radicalized student movement two years of meticulous work to prepare for this uprising through systematic consultations, policy debates and extensive production of studies and analyses, thereby 'winning the battle of ideas' not only with students but also with a large chunk of popular opinion.[17] Parallel to that preparation, ASSÉ reinvented an organizational culture promoting the supremacy of the general assembly against more traditional modes dependent on elected officials and core activists. Information on the process, including negotiations, was as transparent as it could be. The methods of organizing debates were constantly renewed, going back-and-forth between working groups and mandated (and revocable) structures. During the 2012 strikes, in educational institutions where ASSE was predominant, there were weekly assemblies where everything was discussed at length. This was achieved without exaggerated procedural debates, focusing discussions on goals and results. At the end of these discussions, votes were taken, identifying a majority perspective and not some vague implicit consensus.

The movement was able to identify a clear and achievable target: freezing student fees. And at the same time, it worked on raising the larger issue of accessibility to post-secondary education, implicating a large part of the population. By April 2012, the strike movement became unstoppable, especially once the other student federations accepted the leadership of ASSÉ, which for a while had agreed to become absorbed into a larger coalition, CLASSÉ (Coalition large de l'ASSÉ), incorporating important associations that had not been affiliated before. The political imperative overran the organizational boundaries, bringing into the centre of the battle many student groups that had been on the margins, but accepting that ASSÉ/CLASSÉ was the hegemonic pole. Every single day of the week, thousands of students blocked entry to universities and colleges and invaded the streets, very often with the support of teachers, professors and even parents, despite police repression. Pitched battles were engaged time and again with the police, but most of the time it was the sheer size of the mobilization that left a mark on the ground.

In May, faced with an impasse, the right-wing government followed up its threats by passing repressive laws and regulations curbing public demonstrations and prohibiting mass picketing around schools and colleges. This in turn led many thousands of people to join in street protests for weeks, more than once bringing 100,000 and even 200,000 people behind the banner of ASSÉ/CLASSÉ: 'Le mouvement est étudiant, mais la lutte est populaire' ('this is a student movement, but the battle concerns the whole people').

Apart from its multiple social expressions, the movement that came to be known as the 'Carrés rouges' (after the red squares of fabric worn by the students) was embraced by thousands of people, many sporting the red square in public. Very visible and loud demonstrations, large and small, took place simultaneously in many locations (sometimes 5 or 6 in various districts of Montréal alone), often accompanied by various artistic signs of solidarity. This was even visible in official media, where famous artists performed with the *carrés rouges* clearly evident on their clothing. Apparently coming out of the blue, this movement was in fact organized through a dense network of civic associations and trade unions, even if the call to demonstrate did not come directly from the leadership of these movements. Beginning as a way of subverting a ban on unannounced street protests, urban neighbourhoods across Quebec were soon rocked by what became known as the 'Casseroles', nightly festivals of local protest in which residents stood on their balconies or marched through the streets banging pots and pans.

It should also be noted that the mass demonstrations were organized peacefully, usually avoiding confrontations with the police. The organizations at the heart of the mobilization such as ASSÉ and CLASSÉ were not in favour of the 'principle' of the diversity of tactics promoted by anarchists, leading to small 'direct actions', like smashing storefront windows. They thought this was counter-productive, and without going to the extent of chasing out Black Bloc activists, they strongly tried to persuade activists not to disturb demonstrations. At the same time, they always refused to collaborate with the police or to denounce anarchists publicly. This did not prevent police provocation (undercover policemen dressed in black with masks encouraging destruction) and intimidation, as hundreds of peaceful demonstrators (not just black bloc participants) were arrested and charged under the new repressive laws (all charges were later dropped by judicial authorities). Despite this, repression and provocation did not have a substantial impact on the mass mobilizations.

The attempts by anarchists to set up spontaneous and non-hierarchical 'assemblies' following the methods adopted by Occupy had limited impact. There were not enough people to sit in these discussions, as the dominant attitude was that they were unnecessary unless one wanted to function within a strict anarchist framework. The fact that anarchists tried to prevent people with other perspectives from speaking, including those advocating political action, did not help. On the other hand, the student core of the movement was already organized through its own structures, including rigorous consultations and debates, but with an emphasis on taking decisions and elaborating strategies rather than confining themselves to the formal exercise of direct democracy. Anarchist activists and intellectuals did not consider the fact that the vast student movement had a history with organizational references, norms and methods which combined mass participation and leadership. Most people accepted these structures, not as individuals, but as members of a collective bound by a collective will and discipline.

These democratic processes did not fetishize forcing a 'consensus'. In most cases, votes were taken after detailed discussions, expressing the opinion of the majority and allowing organizations to move on. The key issue, beyond allowing the necessary time and resources for several opinions to be expressed, was to create a common will. Parallel methods to widen participation and avoid the monopolization of the discussion by more articulate activists were put in place: obligatory rotation between male and female speakers, limited speaking time for everyone, suspension of plenary debates to allow small groups to consult, systematic informational systems informing people about discussions to be undertaken in advance of meetings (which means they had not only the right to speak, but also the duty to prepare themselves), and the creation of 'working committees' besides elected councils and executives to prepare discussions and investigate various methods and strategies. All of this was 'irrigated', so to speak, by a dense network of social media and publications.

The insistence on 'horizontality' was grounded in the principle that anyone could have a say. However, when it was felt that the discussion had sufficiently included the different perspectives, it was time to make binding decisions based on the strategies that the majority found most suitable, while indicating the boundaries within which the actions were to take place; in other words, not leaving things 'vague' and open to 'interpretation', or relying on the false principle of the 'diversity of tactics'. In the end, the modes of operation adopted by the students were able, to a large extent, to overcome the genuine fear and anxiety shared by many activists, especially the youth, that their capacities would be stifled, as in other large organizations trapped by hierarchy, closed leadership, ultra-institutionalization and centralization. This process thereby invented an organizational culture that encouraged the transcending of the 'individual' in the production of a 'collective subject'.[18]

The immense and hostile media barrage against the movement had an impact, especially outside the metropolitan areas. The PQ government relied on this, hoping to recover the initiative after an election it called to 're-establish order'. In the end however, the bet was lost and the government was defeated. The student victory was far from total, but some of their main demands were forced on the government, which lost face twice: first when it sought to impose a substantial increase in fees, and then when it proved unable to crush the movement.

The right-wing Liberal party returned to power in April 2014 with a promise of 'clean' governance, by which they had in mind the kind of neoliberal 'revolution' that had 're-engineered' public administration elsewhere. Although the social movements have to date partially blocked the implementation of this agenda, there is currently in Québec a clear trend towards authoritarian crisis management. While basic freedoms are undermined, there is a new ideological offensive that in some ways resembles the 'clash of civilizations' thesis upheld by US conservative intellectuals such as Samuel Huntington, advanced since the beginning of the 'endless war' now spreading across Asia and Africa. In Québec, right-wing nationalists hope to manipulate fears of immigrants and religious minorities (especially Muslims) to counter the drift from nationalism and the PQ. There is a partial return to the right-wing nationalism that preceded the Quiet Revolution, substituting ethnic 'identity', conservative values and hostility to popular movements for the struggle for an independent state. This right-wing populism constitutes a real threat in that it instrumentalizes Islamophobia and the fear of 'terrorism', ideas gaining ground in Québec and elsewhere, to advance a range of anti-immigrant and anti-refugee policies.

We could say that currently the social movements are on the defensive. They are however still able, to a certain extent, to slow down and sometimes even defeat neoliberal reforms. This was evident throughout the spring and fall of 2015, when another massive coalition was built around public sector unions and community groups in fightbacks against government austerity. About 400,000 public servants, teachers and health personnel were involved. The three largest federations (CSN, FTQ and CSQ), supported by a host of smaller unions, set up an unprecedented mobilization entailing over 700 local actions (strikes, pickets, occupations and blockades) with major demonstrations in Montréal and Québec City. Many of these actions were decentralized, planned and implemented by local unions, often in conjunction with community organizations struggling to defend public education and health services. The government was forced to backtrack on its aggressive plans to erode working conditions, but it stuck to its mantra of reducing costs and salaries under the mantle of a necessary policy of 'austerity'. Public opinion leaned heavily toward the unions. However, the trade union leadership signed a half-hearted agreement that angered militant trade unionists. It remains to be seen if this partial defeat will have a larger impact on coalition-building and mass struggles, but it is notable that new mass mobilizations are forming around resistance to pipeline projects, including forcing TransCanada Pipelines to cancel plans to build a port at Cacouna (a small town on the eastern south shore of the St. Lawrence) from which to export bitumen from the Alberta tar sands.[19]

THINKING STRATEGICALLY

In the meantime, debate continues around the 'political tool' of Québec Solidaire. How can it be more active in popular struggles outside the parliamentary arena without pretending to 'lead' the popular movement? What best can be done in this narrowly confined parliamentary political space of the Québec National Assembly? Is the priority widening the alliance to encompass the left nationalists, as in Catalonia for example? Or should the focus remain on social and gender issues, attempting to win support in the immigrant communities that are now a very important segment of both the proletariat and precariat in Quebec? What kinds of alliances can be built with like-minded organizations and networks at the Canada-wide level, given the fact that whatever the political status of Québec, there has to be strong solidarity between working peoples across the existing 'federal' state? What is the 'common struggle' to wage with First Nations, beyond vague statements about their right to self-determination?

Many activists and movements in Québec are uncertain, to say the least, about these developments, pointing to the impossibility of serious regime change without a collapse of the power structure. Realistically, this is unlikely in the present local and international correlation of forces. This is not to say that changes are impossible. At this point, socialism, or 'communism' – in the sense that capitalism needs to be replaced by a society where the 'commons' will prevail over the laws of accumulation, destruction and oppression – is a horizon or an ideological perspective, not a political programme.

The priority, for many years to come, is to build a broad-based people's alliance resisting the neoliberal onslaught, promoting transformations that can be effectively implemented. This is well captured by the QS programme, which converges, by and large, with the 'Leap Manifesto' published by left environmentalists, social-democrats and socialists (animated by Naomi Klein and Avi Lewis) during the fall 2015 Canadian federal election campaign.[20] These platforms stress rebooting the public sector while opposing privatization, leaving behind extractivism and quickly advancing energy industry conversion, focusing on local economic development, reforming current anti-democratic institutions and processes, and re-establishing external relations on the basis of solidarity and cooperation, away from Canada's traditional role as a US surrogate and ally in military relations and in defence of globalization.

But what has happened through the Carriers rouge movement in Québec promises to go much deeper than this. It has represented, and sometimes prefigured in embryonic form, new forms of democratic and popular representation and participation, inspired by the notion, best articulated by the Asamblea popular de los pueblos de Oaxaca in Mexico, that 'power, in the process of self-affirmation of individual and social classes does not signify oppression. The permanent challenge for oppressed classes is to coordinate without authoritarianism, to conduct without manipulation, to lead in sharing power so that it becomes a collective reality.'[21] This is directed at building the revolutionary subjectivity of the masses, not simply multiplying social movements hoping that they, by their eventual growth, can marginalize or transform state power. It means developing means to confront state power, which requires a strategic perspective to neutralise its capacities and eventually to replace it. It recognizes that the political space is not some 'external' domain that can be avoided; that the movement cannot stand 'beside' or on the 'outside'; otherwise it becomes 'fantasy', or at best confined to dealing with 'authentic social relations, a revolution in personal life and a bouquet of cultural experiments'.[22] Carrying this further requires remaining steadfast, obstinate but not obsessed, and continuing the exhausting 'war of position' by building popular movements on the basis of the original socialist project, led by the working and popular classes themselves (self-emancipation). We should not forget, as Hal Draper put it in the *Socialist Register* over four decades ago, that socialists, the left, the 'modern prince', in brief, the 'educators', always need to be 'educated' by the masses.[23]

Many of us in Québec involved in the social struggles and movements recognize the importance of taking our distance, on the one hand, from a certain obsession with horizontality and procedure, and an incapacity – even hostility – to thinking strategically to identify lines of fractures and convergences. On the other, the development of the mechanisms for indepth and sustainable participation requires opening up structures, designing new methods for including the invisible and voiceless and thereby opening up the political process beyond traditionally dominant voices.

In that sense, structures need to be made flexible and movements have to learn how, as the Zapatistas say, to 'command by obeying'. This includes a strong dose of horizontality in the decision-making process, which is different than 'horizontalism'. In the anarchist narrative, horizontalism becomes an obligatory procedure; a 'one-size fits-all' recipe. In our experience, breaking down top-down (and most of the time opaque) decision-making habits is necessary to 'get to the point': that is, to elaborate strategies by and for anti-systemic popular movements. This requires going beyond the point where movements are a collection of individualities and to a place where the collective will prevails. That collective will has to materialize itself through mandates and representative mechanisms, and understand that the process cannot go ahead with general assemblies alone.

This is a global trend: popular movements and the left are recognizing that they have to search for the points of intersection, and not remain satisfied because lots of people are on the streets talking freely about liberation without a strategy. We need strategies, and therefore we need the 'party'. In fact, we need two 'parties'.

The first is a political party, which cannot at this point be anything other than wide anti-neoliberal coalitions like QS, which have also emerged elsewhere under different names and labels. These are based on the understanding that the party is a tool and not a substitute, an interface subordinated to the movements, helping to sort out wider strategies and convergences.[24] For Álvaro García Linera, this means that 'the frontier between social movement and party is very ambiguous, porous; and that the party structures (which provide a certain scope for cohesion, unity, principles and organization) maintain very direct, free-flowing and organic links with the social organizing structures and with the emerging social movements.'[25] In the Bolivian laboratory, these porous boundaries mean that the governing MAS party (sometimes defined as the 'tool of the popular movement'), includes members of mass movements, not just members of the party per se. The process advanced through its ability to focus, make strategic headway, challenge power and build counter-hegemonic people's power. That 'party' might even, in certain cases (as in Bolivia) insert itself in the circuits of power and accelerate a transformative project.

The other 'party' is where socialists combine to act not within a centralized organizational structure, and not to 'lead' social movements, but to advance a broad and deep intellectual process, in the best Gramscian sense, that facilitates the convergence of the movements. Its task is 'to make an actuality of the communist horizon in everyday life and thought'.[26] This 'party' is not a separate entity or a relatively secluded structure; even less does it pretend to be the 'owner' of some 'Marxist science'. Being in the 'party' means being 'partisan'. This is the idea in the *Communist Manifesto* in which communists are advised not to form 'a separate party opposed to other working-class parties [because] they have no interests separate and apart from those of the proletariat as a whole', nor to 'set up any sectarian principles of their own, by which to shape and mould the proletarian movement'. They rather act as an intellectual incubator, 'bringing to the front the common interests of the entire proletariat, independently of all nationality'.[27]

This 'non-party party' participates in the production of useful knowledge by and for popular struggles, as 'a mobilized structure capable of integrating into its own resources, internal dynamic, deliberation process and lines of actions other individuals and associations to the end of a common goal ... [to] become a form of democracy and direct political sovereignty'.[28] The Gramscian metaphor of the 'modern prince' suggests a type of party that is consistent with this, one that encourages the formation of 'organic intellectuals' to help in empowering and building the capacities of the social movements. It is designed to become 'the proclaimer and organiser of an intellectual and moral reform, which also means creating the terrain for a subsequent development of the national-popular collective will towards the realisation of a superior, total form of modern civilization'.[29] What has been so exciting about living in Québec in recent years is how far one can see the spirit of such ideas at work.

NOTES

1   I would like to thank Richard Fidler and Roger Etkind for their critical remarks on earlier drafts of this text. The People's Summit was organized by the Réseau Québécois sur l'intégration des Amériques in conjunction with networks in English Canada, the USA, Mexico, Brazil, Chile and Argentina, brought more than 50,000 people to Québec City.
2   André C. Drainville, 'Québec City 2001 and the making of transnational subjects', in Leo Panitch and Colin Leys, eds., *The Socialist Register 2002: A World of Contradictions*, London: Merlin Press, 2001.
3   After its initial South American phase, the WSF attempted to expand into other continents, with unequal success. See Massiah Gustave, *Strategy for the Alternative to Globalisation*, Montréal: Black Rose Books, 2015.
4   Front d'action populaire en réaménagement urbain (see www.frapru.qc.ca).
5   Including the bi-monthly *A Bâbord*, the daily news service on line *Presse-toi-a-gauche*, the journal *Nouveaux Cahiers du socialisme*, the economic research group IRIS and others.
6   Peter Thomas, 'The Communist hypothesis and the question of organization', *Theory and Event*, 16, 2013.
7   The creation of a radical subjectivity was inspired by a widely read journal of that time, *Parti pris*.
8   In 1970, the Canadian state imposed a state of siege on the pretext of the activities of a small, militarized FLQ, but the real target was the rising social movement. Two years later, a general strike preceded by a wave of occupations of cities and radio stations confronted the government.
9   Pierre Beaudet, *Quel socialisme ? Quelle démocratie ? La gauche québécoise au tournant des années 1970-1980*, Montréal: Nota Bene, 2016.
10 The PQ was finally elected in 1976 after two unsuccessful attempts. The affirmed goal of the new government was to prepare the accession to sovereignty. In parallel, it passed legislation responding to popular demands. The PQ was not social-democratic like European parties, but included social-democratic elements within its programme and its membership.
11 In 1980, a referendum called by the PQ on sovereignty was defeated by a coalition of conservative and bourgeois liberal parties. There was a second referendum in 1995 that ended in a draw.
12 Two 'Marxist-Leninist' organizations, by and large exclusive to Québec, which grew in the late 1970s and collapsed by the early 1980s, promoted this view: the 'Workers Communist Party' (Parti communiste ouvrier) and 'In Struggle' (En Lutte!),
13 See Diane Lamoureux, 'Féminisme et mouvement des femmes : entre émancipation et libération', dans Gaëtan Tremblay (dir.), *L'émancipation hier et aujourd'hui*, Québec: Presses de l'Université du Québec, 2009.
14 Richard Fidler, 'Québec Solidaire, a Québécois approach to building a broad left party', in Carlo Fanelli and Priscillia Lefebvre, eds., *Uniting Struggles: Critical Social Research in Critical Times*, Ottawa: Red Quill Books, 2011.
15 Elise Thorburn, Adrie Naylor, and Robyn Letson, 'Notes on spontaneity and organization', *Upping the Anti*, 14 2012.
16 Alex Levant, 'Rethinking spontaneity beyond classical Marxism: Re-reading Luxemburg through Benjamin, Gramsci and Thompson', *Critique: Journal of Socialist Theory*, 40, 2012, p. 383.
17 See the comments on this by one of the most prominent leaders of the student strike, Gabriel Nadeau-Dubois, *In Defiance*, Toronto: Between the Lines, 2015.
18 See in this respect Stephanie Ross's critique of anarchism's inherent individualism in

Stephanie Ross, 'Is this what democracy looks like? The politics of the anti-globalization movement in North America', in Leo Panitch and Colin Leys, eds., *The Socialist Register 2003: Fighting Identities*, London: Merlin, 2002; and Jodi Dean's articulation of the collective subject in Jodi Dean, 'Division and desire: Jodi Dean discusses the *Communist Horizon*', *Socialism and Democracy*, 27, 2013, pp. 23-41.

19 The energy giants exploiting the tar-sands in Alberta are working strenuously to win regulatory approval for building and converting pipelines to get bitumen 'to sea water' on both the Pacific and Atlantic coasts. A major project, Energy East, would convert an existing gas pipeline to Québec, and build a new pipeline across Québec to the Atlantic. The coalition opposing the project includes environmental groups, popular movements and indigenous communities.

20 Richard Fidler, 'Climate justice movement shakes Canada's New Democratic Party', *Life on the Left*, April 11, 2016. Available at: lifeonleft.blogspot.ca.

21 My translation, from Red mesoamericana de educacion popular, at: www.redalfja.net.

22 Contrast John Holloway in *Change the World Without Taking Power*, London: Pluto Press, 2002, with Jodi Dean, 'Response: the question of organization', *South Atlantic Quarterly*, 113(Fall), 2004.

23 Hal Draper, 'The Principle of Self-Emancipation in Marx and Engels', in Ralph Miliband and John Saville, eds., *The Socialist Register 1971*, London: Merlin Press, 1971, pp. 81-109.

24 In the greater Montréal area (where 50 per cent of the Québec population resides), QS enjoys significant support (in the range of 15-18 per cent of the electorate). It battles mostly with the PQ, which has long been established in these working- and lower-middle-class francophone districts. In the rest of Québec, QS has a weak base.

25 Álvaro Linera Garcia, 'Challenges for a new left', *La Migraña*, 15(June), 2015. Translation by Richard Fidler available on his blog, *Life On the Left*, at: lifeonleft.blogspot.ca.

26 Jodi Dean, 'The Party and Communist Solidarity', *Rethinking Marxism*, 27, 2015, pp. 332-42

27 'Manifesto of the Communist Party', in Karl Marx, *The Revolutions of 1848, Political Writings Volume I*, David Fernbach, ed., New York: Vintage, 1973, p. 79.

28 Alvaro Garcia Linera, 'Imagining a New World', *l'Humanite in English*, Translated by Harry Cross, 5 August 2013. Available at: www.humaniteinenglish.com. See also Nick Dyer-Witherford, 'Networked Leninism? The circulation of capital, crisis, struggle and the common''', *Upping the Anti*, 13 2011.

29 Antonio Gramsci, *Selections from the Prison Notebooks*, Translated and edited by Quentin Hoare and Geoffrey Nowell Smith, London: Lawrence and Wishart, 1972.

MARX AND ENGELS ON THE REVOLUTIONARY PARTY

AUGUST H. NIMTZ

Engels began his brief remarks at Marx's funeral in 1883 by describing his life-long political companion's 'scientific' accomplishments. 'But he looked upon science above all things as a grand historical lever, as a revolutionary power in the most eminent sense of the word ... For he was indeed, what he called himself, a Revolutionist'.[1] As his closest collaborator, Engels knew better than anyone about this indispensable dimension of Marx's project. If it wasn't enough, as the young Marx had concluded in 1845, to 'interpret the world' but also necessary 'to change it', then action and organization were essential. Yet nowhere did Marx lay out a set of clearly articulated principles for revolutionary organization. But if all of his organized political activities are examined – along with those of Engels after Marx's death – this essay demonstrates it is possible to distill in broad outlines the norms that guided Marx's approach to revolutionary organizing.

Almost fifty years ago, in the 1967 *Socialist Register*, Monty Johnstone performed an invaluable service in synthesizing for the first time – certainly in English – Marx and Engels's views on the revolutionary party.[2] But aside from materials Johnstone didn't have access to when he published his still quite valuable essay (above all the *Marx-Engels Collected Works* (*MECW*), the most complete compilation of their writings in any language) it's now easier to verify citations of their writings and, more importantly, to see the larger context in which the citations were originally written. Also, much has passed in real world politics since 1967, not least the collapse of the Soviet Union and its satellite regimes after 1989, reigniting much-debated questions (which Johnstone didn't address) about whether the actions of Lenin, let alone Stalin and his successors, were consistent with the views of Marx and Engels. For today's activists, what are – the question Marx and Engels would have posed – the organizational lessons inspired by their example?

THE COMMUNIST CORRESPONDENCE COMMITTEES

Once the Marx-Engels partnership was formed and armed with a jointly written theoretical statement, *The German Ideology* (1845-1846), the next task, as Engels recounted four decades later, was 'to win over the European, and in the first place the German, proletariat to our conviction'.[3] Growing evidence that revolutionary winds were about to blow across Europe made that an urgent undertaking. Political clarity and differentiation – the need to know who was committed to a revolutionary course, potential comrades; and who not, potential opponents – was necessary. The means for doing so was the Communist Correspondence Committees, established by the Marx-Engels team at the beginning of 1846 in Brussels where the two lived, their first organizational venture.[4] Named after the internationally oriented Jacobinic Corresponding Societies, the Committees' mission was to promote communication (Jenny, Marx's wife, constituted the secretariat) and 'impartial criticism' between self-styled socialist and communist currents in various European settings in order to be acquainted with one another 'when the moment for action comes'.[5] This international character became a hallmark of the Marx-Engels team's subsequent political activities, as did the emphasis on communication and discussion not for its own sake, but for 'when the moment of action comes'. There's no evidence that the Committees were guided, at least initially, by formal rules; they were clearly a work in progress.[6] The Committees, at least the Brussels chapter that Marx and Engels headed, tolerated diverse, and even contradictory, views, and disputes (such as Marx had with Wilhelm Weitling in March 1846) were settled by a simple majority vote, without the losers being expelled or even expected to leave.

A request for advice from a hopeful organizer of a German Committee branch gave Marx and Engels the opportunity to formulate their first joint political and organizational statement – positions that would forever inform their practice. Their two-and-a-half-page letter to Gustave Köttgen, dated 15 June 1846, constitutes a foundational document for what came to be called, by friend and foe, 'the Marx party'. The organizational advice – the need for regular meetings where discussions and debates informed by 'communist' literature could take place, for a movement that financed itself and didn't privilege, materially, its 'authors,' that had a clearly defined membership, that should convene a delegated congress only after real work at the local level, and free of 'personal considerations' – anticipated norms they'd employ in all subsequent political activities. In addition to organizational advice, Köttgen wanted political direction – whether workers should petition Prussian authorities to win reforms. That would only be effective, Marx and

Engels replied, 'if there already existed in Germany a strong and organized Communist Party, but neither is the case'. In the postscript, they proposed a remedy – take part in the petition campaigns of the bourgeoisie: 'join them for the time being in public demonstrations, proceed jesuitically, put aside Teutonic probity, true-heartedness and decency, and sign and push forward the bourgeois petitions for freedom of the press, a constitution, and so on. When this has been achieved a new era will dawn for c[ommunist] propaganda. Our means will be increased, the antithesis between bourgeoisie and proletariat will be sharpened.'

This idea of how the nascent communist movement in Germany should relate to the bourgeoisie for the democratic revolution would remain at the very core of Marx and Engels's life-long politics. As Engels explained in 1892: 'Marx and I, for forty years, repeated ad nauseam that for us the democratic republic is the only political form in which the struggle between the working class and the capitalist class can first be universalized and then culminate in the decisive victory of the proletariat'. In many ways, their letter anticipated Lenin's *What is to be Done?*(1902), which too offered an answer for how to construct a countrywide social democratic or communist party for the first time in a setting where the democratic and not the socialist revolution was on the immediate agenda. The advice for regular meetings, a determinate membership, having 'communist' literature to forge such a movement, and the need for workers to join with other classes (including the bourgeoisie) to fight for political democracy was later captured in the spirit of Lenin's famous pamphlet. And not the least, in quintessential Leninist sensibility, an organization meant for 'when the moment of action comes'.

THE COMMUNIST LEAGUE

The short-lived Communist Correspondence Committees' most consequential achievement was to bring Marx and Engels in contact with Western Europe's most class conscious workers. Having bested in debate the utopian ideas and schemas that many of them subscribed to, the two middle-class revolutionaries were increasingly seen as a pole of attraction. In early 1847, the League of the Just, the mainly German exile worker/artisan group founded in 1836 and with branches in London, Paris, and elsewhere, invited the two to join them. Marx and Engels agreed but on one condition – that the League end its conspiratorial modus operandi. The leadership readily agreed, since the organization had already done so. In turn, the two had to make clear what their 'plans' were and how they would 'go about achieving' them; also, they were expected to commit to the proletarian discipline of the forces they had now fused with. Two delegated conferences in 1847 resulted, at Marx and Engels's urging, in the organization's renaming, now the Communist League.

For its organizational norms, which included the stipulation that membership entailed 'revolutionary energy and zeal in propaganda' and 'subordination to the decisions of the League',[7] Marx and Engels proposed only two changes, both of which were adopted. The first was that the delegated congress, 'the legislative authority' to which the League's Central Authority (its 'executive organ') was subordinate, should be the organization's supreme authority. The second, that members be allowed to join other organizations to advance the Communist League's agenda, made it possible for Marx and Engels to help organize and be active in the broader worker's movement and the petit bourgeois democratic associations on behalf of the League in Brussels, Paris and eventually Cologne. The Brussels duo was also commissioned to compose a theoretical/action program for the League. When Marx failed to deliver on time what came to be called the *Manifesto of the Communist Party*, fellow Central Authority leaders warned that 'measures would be taken' if he didn't get it written – evidence that he was indeed subordinate to the discipline of the League. Never before in the annals of the class struggle had the toilers displayed such self-confidence vis-à-vis their literary representatives – powerful testimony to what distinguished the proletariat from other toilers.

The ink was barely dry on the *Manifesto* when the long-expected upheavals in Europe erupted. Once Paris exploded in February 1848, followed by Vienna and, shortly afterwards, Berlin, it became increasingly apparent that a new era had dawned, whatever the outcome. 'The European Spring' made centuries-old autocratic rule an endangered species. The League's leadership realized that it needed to supplement the *Manifesto* and commissioned, once again, Marx and Engels to compose *The Demands of the Communist Party in Germany*. As Marx explained years later, both documents were written for 'the Communist Party', that is, 'the party in the broad historical sense' of which the League 'was simply an episode'.[8] The organizational expression of 'the party' could therefore take different forms and names in time and place. Marx's understanding of 'the party' helps to clarify what one key sentence in the *Manifesto* actually means – that communists aren't sectarian towards the workers' movement: 'The Communists do not form a separate party opposed to other working-class parties.'[9]

Armed with a concrete program, the Central Authority of the League organized its forces for a return to Germany in April 1848. *The Demands*, seventeen in number and two pages in length, recognized that a bourgeois democratic revolution was on Germany's immediate agenda and not a socialist revolution. That meant aligning the worker's movement with the peasantry and the petit bourgeoisie during its course. In leading the League for the duration of the German Revolution, Marx and Engels made their first venture into the electoral arena. Having been conferred by the Central Authority with 'full discretionary power' for the direction of the League until 'the next congress,' Marx decided sometime in the summer of 1848 to put the organization on hold.[10] Forging the 'people's alliance,' the worker-peasant-petit bourgeois coalition to fight for the democratic revolution, in his opinion could best be done through the editorial board of the Cologne-based *Neue Rheinische Zeitung,* the newspaper Marx began publishing on 1 June. Too many of the League's members were still operating in a conspiratorial manner, or had become absorbed in the larger democratic movement, or simply had dropped out of politics. Though Marx and his comrades did all they could to push Germany's democratic revolution to fruition, it became increasingly clear in the first months of 1849 that the process was ebbing. Marx and Engels and the rest of the League leadership were forced to relocate to London by September.

An essential task was to draw a balance sheet on the previous year and a half and to prepare for an expected revival of Europe's 'Spring'. Marx and Engels's *Address of the Central Authority to the League, March 1850* drew the key lessons of the upheavals: first, the liberal bourgeoisie could not be counted on to push forward the bourgeois democratic revolution (the *Manifesto* held open the possibility that it could be); and second, the petit-bourgeoisie could not be trusted. Yet, it would be with the latter that the still small working class would have to ally in the expected renewal to overthrow 'the reactionary party'. To avoid betrayal, workers would have to be organized 'independently,' a word that appears on virtually every one of the document's eleven pages: hence, a self-criticism of the decision to suspend the League in the course of pursuing an alliance with the petit bourgeoisie.

The *Address* advised the workers' movement and the League to have 'unconcealed mistrust in the new government' that would issue from the overthrow of the old regime. 'Alongside the new official governments they must immediately establish their own revolutionary workers' governments, whether in the form of ... municipal councils ... workers' committees' etc. – what Lenin would later call 'dual power'. The document also advised on how the League should conduct itself in the electoral arena during the next upheaval. It should run League members, when possible, as candidates 'even where there is no prospect whatever of their being elected' and not be persuaded by the petit bourgeoisie that in so doing 'they are splitting the democratic party and giving the reactionaries the possibility of victory' – in other words, the time-worn wasted vote/lesser-evil argument. There was more to be gained than to be lost for the long term interests of the workers' movement in independent electoral action – an opportunity 'to count their forces and to lay before the public their revolutionary attitude and party standpoint'.

That this advice followed almost immediately details on how workers should be 'armed and organized' made clear why the need 'to count their forces'. Only an independently organized and armed working class could assure that the next revolution in Germany would be, in the very last words of the document, 'The Revolution in Permanence' – that is, a socialist revolution.[11] Along with the letter to Köttgen and the *Manifesto*, the *Address* constitutes the third key document in the Marx-Engels arsenal on the organizational question.[12] Significantly, Lenin committed it to memory and 'used to delight in quoting' it.[13] I argue that with regard to 'dual power,' independent electoral action, and armed organization of the proletariat, the *Address* informed, unlike any other of their writings, the Bolshevik course in 1917. It is thus crucial in explaining the Bolshevik's success in leading Russia's workers and peasants to power in October – the first time ever anywhere.[14]

THE INTERNATIONAL WORKINGMEN'S ASSOCIATION

After a more than decade-long lull in Europe's revolutionary process and the end of the Communist League, the United States Civil War (1861-1865) brought the Marx party back into active public political work. The precipitating issue was whether Europe's proletariat should follow their ruling classes in supporting the southern slavocracy. Textile workers in England, many of whom had been made redundant by the Union blockade of Confederate cotton, said no, much to the joy of Marx and Engels. Working-class opposition to the pro-Confederacy interventionist sentiments of Europe's ruling classes registered the growing recognition that the proletariat needed its own foreign policy – not only for the Civil War, but also for other international issues such as Polish and Italian self-determination. That sentiment spurred the establishment of the International Workingmen's Association (IWA), which would become known as the First International.[15] Since Marx had already put aside work on his long-promised magnum opus, *Capital,* to mount a 'struggle in the press' against supporters of the Confederacy, it didn't take much convincing to get him on board for the project's founding in London in September 1864. This was especially so because, as he explained to his comrades, 'real workers' leaders' were so centrally involved. Coming out of the broadly sponsored London meeting that called for fraternal ties among Europe's proletariat, to which Marx had been invited as the representative of the German workers' movement, was the decision that the various national representatives compose a mission statement and organizational norms. That Marx was in a position to draft the founding documents for the new body reflected the experience and skills he acquired in the 1848-49 upsurge, as well as informal organizational ties he maintained even while concentrating during the 1850s on 'scientific work'. Marx was able to quickly emerge as 'the acknowledged leader' of the International Workingmen's Association from 1864-72, as Engels would put it at his comrade's funeral, the 'crowning effort' of his revolutionary work.

The political conclusion Marx and Engels drew from 1848 concerning the indispensability of independent working-class political action directly informed the *Inaugural Address* and the *Provisional Rules of the Association* Marx drafted. After surveying, in the former, Europe's economic reality following the demise of the 1848-49 upheavals, Marx pointed not only to the growing inequalities between 'the industrial masses' and the capitalists but also to the gains workers had made, particularly in England, to defend their class interests. 'Yet,' in words that resonate all too well today, 'the lords of the land and the lords of capital will always use their political privileges for the defense and perpetuation of their economical monopolies. So far from promoting, they will continue to lay every possible impediment in the way of the emancipation of labor.' There was only one answer to this, Marx concluded: 'To conquer political power has therefore become the great duty of the working classes.' And in the opening sentence of the preface to the accompanying rules for the new organization, he wrote: 'The emancipation of the working classes must be conquered by the working classes themselves.'[16]

These claims became the axis around which Marx's work for the next decade in the IWA revolved. When his drafts were adopted unanimously by the other national representatives to the London meeting, Engels, who lived in Manchester, was surprised that his partner could write something that could pass muster with all of the diverse political tendencies represented at the initial gathering. It wasn't that difficult, Marx replied, 'because we are dealing with "workers" all the time'. His modus operandi, as he described it to Engels, was *fortiter en re, suaviter en modo*, strong in deed and mild in manner – what allowed him to become the new organization's unofficial head.

Within weeks of the IWA's founding, Marx, a member of the General

Council (GC), its executive and highest decision-making body in between congresses, moved to enforce the norm that introduced the body's just adopted rules. When a prominent lawyer sought a seat on the GC, it became clear that not all had fully understood what Marx proposed. Yet Marx was able to convince other members to reject the request. 'I believe him an honest and sincere man; at the same time, he is nothing and can be nothing save a Bourgeois politician.' Exactly because the suitor aspired to a seat in Parliament, 'he ought to be excluded from entering our committee. We cannot become *le piedestal* for small parliamentary ambitions .... [Otherwise] others of his class will follow, and our efforts, till now successful at freeing the English working class movement from all middle class or aristocratic patronage, will have been in vain.'[17] From its commencement Marx opposed any attempts to turn the IWA into an electoral conduit for any class other than the proletariat; whether it should and could be such a vehicle even for the proletariat was a discussion and debate that lay ahead.

Exactly because of the diverse currents and tendencies that came together to form the IWA – unlike in the case of the Communist League – it required a fairly flexible organizational framework. To accommodate that heterogeneity in such a way as to secure political homogeneity was certainly Marx and Engels's long-term goal, not unlike their approach to the Correspondence Committees. Differences about the appropriate norms for such a framework provoked the most famous fight within the IWA, between the 'Marx party' and Mikhail Bakunin's anarchist current.[18] It began with Bakunin's proposal to the GC in 1868 to erect alongside the IWA a parallel body of anarchist affiliates. Marx demurred: such an arrangement would be a threat to the IWA's sovereignty, or, as Engels put it, 'a state within the state'. The rest of the GC without exception agreed with this, seeing that by operating independently of the GC, Bakunin's network could avoid engaging other sections in debate and common work – the necessary process toward political homogeneity – and could insulate his forces from the arguments of Marx's current and, of course, the discipline of the GC.

Bakunin tried another angle in response. He was prepared to disband his network if the GC was willing to approve its program – a not too subtle attempt to have his anarchist views be made official IWA policy. Marx saw through the ruse and responded tactfully and adroitly. The sections of the would-be disbanded network could be admitted to the IWA as individual affiliates. As for their programmatic views, he pointed out that given the heterogeneous character of the forces that comprised the organization it was to be expected that 'their theoretical notions, which reflect the real movement, should also diverge'. At the same time, 'the exchange of ideas facilitated by the public organs of the different national sections, and the direct debates at the [congresses], are sure by and by to engender a common theoretical program'. Thus, there was no need for the GC to rule on any section's program as long as 'its *general tendency* does not run against' that of the International, '*the complete emancipation of the working class*'.[19]

Engels explained to a Bakunin protégé the advantages of a theoretically diverse IWA at this stage in its development: 'Our power lies in the liberality with which the [IWA's] first rule in interpreted, namely that all men who are admitted aim for the complete emancipation of the working classes .... Unfortunately the Bakuninists, with the narrowness of mentality common to all sects, were not satisfied with this. In their view the [GC] consisted of reactionaries, the program of the Association was too vague. Atheism and materialism ... had to become compulsory, the abolition of inheritance and the state, etc., had to be part of our program ... But to put all these things into our program would mean alienating an enormous number of our members, and dividing rather than uniting the European proletariat.'[20] A more programmatically open organization was the means, through discussions and debates, to 'engender a common theoretical program'.

Bakunin's assurances notwithstanding, he reconstituted his supposedly disbanded network as a secret organization – which explains in part his next move. At the Basel Congress of the IWA in 1869, the only one he ever attended, Bakunin vigorously campaigned to have the powers of the GC vis-à-vis the sections of the IWA be expanded – a very surprising move which, as Hal Draper convincingly shows, indicated that Bakunin was planning a takeover of the GC by his partisans.[21] The proposal, like his two other organizational initiatives, was defeated. Bakunin's machinations eventually led to the expulsion of his current from the IWA at the Hague Congress in 1872. Marx and Engels were able to present enough evidence to convince delegates that the anarchist leader had organized a covert operation against the GC, in clear violation of the international's rules. Documents discovered since then make for an even more damning case. Bakunin, Draper instructively points out, has the dubious distinction of having formed 'the first leftist movement to apply its conspiratorial pattern of subversion not to assail society at large or to defend itself against the police, but to destroy other socialists' organizations'.[22]

Only on two occasions were the political rather than organizational differences between the Marxists and Bakunin's current in the IWA publicly debated. One came at an expanded GC meeting in London in September 1871. Due largely to the impact of the Paris Commune five months earlier – Marx's *The Civil War in France*, written for the IWA, distilled its political significance – Marx and Engels made their most forceful case to date in favour of workers forming their own political parties and participating in the electoral and parliamentary arenas: that is, independent working-class political action, the core of their *Address of March, 1850* as well as the key point Marx wrote into the IWA's founding documents. 'To preach abstention' from political action, as Engels accused the Bakuninists of doing, 'would be to push [workers] into the arms of bourgeois politics. Especially in the aftermath of the Paris Commune, which placed the political action of the proletariat on the agenda, abstention is quite impossible.'[23] They won not only the majority of the GC to their position but also the delegates to The Hague Congress less than a year later.

The other occasion for a public airing of political differences with the Bakuninists came when the latter, in response to one of the decisions of the 1871 London Conference – specifically, the condemnation of the covert operation – charged the GC with being 'authoritarian'. It argued that the International, 'embryo of the future human society, must be, from now on, the faithful image of our principles of liberty and federation'. Marx and Engels, on behalf of the GC, countered that the IWA or any revolutionary organization could not serve as a model for a socialist society since it was absurd to think that the working classes could organize itself to take and defend state power without the centralization of authority. Drawing on the lessons of the Paris Commune, they noted sarcastically that, according to Bakunin's logic, the 'Communards would not have failed if they had understood that the Commune was "the embryo of the future human society" and had cast away all discipline and all arms, that is, the things which must disappear when there are no more wars!' [24]

Largely in response to Bakunin's subterfuges, Marx and Engels initiated and supported moves in the GC to make it more disciplined and centralized. Both steps were not, however, ends in themselves. When in July 1872 the GC codified the IWA's administrative rules, Engels proposed that the right of the GC to suspend sections be surrounded with safeguards to ensure, as Marx said at the same meeting, that the GC 'never could constitute itself a power in opposition to the Association'.[25] Whether the IWA would have become an organization with the kind of centralization, discipline and political homogeneity of the Communist League will never be known. The IWA's move to the United States after The Hague gathering – Marx and Engel's solution to keep the Bakuninists at bay – effectively meant, in hindsight, its de facto end.[26]

Marx and Engels, especially Marx, spent more time in the IWA than any other political formation, and it is therefore the richest source for examining their organizational norms. It is noteworthy that during the entire course of its existence they almost never referred to 'our party' or the 'Marx party' as a faction within the IWA. This suggests that they saw the IWA itself as *their party*, or more correctly, their party in the making. Indeed, in a highly didactic letter to a supporter in the United States, Marx distilled the essence of the political struggle: 'The political movement of the working class naturally has as its final object the conquest of political power for this class, and this requires, of course, a previous organization of the working class developed up to a certain point, which arises from the economic struggles themselves.'[27] For the working class to seize political power, in other words, it must have an organization already in place.

AFTER THE INTERNATIONAL WORKINGMEN'S ASSOCIATION

The victory Marx and Engels scored at The Hague in having the IWA call for working-class political action helped plant the seeds for Europe's mass working-class political parties. While much would need to be done to make that call a reality, it nevertheless gave those predisposed to move in that direction the authority (i.e., the prestige of the IWA) to go forth boldly. The end of the IWA, Marx and Engels soon recognized, allowed the various sections to do the necessary spadework at the national level to make the next round in international organizing more fruitful – to recall the advice they gave to Köttgen almost thirty years earlier, not to rush prematurely into holding a national congress for the German sections of the Correspondence Committees.

The German movement, which was in the vanguard beginning in 1869, revealed after a decade of organizing that the 'independent' in the independent working-class political action formula was very much a work in progress. Marx and Engels became increasingly concerned about what was taking place and wrote a stinging critique of the leadership's conduct, above all for its opportunism (what would later be called revisionism or reformism). Generally known as the *Circular Letter of 1879*, it constitutes – after the Köttgen letter, the *Manifesto*, the *1850 Address*, the *Inaugural Address*, and the *Civil War in France* – one of their major programmatic statements. Not intended for public eyes, the letter reprimanded the German leaders for bending, as a way to make the party more popular, to petit bourgeois interests at the expense of those of the proletariat. One of the addressees was the young Edward Bernstein, who would later lead the revisionist charge against the revolutionary strategy of the two founders of the modern communist movement.

A major issue the *Circular* raised spoke to an organizational matter, specifically how to make the party's Reichstag group or *Fraktion* accountable to the party as a whole – a challenge that would bedevil many a twentieth/twenty-first century workers' party wherever it had a parliamentary group. Engels came to the defense of a rank-and-file member who charged a Reichstag representative with having violated the party's principles by voting for one of Chancellor Otto Bismarck's capitalism-from-above ventures. But the bigger problem for Marx and Engels was the uproar among the party leadership that the critique had been issued at all: '[H]as German Social-Democracy indeed been infected with the parliamentary disease, believing that, with the popular vote, the Holy Ghost is poured upon those elected, that meetings of the [*Fraktion*] are transformed into infallible councils and factional resolutions into sacrosanct dogma?'[28] To combat the 'disease' of 'parliamentary cretinism,' as Engels had called it in 1850, the party had to uphold the norm that parliamentary representatives be subordinate to the will of the party rank and file.

The *Circular* reveals that even before Marx's death in 1883 it fell largely to Engels, its main author, to counsel the new parties – a 'bounden duty that brooks no delay,' as he put it less than a year before his own death in 1895. His advice to a supporter in Denmark in 1889 about the value of internal party debate is exemplary: 'No party can live and prosper unless moderate and extreme tendencies grow up and even combat one another within its ranks.' In the absence of 'convincing proof of *activities* harmful to the party', it would be an act of 'imprudence,' he opined a year later, if the leadership of the German party expelled a group of its critics. Context, as always with Marx and Engels, was primary. When Bismarck's Anti-Socialist Law, in place from 1878-90, forced the German party into a virtually underground existence while permitting its *Fraktion* room for manoeuvre, 'the parliamentary group's dictatorship … was essential and excellently managed'.[29] But once the prohibition ended, it was 'imperative that the chaps should at long last throw off the habit of handling the party officials – their servants – with kid gloves and kow-towing to them as infallible bureaucrats, instead of confronting them critically'.[30]

> The party is so big that complete freedom of discussion within its ranks is imperative …. [It] cannot remain in existence unless every shade of opinion is allowed complete freedom of expression …. Do not make martyrs unnecessarily, show that there is freedom of criticism, and *if* you have to throw anyone out, do so in cases where the *facts* – OVERT ACTS of turpitude and betrayal – are quite blatant and completely demonstrable …. One must give the rotten elements time to become so rotten that they

defect virtually on their own accord. The discipline of a party numbered in millions is quite different from that of a sect numbered in hundreds.³¹

Freedom of expression also required 'a *formally* independent party press ... which is not *directly* dependent on the Executive or even the Party Congress, i.e. which is in a position unreservedly to oppose individual party measures *within* the programme and accepted tactics, and freely to criticise that programme and those tactics, within the limits of party decorum'.³² Nota bene Engels's italicized/small capitalization 'activities,' 'facts,' and 'overt acts'. As was true when Marx asked Andreas Gottschalk to tender his resignation from the Communist League four decades earlier, actions and not opinions were the condition for party membership.

Engels was elated when the workers' movement in England began finally in 1892 to break with the Liberal Party, allowing him to reaffirm the most basic of the Marx party's organizational principles: 'We have one firm rule for all modern countries and for all times and that is to prevail upon the workers to form their own independent party in opposition to all bourgeois parties'.³³ The Social Democratic Party of Germany, the largest of the workers' parties, which he and Marx helped nurture, was the paragon. But he objected, five months before his death, to what he detected as the leadership's quest for 'absolute legality' at the expense of the right to armed struggle: '[Y]ou have nothing to gain by advocating complete abstention from force. Nobody would believe you, *nor would any* party in any country go so far as to forfeit the right to resist illegality by force of arms .... [N]ot legality at any price, not even as a manner of speech!'³⁴ In hindsight, his admonition anticipated the reformist course of twentieth-century German Social Democracy.

As national parties emerged in the wake of the IWA, there were understandable urges to resurrect the IWA. Engels declared in 1874 that 'the next International,' unlike the IWA, 'will be directly Communist' but only 'after Marx's writings have been at work for some years'. Thus, it was too soon to take the leap even by 1882. Wait, he cautioned, for 'when events in Europe provoke it .... [S]uch events are already taking shape in Russia where the avant-garde of the revolution will be going into battle. You should – or so we think – wait for this and its inevitable repercussions on Germany, and then the moment will also have come for a big manifesto and the establishment of an *official*, formal International which can, however, no longer be a propaganda association but simply an association for action.'³⁵

By 1900 a new organization, the Socialist, or Second, International, was in place, grouping affiliates in at least most European countries. The International's most consequential action was helping to nurture a Russian party, whose left wing would come to be what Engels had predicted, 'the avant-garde of the revolution ... going into battle'. Notably, in Lenin's debates with the so-called Economists in 1901, he countered their view that political agitation and building revolutionary organizations weren't essential in quiescent times: 'it is precisely in such periods and under such circumstances that work of this kind is particularly necessary, since it is too late to form the organization in times of explosion and outbursts; the party must be in a state of readiness to launch activity at a moment's notice'.[36] In this he sounded very much like Marx had in his 1871 letter to the IWA's supporter in the US. Many of the positions Marx and Engels took about how the IWA should function – at least the GC if not the body as a whole – particularly the need for more centralization and discipline in the wake of the Bakunin operation, anticipated norms that Lenin would espouse and practice in the course of leading the Bolshevik party to the Russian Revolution of October 1917.

The defeat of the German Revolution in 1919 – along with the murders of Rosa Luxemburg and Karl Liebknecht – tragically confirmed the long-term perspective that Lenin shared with Marx and Engels on party building: unless the working class had a 'previous organization' to take power it would be 'too late' to try to construct one in the heat of revolutionary turbulence. In founding the Communist, or Third, International in Moscow in 1919, the Bolsheviks under Lenin's leadership did exactly what Engels foresaw: 'the establishment of an official, formal International ... an association for action' and one that 'will be directly Communist'. Inspired by the Bolshevik example and most cognizant of the political degeneration and betrayal of the Socialist International – specifically, the vote of the parliamentary representatives of the vast majority of its affiliates (with the German party in the lead) to fund the First World War – the Communist International at its Second Congress in 1920 adopted a set of party organizational norms required for affiliation – the so-called 'Twenty-One Conditions'. At the Third Congress in 1921 delegates debated and voted on a set of theses on party organizational principles, 'democratic centralism' being of primary importance.[37] Regarding the 'Theses on the Organizational Structure of the Communist Parties' adopted at the Third Congress, Lenin, a year later at the Fourth Congress, said the 'resolution is an excellent one ... but it is almost entirely Russian ... too Russian, it reflects the Russian experience ... quite unintelligible to foreigners' who 'cannot be content with hanging it in a corner like an icon and praying to it'.[38]

Indeed, in 1921 the Bolsheviks at their Tenth Congress had already made a fateful decision owing to the still precarious situation the Revolution faced in the immediate wake of the brutally debilitating civil war. The party overwhelming voted to temporarily suspend the right to form factions, giving more weight to centralism in the democratic centralist formula that the party had long operated under. Factions had allowed for organized challenges to the party leadership, an essential requirement for the 'democratic' in the democratic centralist formula. Fifteen years later, with the advantage of hindsight, Leon Trotsky, Lenin's second in command in the October Revolution, acknowledged that the organizational means for the subsequent Stalinist counterrevolution and all of its horrors had its origins in that decision, which he too had voted for and still defended given the circumstances: 'one thing is absolutely clear: the banning of factions brought the heroic history of Bolshevism to an end and made way for its bureaucratic degeneration'.

The damage went beyond the USSR. 'Beginning in 1923 [Stalin's] epigones extended the banning and stifling of factional struggle from the ruling party in the USSR to the young sections of the [Communist International], thus dooming them to degeneration before they had time to grow and develop.'[39] Trotsky's sober assessment, made in 1935, proved to be all too accurate: not just about the Bolshevik Party in Russia, but also about the tragic trajectory of the vast majority of parties that called themselves 'Marxist,' 'Communist,' 'Leninist,' or some variant in whatever corner of the planet. When the international, by then moribund, no longer served as a pawn in Stalin's diplomatic manoeuvres he unceremoniously pulled the plug on it in 1943, three years after one of his many assassins had put an ice pick into Trotsky's brain. Johnstone in his final pages was all so right about Stalinism in relation to the project of Marx and Engels: 'There is nothing in their work to justify Stalin's attempt to present as Marxist his theory that Socialism demands a one party system, least of all in the form operated by him where a small tyrannical clique substituted itself for the working class in laying some of the foundations of Socialism.'[40]

A TIMELY REVISIT?

Johnstone's classic essay in the 1967 *Socialist Register* was published amidst a swell of political agitation. Most radicalizing youth in that period chose not to embrace what they understood to be Marxist-Leninist parties – the 'old left' versus 'new left' debate.[41] But the reality of capitalism, specifically the global financial crisis that began in 2008 and the depression-like conditions which followed in its wake, alongside the limits of the 'occupy' and other protest movements as politically effective counters to the crisis, have reawakened interest in a revolutionary party.[42]

Communist party-building in the future will involve the coming together of prior organizations that bring with them an assortment of experiences – not unlike what has happened before. Among them will be the few remaining nuclei that trace their origins to the Bolsheviks via Trotsky's Left Opposition, and who still retain Leninist organizational norms. The vast majority of those coming to the process, however, will bring very different norms and traditions (e.g., anarchists), but who increasingly recognize that protest alone isn't sufficient for real liberation. Hopefully they will be open to knowing more about the rich Marxist heritage. This is what this essay purports to aid and abet: that is, the taking and transforming of state power so as to eventually end class societies and their antagonisms, and to make it possible that, in Johnstone's final words, 'the continued existence of a proletarian party would clearly be an anachronism'.[43]

NOTES

1 Karl Marx and Friedrich Engels, *Karl Marx and Frederick Engels: Collected Works* Volume 24, New York: International Publishers, 1975, p. 464.
2 Monty Johnstone, 'Marx and Engels and the Concept of the Party', *The Socialist Register*, New York: Monthly Review Press, 1967.
3 Karl Marx and Friedrich Engels, *MECW* Volume 26, pp. 318-19.
4 Both had a role in founding in London in September 1845, the short-lived Society of Fraternal Democrats, the first international proletariat organization.
5 Karl Marx and Friedrich Engels, *MECW* Volume 38, pp. 38-39.
6 See my *Marx and Engels: Their Contribution to the Democratic Breakthrough*, Albany, N.Y.: State University of New York Press, 2000, pp. 30-38, for details.
7 Bolshevik archivist and biographer of Marx and Engels, David Riazanov, claims that with this stipulation the CL had adopted the 'democratic centralism' usually associated with Leninist norms, in his *Karl Marx and Friedrich Engels*, New York: Monthly Review Press, 1973, p. 75. I have argued, as Riazanov admits, that owing to how the League's 'executive authority' was elected by the local organization, as opposed to by the congress, the Bolshevik norm, that there was effectively more democratic content to the Bolshevik modus operandi than that of the League. See: *Marx and Engels*, p. 54.
8 Karl Marx and Friedrich Engels, *MECW* Volume 41, pp. 87, 82.
9 See Hal Draper, *The Adventures of the Communist Manifesto*, Berkeley: Center for Socialist History, 1994, pp. 236-39, on the translation and meaning of the passage.
10 Regarding the debate about the decision, see John Cunliffe, 'The Communist League and the 'Dissolution Question'', *Journal of Modern History*, 53:1 (March 1981).
11 Karl Marx and Friedrich Engels, *MECW* Volume 10, pp. 283-87.
12 Hal Draper convincingly argues that Marx and Engels, contrary to some claims, never disowned the document: *Karl Marx's Theory of Revolution, Vol. 1*, New York: Monthly Review Press, 1977, pp. 599-612. See also Johnstone, 'Marx and Engels', pp. 127-28.
13 Riazanov, *Karl Marx and Friedrich Engels*, p. 100.
14 See my: *Lenin's Electoral Strategy from 1907 to the October Revolution of 1917: The Ballot, The Streets – Or, Both*, New York: Palgrave Macmillan, 2014, especially chapter three. Absent in the *Address* is the worker-peasant alliance, all so vital in the success of the Bolsheviks. That omission was partly corrected in the subsequent Central Authority

Address of June, 1850, that Marx and Engels wrote. For details see Nimtz, *Marx and Engels*, p. 106.
15 On Marx and Engels's role and the organizational issues see my *Marx and Engels*, and 'Marxism Versus Anarchism: The First Encounter', *Science & Society*, 79:2 (April 2015).
16 Karl Marx and Friedrich Engels, *MECW* Volume 20, pp. 5-14.
17 Karl Marx and Friedrich Engels, *MECW* Volume 42, pp. 92-93. For how Marx dealt with the fact of his own class origins in his role in the IWA, see Nimtz, *Marx and Engels*, pp. 185-8.
18 Much more is now known about this conflict since Johnstone penned his brief comments.
19 Karl Marx and Friedrich Engels, *MECW* Volume 21, pp. 45-46.
20 Karl Marx and Friedrich Engels, *MECW* Volume 44, pp. 162-63.
21 Draper, *Karl Marx's Theory of Revolution* Volume 4, pp. 270-304 makes the most detailed case against the anarchist.
22 Draper, *Karl Marx's Theory of Revolution* Volume 4, p. 271.
23 Karl Marx and Friedrich Engels, *MECW* Volume 22, pp. 417-18.
24 Karl Marx and Friedrich Engels, *MECW* Volume 23, pp. 115, 121.
25 *General Council of the IWA, 1871-1872: Minutes*, Moscow: Progress Publishers, 1974, p. 242.
26 Regarding the charge that a more centralized and disciplined IWA effectively meant its demise because it resulted in the expulsion of the Bakuninists, see Nimtz, 'Marxism versus Anarchism', pp. 171-3.
27 Karl Marx and Friedrich Engels, *MECW* Volume 44, p. 258.
28 Karl Marx and Friedrich Engels, *MECW* Volume 45, p. 400.
29 Karl Marx and Friedrich Engels, *MECW* Volume 49, p. 135.
30 Karl Marx and Friedrich Engels, *MECW* Volume 49, p. 131.
31 Karl Marx and Friedrich Engels, *MECW* Volume 48, p. 425; and *MECW* Volume 49, pp. 11, 16-17, 516-17.
32 Karl Marx and Friedrich Engels, *MECW* Volume 50, p. 33.
33 Karl Marx and Friedrich Engels *MECW* Volume 49, p. 515.
34 Karl Marx and Friedrich Engels, *MECW* Volume 50, pp. 457-9. Engels's reprimand had to do with the most famous bowdlerization in the annals of Marxism – Wilhelm Liebknecht's cut and paste job on his 'Introduction' to the 1895 edition of Marx's *Class Struggles in France*, done 'in such a way as to present me as a peace-loving proponent of legality quand même' (*MECW* Volume 50, p. 486).
35 Karl Marx and Friedrich Engels, *MECW* Volume 46, p. 198. It is true, as Johnstone notes, that Engels gave 'enthusiastic support' (p. 135) to the 1889 meeting that inaugurated what would be the Second International. But that's a hindsight observation. There is nothing in the record that suggests Engels saw the meeting as in fact an inauguration. His counsel to 'wait,' I argue, was still operative.
36 Vladimir Lenin, *Collected Works* Volume 5, Moscow: Progress Publishers, 1977, p. 18.
37 For details on the Second Congress, see John Riddell, ed., *Workers of the World and Oppressed Peoples, United!: Proceedings and Documents of the Second Congress, 1920*, New York: Pathfinder Press, 1991.
38 Vladimir Lenin, *Collected Works* Volume 33, p. 431. There is no mention of this crucially important fact about Lenin's understanding of party organization in Tamás Krausz's *Reconstructing Lenin: An Intellectual Biography*, New York: Monthly Review Press, 2015. What he does supply isn't necessarily erroneous but mainly inadequate and largely bereft of historical context, such as his too brief discussion of 'democratic centralism' (p. 118). See my *Lenin's Electoral Strategy*, vol. 1, for understanding of how the norm developed.

39 Leon Trotsky, *Writings of Leon Trotsky, 1935-36*, New York: Pathfinder Press, 1977, p. 186.
40 Johnstone, 'Marx and Engels', p. 144.
41 Notably, the new communist party, with no organic links to the Bolsheviks, that was birthed in 1965 in Cuba, arguably the most significant revolutionary breakthrough in the second half of the twentieth century, largely escaped the opprobrium of the new left. Despite having been born with a Stalinist defect – one of the three currents that came together for its formation after the overthrow of the old regime – the party's revolutionary wing led by Fidel Castro was, despite Moscow's embrace, able to avoid the degeneration that had occurred elsewhere. It was because the Cuban revolution was healthy enough at birth that it was able to survive for so long after the collapse of the Stalinist regimes.
42 Jodi Dean makes the most cogent case in her latest book, *Crowds and Party: How Do Mass Protests Become an Organized Activist Collective*, New York: Verso, 2016.
43 Johnstone, 'Marx and Engels', p. 145. My *Marx and Engels* and *Lenin's Electoral Strategy* were written just for that reason.

1917 AND THE 'WORKERS' STATE': LOOKING BACK

A W ZURBRUGG

Lenin's *State and Revolution* was one of the most famous texts of the twentieth century. Written in 1917 before the October revolution and published shortly after, it looked forward to a new polity, one that should be fully democratic, with a 'dictatorship of the proletariat' creating 'democracy for the people'.[1] The substance of the work was a review of Marx and Engels texts (the Paris Commune especially). Lenin did not ask if these texts were suited to framing a discussion of current issues. His discussion assumed that a Marxist party's thinking should predominate. He did not consider differences between artisan Paris in 1871, and industrial St. Petersburg and Moscow in 1917; between the older (commune) and newer forms of mass participatory organisation. He did not consider the pressing issues of what role factory committees might play, how they might relate to unions, Soviets and other structures, and how these various organisations could work together.

Lenin often took his cue from the German model of social democracy before the war. Notably, in *State and Revolution* he still refers to the German post office – under socialist guidance – as a model,[2] without noting the post office's hierarchal status-proud culture, with officials recruited from the army; ex-soldiers inured to military discipline. It is telling that he refers to *beamte* (state officials delivering letters) proud of their status, rather than organised workers. Lenin called for the destruction of autocratic and parliamentary state forms. But he also admired orderly hierarchies. So *State and Revolution* contains diverse and somewhat contradictory elements.

The revolution advanced through disorderly local initiative. Women workers, disregarding the advice of activists, initiated the first demonstration that sparked the downfall of the Tsar. Demands for decent housing arose in an unplanned manner. So, for example, the Kronstadt Soviet resolved that housing should be shared out – those who possessed large houses had to give up spare rooms. Local Bolsheviks pressed for this decision to be delayed, urging that no decisions should be made on a local basis; some were recalled by their base organisations for failing to follow the instructions of their electors, others were expelled from the Bolshevik Party for following these instructions.[3]

The October revolution brought such diverse elements to the fore; moreover, as it developed the substance and weight of various elements – old and new – changed, and so too did the interrelation between them. These dynamics were both complex and somewhat unprecedented: there was no single road map for the transition towards socialism, rather several sketchy 'maps' with diverse and somewhat inconsistent signposts.

WORKERS' CONTROL?

The quote below gives a taste of industrial problems in St Petersburg towards the end of 1917. The speaker here is Alexander Shliapnikov, Commissar of Labour, laying down the law when workers protested at the closure of their Nobel oil refinery:

> If the workers resist, so much the worse for them! They will simply be laid off by force, and without indemnity. The most recalcitrant, the leaders, enemies of the proletarian cause in general will expose themselves besides to consequences infinitely graver. And as to the Anarchist gentleman, let them take care! The Government cannot tolerate their mixing in affairs that are none of their business, nor their inciting honest workers to disobedience … The government will know how to penalise them, and will not hesitate.[4]

Initially at least the new government did enjoy widespread goodwill – even when workers were told that redundancies were inevitable. It was understood that the new government could not immediately remedy economic chaos. Yet Shliapnikov's comment that 'honest workers' were being incited reflected a concept that anyone who opposed his party was a corrupting 'un-person'. Behind his bullying language was the view that governments should govern. The new central state had one way streets – orders flowed down, reports flowed up; lower organisations had to obey directives; nothing obliged the centre to consult with or be accountable to local grassroots participatory structures.[5]

Factory committees were the most popular urban organisation formed in the wake of the February revolution. They imposed an eight-hour day. They held meetings during working hours, open to all. At a factory committee conference held in January 1918, delegates made clear they wanted policy and planning co-ordinated by new state organs at the national level while hoping that equality and participatory democracy would be preserved. As one resolution put it:

> [W]e, the proletariat ... build leadership on the principle of complete democratism ... if these organs really do turn away from the masses, then, of course we will have to introduce that amendment. Indeed we would have to overthrow those organs, and perhaps make a new revolution. But so far we feel that the Soviet of People's Commissars is our soviet and the institutions it creates are fully in accord with us.[6]

Among his famous 'April Theses' of 1917, so important for guiding the Bolsheviks' strategic orientation between the February and October revolutions, Lenin had set out a transitional industrial strategy: 'It is not our immediate task to "introduce" socialism, but only to bring social production and the distribution of products at once under the control of the Soviets of Workers' Deputies.'[7] In September, in *The Impending Catastrophe*, he would write: '[S]tate-monopoly capitalism is a complete material preparation for socialism, the threshold of socialism, a rung on the ladder of history between which and the rung called socialism there are no intermediate rungs. ... [S]ocialism is merely state-capitalist monopoly which is made to serve the interests of the whole people ...'[8] State policy from October to mid-1918 was in line with this thinking. It envisaged state centres – *glavki* – guiding industries, leaving managers and owners in possession but subjected to workers' control – defined by Lenin as 'all-embracing, omnipresent, most precise and most conscientious accounting of the production and distribution of goods'.[9]

In fact, in many factories 'workers' control' was much more than this. Factory-committees expanded and took on aspects of management (not least because some bosses ran away), kept enterprises going, shared out work, and sought out sources of food and raw materials. Of some 500 firms nationalised before July 1918, 400 were taken over by initiative of local organisations and only 100 'by decree of the centre'.[10] In these workplaces and even where factory owners remained in place, the committees acquired substantial weight, to such an extent that they sometimes had 'greater power than the official administration in the areas of supplies, output, equipment, labour discipline, purchasing or demobilisation'.[11] As S.A. Smith's *Red Petrograd* goes on to note: 'In a vague, incoherent way, the committee leaders knew that unless the transfer of power to workers at the level of the state was accompanied by a transfer of power at the level of production, then the emancipation of labour would remain a chimera.'[12]

However 'vague' or 'incoherent', this sensibility echoed the challenge that Anton Pannekoek had issued to German Social Democrats in *Vorbote*, in May-June, 1917:

> National ownership of large branches of industry is synonymous with their militarisation. ... To the proletariat this state socialism can mean only an aggravation of its sufferings and increased pressure upon the burden of life. Notwithstanding this, it is to be expected that a large part of our Social-Democracy will not oppose this plan but will lend it its heartiest support. Their old ideals make them the prisoners of this new system of national exploitation. ... *Socialism is not based upon national ownership, but upon the strength, the might of the proletariat.* In the past the conceptions of socialism and state industries have been hopelessly confused in the minds of our Social-Democracy; in the future, this party will face the state socialist plans for the increased enslavement of the working class, with neither mental weapons nor a clearly defined attitude.[13]

Syndicalist railway workers in Russia, like those in Britain and Italy at the time, quickly concluded that nationalization was no panacea. By the spring of 1918, Russian rail workers strongly resented the state's 'railroad dictators'[14] who had been tasked with restoring the transport system. The threat of starvation in cities had motivated the imposition of military discipline on the railways, but the effect of the orders, 'apart from creating another layer of inexperienced, often corrupt security forces, had little, if any, practical impact'.[15]

Syndicalists argued for a national network to manage the economy – but one based on grassroots control and federation. At the first national trade union congress in January 1918, Grigori Maximov, one of the leading anarcho-syndicalists in the 1917 revolution, acknowledged the need 'to create a centre but not a centre of decrees and ordinances but a centre of regulation, of guidance – and only through such a centre to organise the industrial life of the country'.[16] The difference between syndicalists and Bolsheviks (and even sometimes among them, since neither was a monolith) was not over the scale of industrial organisation but over its forms, with syndicalists wanting workplace and community organs, and their federations, invested with substantial grassroots power.

Lenin did not promote these aspirations.[17] Those elements in *State and Revolution* that suggested subordination could not be dispensed with in a period of revolutionary transition now came more clearly to the fore in guiding state practices. Already in 1917 he had argued that that the 'whole of society will have become a single office and a single factory, with equality of labour and pay … *All* citizens become employees and workers of a *single* country-wide state "syndicate"'.[18] As it turned out, Lenin's concept of 'workers' control' in practice meant only a check on official management, curtailing managerial ambitions that factory committees may have held.

In the negotiations held between the new state and Russian industrialists in the spring of 1918, attempts were made to reach some accommodation – leaving ownership of industry in private hands but subjecting it to state control and direction. These negotiations led nowhere. It was feared that German industrialists might take over industries.[19] Nationalisation was decreed to prevent this, as well as to facilitate industrial planning. In this context, trade unions became instruments of government policy. They prevented some abuses, but were not independent. They might both defend a shorter working day and demand paid and unpaid overtime. As early as 23 February 1918, Schmidt, the new Commissar of Labour, declared that unions 'can no longer call strikes'.[20]

Factory committees were merged with unions in early 1918, with some of their leaders becoming union and state officials. There were growing complaints in St. Petersburg plants that the new committees rejected demands from labour assemblies for new elections.[21] Although union membership was compulsory, participation fell away and it became the practice to hold meetings outside working hours. Union officials took on some of the attributes of personnel managers. They helped to enforce workplace rules and implement punishments for absenteeism and other infractions. The agendas of union meetings were controlled – those raising previously unauthorized topics attracted the attention of the police (the Cheka). On 20 March, the critical newspaper *Novaia Zhizn* carried a report of a meeting of 83 delegates in St Petersburg which had raised a series of complaints: workers were 'without hope'. The government had done everything to oppose them, it had blocked new elections, threatened workers with machine guns, brought hunger, economic disorganization, civil war, unemployment, even execution without trial.[22] By 29 April 1918 critical union leaders were asserting that 'organizations can exist only insofar as they subscribe without a murmur' to government policy.[23]

In May 1918 Lenin wrote that the world revolution had born:

> … two unconnected halves of socialism exist[ed] side by side like two future chickens in the single shell of international imperialism. In 1918 Germany and Russia have become the most striking embodiment of

the economic, the productive and the socio-economic conditions for socialism, on the one hand, and the political conditions on the other. ... [O]ur task is to study the state-capitalism of the Germans, to spare no effort in copying it and not shrink from adopting dictatorial methods ... we must not hesitate to use barbarous methods.[24]

In this context, production in Russia was to be promoted through the imposition of managerial power: 'Iron discipline ... is the general and summarising slogan of the moment.'[25] On 4 May an instruction called for 'Obedience during work, and unquestioning obedience at that, to the one-man decisions of the Soviet directors, elected or appointed by Soviet institutions and vested with dictatorial powers ...' Equal wages, as advocated in *State and Revolution*, were abandoned. Productivity was to be raised through piece-work with the application of 'what is scientific and progressive in the Taylor system'.[26]

Urban residents were directed into jobs, without being able to choose between state and non-state employment in a co-op or collective. The Left Communists now wrote that current policies were leading 'in the direction of bureaucratic centralization, of rule by various commissars, of deprivation of independence from local Soviets and of rejection in practice of the type of "Commune state" ruled from below'.[27] They feared that former workers who sat in *glavki* and in the state would not represent the working class. In response to the argument that the stifling of workers was bringing state-capitalism rather than socialism, Lenin asserted: 'state-capitalism would be a *step forward*. If in a small space of time we could achieve state-capitalism in Russia that would be a great victory.'[28]

In April 1918, the twelfth of the theses of the Left Communists, mentioned above, commented:

The introduction of labour discipline in connection with the restoration of capitalist leadership in production cannot essentially increase the productivity of labour, but it will lower the class autonomy, activity and degree of organisation of the proletariat. It threatens the enslavement of the working class, and arouses the dissatisfaction both of the backward sections and of the vanguard of the proletariat.

But in June 1918, at a conference of factory committees and unions, Lenin demanded unquestioning obedience to a single will as an absolute necessity for large-scale industry.[29] The workers' state was to be constituted through workers' submission to industrial managers directed by the state. Workers were to act in ways prescribed by management, party and state; relying on managers and other specialists to bring useful technology into industry, allowing them superior pay and rations. Lenin saw this as conforming with the notion of the dictatorship of the proletariat, since workers 'are the majority on the collegiums of the Supreme Economic Council'.[30]

While many former workers did in fact become officials, specialists and managers in the *glavki* and ministries, it was often remarked at the time that such people were losing touch. As *Kommunist*, a Left Communist journal, put it in June 1918: 'We are far from affirming that Soviet personnel have *already* been transformed into the last word of bureaucracy as irredeemably separated from the masses as has befallen, for example, the upper layers of the German trade-unions, but it is undeniable that this tendency exists.'[31] By October 1918, even a Communist secretary in the People's Commissariat for Internal Affairs (NKVD) (the ministry set up on 7 November 1917 with responsible for security and law enforcement) was expressing his concern that Soviet power was turning into 'All Power to the Chekas'.[32] It was on the basis of these developments that in September 1918 the anarcho-syndicalist leader Maximov summed up what the first year of the revolution had brought about:

> The proletariat is gradually being enserfed by the state. The people are being transformed into servants over whom there has risen a new class of administrators – a new class born mainly from the womb of the so-called intelligentsia ... it is only a matter of time before privileges will pass to the administrators. We do not mean to say that this inequality and these privileges are arbitrary, or that the Bolshevik party set out to create a new class system. But we do say that even the best intentions and aspirations must inevitably be smashed against the evils inherent in any system of centralized power. The separation of management from labour, the division between administrators and workers flows logically from centralization. It cannot be otherwise. There are no other words to the song. The song goes thus: management implies responsibility, and can responsibility be compared with ordinary labour? Responsibility demands special rights and advantages. Such is the source of privilege and of the new anti-socialist morality. Thus we are presently moving not towards socialism but towards state-capitalism. Will state-capitalism lead us to the gates of socialism? Of this we see not the slightest evidence.[33]

WAR COMMUNISM

The revolution had been confronted by tensions between industry and agriculture since February 1917. Years of war had weakened the transport infrastructure that sustained exchanges between town and country. Industry was cut off from areas that supplied food and raw materials. As industry faltered it had little to exchange with rural areas. Measures were established before October to collect and ration food and to secure industrial supplies from rural areas. Peasants – some 85 per cent of Russia's population – had made their own revolution, taking over land for themselves. They had little incentive to produce more for the state. Famine stalked the cities of northern Russia.

The Bolsheviks had won only 25 per cent of the vote in Constituent Assembly elections of November 1917, but had little support outside urban areas. The new voting system was unequal. Rural Russia had one delegate for 125,000 persons, while urban Russia had one delegate for 25,000 electors.[34] The left wing of the Socialist Revolutionary (SR) party, whose base was in the peasantry, was brought into the new government as a minor partner but complained that decisions were being taken without proper debate or procedure. In the summer of 1918, amidst reports of violence against their rural supporters, the Left SR party broke with the Bolsheviks and was ousted from the Soviets. What Lenin proclaimed openly in 1921 was already being asserted in practice at this time: 'We tell the peasants quite openly that they must choose between the rule of the bourgeoisie and the rule of the Bolsheviks.'[35]

In the period of 'War Communism', between 1918 and 1921, the new state focused on the comprehensive direction of people and resources. Barriers were imposed between town and country to regulate trade. An army of food requisition squads was created. It was instructed to target middling and richer peasants, taking grain but offering little or nothing in return. These squads were seen as oppressive outsiders grabbing food and behaving 'as if they were in enemy country'.[36] '[B]lood flowed in torrents: the poor peasants, the middle peasants and the numerically insignificant Kulaks, the rich peasants all rose as one.'[37] Further deaths from hunger and disease followed, perhaps as many as twelve million between 1918 and 1922.[38]

In the cities the state tried to direct all social and economic activity. Unplanned initiative was curtailed or criminalised. There were forests and rivers around St Petersburg that might have provided fuel and fish, but unauthorised fishing, it was said, would produce nothing – and security forces would take the catch.[39] In 1918 only half of workers' food came from official sources.[40] The state was forced to compromise: it tolerated open-air markets and allowed individuals to bring 25 kg food-sacks into cities. Official and unofficial economic systems existed side-by-side. Productivity suffered as urban workers starved. Payment for piece-work had little immediate effect: most of workers' 'income' consisted of inadequate rations. 'Iron discipline' could not remedy the structural problems that had been exacerbated since 1914.

All-too-visible inequalities provoked angry responses. Party leaders in St Petersburg had hot baths while much of the city shivered. Guards protected their hotel woodpiles while other houses were torn apart for fuel. Adolf Ioffe wrote on the privileged nature of party life in May 1920. In Moscow inequality was enormous:

> At the lowest level it means a pair of boots and a tunic; higher up, an automobile, a railcar, access to the Sovnarkom [State Executive] dining room, an apartment in the Kremlin or the National [hotel] ... There is no room here for the old party dedication and self-sacrifice ...[41]

The Bolsheviks saw their political base shrink.[42] There were many strikes. Opposition to the party-state increased. At times, the Bolsheviks did sound out the views of non-party labour, and attempted to respond to complaints, but there were limits to this tolerance, and where their domination was threatened they maintained their rule through intimidation.

The Central Executive Committee of the Soviet Congress did not meet between June 1918 and February 1920.[43] Where Soviets were recalcitrant they were dissolved – they functioned only where the party had a majority. The right of recall lapsed. Elections were fixed. The holding of 'free' unsanctioned elections was penalised. Everything discussed within Soviets and non-party organizations was to be decided beforehand in a party fraction. In its own words, the party wanted 'unquestioned leadership in all organisations of working people, in the unions, co-operatives, village communes, etc. The Communist Party strives especially to carry out its programme and to exercise *unlimited* leadership ... Outright military discipline is needed in the party in the present epoch.'[44] When May Day 1920 came round Mensheviks wanted a day off work and declined to join in a state sponsored day of supplementary 'voluntary' work – a 'Subbotnik'.[45] Lenin's response was:

> [O]nly malicious enemies of the working people, only malicious supporters of the bourgeoisie,[46] can treat the May First Subbotnik with disdain; only the most contemptible people, who have irrevocably sold

themselves to capitalists, can condemn the utilisation of the great First of May festival for a mass-scale attempt to introduce communist labour.[47]

Trotsky now advocated the militarisation of labour as 'the inevitable method of organizing and disciplining labour power during the period of transition from capitalism to socialism'.[48] The dictatorship of the proletariat, as Lenin himself put it, was to be exercised 'only by a vanguard that has absorbed the revolutionary energy of the class'. Lenin's own respect for democracy appeared to have vanished, when in June 1920 he said:

> The proletarian dictatorship should display itself primarily in the advanced, the most class-conscious and most disciplined of the urban and industrial workers – the greatest sufferers from hunger who have made great sacrifices during these two years – educating, training and disciplining all the other proletarians, who are often not class-conscious, and all working people and the peasantry. All sentimentality, all claptrap about democracy must be scrapped.[49]

Not everyone shared this perspective. Many Communist Party members resigned at the time of the Kronstadt revolt. Hermann Kanaiaeff, a Red Army officer explained:

> Communist politics have brought the country to an impasse. The party has become bureaucratic, and evidently it has no desire to listen to popular aspirations. How could it hear the voice of the people, when it seeks only to impose its will? (Just think of 150 million peasants!) If workers are to be revived, electoral methods need transforming, allowing freedom of speech so that the masses can participate freely in the country's reconstruction.[50]

Resistance was also expressed in less violent forms, perhaps because hunger left little energy for protest. A study of the city of Saratov at the time describes routine dissent: abstention, dissimulation and voting against Communist resolutions and candidates; absenteeism, go-slows and pilfering. Conformity became 'ritualistic and opportunistic'; the new state had alienated working people.[51]

Of course, through the years of War Communism the social shape of Russia had changed greatly. Major cities had shrivelled. Tens of thousands of urban workers had joined food requisition squads (60,000 strong); 200,000 workers from Moscow and St Petersburg had been conscripted into the Red

Army. Lenin wrote that the urban proletariat had been declassed.[52]

By the end of 1919 nearly half the workforce in St Petersburg consisted of women.[53] 'Women's work' remained: child-care, cooking, etc. was unpaid, unvalued and often un-recognised. Lenin remarked that 'very few husbands, not even proletarians, think of how much they could lighten the burdens and worries of their wives, or relieve them entirely, if they lent a hand in this "women's work"'.[54] Progressive measures taken by the new regime in urban areas were important in this context, promoting literacy, providing kitchens, nurseries, and care for pregnant women. Abortion and divorce were legalized. But years of war and conflict impacted on family life. Huge numbers of children were abandoned. Venereal disease was rife. Inequalities persisted despite new and progressive legislation. Work done by a peasant family earned some compensation for those who exchanged produce for money, but not so much for those who worked unpaid under the direction of a male family head. For their part, urban women workers were viewed as less class conscious and less proletarian. They had little influence in the unions, party and state, and had little power to defend their interests. Carers and housekeepers might vote but, lacking associations of their own, had no particular representation in Soviets or unions. Some attempts were made to set up unions to defend the particular interests of women, but the party resisted such initiatives.[55]

Meanwhile, the ranks of officialdom mushroomed. In St Petersburg their numbers rose from some 38,000 in 1910, to over 170,000 in 1920 while workers' numbers declined from 411,000 to 150,000. Moscow had some 150,000 officials, more bureaucrats than workers.[56] A new layer of bureaucracy, the Workers' and Peasants Inspectorate, was invented to check older ones. A 200,000-strong Cheka policed everyone. Lenin now talked of old oppressive classes 'hiding out among Soviet government employees'.[57] His argument missed the point: it was not so much the *former* class origins of state officials that was an issue, but rather their current practice. If one had to get a pass to see an official, to get a stamp on a document, and one then had to queue for hours to get another pass and another stamp; if officials turned up late and went home early leaving people frustrated and having to queue again one might come to the conclusion that the state apparatus was self-serving.[58] If one saw off-ration perks and foods going to commissars and was hungry one would conclude that officials were using their *current* status for their own benefit. Former workers, turned officials, were absorbed into the state machine and had 'lost their living links with the masses'.[59] In 1926 Anton Ciliga described these new strata's desiccated egoism, concerned 'to hew themselves out a good place, regardless of others'.[60] Besides the manner in which it operated, the new state was disproportionately large and costly.

Lenin had talked of a 'cheap state'[61] back in 1917, and claimed the *only* 'reason why the functionaries of our political organisations and trade unions are corrupted ... and betray a tendency to become bureaucrats, i.e., privileged persons divorced from the masses and standing above the masses' was due to 'the conditions of capitalism'.[62] Lenin's assessment was short sighted. It became clear after 1917 that it was not just the conditions of capitalism that engendered the 'divorce' of the privileged from the masses, the new state's privileged officials, Cheka operatives, commissars and bureaucrats absorbed an officious energy from their *new* roles.

Many dissidents kept quiet while 'White' fascistic forces were a threat.[63] Some were very aware that there was precious little freedom in other countries at war. In the USA for example, all dissent was suppressed, and IWW activists were largely imprisoned. But as Russia's civil war came to an end in the spring of 1921, dissent revived. For example, in February, at a conference of metalworkers, critics received stormy applause in response to their calls for wage equality, the abolition of privileged rations and for distribution of those rations through unions, suggesting that state structures were distrusted: 'By their words one could sense a complete breach between the masses and the party, between the masses and the union.'[64] The state cracked down on opposition. In Kronstadt a mass meeting called for a return to equal rations and the mass democracy of 1917:

> Having heard reports of delegates sent to Petrograd by the general assembly of ships' companies, to investigate the situation, the assembly decides that, given that the present Soviets do not express the will of workers and peasants, to proceed with the immediate organisation of new elections of Soviets by secret ballot; there should now be complete freedom of expression and propaganda among workers and peasants for the preparatory electoral campaign. Freedom of speech and of the press for workers and peasants, for Anarchists and for Socialist parties of the left; freedom of assembly for unions and peasant organisations is to be guaranteed ...[65]

In the face of such discontent Lenin abandoned War Communism. The New Economic Policy did improve general conditions, especially for rural people, but not so much for urban workers. Unemployment increased and much of the welfare state was dismantled producing dire consequences for women.

One critic, writing in 1923, concluded that unions had become organs of police surveillance and that 'the Communist boss, the State, not only exploits the workers, but also punishes them himself, since both of these functions, exploitation and punishment, are combined in him'.[66] Another, Ciliga, a sympathiser of the Left Opposition, remarked in 1926 that factory workers:

> were prisoners of their foremen and directors, as in capitalist countries. Their lot was indeed worse, for, in the latter countries, the workers can protest in the press and at meetings. Here there was no one to whom to turn. It was not socialism, he concluded, it was slavery.[67]

REASSESSING THE TRANSITION

We have seen that Lenin looked for a process of transition rather than immediate socialism. From this, several overlapping questions arise: Was the shape of the revolution the result of choice or unpredictable circumstance (or both)? Could the Leninist model of transition arrive at socialism?

Russia's economy was a mess before the Bolsheviks took power. In other countries, too, the transition from a wartime to a peacetime economy brought huge disruption. On the other hand, if one compares these circumstances with those of other revolutions, Russia had certain advantages: for one thing, it initially developed over a long period to May 1918, so there was some space for problems to be resolved. Moreover, it had geographical advantages: capital cities were able to provide war materials and act as transport hubs so resources could be redirected from place to place.

Circumstances of war, mass demobilization and economic dislocation would have made any strategy for change very difficult. Disruption was inevitable. However, the policies of War Communism – particularly the agrarian policy of requisitioning food – exacerbated problems. Critics inside and outside the Bolshevik Party called for it to be abandoned.

The swollen state was inefficient. Workers perceived its enormous structures as wasteful, corrupt, ill informed and chaotic[68] – issuing contradictory instructions. Much conflict was a turf war between managers. 'The simplest act of distribution, the provision of matches for the Moscow population for instance, might be held up for weeks or even months as a result of endless quarrels in regard to departmental jurisdiction.'[69] The state, was obsessed with large-scale planning, and its appetites were frequently overambitious, unbalanced, and greater than its capacity, so that resources went to waste. Simultaneously it might obstruct unsanctioned local initiatives, such as individuals growing food for themselves on urban allotments – something that was allowed in the Second World War.

Discipline was imposed to remedy the chaos allegedly introduced by workers' control, but naturally enough this could remedy neither a chaotic state nor the problems that arose from a disorganised economy. Workers' pay was refashioned, using piece-work and payment-by-results; that harsh discipline was not inflicted on failing commissars and managers. Substantial perks remained available for them.

Before October, Lenin had believed that: 'The idea of "direction" by officials "appointed" from above is essentially false and undemocratic ...'[70] In December 1920 he thought: 'Democracy is a category proper only to the political sphere.'[71] Circumstances perhaps determined his focus. But his doctrine setting out distinct spheres – political and economic – did not admit that feedback from the latter would shape the norms of the former. To believe that factory workers would give unquestioning obedience from Monday to Saturday and enjoy power and 'rule' on Sunday; to believe that powerful and privileged elites would facilitate a transition towards socialism rather than seek to fulfil their own interests – all this was fantasy.

By the autumn of 1918, Rosa Luxemburg had already come to her chilling assessment of the Russian revolution: 'Without general elections, without unrestricted freedom of press and assembly, without a free struggle of opinion, life dies out in every public institution, becomes a mere semblance of life, in which only the bureaucracy remains as the active element. Public life gradually falls asleep.'[72]

Fifty years later, Isaac Deutscher concluded in the final pages of *The Prophet Armed* – the first volume of his trilogy on Trotsky – that by 1921 the Bolshevik leadership, having been driven into Communism by unanticipated, harsh circumstances beyond their control, were experiencing 'defeat in victory'.[73] In another text he wrote that revolutionary socialist leaders 'suddenly' found themselves in a situation in which there was no revolutionary class behind them[74] – a possibility none of the classical Marxist theorists had anticipated.[75]

Fifty years later still, Tamás Krausz's *Reconstructing Lenin* – even while concluding that Lenin still 'provides tools for those who still think of the possibility of another, more humane world' – clearly reveals the severe contradictions in Lenin's theory and practice, acknowledging that 'it was a mistake to think that the workers could defend themselves against their own state without democracy'.[76]

Krausz writes that the party does not appear as a concept in *State and Revolution*.[77] Lenin's key message had been to assert the key role of the *commune* as a revolutionary model, superseding parliamentary democracy. But the concept of the party was in fact present in *State and Revolution*, under the rubric of the 'vanguard of the proletariat' educated by Marxism to become *the* teacher, guide and leader.[78] Underlying Lenin's thinking is the concept of the key role of the vanguard party in negating other 'non-proletarian' influences in the labour movement, with truth residing in the party's correct interpretation of Marxist texts. This Marxism assumed a symbiosis between one party and one class. The possibility that the party might articulate the aspirations of a part of the proletariat against another part was not considered. There was no pluralism here, nor any reflection on how conflicting perspectives might be resolved – or not.[79] The notion of a single vanguard for a single class was not derived from consideration of the strengths and weaknesses of various unorganised or organised sectors (and factory committees, unions, housing committees, peasant assemblies, etc.) – structures that were largely absent in *State and Revolution*, a text Krausz calls the 'handbook' of revolution.[80]

Krausz writes 'that the *soviet dictatorship*, "the dictatorship of the majority (dictatorship of the proletariat) vis-à-vis the minority" was politically legitimated by the revolution itself'.[81] And he adds that *State and Revolution* was 'the theoretical "*self-definition*" of an array of social-political forces organized in the framework of the soviets and other spontaneous social organizations ...'[82] Yet Lenin admitted that a minority was disciplining a majority. Dissident spokespeople from an array of social forces felt the untender attentions of the Cheka. Krausz's use of three disparate terms glosses over these problematic realities.

In 1917 Lenin worked with forces of mass direct democracy to destroy the old state machine. Aspects of his thinking already present before October – the admiration of order, discipline and organisation – emerged more clearly thereafter. The party disciplined and commanded a decimated urban proletariat, and working people in general, through a rigged democracy that operated only in the political sphere. This political system was an appropriate fit, perhaps, for a transition to state-capitalism but quite unfit for a socialist purpose. The energy of working people was sapped as they found the new state unresponsive and oppressive; state power facilitated popular apathy and powerlessness.

Of course all transitions are limited by material and social factors. Everything cannot come all at once: one cannot build today's factories with tomorrow's bricks. But whereas older materials may have to be used, and may be used, with a limited impact on the process of transition towards socialism, the same does not hold for social relations. Hierarchical and authoritarian social relations seem destined to create feedback, recreating relations of power and powerlessness and material inequality.

Strategies for transition towards socialism have tended to focus on two central concerns: workers' power and state planning. One set of strategies looked first to the planning of industrial production. Planning was viewed as essentially progressive, and its potential shortcomings were often disregarded. Circumstances – Russia's isolation, economic disruption, the preponderance of peasant farming – did not suit this sort of transition. Lenin and his party chose traditions and priorities, along with iron discipline and one-man management. Their thinking leaned on that of Friedrich Engels, who viewed authority as natural and indispensable, citing railways as an example.[83] But other options might have been taken, and other interests might have been given priority.

Another socialist perspective focused on local accountability and equitable social relations. There was some satisfaction – albeit limited – in choosing between thin or thick cabbage soups. Workers could begin building new social relations and new networks to serve needs that could not be met on a local scale. Subsequent experience with collectives in Republican Spain after July 1936 suggests that a libertarian model could work, even on railways,[84] and with greater success than the Russian system, run on military lines. If events in Spain took another course, with the widespread growth of industrial and agricultural collectives, that development was also not merely accidental. It reflected a different revolutionary perspective and heritage deriving from Bakunin and his legatees, which rejected the Jacobin/bourgeois model and envisaged a self-managed social revolution. In this tradition, authority certainly existed, but efforts were made to socialize it and ensure it was not permanently fixed, so that capacities, expertise and responsibilities were rotated and shared. Grassroots bodies would work to both ensure accountability and build wider federations. As for relations between rural and urban collectives, here too the Spanish experience, while hardly rosy, was still happier than the Russian.

For a short time, the range of political forces that generated the October 1917 revolution came together in factory committees, soviets and other participatory institutions. The shortcomings of the leading players in the new state were not so evident in the early phase of the revolutionary process. But the common purpose that brought these various forces together in October soon fragmented; thereafter this array of forces had no unity. For the most part they continued to defend participatory change, and opposed reaction, but only a fraction of these forces lined up behind Lenin's party. The new state promoted layers of intellectuals and some industrial workers into roles as managers, commissars, officials and officers in security forces facilitating power and privilege.

The Bolsheviks portrayed these forces' bureaucratic and militaristic organisational norms as virtues, setting out that 'iron proletarian centralism' was the basic principle of the Third International in the epoch of the dictatorship of the proletariat, and that iron military discipline must be established in its ranks.[85] Trotsky would say: 'Clearly, the Party is always right ... We can only be right with and by the Party, for history has provided no other way of being in the right.'[86] Thus the former chair of the St Petersburg Soviet himself could not see the soviets as an independent 'way of being right'. Soviets, in this perspective, were not forums where the policies of various layers of working people might be reconciled, but administrative bodies that implemented the directives of a fused party-state leadership. Russia became, in name, a Federalist, Soviet and Socialist Republic, but reality proved quite different. Participatory and egalitarian politics were largely submerged.

Since 1917, there has been a reversal in the balance between the rural and urban worlds. Employment in the service sector is now greater than in industry. Gender relations have changed. Contemporary levels of literacy and education are hugely different. Communication passes through the internet. Such changes – and experience elsewhere – make the Bolshevik model ever more inappropriate. Movements for transformative change may seek out new paths that facilitate new social relations and forms of accountability, with both economic security for particular regions and the benefits of international trade. Democracy may yet be given a new twist towards participation and federalism. Devolution, decentralisation and autonomy may better facilitate participation and accountability.[87] Change in the future may be informed by past history, but may also take on new shapes to adapt to future developments and conform to new hopes and aspirations through a very different strategic imagination.

NOTES

1   Vladimir Lenin, *Collected Works* Volume 25, London: Lawrence & Wishart, 1960, p. 468. Lenin defined 'proletariat' as industrial workers; 'the people' was a wider term including white-collar employees and peasants.
2   Lenin, *Collected Works* Volume 25, pp. 431-2.
3   Efim Yartchouk, 'L'autogestion à Kronstadt en 1917', *Autogestion et socialisme*, No. 18-19, Paris: Martin, 1972, pp. 223-6.
4   Voline, *The Unknown Revolution*, Detroit: Black & Red, 1974, pp. 293-4.
5   James Bunyan and H. H. Fisher, *The Bolshevik Revolution 1917-1918: Documents and Materials*, Redwood City: Stanford University Press, 1934, p. 280.
6   David Mandel, 'The Factory Committee Movement in the Russian Revolution', in Immanuel Ness & Dario Azzellini, eds., *Ours to Master and to Own*, Chicago: Haymarket, 2011, pp. 125-6.

7   Lenin, *Collected Works* Volume 24, p. 24.
8   Lenin, *Collected Works* Volume 25, pp. 362-3.
9   Emphasis added. Lenin, *Collected Works* Volume 26, pp. 106-7.
10 Maurice Dobb, *Soviet Economic Development Since 1917*, London: Routledge, 1966, p. 90.
11 S.A. Smith, *Red Petrograd: Revolution in the Factories 1917-1918*, Cambridge: Cambridge University Press, 1983, pp. 213-14.
12 Smith, *Red Petrograd*, p. 227.
13 Emphasis added. Anton Pannekoek, 'After the War Ends', available at www.marxists.org/archive/pannekoe/1917/after-war-ends.htm. See also my translation in *Not Our War*, London: Merlin Press, 2014, pp. 185-7.
14 This is a term is used in Vladimir Brovkin, 'Politics, Not Economics was the Key', *Slavic Review*, Vol. 44, Issue 2, Urbana: University of Illinois Press, 1985, pp. 244-50. Brovkin notes a series of strikes in the summer of 1918.
15 Alexander Rabinowitch, *The Bolsheviks in Power*, Bloomington: Indiana University Press, 2007, p. 268.
16 Quoted in Maurice Brinton, *The Bolsheviks and Workers' Control*, London: Solidarity, 1970, p. 21.
17 Lenin banned the writings of Pelloutier and other syndicalists. Paul Avrich, *The Russian Anarchists*, Princeton: Princeton University Press, 1967, p. 225.
18 Lenin, *Collected Works* Volume 25, pp. 478-9.
19 Leonard Schapiro, *The Origin of Communist Autocracy*, London: George Bell and Sons, 1966, p. 141.
20 Quoted in Bunyan and Fisher, *The Bolshevik Revolution*, p. 643.
21 Samuel Farber, *Before Stalinism*, London: Polity Press, 1990, p. 69.
22 Bunyan & Fisher, *The Bolshevik Revolution*, pp. 645-6. *Novaia Zhizn* was banned that summer.
23 Bunyan and Fishcer, *The Bolshevik Revolution*, p. 647.
24 Lenin, *Collected Works* Volume 27, p. 340.
25 Lenin, *Collected Works* Volume 27, p. 317.
26 Quoted in Yuri Akhapkin, *First Decrees of Soviet Power*, London: Lawrence & Wishart, 1970, pp. 132-5. Before 1917 Alexander Bogdanov had criticised Taylorism fearing that making workers fit a repetitive mechanical process would dull senses and produce mindlessness. He predicted that the overall productivity of industry would decline if an army of unproductive middle managers was created. See also Steve Smith, 'Taylorism Rules OK?', *Radical Science Journal*, No. 13, 1983.
27 Left Communists' Theses on the Current Situation, *Critique* April 1918, Glasgow. Available at: https://libcom.org.
28 Lenin, *Collected Works*, Volume 27, p. 293.
29 Lenin, *Collected Works*, Volume 27, p. 316.
30 Lenin, *Collected Works*, Volume 27, p. 488.
31 Marc Ferro, *Des soviets au communisme bureaucratique*, Paris: Éditions Gallimard/Julliard, 1980, p. 133.
32 Quoted by Israel Getzler, 'Soviets as Agents of Democratisation', in Edith Rogovin Frankel, et al, eds., *Russia in Revolution*, Cambridge: Cambridge University Press, 1992, p. 30.
33 Published in *Vol'nyi Golos Truda*. This paper, like its predecessor *Golos Truda* was banned. Paul Avrich, ed., *The Anarchists in the Russian Revolution*, London: Thames & Hudson, 1973, pp. 122-5. Maximov fought in the Red Army but was sentenced to death for refusing to do police work. Appeals by the metalworkers' union secured his reprieve.

34 Yuri Akhapkin, *First Decrees*, p. 157.
35 Lenin, *Collected Works*, Volume 32, pp. 495-6.
36 Isaac Steinberg, *Spiridonova*, London: Methuen, 1935, p. 224.
37 Gregory P. Maximov, *The Guillotine at Work*, Vol. 1, Sanday, Orkney: Cienfuegos Press, 1979, p. 69. See also: Jacques Baynac, *La Terreur sous Lénine*, Paris: Le Sagittaire, 1975, p. 137.
38 Alexandre Skirda, *Kronstadt 1921*, Éditions de Paris, 2012, p. 74.
39 Marcel Body, *Au Cœur de la Révolution*, Éditions de Paris, 2003, pp. 181-2.
40 Roy Medvedev, *The October Revolution*, London: Constable, 1979, p. 141.
41 Quoted in Dmitri Volkogonov, *Trotsky: The Eternal Revolutionary*, London: HarperCollins, 1997, p. 237; see also Emma Goldman, *Living My Life*, Vol. 2, New York: Dover Publications, 1970, pp. 753-754.
42 Vladimir Brovkin, 'The Mensheviks' Political Comeback: The Elections to the Provincial City Soviets in Spring 1918', *Russian Review*, Vol. 42, Issue 1, Lawrence, Kansas: Wiley, pp. 1-50. Roy Medvedev, *The October Revolution*, p. 148.
43 Marcel Liebman, *Leninism Under Lenin*, London: Merlin Press, 1980, p. 230.
44 Oskar Anweiler, *The Soviets*, New York: Pantheon, 1974, p. 241; Mervyn Matthews, *Soviet Government: A Selection of Official Documents*, London: Jonathan Cape, 1974, pp. 134-5, 144.
45 Subbotniks were rewarded by free meal, no small matter in hungry times. Participation was obligatory for members of the Communist Party, others would have anticipated troubles if they desisted. Lenin's violent language is itself evidence of coercive intent.
46 Mensheviks were not 'malicious supporters of the bourgeoisie'. Stalinist propaganda would go on to use such mendacious discourse and the mechanism of the amalgam. These methods were already being used at this time.
47 Lenin, *Collected Works* Volume 31, pp. 123-5.
48 Leon Trotsky, *Terrorism and Communism*, London: New Park, 1975, p. 154. See also chapter 8, Nikolai Ivanovich Bukharin, *Economics of the Transformation Period*, London: Pluto Press, 1978.
49 Lenin, *Collected Works* Volume 31, p. 176.
50 *Kronstadt Izvestia*, No. 3, 5:3, 1921.
51 Donald J. Raleigh, *Experiencing Russia's Civil War: Politics, Society, and Revolutionary Culture in Saratov*, Princeton University Press, 2002, pp. 376-7, 408, 413-6.
52 See for instance the speeches in March and May 1921. Lenin *Collected Works* Volume 32, 1973, pp. 199, 412.
53 See comments on a 'sea of women' in Mary McAuley, *Bread And Justice*, Oxford: Oxford University Press, 1991, p. 244.
54 Clara Zetkin, 'My Recollections of Lenin', in Vladimir Lenin, *On the Emancipation of Women*, Moscow: Progress Publishers, 1977, p. 114.
55 Samuel Farber, *Before Stalinism*, p. 86.
56 William J. Chase, *Workers, Society and the Soviet State,* Bloomington: University of Illinois Press, 1990, p. 50.
57 Lenin, *Collected Works* Volume 32, p. 455.
58 Alexander Berkman, *The Bolshevik Myth*, London: Pluto Press, 1987, pp. 180, 219-21.
59 *Petrogradskii Pravda*, quoted in Mary McAuley, *Bread and Justice*, p. 254.
60 Ante Ciliga, *The Russian Enigma*, pp. 12-13. Bakunin had anticipated as much: former workers, 'once they become popular representatives or rulers cease to be workers. They begin to regard the proletarian world from the heights of the State, they represent themselves and their pretension to govern the people, but no longer represent the people'. See Michael Bakunin, *Selected Texts*, London: Merlin/Annares, 2016, p. 245.
61 Lenin, *Collected Works* Volume 25, p. 426.

62 Emphasis added. Lenin, *Collected Works* Volume 25, p. 491.
63 Chase, *Workers, Society*, pp. 51-2; Walter Henry Chamberlin, *The Russian Revolution 1917-1921*, Vol. 2, New York: Macmillan, 1954, p. 109.
64 Chase, *Workers, Society*, p. 50.
65 Skirda, *Kronstadt 1921*, pp. 125-6.
66 Peter Arshinov, *History of the Makhnovist Movement 1918-1921*, Detroit & Chicago: Black & Red, 1974, p. 71.
67 Ante Ciliga, *The Russian Enigma*, London: Ink Links, 1979, pp. 11-12.
68 Thomas F. Remington, 'Institution Building in Bolshevik Russia: The Case of "State Kontrol"', *Slavic Review*, Vol. 41, Issue 1, Urbana: University of Illinois Press, 1982, pp. 91-105.
69 Chamberlin, *The Russian Revolution*, pp. 2, 99 and 112-13.
70 Lenin, *Collected Works* Volume 24, p. 322.
71 Lenin, *Collected Works* Volume 32, pp. 32, 26.
72 Rosa Luxemburg, *The Russian Revolution*, London: Carl Slienger, 1977, p. 47.
73 Left SRs, Maximalists and Anarchist were winning influence—Deutscher writes: 'People listened even more sympathetically to anarchists violently denouncing the Bolshevik regime. If the Bolsheviks had now permitted free elections to the Soviets, they would almost certainly have been swept from power'. Isaac Deutscher, *The Prophet Armed*, Oxford: Oxford University Press, 1976, pp. 504-5 and 515-17.
74 Isaac Deutscher, *Die unvollendete Revolution*, Frankfurt: Fischer Bücherei, 1967, p. 31. The events of 1921 did not come suddenly, 'out of the blue'—they flowed from the conflicts and tensions that had been building since 1918.
75 Fifty years earlier Bakunin had anticipated potential conflict between town and country in the course of revolution if rule by decree prevailed. An alliance between rural and urban workers was imperative. 'The entire revolutionary question lies here, one must resolve it or perish'. Bakunin, *Selected Texts*, p. 183.
76 Tamás Krausz, *Reconstructing Lenin: An Intellectual Biography*, New York: Monthly Review Press, 2015, pp. 331, 370. Krausz comments on workers' supervision (in English language texts this is usually rendered as 'workers' control') and suggests incorrectly that Lenin borrowed this concept from the anarchists (p. 202). Anarchists and syndicalists, as we have seen, wanted much more than mere accounting and checking, while Lenin, concerned with the growing influence of libertarians in the latter half of 1917, had carefully and deliberately asserted strictly limited forms of workers' control, subordinated to state power. As was noted above, developments exceeded this agenda and led to incipient forms of workers' management. There is another error, perhaps an error in translation, on page 191: 'In a study from 1910, Bakunin acknowledged that …' Bakunin died in 1876.
77 Krausz, *Reconstructing Lenin*, p. 196
78 Emphasis added. Lenin, *Collected Works* Volume 25, p. 409.
79 The Sixth Congress of the International Workers' Association, meeting in Geneva, 1-6 September 1873, had adopted the view that the purpose of workers' congresses was to discuss and to attempt to bring some degree of harmony between various points of view. Rene Berthier, *Social-Democracy and Anarchism in the International Workers' Association, 1864-1877*, London: Merlin/Anarres, 2015, p.185
80 Krausz, *Reconstructing Lenin*, p. 178.
81 Krausz, *Reconstructing Lenin*, p. 196. Krausz notes that there were only some four million industrial workers in Russia, so, even if all proletarians had supported the Bolshevik party (never the case), the dictatorship of this proletariat could never have amounted to the dictatorship of a majority of working people.
82 Emphasis added. Krausz, *Reconstructing Lenin*, p. 197.

83 For a critical perspective see Anthony Zurbrugg, 'Socialism and Strategy: A Libertarian Critique of Leninism,' *Anarchist Studies*, 22.1, 2014.
84 For an example—on railways—see: Gaston Leval, *Collectives in the Spanish Revolution*, London: Freedom Press, 1975, p. 247.
85 *Theses, Resolutions and Manifestos of the First Four Congress of the Third International*, translated by Alix Holt & Barbara Holland, London: Ink Links, 1980, p. 73
86 Boris Souvarine, *Stalin*, London: Secker & Warburg, 1939, pp. 362-363.
87 For example: http://zcomm.org/category/topic/parecon, www.solidaires.org, and www.cgt.es.

THE 'PEOPLE'S WAR' AND THE LEGACY OF THE CHINESE REVOLUTION

WANG HUI

The disintegration of the Soviet bloc after 1989 marked the beginning of the end of the revolutionary socialist movement that originated in the nineteenth century and was consolidated by the twentieth-century Communist regimes. The end of the ideological confrontations of the cold war brought proclamations both of the 'end of history' as well as of a new 'clash of civilizations'. These two opposing theses together declared the end of twentieth-century politics: national liberation, land reform, class struggle, state and revolution have all apparently become anachronisms. In parallel with this, the power of capital overwhelmed the obstacles that the socialist movement had played so large a part in constructing, and began to reorganize all social and political forms. In the present conditions of financialized monopoly capitalism, the most salient project for capital is to erode any substantive differences among political forms so as to realize its project of 'globalization'. In twenty-first century capitalism, whether characterized by single-party or parliamentary multiparty systems, ideological conflicts have been muted or eliminated. Even the socialist and capitalist systems themselves are no longer seen as mutually irreconcilable. These diverse formations can apparently all be contained and tamed within an increasingly homogenous capitalism, in which the division of the international order into 'three worlds' has also increasingly lost its political significance. Meanwhile, anticapitalist movements, symbolized by Occupy Wall Street, however loud and visible, have been weak in reality. Trapped by the prevailing media, most such movements pay no attention to the legacy of fierce political struggle of the last century.

All of this applies to China as well, where many show disdain for the political innovations of the revolution almost seven decades on. This is hardly surprising given that the Communist revolutions of East Asia have fallen into ambiguous betrayal, almost buried in the shadows of the market. But Marx's spectre of the communist revolutionary movement has by no means entirely disappeared. And it is significant that it has most often taken a Maoist shape, as could be seen from the spectacle of parties and movements of which revolutionary violence remained a feature, and which have led or promoted a protracted people's war in Peru, Colombia, the Philippines, Turkey, and the entire South Asian region. Very differently from the protest movements in the developed countries, the Maoist movements did not hesitate to declare their roots in the twentieth-century revolutionary movement they sought to continue, especially the Chinese revolution. In the capitalist peripheries, questions of land, national liberation, democratic revolution and economic growth still form the basic agenda. Especially in South Asia, the Maoist movement's deployment of the twentieth century's basic political vocabulary of anti-imperialism and anti-feudalism appears still valid and effective, as the caste system, land relations, national independence and other issues continue to be central concerns.

Like the revolutionary movements of the twentieth century, contemporary Maoist movements have combined peaceful protest, armed struggle, relations with the workers and peasants, and 'the line struggle' through practice and theoretical debate, striving to achieve political unity and forge a new political subject through a dynamic process of division and integration. These features hardly find any equivalent in the contemporary social movements centred in urban middle classes. Such movements are often short-lived, fragmented, and based on immediate interests and mainstream values. The lack of a process of remolding the subject (or of self-negation in order to form a new self) makes it impossible for social struggle to be sustained. The scale, longevity, intensity and political innovation of the Maoist movement distinguishes it from the various Occupy movements in the west.

Calling this persistence of Maoist practice a 'spectacle' is deliberate, intended to contrast it with both the spectacular collapse of most Communist parties or their degeneration through an embrace of neoliberal globalization, as well as the spectacle of protest movements like Occupy. The 'spectacle' of Maoist movements also offers a sharp contrast to the overwhelming focus of contemporary scholarship on globalization, the rise of Chinese capitalism, financial crises, etc. Even the more critical currents leave little, if any, space for the possibility of overcoming capitalism through revolutionary means. As such, old categories, from class to nation, autonomism to internationalism, become the subjects of negative reflection and deconstruction. In the context of contemporary thinking, we can hardly find traces of the Maoist movement; or else it is no more than a synonym of terrorism. We have become accustomed to observing our world through the lens of the 'end of history', even for many people who firmly reject such a theory. This is why it is especially important to insist on asking whether Maoism as movement and party still bears lessons for people engaged in various forms of struggle.

THE PEOPLE'S WAR AS POLITICAL CATEGORY

People's war was an innovation particular to the Chinese Revolution, unlike political phenomena elsewhere of parties, party politics, and governments, which originated in nineteenth-century Europe and twentieth-century Russia. Without understanding people's war, one cannot comprehend the uniqueness of the Chinese revolution or grasp the deep differences between revolutionary 'party construction' and other forms of party politics. Without understanding people's war, one also cannot understand the historical implications of such distinctive political concepts produced in twentieth-century China as the mass line and the united front.

The party described its articulation in the Chinese Communist revolution as 'new democratic'. In specifying its basic tasks as that of overthrowing imperialist powers and 'feudal' relations, the revolution was simultaneously national and social in nature, lifting up an oppressed nation and its toiling masses, building momentum and gaining strength from the rural margins, encircling the cities from the countryside and seizing state power through a people's war. The revolution paved the way for China's subsequent modern industrial and social development, contravening the supposedly universal paradigm of capitalist development. Meanwhile, the Chinese revolution was also 'part of the world revolution' as Mao noted in 1940 in *On New Democracy*. Its world-historical significance lay in its transformative and emancipatory effects on China and its immense influence on the third world. The 'New China' signified it was possible to make a break with the old world.

The Chinese Communist party, founded in 1921, was left with the tasks that the republican revolution of 1911 had been unable to accomplish. The tragic defeat of the communists in 1927, when the counterrevolutionary force within the Kuomintang party (KMT) slaughtered workers and communist sympathizers, compelled a major shift in revolutionary strategy. Since the working class only constituted a tiny minority of the population, with the majority being peasants, revolutionary workers and intellectuals in the urban centres began to move to the countryside. A new theory of a staged revolution accompanied this, involving a differentiation between minimum and maximum party programmes: the first step towards socialism and communism would be land redistribution. There was also a change from conceiving a political movement centred around a vanguard party to organizing a people's war based on the close intertwining of party and army, with both seen as based in the people. And starting around 1930, the Chinese revolution began running local governments in its base areas. All three – party, army, and local government – were seen as closely linked in the process of state building even before securing national power.

In 1925-26, the KMT adopted the policy of allying with the Soviet Union and the CCP, and the two parties cooperated to promote peasant and workers' movements. The Peasant Movement Training Institute at Guangzhou led by Mao Zedong was only one of a dozen of similar institutes to train peasant activists. During the period of the Northern Expedition, the KMT focused on two goals: constructing a political army for the party free of the influence of the old warlords, and building peasants' and workers' movements in cooperation with the CCP. Thus the notions of a politicized army for the party, and of resisting armed counterrevolution with armed revolution, were initially formulated not by the CCP but rather the early KMT, still under the influence of the Comintern. But critically, the transformation of the CCP would not have been possible without the concept of people's war, which was developed only after it was betrayed by the KMT and its activity in the cities was brutally suppressed in 1927.

The CCP was initially composed of petty bourgeois intellectuals who were even less connected with the peasants and workers than the KMT. This was worlds apart from what emerged later in the Jiangxi Soviet period (1931-34). Likewise, the urban uprisings and workers' struggles led by Qu Qiubai, Li Lisan and Wang Ming among others after Chiang Kai-shek's all-out attack on the CCP in 1927 differed markedly from the strategy of 'encircling the cities from the countryside' later deployed during the people's war. The party's unification with the army, the 'red political power' of the soviet governments it established in the base areas, and the peasant masses through the agrarian revolution, as well as its relationship with other parties, social classes and their political representatives, all took shape through the people's war, which created a type of political party that differed from all political parties of the past. This party also created a class subject different from all working-class parties of the past, a class subject structured by a membership composed mainly of peasants.

Mao's famous 'Sanwan reorganization' of the Red Army in 1927 was centred on the project of making 'party branches within the regiment' and setting up 'soldiers' committees' oriented toward creating equality between officers and soldiers. The reorganization facilitated an organic, integral relationship between the party, army and masses. The joining of two armies that had participated in the Nanchang and Autumn Harvest Uprisings and created the Jiangxi Soviet Revolutionary Base Area in 1928 was a milestone for the people's war. Within the base areas, party politics morphed into a mass movement through the military struggle for land reform. While the army implemented land reform, the party (or at least the rural soviets under the guidance of the party) administered economic life and promoted cultural and ideological activities among the people. This complex intertwining of the party, army, government and peasant movement facilitated the creation of a completely new revolutionary political subject: 'the people' (*renmin*). Forging the peasantry into a revolutionary political subject required a continual process of politicization. Since the interests of the peasants lay in land redistribution, they could not be expected to devote themselves to a project of ultimately abolishing private property, the ultimate political goal of the communists. Precisely because of this, the emergence of a new political subject would be impossible without integrating the party, army, soviets and masses into a coherent unity. With the peasants as its main constituent and the worker-peasant alliance as its foundation, the emergence of this new revolutionary subject facilitated the transformation of all forms of politics (including local governments, the party, peasant associations, and labor unions). People's war, therefore, was not a purely military concept, but also a profoundly political one, which fundamentally reconceived party representation in modern politics.

One of the crucial achievements of the people's war was the establishment of 'red regimes', most often in the form of independent soviet governments in the border regions between provinces, which became organizational centres of daily life. While they took what they could from foreign and Chinese historical experiences, this form of government differed from the conventional bourgeois state: it was the political expression of a class that had acquired self-consciousness through continuous political and military mobilization.

In his well-known article 'Why is it that the red regime can exist in China?' Mao pointed out that China was neither an imperialist country nor one ruled directly by imperialism; it was an internally unevenly developed country divided by warlords, dependent on different imperialist powers that thus controlled the country indirectly. But this situation also weakened class domination, and produced external conditions for the survival of red regimes in rural China. Frustrated by the failure of the Great Revolution (1924-27), the CCP attempted to establish red regimes in the war zones, based on the integration of the party, the army, the government and mass politics. The CCP and its local governments developed further during the War of Resistance against Japan, in which military struggle, the mass line and the united front became the guarantees of success. Later, during the Civil War in the late 1940s, anti-Japanese guerrilla warfare evolved into large-scale armed conflict, even as the war of position continued.

In the course of organizing this people's war, the CCP and the base area governments not only attended to military issues but also questions of social organization. The party created the concept of the mass line with several principles in mind. First, serving the needs of the largest number of people would be the starting point and ultimate goal of party work. Second, only if the border region government solved the people's problems, improved their lives and won their trust could it mobilize the broad masses to join the Red Army, support the revolutionary war and defeat the Encirclement Campaigns launched by the KMT. Thus people's war was not only an effective military tactic to defeat the enemy, but also dealt out of necessity with crucial issues that immediately affected people's lives, including land ownership, labour issues, gender equality, daily necessities, education, trade and money and finance. The interpenetration of the military and ordinary social life was thus a core component of people's war. Mao repeatedly reminded CCP members that they must stay with the people, mobilize them, care for them, sincerely work for their interests, and solve problems they encountered in daily life, such as housing, rice and salt, clothing and childbirth, in order to win the support of those who would risk their lives on the battlefield.[1]

The mass line was the basic strategy of people's war. It was a party policy as well as a way to reconstruct the party: without the party organization, it would not be possible to define the masses; while if the party did not mix with and learn from the masses, it would become a cumbersome structure riding on the backs of the people. In the vast countryside, this peasant-based party acquired its political and discursive position through its movements and campaigns. In this sense, it was the party and its mass line under the conditions of people's war that created the self-consciousness of a class, and thus created a class in the political sense. Only a party that had reconstructed itself through people's war could have created a proletarian class composed primarily of peasants. It was this unprecedented people's war that consolidated military struggle, land revolution, base area development and the construction of a revolutionary state, through political strategies including military struggle, the mass line and the united front. With its class politics based on the alliance of workers and peasants as well as the united front of national liberation, the CCP eventually overtook the KMT, which had moved away from the peasant movement and revolutionary politics.

PARTIES AND POLITICAL REPRESENTATION: THE CONTINUING RELEVANCE OF MAOISM

Party politics took its modern shape in nineteenth-century Europe. In China, this was a most important political innovation of the twentieth century, although distinctively shaped by the people's war and its political aftermath.

There were four prerequisites for the formation of modern Chinese party politics. Firstly, the conditions of the early Republican era rendered crucial the formation of a new national politics. The party politics of the 1911 Revolution attempted to emulate the multi-party parliamentary system developed within the framework of European constitutional politics. But faced with the challenges of secessionism, monarchical restoration, and the crisis of republicanism, the revolutionaries and many political elites moved away from their original political objective. Secondly, during the First World War, many political parties in the West participated in nationalist war mobilization. Consequently, reflection on traditional modes of party politics peaked among European intellectuals after the war, forming part of the intellectual atmosphere in which Chinese party politics was reconstructed. Thirdly, the eruption of the Russian Revolution during the war led some Chinese revolutionaries to believe that Bolshevism could overcome the limits of bourgeois party politics. Lastly, modern Chinese revolutionary parties (including the KMT before 1927) gradually formed the political practice of people's war, a new type of politics that transcended traditional political parties and their representative relations.

In other words, the crisis of party politics gave birth to the party system that was the political nucleus of this revolutionary century. This new model of political party, influenced by Leninism and the Russian revolution, bore the dual features of 'super political party' (*chaoji zhengdang*) and 'supra party' (*chaozhengdang*). The term 'super political party' refers to the fact that although the KMT and the CCP both had to adopt some of the elements of party politics, neither intended to limit themselves to working within competitive parliamentary structures. Instead, both aimed to become the hegemonic or 'leading' party. That these organizations also had a 'supra party' orientation means that the form of political representation they articulated differed from that in conventional parliamentary systems, and was much more similar to the Bolshevik party, with an element of the Gramscian 'modern prince' in representing both the people and the future.

In both Western multiparty systems and the Chinese system of multiparty cooperation under one party rule, the representativeness of political parties has become increasingly obscure. In the case of China, the representativeness of the party has diminished alongside the lucidity of such traditional categories as the proletariat, the worker-peasant alliance, and the united front.[2] The most severe symptom of what might be called this 'rupture of representativeness' is the 'statification' of the party, or the integration of the party into the framework of state. As both its function and form of organization become ever more assimilated with the state apparatus, the party has been deprived of the independent essence needed for political organization and mobilization. This process implies the end of the mass line, which had engendered the political dynamism of the CCP.

Two interrelated forms of the statification of the party can be identified: first, the bureaucratization of the party beginning in the early days of the People's Republic, which was one of the pivotal reasons for the Cultural Revolution; and second, the marriage of the party and capital through the corporatization of the government which accompanied market reforms. The 'rupture of representativeness' manifests itself most intensely in the incongruity between the party's claim to general representation transcending the old class categories, and its increasing distance from the people, especially those from lower social strata. There are of course still policies protective of workers and peasants; however, one can barely discern any organic connection between party politics and the politics of workers and peasants.

The detachment of the political system from society has happened not only in the socialist or post-socialist countries, but also in Western party systems and other systems based on these. Just as in China the relationship between the party and its class basis becomes ever more vague, the distinction between left and right among Western political parties has become blurred. Unlike in the nineteenth century and in the early twentieth century, it is hard to find political movements with clear agendas in today's party politics. The fracturing of representativeness has so intensified that one might even conclude that the party politics, which flourished in the nineteenth and twentieth centuries, has either disappeared completely or persists only in limited areas. Conventional party politics either is transforming, or has already transformed, into a state-party politics, with parties serving as a structure of state power. If one investigates whether it is political parties that control the state, or conversely the logic of the state that dictates to parties, the latter may be a better answer.

The boundary between party and state is vanishing, and the outcome of their assimilation is the dissolution of political representativeness, which in turn renders ever more asymmetrical the power relations in the political sphere. Rather than balancing or reducing inequalities in the socioeconomic sphere, this conflation of party and state actually provides an effective institutional support for this. The fracture of representativeness allows the rhetoric of politicians to degenerate into a performance aimed at grabbing power, while techno-bureaucrats strive for higher political positions. In the Western multi-party or dual party structure, the role of political parties is fundamentally social mobilization pivoting on elections that take place every four or five years. In these contexts, the party is more like a state apparatus for the rotation of leaders.

The super political party in China was originally sustained by rigorous organization, straightforward value orientation, and mass movements characterized by vigorous interaction between theory and practice. However, today the CCP has almost been reduced to an administrative organization. The party has become a component of the management apparatus, with its function of mobilization and supervision being increasingly identical with the state mechanism, as its bureaucratic form intensifies and its political distinctiveness diminishes. Additionally, the crisis of representativeness afflicts ruling parties as well as non-ruling parties the world over. In present day China, any representativeness of the eight small 'democratic parties' has also become unprecedentedly elusive.

The waning of the representativeness of those public institutions that mediate between state and political society (parliament in the West and the National People's Congress and the Chinese People's Political Consultative Conference in China) echoes the statification of parties. In parliamentary democracy, seats in the parliament usually reflect party constituencies. But with the decline of distinctions between political parties, the connection between parliament and society is gradually severed. In theory, the notion of proportional representation in the People's Congress of China seems more removed from the reality of party politics than in party-centred parliamentary systems. In practice, the Chinese model needs to be buttressed by politics based in the mass line, the decline of which will undermine the process of selecting people's deputies and the role of the Congress in China's political life. The People's Congress has been rightly criticized for the fact that the percentage of worker and peasant deputies in the body is radically disproportionate to the broader makeup of Chinese society.

The consequence of the crisis of representative politics has been depoliticization. As party politics has degenerated into the politics of state-party or state-parties, is 'post-party politics' possible? 'Post-party politics' refers not to any politics after political parties disappear, but to the fact that they have taken on new roles in the context of depoliticization. The idea of 'post-political parties' indicates that although parties still act as leading political entities, they have lost their earlier representativeness and original logic of identity. At the same time, political form remains stable, as major political institutions are still based on the principle of party representation. Precisely because of this, the fracture of representativeness is the main symptom of today's political crisis.

The reality of 'post-party politics' implies the necessity to devise a new practice beyond the framework of party politics. The key issues are how to reconstruct representativeness, at what level, and whether we should think differently about representation altogether. In the political practice of twentieth-century China, elements of 'post-party politics' were present, but only as the practice of a 'super-political party' in the people's war, based on the mass line and the united front. These practices attempted to transcend conventional representative relations. Today's party politics in China is also generated by the degradation of a 'super-party' into a state-party system. In order to overcome the crisis of representation, we need to reconstruct representativeness and to explore new paths of post-party politics. Two dimensions of 'post-party politics' need to be tackled: a re-examination of the principles of representative politics in twentieth-century China, and an exploration of the conditions and possibilities of 'post-party politics'.

Such re-examination and exploration may yield important lessons for contemporary social movements. The Occupy movement did not only have a huge impact in the United States, but also inspired anti-capitalist movements in other regions. However, these movements have several obvious weaknesses. First, with the end of the twentieth-century socialist movements, contemporary movements are deeply skeptical about the organizational morphology of political parties. This has resulted in their lack of real leadership, clear political programme and accompanying short-term strategy. Moreover, due to their inability to link protests with long-term social experimentation, the Occupy movements have not nurtured a coherent new political subject: the 'we' is only a temporarily aggregated group and not a sustainable political process. This is one of the differences between the mass movement in the conditions of people's war and the mass movements of today. Still, we cannot use the former case to denigrate the latter, nor should we use the latter to negate the former, since the foundational historical situations are different in each case.

However, can we learn something from the mass movements of the previous era? In the discursive context of the Chinese revolution, Mao's basic slogan was 'from the masses, to the masses'. In fact, 'to the masses' was an idea of the Comintern, which called on the revolutionaries, especially the elite elements (professors, doctors, lawyers, teachers, etc.) to join the mass movements. But 'from the masses' was a product of the people's war. The masses did not emerge spontaneously, but were rather organized as a politically meaningful category of subjective agency (recall the principles of Sanwan Reorganization: only when the soldiers formed their own soldiers' committees could the party find its masses in the army). The formation of the masses is the formation of the 'we' – not as an old, spontaneous existence, but as a brand new subject. The 'mass line' did not only change the masses, but also the elites joining in the mass movement. Together they formed the new 'we'.

Today, the political logic of the twentieth century has receded. The intellectuals mostly look at the stratification of Chinese society and its politics in a positivist manner, forgetting that class politics in twentieth-century China had elements of a supra-representative politics. In the struggle between the KMT and the CCP, and in the war of resistance against the Japanese, the united front, armed struggle, party construction, and so on became the CCP's political assets. The mass line, summarized as 'all for the masses, all relies on the masses; from the masses and to the masses', was the main pathway through which the politics of this 'supra-' and 'super-' political party was constructed. Apart from the Soviet tradition, the project of state building in the base areas in preparation for the future national power also borrowed from western representation systems, including the election of representatives and the very narrative of representativeness itself (not only of the CCP but of the other democratic parties). However, obviously this political praxis contained supra- or post-political party elements as well. The supra-party aspect of party politics can also be interpreted as a feature of supra-representativeness: it encapsulates the relationship between politics and culture, and between political party and masses.

THEORETICAL DEBATE, SOCIAL STRUGGLE, AND REPOLITICIZATION

The experience of the Chinese revolution was based on praxis, correcting its mistakes through theoretical debates and political struggle, and consequently creating the premises for new strategies and new practice. When theoretical debates were more active, the political realm was more lively and innovations in political structure more dynamic. Mao's conceptions of principal and secondary contradictions, the principal and secondary aspects of a contradiction, the transformation of a contradiction, the epistemology of split of one into two, and so on – all intrinsically related to the military strategy of the people's war – were indicative of the kind of space for debate and reflection, which opened the possibility of new politics and strategies.

Highlighting the role of such theoretical and political struggles does not obviate the need for criticisms of excessive and arbitrary violence. Political persecution is the end of theoretical struggle and party line debate, and is therefore the end of inner-party competitive practice. Today, the suppression of political debate is also the end of politics. Many publications in today's China which pretend to be conclusive about violence in history ignore the necessity of theoretical struggle over the party line, seeming to forget that shutting down the political arena results in the absence of any self-corrective mechanism in politics. This kind of research is the product of the politics of depoliticization.

The statification of political parties also marks the end of an era of mass line politics. In the context of globalization and market conditions, returning to the question of the mass line is not so much about lamenting a historical episode as about undertaking a new quest for a possible and uncertain future. The one sure thing is that some foundational concepts for understanding the construction of modern states and power systems – from sovereignty to citizenship, class to labour, etc. – need to be redefined in accordance with changed global socio-economic conditions. For example, in the Chinese discursive context, are the concepts of the working class or the worker-peasant alliance necessary to reestablish representativeness? In the conditions of a financialized capitalism, the developed countries are experiencing a process of de-industrialization. If the working class as a revolutionary class is radically shrinking or has even disappeared, what is the new political subject? In China and many other non-Western countries, large-scale industrialization has produced a massive working class constituted to a large extent by migrant workers. The re-emergence of classes is a hugely important phenomenon of contemporary Chinese society. The reuse of the language of class is inevitable. However, the expansion and restructuring of the working class is a process that is almost coextensive with the decline of working-class politics.

Not only is the newborn working-class politics very far from reaching the depth and scale of that of the earlier era, it also will most likely not repeat the twentieth-century experience. We can discern at least two features of present day working-class politics: one is the missing link between working-class politics and party politics, the other is the relative instability of loosely organized workers in a fluid production system. These features distinguish today's workers not only from the working class during the period of socialist industrialization, but also from the earlier period of working-class formation. If the 'rupture of representativeness' is the expression of a disjuncture between political and social forms, then what political form could be organically linked with current social forms?

Reconstructing representativeness is inevitably and directly a matter of solving the problem of the reemergence of social classes and class conflicts. However, capitalist globalization and the deepening of statification of political parties mean that this task is not simply about reconstructing a class-based party. Rather, it is about forming a more autonomous social sphere of politics (including trade unions, peasant associations, and other social groupings broadly considered political organizations), and especially an active labour politics aimed at transforming the relations of production. The rural-urban divide and its transformation, regional disparities, rising tensions in class relations, and the destruction of the eco-environmental system by the prevailing modes of production and consumption all demonstrate the contradictions of contemporary capitalism. As such, rural construction, environmental protection, a changed growth model, the pursuit of ethnic equality and cultural diversity, and reversing the degradation of the working class should all be the driving forces of a needed politics of equality.

New political and economic realities mean that we cannot simply return to the political models of the nineteenth or twentieth century. However, ideological debate and organizational construction on the basis of an open politics remain indispensable. Even if those organizations which call themselves political parties still exist, their political meaning has changed significantly. How to make broad social forces participate in political processes more directly is a necessary question that should guide our search for a new political framework. This is also a basic precondition for the CCP to practice the mass line in a different style. Repoliticization cannot rely on old party politics, but must embrace the practice of a 'post-party politics'. Such a politics does not negate any function of political organizations, but will emphasize their openness, looseness, and non-bureaucratic nature. The mass line and mass politics are sources of political vitality, cornerstones against right-wing populism, and the bases of the process of repoliticization and the creation of universality. This is the perspective in which the Chinese Communist revolution still makes immediate sense.

NOTES

This essay draws on the chapter on the Korean War in my book *China's Twentieth Century*, London: Verso, 2016 as well as my earlier essay on 'The Crisis of Representativeness and Post-party Politics', *Modern China*, 40(March), 2014, pp. 214-39.

1   Mao Tse-tung, 'Be Concerned with the Well-Being of the Masses, Pay Attention to Methods of Work', *Selected Works of Mao Tse-tung*, Vol. I, Beijing: Foreign Languages Press, 1965, pp. 147-52.

2   The 'decline of representation', which suggests the detachment between political system and social form, is an issue that I have discussed on various occasions. In 'Depoliticized Politics, the Multiple Components of Hegemony, and the Eclipse of the Sixties' I discuss the question of depoliticized politics. See *Inter-Asia Cultural Studies*, 7.4(December), 2006, pp. 683-700. In 'The Decline of Representation: Another Inquiry on "Equality of What"', *Beijing Cultural Review*, 5(October), 2011, pp. 66-81 and 6(December), 2011, pp. 98-113, I explore the different types of equality crisis and its relationship with the crisis of representativeness.

REVOLUTION AS 'NATIONAL LIBERATION' AND THE ORIGINS OF NEOLIBERAL ANTIRACISM

ADOLPH REED, JR

This essay, like this volume as a whole, is motivated by the centennial of 1917 providing occasion for reflection on the great revolutionary projects of the last century and rumination on the status of the notion of revolution now. My concern is fundamentally 'presentist' and best characterized as demystification or ideology-critique. Specifically, my interest is in reflecting on the emergence of antiracism as a discrete political stance – that is, not simply a principled opposition to discrimination and bigotry – and the impact that it, along with other strains of what is commonly called identity politics, has had on contemporary left political thought and practice, including dominant ways of conceptualizing social transformation and revolution. I believe, for reasons that I trust this examination will make clear, taking critical stock of antiracist politics is a crucial task for the left, especially in the United States, where antiracism arguably emerged as a claim to a discrete politics, but elsewhere as well. Antiracist politics, and its corollary commitment to diversity, has become a significant American cultural export, as Bourdieu and Wacquant noted nearly two decades ago.[1]

Whatever it may have been at earlier historical moments, antiracism as a contemporary politics is not necessarily aligned with projects of broad social transformation animated by the egalitarian vision that prompted the twentieth century's iconic revolutions. Rather, antiracist politics in the United States and elsewhere in the West and much of Latin America can be, and often enough has been, an antagonistic *alternative* to such projects of broad transformation. That is, notwithstanding a persistent inclination among leftists to consider it a discourse at least in dialogue with the left, antiracism is as likely now to be an ideological and practical programme that fits more comfortably within neoliberalism than with a socialist left. In the United States especially, but increasingly in Western Europe and Canada also, antiracism and other political tendencies based on ascriptive identities – that is, those expressing what one supposedly *is* rather than what one does[2] –

commonly reject Marxist and other socialist politics as insufficiently attentive, if not inimical, to the special position and needs of racial or other ascriptively defined populations understood to be oppressed in ways that are not causally or most consequentially rooted in capitalist political economy. In fact, these tendencies commonly object to the universalizing perspectives associated with socialism and Marxism in particular as Eurocentric (or phallocentric, or heteronormative) homogenization that denies the specificity of ascriptive groups' distinctive perspectives, grievances and demands.

To the extent the political orientation from which antiracist and other identity-based tendencies proceed is more 'groupist' than broadly solidaristic, the vision of a just society around which they cohere can be more in line with liberal interest-group pluralism than with a left that relates its lineage or marks its affinities to the broad tradition that generated the revolutionary movements of the last century. Eric Hobsbawm pointed to this tension in the mid-1990s indicating that, while the left naturally has supported movements advocating for the rights of stigmatized groups, identity groups 'are not committed to the Left as such, but only to get support for their cause wherever they can'.[3]

Openness to this kind of politics stems partly, as Hobsbawm points out, from the left reflex to support the cause of the oppressed. The victories won in the second half of the twentieth century against ideologies and regimes of ascriptive hierarchy, chiefly those grounded on narratives of race and gender, made leftists, and labour, all the more conscious of past failings with respect to inattentiveness to, acceptance or even overt embrace of ascriptive inegalitarianism. The generation of leftists who emerged in the 1960s came of age with the militant anti-colonial movements and national liberation struggles in what was then known as the Third World, the civil rights struggle in the United States, and anti-apartheid struggles in South Africa, as well as the resurgent women's movement. That generation was also likely to be self-critical regarding what were perceived as failings and limitations – some would say ossification, even debasement or perversion – of the dominant practical models of socialism in Eastern Europe and elsewhere on the capitalist periphery. The New Left generation's inclination to criticize 'really existing socialism' extended also to the orthodox Marxist parties in the West, which were easily enough seen as out of touch with the new spirit of insurgency coming from youth, minority groups in advanced capitalist societies, and Third World movements of national liberation. In the US, many displayed similar scepticism toward the trade union movement, which in the eyes of many radicals had settled into a narrow, self-interested class collaborationism.

This is a familiar story to *Socialist Register* readers, and one I summarize very schematically. In addition to Hobsbawm's account mentioned above, Leo Panitch and the late Ellen Meiksins Wood have discussed these developments more extensively, especially the impact of the intellectual left's movement both into the academy and away from an intellectual and epistemic commitment to class struggle.[4] Several features of that moment are pertinent for making sense of the subsequent development of antiracist politics in itself and the left's embrace of it. Disillusionment with democratic centralism and sclerotic bureaucratism fed a skeptical attitude toward organizational and intellectual discipline, as well as toward commitment to specific visions and programmes of social transformation. Those tendencies became exacerbated over the 1980s and 1990s as left activity retreated increasingly into universities. In that climate, as more and more of the left came to be defined by moral stance rather than strategic politics and practical programme, self-criticism and atonement regarding racism and sexism on the part of labour and the left in the past, and bearing witness against injustice in the present, loomed steadily larger as an element of left political discourse, especially in the US. And then, with rote repetition of ever more deeply embedded commonsense knowledge, the narrative of labour's and the left's past failings with respect to racial and gender inequalities was increasingly shed of nuance, to the point that in recent decades it has become a truism in some activist circles that failure to challenge ascriptive inequalities, or even active reproduction of them, has been a definitive characteristic of the working-class-based left and trade unions, and is substantially responsible for the decline of either or both.[5] Commitment to the accusatory narrative can underwrite extraordinary historical misrepresentation, for example, Eugene Debs's statement that socialism has 'nothing special to offer the Negro' is taken as evidence of his indifference to racial inequality – when his intent was exactly the opposite.[6]

A left that had by and large given up the goal of radical social transformation and the objective of pursuing political power for the purpose of realizing that goal became less distinct from liberalism. Such a left, as Russell Jacoby notes, 'ineluctably retreats to smaller ideas, seeking to expand the options within the existing society'.[7] Militant embrace of the discourses of identity politics, most notably antiracism, has helped to sustain an appearance that the left is not in retreat but remains on the cutting edge of transformational politics. That is because of the prominence of a view that construes 'oppressions' rooted in race and gender, etc., as both foundational to American society – or the West – and so deeply embedded that most whites/men are in denial about their power. From that perspective the civil rights movement's legislative victories in the 1960s were superficial and could not address the deep-structural sources of racism and sexism, which are effectively ontological and therefore beyond the reach of normal political or social intervention. Thus the struggle against these sources of inequality is always insurgent because their power never diminishes.

CONTEMPORARY ANTIRACISM'S AHISTORICAL CHARACTER

Representing racism as a transhistorical phenomenon, sometimes characterized as a 'national disease' or 'original sin', underwrites a claim that it continues to shape life chances for blacks and other nonwhites as it did in earlier periods when, as W. E. B. Du Bois put it, 'the walls of race were clear and straight; when the world consisted of mutually exclusive races; and even though the exact edges might be blurred there was no question of exact definition and understanding of the meaning of the word', that is, when notions of racial hierarchy were hegemonic and were open and explicit principles of social and political organization.[8] That view, to the extent that it understands racism as transcending patterns of historically specific social relations, presumes primordial understandings of race/racism as a phenomenon shared by both postwar racial liberalism and the earlier racial determinism it challenged. This is, moreover, a political problem as well as an intellectual one.

The politics crafted in this antiracist framework has a rearguard character that is expressed in its proponents' tendency to rely on evocation of past racist practices – law professor Michelle Alexander's book *The New Jim Crow* is one prominent illustration[9] – to mobilize outrage about injustices in the present. The argument by means of historical analogy, i.e., that current injustices that may seem to derive most directly from different, more complex sources are more significantly understood as like latter-day instances of racist practices in the past, rests on the trope that the current outrages demonstrate the deep continuity of racism as a force and at least suggests the inadequacy of the victories of the civil rights struggle. Yet that trope is also in effect an acknowledgment that big victories on that front have indeed been won. Otherwise there would be no basis for assuming that the comparison would have rhetorical force. Condemnation of an act or practice by comparing it to slavery or Jim Crow could provoke the desired effect only if we can assume consensus that slavery and Jim Crow were bad things. Moreover, sustaining the conviction that racism remains most significantly causal of contemporary patterns of inequality requires terminological gymnastics which enable positing racism – 'institutional', 'structural', even 'post-racial'

– as, at least by default, the causal explanation for inequalities that appear statistically as racial disparity and are lived as such in day-to-day life. In fact, historical analogy typically stands in lieu of empirical argument to explain why we should automatically see contemporary disparities as evidence of the unspecified workings of a generic racism rather than as products of current and concrete political-economic processes that are very much 'presentist' elements of the regime of steadily intensifying regressive redistribution, the mechanisms, that is, that constitute the *telos* of neoliberalism.

Assertion of the centrality of racist ideas and practices among labour and the left is similarly ahistorical both as a representation of the past and in its implications of continuity in the present. It is more allegory or fable than historical account. Presumptions, stances, and practices that now would be clearly recognized and negatively sanctioned as racist certainly were common enough in the Marxist left and the labour movement in the nineteenth and early twentieth centuries. The appropriate basis of comparison – if one wants to make the sort of moral assessment that many critics of those institutions intend – would, however, not be early twenty-first century sensibilities, but whether racism and sexism were more prominent within unions and left politics than within other contemporaneous institutions. Frankly, from an historicist perspective this sort of exercise in moralistic calculation seems rather puerile, but, because antiracist criticisms of the left in the present depend so heavily on claims regarding the past, it is necessary to address them. Toward that end an important first step is recognizing that what race means and does not, how it has operated as a politically and ideologically potent category, as well as its meanings and significance, have evolved over time and context.

The period of revolutionary ferment out of which the Bolshevik revolution emerged coincided with the historical moment when the race idea was at or approaching its apogee in the history of the world, before or since. At the beginning of the twentieth century race science identified between three and sixty-three 'basic' races in the world, including between three and six, or even thirty-six, in Europe alone.[10] That ambiguity was the inevitable result of efforts to establish precise characteristics of a nonexistent phenomenon: 'races' simply do not exist as natural populations. Race theorists assumed that their efforts at taxonomic specification failed because generations of population movement and mixing had diluted original, 'pure' racial types; so they looked for racial essences beneath national or linguistic affiliations. This conviction in turn supported the manifestly unscientific approach of positing a priori ideal types and attempting to classify existing populations 'racially' by comparing the frequencies of geographical distribution of physical characteristics imputed to the ideal racial types constructed in the race scientists' taxonomies.[11]

Marxists and other leftists were more likely to dissent from hegemonic racialism than others, but race-thinking permeated political and intellectual discourse and everyday common sense. It was reproduced among progressives, Fabians and many socialist reformers, as well as conservatives, in dominant notions of evolution as progress. Teleological presumptions about fixed stages of cultural and social evolution and the comparative method in Victorian anthropology that considered contemporary 'primitives' as living versions of ancestral Europeans reinforced the tendency – convenient for proponents of colonial expansion – to rank populations hierarchically on the basis of natural limits and capacities ascribed to them. And even many revolutionaries believed that colonial domination was justified because 'backward' peoples needed periods of tutelage to prepare them for the modern world. Many English race scientists were convinced that the indigenous working class was racially different from the aristocracy. Just as some socialists opposed imperialist expansionism on egalitarian grounds, others opposed it on racial grounds, expressing fear of degeneration through contact with racially inferior populations.[12] Often class struggle was fought at least partly on the terrain of racialist ideology.

In the latter half of the nineteenth century fights in the American West over importation of Chinese labour and Japanese immigration also centred around racialist ideologies. Railroad operators and other importers of Chinese labour imagined and openly asserted that those workers' distinctive racial characteristics made them more tractable and able to live on less than white Americans; opponents, including the California labour movement, argued that those very racial characteristics would degrade American labour and that Chinese were racially 'unassimilable'. But it was the employer class, not the workers likely to be displaced or impoverished, who established the debate on racial terms. Post-bellum southern planters imported Chinese to the Mississippi Delta region to compete with black sharecroppers out of the same racialist presumptions of greater tractability, as did later importers of Sicilian labour to Louisiana sugarcane and cotton fields.[13]

Large-scale industrial production in the late nineteenth and early twentieth centuries depended on mass labour immigration mainly from the eastern and southern fringes of Europe. The innovations of race science – that is, of racialist folk ideology transformed into an academic profession – promised to assist employers' needs for rational labour force management and were present in the foundation of the fields of industrial relations and industrial psychology. Hugo Münsterberg, a founding luminary of industrial psychology, included 'race psychological diagnosis' as an element in assessment of employees' capabilities, although he stressed that racial or national temperaments are averages and considerable individual variation exists within groups. He argued that assessment, therefore, should be leavened with consideration of individuals' characteristics and that the influence of 'group psychology' would be significant 'only if the employment not of a single person, but of a large number, is in question, as it is most probable that the average character will show itself in a sufficient degree as soon as many members of the group are involved.'[14]

As scholarship on race science and its kissing cousin, eugenics, has shown, research that sets out to find evidence of racial difference will find it, whether or not it exists. Thus race science produced increasingly refined taxonomies of racial groups, and the apparent specificity of race theorists' just-so stories about differential racial capacities provided rationales for immigration restriction, sterilization, segregation and other regimes of inequality and subordination, including genocide. It also generated practical applications to assist employers in assigning workers to jobs for which they were racially suited. A 'racial adaptability' chart used by a Pittsburgh company in the 1920s mapped thirty-six different racial groups' capacities for twenty-two distinct jobs, eight different atmospheric conditions, jobs requiring speed or precision, and day or night shift work.[15]

Of course, all this was bogus, nothing more than narrow upper-class prejudices parading about as science. It was convincing only if one shared the folk narratives of essential hierarchy that the research assumed from the outset. But the race theories did not have to be true to be effective. They had only to be used as if they were true to produce the material effects that gave the ideology an authenticating verisimilitude. Poles became steel workers in Pittsburgh, Baltimore, Buffalo, Chicago, and Gary, not for any natural aptitude or affinity but because employers and labour recruiters sorted them into work in steel mills.

RACIALIST IDEOLOGY'S MATERIAL FOUNDATIONS

As a significant social force, racialist ideology has always been anchored to material imperatives, in both domestic and international domains. It became commonsense truth to the extent that it connected with the perspectives and interests of powerful elites. Like all ideologies of ascriptive difference, it would pre-empt debate over evolving programmes of exploitation and domination by reading them into nature. While the discourse of white supremacy certainly has had no shortage of sincere adherents, it became hegemonic over the second half of the nineteenth century because it comported well with upper-class prejudices and capitalists' economic programmes. That is how, as the Pittsburgh racial adaptability chart illustrates, it became the conceptual frame of reference within which other groups and strata came to understand their social position, articulate their own interests and thus constitute themselves practically as groups.

In the US for instance, in the late 1830s and 1840s, in a context of rising abolitionist sentiment and the democratization of public discourse associated with the spread of universal (white male) suffrage, white supremacist ideology undergirded and propelled a shift in defences of slavery. Previously, pro-slavery arguments centred on defending the institution as a 'necessary evil', an unpleasant and even morally dubious requirement of the plantation-based economic order of the southern states. One antebellum planter put the matter succinctly: 'For what purpose does the master hold the servant? Is it not that by his labor, he, the master, may accumulate wealth?'[16] In the changing political climate, the rhetorical centre of gravity of defences of slavery shifted to an argument that the institution was indeed a positive good for all involved, including the enslaved. This moment coincided with the formation of the embryo of what by the end of the century would become race science. As the sectional crisis sharpened in the late 1840s and early 1850s, propagation of white supremacist ideology – both rhetorically and institutionally, through carrots and sticks – became important as a basis for accommodating non-slaveholding southern whites to the possibility of secession. Appeals to racial solidarity provided a narrative of political cohesion and negatively sanctioned dissent.

To be clear, indicating that it had a material foundation is not to suggest that embrace of white supremacy was 'purely' instrumental, even among proto-race scientists and pro-slavery ideologues. An important feature of ideologies of ascriptive difference is that they hopelessly cloud the distinction between principled belief and pursuit of self-interest. Josiah C. Nott and George R. Gliddon, the authors of *Types of Mankind,* one of the most prominent texts of mid-nineteenth century race theory, both no doubt believed sincerely that the races they identified were equivalent to separate species and that blacks were naturally fit for enslavement. They were also, respectively, a wealthy slave-owning Alabama physician and an English Egyptologist who also wrote on the cotton economy in Egypt.[17] A striking testament to the harmonizing power of ideology is the appearance of an antebellum field of slave medicine, devoted to identification and treatment of conditions peculiar to blacks. Among those was *drapetomania,* a 'disease of the mind' that afflicted slaves with an irrational inclination to 'run away from service'. Samuel A. Cartwright, the slave-owning Louisiana physician who discovered and reported the malady in the early 1850s, when 'positive good' arguments had become dominant among slavery's defenders, was convinced that he had identified a genuine medical condition, preposterously transparent as it seems to a twenty-first century sensibility.[18]

White supremacist ideology, and the racialism in which it was embedded, operated similarly, of course, in relation to European and American colonialism in the late nineteenth century. Pioneer sociologist Edward A. Ross in 1901 laid out an especially clear account that links scientific race theory, rooted in the neo-Lamarckian evolutionism common in the early social sciences, and an argument for imperialism and colonization as inexorable imperatives of the 'vigorous' races.[19] In an illustration of the complex ways that hegemonic racialism could work, Ross had been fired from the Stanford University faculty the year before for having run afoul of Jane Lathrop Stanford, widow of Leland Stanford of the Union Pacific railroad and domineering force on the University's board of trustees. Ross had earned Mrs Stanford's ire for two particular transgressions: he militantly advocated, in league with trade unions, intensified enforcement of Chinese exclusion on racial grounds (Union Pacific was a principal proponent of importing Chinese labour, also on racial grounds); and he advocated with equal militancy public ownership of utilities.[20] Rudyard Kipling, a literal product of British imperialism, extolled 'The White Man's Burden', which – in a gush of enthusiasm at the US's recent acquisitions from the Spanish-Cuban-American War – he urged Americans to take up. I am agnostic with respect to how earnestly Kipling held the brew of condescension dressed as altruism projected in his infamous contention. We can say with certitude, though, that he understood that there was much more to colonialism than altruistic tutelage. In response to Kipling, one of the most emphatic racists of the day in American politics, Democratic US Senator from South Carolina Benjamin R. 'Pitchfork Ben' Tillman, denounced imperialist expansionism on racial grounds, stressing concerns that sustained contact with inferior populations would lead to white racial degeneration.[21]

By the turn of the twentieth century racialist ideology had become a global frame of reference through which arguments about colonialism and economic and political hierarchy were commonly conducted. Therefore, it should not be surprising that opposition to those hierarchies would be expressed, at least initially, in that same language. An oft-cited instance of that perception is W. E. B. Du Bois's 1903 observation that 'the problem of the Twentieth Century is the problem of the colour line', which he went on to specify as 'the relation of the darker and lighter races of men in Asia and Africa and the islands of the sea'.[22] In the US, mass disfranchisement of blacks and imposition of strictly codified white supremacist apartheid in nearly all the South made the colour line particularly salient as a bulwark against egalitarian political interests. This is consistent with how ascriptive ideologies naturalize contingent material relations of inequality by making them invisible within narratives of fixed hierarchy. The racialized discourse of tutelage, persistence of the presumptions of the Victorian comparative method, and direct and overt racialized domination all reinforced a similar understanding of the driving impetus of colonialism. It was reasonable for egalitarian opponents to assume either that racialist ideology was the proximate source of the inequality and exploitation, or that combating that ideology was a necessary precondition for attacking the inequality.

It is noteworthy that both in the US and in much of the *fin-de-siècle* colonial world, as Du Bois's colour line apothegm illustrates, the first tentative expressions of modern political assertiveness from the dominated populations were formulated within the paradigm of tutelage of the underdeveloped. The nascent professional and functionary classes in the colonies and the American South, the 'new men', as Judith Stein describes them, began to yield a stratum who pursued advocacy for subordinate populations alongside managerial authority over, and organized guidance of, their progress toward self-government. In the US that stratum of racial advocates, often describing themselves as 'race men' and 'race women', attained civic voice in the context of mass disfranchisement and shared a commitment to the large ideal of 'racial uplift'.[23] This established a recognized social role and occupational niche for the race or ethnic group leader as a sort of freelance broker or ethnic-group entrepreneur. Booker T. Washington and Du Bois were prominent voices of this stratum. Both in the US and colonial territories this politics of group advocacy often rested on racialist presumptions about the subordinate populations' general backwardness and the stewardship role the group's more cultivated and advanced members should play in leading the masses out of their benighted state. This was a petition politics that addressed governing elites as its principal audience because it understood them to be the only source of effective political agency. That meant as well that the mission of group uplift was defined within parameters set by the ruling class.

By the 1930s racialist ideology was increasingly under attack on biological, anthropological, and political fronts, in part as an expression of the left's social momentum, which helped to buttress and disseminate egalitarian ideas and sensibilities. In that environment, the Great Migration from the Jim Crow South to big cities in the North and Midwest encouraged popular mass politics among black Americans, particularly as black workers were incorporated into the new industrial unionism. Mass organization as a political form as well as trade unionism also spread through much of the colonial world. In both settings, insurgent politics understandably joined opposition to racism with opposition to exploitation, as defences of those hierarchical regimes still depended on racialist arguments and would continue to do so for several decades. But the cultural and ideological victory of egalitarianism over racialism that consolidated in post-Second World War intellectual life came with a very large asterisk. What was largely defeated was the historically specific strict bio-determinist discourse of race that had prevailed as common sense between the last decades of the nineteenth century and the first quarter of the twentieth. Walter Benn Michaels and Werner Sollors have shown that the retreat from race to culture in theories of social difference that began in the 1920s was in some ways more an exchange of one metaphor of essential difference for another than a rejection of the notion of essential group difference. As historian of anthropology George Stocking, Jr points out, from its origins in the early twentieth century the modern culture idea never fully escaped race theory's presumptions.[24]

In the postwar years, culture increasingly supplanted race in discourses legitimating inequality, particularly regarding exploitation of colonized societies and racial minorities in the US. In its taxonomy of 'stages of development', modernization theory in the academic study of comparative political development merely rehearsed hoary racialist accounts, such as that by E. A. Ross cited above, and the logic of the Victorian comparative method, while dressing them in a later generation's scientistic raiment. Robert Vitalis has shown recently how the academic field and political practice of international politics in the US remained rooted in substantively racialist paradigms well into the 1960s.[25] And the State Department's and other national elites' concerns about the impact that domestic civil rights agitation could have on US imperial designs in former colonial territories led to a concern with damage control that generated, on the one hand, censorship of news broadcast abroad and intense monitoring and policing of domestic activists' overseas engagements and, on the other, liberal Cold Warriors' pressure on the domestic front in support of some versions of the movement's aims.[26]

AMBIGUITIES OF RACE AND CLASS IN POSTWAR INSURGENCIES

Anti-colonial and national liberation movements also paid attention and to some extent drew inspiration from the postwar black American insurgency and vice versa. At least through the 1950s, movements on both planes of insurgency mobilized in general terms on a popular front basis. In both spheres – economic position and racial or national category – each signified the other. In the black American case, the postwar insurgency, which had germinated since the mid-1930s, incubated by industrial unionism and socialist agitation, was propelled partly by a tension between what Preston Smith characterizes as racial democratic (i.e., committed to radical equality of opportunity within American capitalism) and social democratic tendencies and programmes.[27] Occasionally, the ultimate contradiction between those tendencies would erupt as open conflict around specific initiatives. However, in quotidian experience racial discrimination and subordination and economic exploitation and degradation seemed, and on one level were, elements in a singular system of oppression. For leftists in both loci of insurgency, pursuit of redistribution along racial and class lines each seemed to be a necessary condition for successful pursuit of the other, if they were not treated as indistinguishable. By the end of the Second World War, even very conventional black liberals and moderates were emphatic that continued growth of industrial unionism and expansion of public social wage policies were indispensable for black Americans' advancement toward equality.[28]

For many, including activists, the social-democratic and racial-democratic imperatives were so tightly melded that, even on those occasions when tension between them erupted into explicit conflict in relation to specific initiatives, the sources of conflict typically were interpreted as deriving from individual, idiosyncratic differences rather than more portentous ideological contradiction. A downside of the popular front style of politics, which was very successful through the major legislative victories of the mid-1960s, was that it proceeded from an abstract commitment to the interests of the race as a whole as a governing norm for political judgment, which was by definition murky and facilitated evasion of those sharp, potentially zero-sum disagreements over political vision that would surface in strategic or even tactical debates. This murkiness left many popular front black radicals ill-prepared for a critical moment in the mid-1960s when the submerged class contradiction sharpened in debate over ways forward after the legislative victories against segregation.

THE CLASS CONTRADICTION

That tension in black politics was at its core a class contradiction; racial democracy is the social ideal of the aspiring professional-managerial and business strata. Failure, inability or reluctance to address class dynamics in black politics as such, while understandable in the context of dynamic racial popular front insurgency as a strategic desideratum or even simple oversight, nonetheless has had consequences for subsequent understandings of the relation of race and politics and assertions of the scope of authentically black political interests that eventually undermined possibilities for sustaining a working-class agenda in black politics. Antagonistic reactions from both antiracist activists and political elites to Senator Bernie Sanders's campaign for the 2016 Democratic presidential nomination, on a platform inspired by social democracy, threw into bold relief the extent to which what is now generally recognized as black politics is fundamentally a professional-managerial class programme that constitutes the left-wing of neoliberalism.

This politics actively invokes the cultural authority of earlier moments of black insurgency, shorn of their working-class programmatic character, and spectres of the racial order it opposed, to align with a neoliberal ideal of social justice – parity in the distribution of capitalism's costs and benefits among recognized ascriptive categories – as the boundary of the politically thinkable, even among a nominal left. This odd state of affairs is the product of several developments in postwar American politics, beginning with the impact of the business counterattack on labour in the years after the war and the aggressive anti-communism of the late 1940s and 1950s, and including the terms on which the victories of the mid-1960s were consolidated institutionally within black politics and the country at large. And, perhaps counter-intuitively, identification with Third World anti-colonial and national liberation movements in the 1960s and 1970s played a significant role in rendering invisible the class dynamics that shaped the thrust and impact of post-segregation black politics.

The decade after the end of the Second World War was a key moment in helping form the trajectory that has culminated in contemporary antiracist politics in the US. Two linked pressures, one suppressive and the other affirmative, shifted the balance in black popular front radicalism sharply in favour of the racial-democratic tendency. The reactionary anti-communist offensive of those years, as was its domestic intent, stigmatized and suppressed expressions of socialist or anti-capitalist politics or critique. Its effects on accelerating purges of the left from the labour movement are well known. Leah N. Gordon and Risa Goluboff have examined its impact on the strategic orientation of black politics and racial advocacy.[29] Crucially, aggressive, putschist anti-communism and its 'loyalty' apparatus drove a retreat from political-economic interpretations of the bases of racial inequality and toward an individualist, psychologistic perspective focused on racism as prejudice, bigotry, or intolerance. On the affirmative side of the ledger, that new racial liberalism divorced from political economy encouraged a litigation strategy of challenging the codified apartheid in the

South as violating the guarantees of equal protection against discriminatory state action provided by the Fourteenth Amendment of the Constitution. By the mid-1940s the federal courts had shown that that direction could produce positive results for litigants, and that potential opening impelled a focus on the segregationist southern order and its infringements on the civil rights of blacks as a class of individuals.

Of course, segregation violated the Fourteenth Amendment no more in 1954, when the US Supreme Court found state-sponsored racially segregated education unconstitutional by definition, than it had in 1896, when the Court's ruling in *Plessy v. Ferguson* upheld codified segregation in the 'separate but equal' doctrine. Moreover, black activists had fought against the segregationist regime with whatever means available since before *Plessy* had established it as legitimate. What had changed was the political and cultural centre of gravity with regard to racial inequality and discrimination.

To be sure, the social-democratic tendency in black politics did not disappear. It remained an important engine of popular political action through the 1960s. The fabled 1963 March on Washington was organized principally by labour leader A. Philip Randolph's Negro American Labor Council, and was officially called the March on Washington for Jobs and Freedom, organized and carried out with considerable trade union support. The impetus for the protest in Memphis at which Martin Luther King, Jr was assassinated was a sanitation workers' strike that was an outcropping of a regional organizing campaign of the American Federation of State, County, and Municipal Employees (AFSCME). Labour and class-related issues were central to much of the militant action that made up the high period of southern civil rights activism from the 1940s through the 1960s, as well as a two-decade long struggle – mainly outside the South, where ruling-class dominance was too complete – for local, state, and federal Fair Employment Practices legislation. This would extend beyond anti-discrimination efforts to authorize public intervention in labour markets to pursue full employment, which had been a central goal of black political agitation – and the black-labour-left alliance in which it was embedded – since the war years. Even in the South, however, as the Memphis case illustrates, labour and class issues were often as not high on the movement's agenda. Even such proceduralist liberal staples of the anti-segregation struggle as restoration of voting rights were linked in the minds of activists and rank-and-file movement supporters to working-class and labour objectives.

NATIONAL LIBERATION, BLACK POWER AND CLASS POLITICS

As Cold War liberalism and postwar racial liberalism converged, activists increasingly tended to link the civil rights agenda to the Cold War international agenda, especially regarding the decolonizing Third World, characterizing southern segregationists as out of step with world opinion and harmful to national security. Thus, at the same time as politically attentive black Americans drew inspiration from and inspired decolonization and national liberation movements abroad, many also found it at least instrumentally useful to identify their domestic struggles with US international aspirations. Not many perceived that there was a possible contradiction between those positions.

Black Americans' identification with anti-colonial struggles rested on an almost unavoidable and affectively powerful sense of common, or at least comparable condition. I recall, on first seeing the film soon after its release, finding the 'Battle of Algiers' immensely resonant; it seemed that I had lived some of it as a child and adolescent in New Orleans and other American cities. But that general identification was also in important ways superficial and naïve, and it would eventually become implicated in the critical defeat of the social-democratic tendency in black politics in the late 1960s and 1970s.

Black American Third Worldism was more nationalist than revolutionary. Going back to Du Bois's apothegm about the colour line – and it is much less known that he essentially recanted it by the early 1950s, specifically describing race as an 'excuse' in class war[30] – black identification with colonized populations stemmed partly from an idealized racial nationalism that presumed white supremacist constructions of the stakes of western imperialism. Du Bois's 1928 novel *Dark Princess* is a romance based on the premise of a global rising of united peoples of colour.[31] In the 1930s and even into the war, many black Americans cheered on Japanese imperialism as a non-white challenge to white supremacy.[32] The roots of the characterization of black Americans' position as an instance of 'domestic colonialism' in the early 1960s lay in an effort not merely to elevate the black insurgency's power and significance through association with Third World struggles, but also to advocate a model of national liberation as a programme and approach for black politics in the US.[33]

Third Worldism was in general more a rhetorical phenomenon than a substantively programmatic one. Marxist revolutionaries on the capitalist periphery embraced it as an aspiration. Mao propounded a 'three worlds' theory, and Cuba still maintains the *Organización de Solidaridad con los Pueblos de Asia, África, y América Latina* (OSPAAL). Left governments in Venezuela and elsewhere have drawn on imagery at least evocative of Third Worldism and Non-Alignment in their efforts to organize regional and supra-regional (typically based on common export commodities) economic and political blocs. The *Alianza Bolivariana para los Pueblos de Nuestra América* (ALBA), with member states in South America, Central America, and the Caribbean, is arguably the most extensive and successful of those efforts. For the most part, however, the history of Third Worldism and the Non-Aligned Movement as predicated on the goal of global alliance of 'peoples of colour' – anti-imperialist or otherwise – has been very much oversold.[34] Moreover, the view that non-whiteness provides a basis for transnational political alliance simply rehearses the mystification that colonialism had been driven fundamentally by white supremacist ideology. As Fanon observed early in the period of decolonization, that mystification, in identifying racial transfer of formal authority as the essence of national liberation, also obscured the extent to which imperialism was always first and foremost a class project, of which colonialism buttressed by racialist fables was only one historically specific form.

In any event, as anti-colonial and national liberation struggles intensified in the 1960s against the backdrop of the escalating Indochina War, Western leftists, almost as a reflex, generally supported those insurgent movements and defended them against inegalitarian critics and imperialist state power; doing so was consistent with the left's egalitarian and democratic values. Many of those movements contained different ideological and class tendencies, a complexity often obscured by their populist rhetoric, which posited claims to represent the authentic 'people'. How class dynamics played out in national liberation movements that succeeded in winning independence and official self-determination is well known. Even several of those movements that embraced socialism and attempted to link the national liberation struggle to a popular class politics – e.g., the FLN in Algeria, the African National Congress in South Africa and those that came to power in the former Portuguese colonies in Africa – were ultimately incorporated into the logic of capitalist globalization in ways that articulated with domestic class contradictions.[35]

In the US, escalation of the war on Vietnam encouraged greater attentiveness in the left to imperialist interventionism, and over that decade armed national liberation or revolutionary struggles intensified in much of the former colonial world and Latin America. At the same time the Black Power nationalist embrace of the domestic colonial analogy and the discourse of national liberation gave a radical halo to what was, militant rhetorical flourishes aside, programmatically an ethnic politics fully incorporable with the pluralist interest-group system. Notwithstanding the sincere convictions of adherents, Black Power was, consistent with ethnic politics in general, very much a class-based affair, harnessing an abstract and symbolic racial populism to an agenda that centred concretely on advancing the interests and aspirations of new political and entrepreneurial strata which emerged from the victories of the civil rights movement and demographic racial transition in American cities.[36] In relation to a history of racial exclusion, it was reasonable and appropriate that many leftists supported what was substantively a programme for inclusion on a racial-democratic model. And the rhetorical militancy and racial-populist symbolism associated with Black Power, including the tropes of national liberation, reinforced the sense that it was a radical or revolutionary tendency that leftists should support.

For more than half a century that view of Black Power has obscured the significance of the mid-1960s debate in black politics over the movement's direction in the wake of the legislative victories. On one side, a working-class and labour-based black radicalism, propounded principally by A. Philip Randolph and his associate and longtime civil rights activist Bayard Rustin, argued that the struggle for black equality faced new, larger challenges opened by the defeat of Jim Crow that required building a different sort of movement centred on the familiar black-liberal-labour-left alliance. In questioning whether 'civil rights movement' even remained an accurate description, Rustin argued, in a widely read essay published a year before Stokely Carmichael introduced the Black Power slogan to the world, that the next phase of the struggle called for expanding the movement's vision 'beyond race relations to economic relations'. He argued that it could not succeed 'in the absence of radical programs for full employment, abolition of slums, the reconstruction of our educational system, new definitions of work and leisure. Adding up the cost of such programs, we can only conclude that we are talking about a refashioning of our political economy.' For that reason, he contended: 'The future of the Negro struggle depends on whether the contradictions of this society can be resolved by a coalition of progressive forces which becomes the *effective* political majority in the United States. I speak of the coalition which staged the March on Washington, passed the Civil Rights Act, and laid the basis for the Johnson landslide – Negroes, trade unionists, liberals, and religious groups.'[37]

This was an unambiguous assertion of the social-democratic tendency in black politics, which Randolph and Rustin followed up with introduction of a 'Freedom Budget' that laid out an agenda for realizing a full-employment economy and its benefits for the society as a whole, noting that black

Americans' circumstances would be improved disproportionately if the Budget were implemented.[38] For a variety of structural and idiosyncratic reasons, their call did not gain social traction.[39] Contributing to its defeat was that the racial-democratic tendency aligned more comfortably with new institutional opportunities made available by the Voting Rights Act, racial transition in cities, anti-discrimination enforcement and the War on Poverty, all of which constituted a class-based racial redistribution that comported with the material aspirations of the emerging, post-segregation black professional-managerial class.[40] Incipient Black Power racial populism obscured the class character of those developments. Particularly ironic, in light of the subsequent development of black politics, is that many radicals successfully deployed racial populism, reinforced by allusions to anti-colonial and national liberation struggles, to portray the social-democratic approach advocated by Randolph and Rustin as a conservative 'integrationist' call for subordination to white interests.

Because black radicals never had the political capacity to challenge for state power or a broad and deep popular base, the movement's class tensions seldom surfaced in political debate. By the mid-1960s the racial-democratic tendency's cultural force and institutional clout – including its incorporation within postwar liberalism – had made its commitment to racial redistribution practically hegemonic as the standard of justice and equality for black Americans. In retrospect, that moment marked the birth of antiracism as a claim to a discrete politics. The ambiguity and murkiness in black popular front radicalism regarding intra-racial class dynamics undercut the ability of social-democratic advocates to mount appropriate critical responses. For the most part, such advocates also fell back on a discourse of racial authenticity and objections that the strategies and objectives of the emerging political class did not properly represent the interests of the 'community' or the 'people'.

The conceptual limitations imposed by that fetishized racial populism testified to and reinforced professional-managerial class hegemony in black politics. Partly from ideological purblindness, partly from material imperatives, the expressions of political radicalism that purported to dissent from the consolidating new black class politics – openly idealist cultural nationalism, a new, anti-imperialist Pan-Africanism, and a potted Marxism-Leninism – defined their radicalism through withdrawal from mundane political dynamics and embrace of one or another flavour of millenarian revolutionary catechism.[41] Some black radicals, particularly in the 1970s moment of the largely Maoist New Communist movement in the US, strove to meld their fundamentally nationalist discourse of national liberation with a Marxist anti-imperialism. The Black Panther Party had been an early expression of this inclination.[42] However, that turn retained the crucial assumptions of national liberation discourse, especially the most significant one – the nationalist premise that posits the group as an authentically communitarian and singular 'people' united against external oppression, and represents the character of class struggle within the population (e.g., black Americans) as that 'people' arrayed against inauthentic 'misleaders' or a co-opted, comprador element. That view originated in the 'domestic colonialism' analogy that emerged from some radicals' early 1960s identification with Third World insurgencies. The great irony of this apparently radical tendency is that the communitarian populism on which it rested worked mainly to obscure class dynamics within black politics.

It is a marker of retreat from programmatic commitment to social transformation that many who consider themselves on the left accept the stance that racial politics is more radical or inclusive than class politics and that pursuit of socialism is suspect on identitarian grounds. Ascriptive identity becomes the primary basis for political commitment, and solidarity on the basis of who we are trumps solidarity on the basis of what we believe only when the left no longer has a transformative vision around which to cohere as a basis for political judgment. Antiracism does not have an affirmative agenda, a fact that complements a left that by and large has little clarity of social vision itself. Antiracist politics mimes radicalism with posture and performative evocation of earlier insurgent politics like Black Power radicalism in the US and the national liberation movements of the 1960s and 1970s, but with complete erasure of the class and political-economic tensions in which those movements were immersed.

CONCLUSION

Positing a singular black community or racial political aspiration has had long-reaching effects on black politics, and leftist scholarship on black Americans, that have facilitated accommodation to neoliberal imperatives often while intending quite the opposite. Proliferation of a literature that presumes a singular 'black freedom movement', 'black liberation movement' or even a 'long civil rights movement' divests black Americans' political activity of its tensions and structural contradictions. The effect is to de-historicize examination of black politics. Politically, this tendency has obscured thirty years or more of steadily lowered expectations for what can be gained from political action. This was exemplified clearly during the 2016 campaign for the Democratic presidential nomination when in South Carolina, longtime Georgia Congressman and former civil rights movement icon John Lewis and his fellow black Congressman James Clyburn from South Carolina denounced the Sanders campaign's proposal for free public higher education as irresponsible because it sent the bad message that people should expect free things – that is, decommodified public goods and services – from government. 'Nothing is free in America', Lewis snarled.[43] Left-neoliberal exuberance surrounding the Democratic National Convention's official nomination of Hillary Clinton as its presidential candidate made undeniably clear that antiracism and other identitarian expressions are more than simply compatible with neoliberalism but are most meaningfully active components of its ideological reproduction. Dara Lind, writing in vox.com, exulted that 'a commitment to diversity has become the [Democratic] party's unifying principle', and Jeet Heer gushed in *The New Republic* that 'the Democratic Party opened their arms to Republicans – without compromising their liberal values'.[44] Identity and social liberalism in this happy vision will completely override the Democrats' enduring class loyalties, and contradictions.

There are two final ironies to note regarding the left embrace of antiracist politics. First, all politics in a class society is class politics. Antiracism is not exempt from that reality. What its proponents will not admit is that it is a class politics but not a working-class politics. Second, representing race as a primordial identity also elevates it as a social force above the dynamics of the reproduction of capitalist social relations; in that sense, antiracist politics of the contemporary sort proceeds from the same primordialist view of race as did *fin-de-siècle* race theorists. And that is also a case of argument by historical analogy coming home to roost.

NOTES

1   Pierre Bourdieu and Loïc Wacquant, 'On the Cunning of Imperialist Reason', *Theory, Culture, & Society*, 16, 1999, pp. 41-58. A recent, striking illustration of US cultural imperialism propelled through antiracist political discourse, though one long gestating, is exemplified in Sujatha Fernandes, 'Afro-Cuban Activists Fight Racism Between Two Fires', *The Nation*, 24 May 2016. Fernandes notes that among the activists' foes are 'fellow Cubans who lack racial consciousness'.
2   I have discussed this distinction extensively elsewhere. See Adolph Reed, Jr., 'Marx, Race, and Neoliberalism', *New Labor Forum*, 22(Winter), 2013, pp. 49-50.
3   Eric Hobsbawm, 'Identity Politics and the Left', *New Left Review*, 217(May/June), 1996, p. 44.
4   Ellen Meiksins Wood, 'Marxism Without Class Struggle', in Ralph Miliband and John Saville, eds., *The Socialist Register 1983*, London: Merlin Press, 1983, pp. 239-71; Wood, *The Retreat from Class: A New 'True' Socialism*, London: Verso, 1999; and Leo Panitch, 'The Impoverishment of State Theory', in S. Aronowitz and P. Bratsis, eds., *Paradigm Lost: State Theory Reconsidered*, London: University of Minnesota Press, 2002, pp. 89-104. On the US case in particular, see also Adolph Reed, Jr. *Class Notes: Posing as Politics and Other Thoughts on the American Scene*, New York: The New Press, 2000, pp. viii-xxviii.

5   An ur-text of this line of argument is Robert L. Allen, *Reluctant Reformers: The Impact of Racism on American Social Reform Movements,* Washington, DC: Howard University Press, 1974. In a line of argument that Roediger and others have continued and elaborated, Allen contends that American progressive and popular movements consistently have been undone by whites' deeper commitments to white supremacy than to the egalitarian projects they pursued. See also David Roediger, *The Wages of Whiteness: Race and the Making of the American Working Class,* London: Verso, 1991; Herbert Hill, 'The Problem of Race in American Labor History', *Reviews in American History*, 24(June), 1996, pp. 189-208; Bill Fletcher, Jr. and Fernando Gapasin, 'The Politics of Labour and Race in the USA', in Leo Panitch and Colin Leys, eds., *Socialist Register 2009: Violence Today,* London: Merlin Press,, 2008, pp. 245-64; Fletcher and Gapasin, *Solidarity Divided: The Crisis in Organized Labor and a New Path Toward Social Justice,* Berkeley: University of California Press, 2009; and Michael Goldfield, *The Color of Politics: Race and the Mainsprings of American Politics,* New York: The New Press, 1997.

6   William P. Jones, 'Nothing Special to Offer the Negro: Revisiting the "Debsian View" of the Negro Question', *International Labor and Working-Class History*, 74(Fall), 2008, pp. 212-24.

7   Russell Jacoby, *The End of Utopia: Politics and Culture in an Age of Apathy,* New York: Basic Books, 1999, p. 13.

8   W. E. B. Du Bois, *Dusk of Dawn: An Essay Toward an Autobiography of a Race Concept,* New York: Harcourt, Brace & World, 1940, p. 116. For a succinct description of the state of racial thinking and practice among American elites at the end of the nineteenth century, see Charles A. Lofgren, *The Plessy Case: A Legal-Historical Interpretation,* New York & Oxford: Oxford University Press, 1988, pp. 93-115.

9   Michelle Alexander, *The New Jim Crow: Mass Incarceration in the Age of Colorblindness,* New York: The New Press, 2012.

10 Joseph Deniker, *The Races of Man: An Outline of Anthropology and Ethnography,* New York: Charles Scribner's Sons, 1900, identified six 'races' – two fair-haired and four dark-haired – more or less indigenous to Europe with four 'secondary races' – two of which were attached to a fair-haired race and two 'intermediate' between the fair-haired and dark-haired races. William Z. Ripley, *The Races of Europe: A Sociological Study,* London: Kegan Paul, Trench, Trübner & Company, 1900, by contrast found three basic European races, the familiar Teutonic, Alpine and Mediterranean. Deniker and Ripley were among the most prominent race scientists of the day, and the extent of their disagreement on such a basic issue might have suggested questioning the race idea's scientific status. Moreover, the United States Immigration Commission in 1913 counted thirty-six races indigenous to Europe among immigrants to the country. William P. Dillngham, *Reports of the Immigration Commission: Dictionary of Races or Peoples,* Washington, DC: GPO, 1911, pp. 2-3; and Daniel G. Brinton, *Races and Peoples: Lectures on the Science of Ethnography,* Philadelphia: David McKay, 1901, pp. 17-50. However, commitment to race as a natural category, then as now, is ontological and therefore impervious to empirical evidence or lack thereof. On the history and logic of race science, see Jonathan Marks, *What It Means to Be 98% Chimpanzee: Apes, People and Their Genes,* Berkeley: University of California Press, 2003.

11 Ripley, *The Races of Europe,* pp. 103-30 is a classic illustration of this phenomenon.

12 For discussions of the sweep and depth of racialist ideology in the late nineteenth and early twentieth centuries see: Mark Pittenger, *American Socialists and Evolutionary Thought, 1870-1920,* Madison, WI: University of Wisconsin Press, 1993; Elazar Barkan, *The Retreat of Scientific Racism: Changing Concepts or Race in Britain and the United States Between the World Wars,* Cambridge: Cambridge University Press, 1993.

13 See, for example, Robert Seto Quan, *Lotus Among the Magnolias: The Mississippi Chinese*, Jackson: University Press of Mississippi, 1982; Alexander Saxton, *The Indispensable Enemy: Labor and the Anti-Chinese Movement in California*, Berkeley & Los Angeles: California University Press, 1971; Vicenza Scarpaci and Jean Ann Scarpaci, *Italian Immigrants in Louisiana Sugar Parishes: Recruitment, Labor Conditions and Community Relations, 1880-1910*, New York: Ayer, 1981.

14 Hugo Münsterberg, *Psychology and Industrial Efficiency*, Boston & New York: Houghton-Mifflin, 1913, p. 130.

15 For example, Letts were supposedly 'fair' with pick and shovel, concrete and wheelbarrow, as well as in working in oily or dirty processes; 'bad' as hod carriers, cleaners and caretakers, and boilermaker's helpers; 'good' as coal passers and blacksmiths as well as at jobs requiring speed or precision; 'good' at working in cool and dry, smoky or dusty conditions; and 'good' on both day and night shift. John Bodnar, Roger Simon, and Michael P. Weber, *Lives of Their Own: Blacks, Italians, and Poles in Pittsburgh, 1900-1960*, Chicago: University of Illinois Press, 1983, p. 240. Pertinent recent histories of the eugenics movement and the extent of its social impact include: Edwin Black, *War Against the Weak: Eugenics and America's Campaign to Create a Master Race*, New York: Dialog Press, 2012; Alexandra Minna Stern, *Eugenic Nation: Faults and Frontiers of Better Breeding in Modern America*, Berkeley & Los Angeles: University of California Press, 2005.

16 Kenneth M. Stampp, *The Peculiar Institution: Slavery in the Ante-Bellum South*, New York: Random House, 1956, p. 5.

17 Josiah C. Nott and George R. Gliddon, *Types of Mankind, or Ethnological Researches*, Philadelphia: Lippincott, Grambo & Co., 1854. See also Reginald Horsman, *Josiah Nott of Mobile: Southerner, Physician and Racial Theorist*, Baton Rouge, LA: Louisiana State University Press, 1987, pp. 130 and 258.

18 Samuel A. Cartwright, 'Diseases and Peculiarities of the Negro Race', *De Bow's Review*, XI(July), 1851, pp. 64-69, and (September), 1851, pp. 331-6. It is reprinted in Paul F. Paskoff and Daniel J. Wilson, eds., *The Cause of the South: Selections from De Bow's Review, 1846-1867*, Baton Rouge, La., and London: Louisiana State University Press, 1982. On Cartwright's place among antebellum southern apologists, see James Denny Guillory, 'The Pro-Slavery Arguments of Dr. Samuel A. Cartwright', *Louisiana History*, 9(Summer), 1968, pp. 209-27.

19 Edward A. Ross, 'The Causes of Race Superiority', *Annals of the American Academy of Political and Social Science*, 18(June), 1901, pp. 67-89.

20 James C. Mohr, 'Academic Turmoil and Public Opinion: The Ross Case at Stanford', *Pacific Historical Review*, 39(February), 1970, pp. 39-61.

21 Benjamin R. Tillman, Speech on the floor of the US Senate, February 7, 1899, available at wikisource.org. See also Daniel E. Bender, *American Abyss: Savagery and Civilization in the Age of Industry*, Ithaca: Cornell University Press, 2013, pp. 41-98.

22 W. E. B. Du Bois, *The Souls of Black Folk: Essays and Sketches*, Chicago: McClurg, 1907, pp. vii and 13.

23 Judith Stein, *The World of Marcus Garvey: Race and Class in Modern Society*, Baton Rouge: Louisiana State University Press, 1986, pp. 7-23; Judith Stein, '"Of Mr. Booker T. Washington and Others": The Political Economy of Racism in the United States', *Science & Society*, 38(Winter), 1975, pp. 422-63.

24 Walter Benn Michaels, 'Race Into Culture: A Genealogy of Cultural Identity', *Critical Inquiry*, 18(Summer), 1992, pp. 655-85; Walter Benn Michaels, *Our America: Nativism, Modernism and Pluralism*, Durham, NC: Duke University Press, 1997; Werner Sollors, 'A Critique of Pure Pluralism', in Sacvan Bercovitch, ed., *Reconstructing American Literary History*, Cambridge: Harvard University Press, 1986, pp. 250-79; and George Stocking,

Jr., *Race, Culture, and Evolution: Essays in the History of Anthropology*, Chicago: University of Chicago Press, 1968, pp. 265-6.
25 Robert Vitalis, *White World Order, Black Power Politics*, Ithaca: Cornell University Press, 2015. On the frankly racialist origins of the international politics field see: Jessica Blatt, '"To Bring Out the Best That Is In Their Blood": Race, Reform, and Civilization in the *Journal of Race Development* (1900-1919)', *Ethnic & Racial Studies*, 27(September), 2004, pp. 691-709. In 1922, after an intermediate name change, the journal became and remains *Foreign Affairs*.
26 Mary L. Dudziak, *Cold War Civil Rights: Race and the Image of American Democracy*, Princeton & Oxford: Princeton University Press, 2011.
27 Preston H. Smith, II, *Racial Democracy and the Black Metropolis: Housing Policy in Postwar Chicago*, Minneapolis & London: University of Minnesota Press, 2012.
28 See, for example, the essays collected in Rayford Logan, ed., *What the Negro Wants*, Chapel Hill, NC: University of North Carolina Press, 1944.
29 Leah N. Gordon, *From Power to Prejudice: The Rise of Racial Individualism in Midcentury America*, Chicago & London: University of Chicago Press, 2015; Risa Goluboff, *The Lost Promise of Civil Rights*, Cambridge, MA & London: Harvard University Press, 2007.
30 W. E. B. Du Bois, 'Fifty Years After', in *Souls of Black Folk*, Milwood, NY: Kraus-Thompson, 1973, p. xi. This retrospective originally appeared in the 1953 edition of *Souls* published by Blue Heron.
31 W. E. B. Du Bois, *Dark Princess: A Romance*, New York: Harcourt, Brace, 1928; Kenneth W. Warren, 'An Inevitable Drift? Oligarchy, Du Bois, and the Prospect of Democracy between the Wars', in A. Reed and K. Warren, eds., *Renewing Black Intellectual History: The Ideological and Material Foundations of African American Thought*, Boulder, CO: Paradigm Press, 2010, pp. 80-94.
32 Lee Finkle, 'The Conservative Aims of Militant Rhetoric: Black Protest During World War II', *Journal of American History*, 60(December), 1973, pp. 692-713; Gerald Horne, 'Tokyo Bound: African Americans and Japan Confront White Supremacy', *Souls*, 3(Summer), 2001, pp. 16-28 and Reginald Kearney, 'The Pro-Japanese Utterances of W. E. B. Du Bois', *Contributions in Black Studies*, 13, 1995, available at scholarworks umass.edu..
33 For early expressions of this tendency, see essays in: Harold Cruse, *Rebellion or Revolution?*, New York: William Morrow, 1968, pp. 74-96; Jack H. O'Dell, 'Colonialism and the Negro American Experience', *Freedomways*, 6(Fall), 1966, pp. 297-308; Jack H. O'Dell, 'A Special Variety of Colonialism', *Freedomways*, 7(Winter), 1967, pp. 7-15; Cedric Johnson, 'Between Revolution and the Racial Ghetto: Harold Cruse and Harry Haywood Debate Class Struggle and the "Negro Question", 1962-8', *Historical Materialism*, 24, 2016, pp. 165-203.
34 Robert Vitalis, 'The Midnight Ride of Kwame Nkrumah and Other Fables of Bandung (Ban-doong)', *Humanity*, 4(Summer), 2013, pp. 261-88.
35 Frantz Fanon, *The Wretched of the Earth*, New York: Grove Press, 1966, pp. 119-63. The theory of neocolonialism was one attempt to take account of the class dynamics in decolonizing societies. Although it was elaborated in relation to Latin American societies, which were not actual colonies, dependency theory also sought to generate structural accounts that situated imperialist domination within an analysis of domestic class dynamics.
36 Dean E. Robinson, 'Black Power Nationalism as Ethnic Pluralism: Postwar Liberalism's Ethnic Paradigm in Black Nationalism', in A. Reed and K. Warren, eds., *Renewing Black Intellectual History*, pp. 184-214.
37 Bayard Rustin, 'From Protest to Politics: The Future of the Civil Rights Movement', *Commentary*, (February), 1965, pp. 27-8.

38 *A 'Freedom Budget' for All Americans: Budgeting Our Resources 1965-1975 to Achieve 'Freedom from Want'*, New York: A Philip Randolph Institute, 1966.
39 Paul Le Blanc and Michael D. Yates, *A Freedom Budget for All Americans,* New York: Monthly Review Press, 2013, examines in helpful detail the Freedom Budget's genesis and the politics around it and the failure of the campaign for it.
40 I examine this transition and Black Power's relation to class formation in: *Stirrings in the Jug: Black Politics in the Post-Segregation Era,* Minneapolis: University of Minnesota Press, 1999; and 'The Post-1965 Trajectory of Race, Class, and Urban Politics in the United States Reconsidered', *Labor Studies Journal,* 41(September), 2016.
41 For critical reconstruction of this discourse of authenticity among black radicals and its impact on subsequent black political development in the US see: Cedric Johnson, *Revolutionaries to Race Leaders: Black Power and the Making of African American Politics,* Minneapolis: University of Minnesota Press, 2007; Alex Willingham, 'Ideology and Politics: Their Status in Afro-American Social Theory', *Endarch,* 1(Spring), 1975, pp. 4-25.
42 Max Elbaum, *Revolution in the Air: Sixties Radicals Turn to Lenin, Mao and Che,* London: Verso, 2002; Johnson, *Revolutionaries to Race Leaders.*
43 Aaron Gould Sheinin, 'John Lewis on Bernie Sanders: "There's Not Anything Free in America"', *Atlanta Journal-Constitution,* 17 February 2015; Cedric Johnson, 'Fear and Loathing in the Palmetto State', *Jacobin,* 29 February 2016.
44 Dara Lind, 'How Democrats Learned to Love Identity Politics', vox.com, July 26, 2016; Jeet Heer, 'Welcome to the New Party of Lincoln', *New Republic,* 28 July 2016. These enthusiastic assessments are disturbingly close to my quip in early 2015 that Clinton and Jeb Bush would wind up running together as a National Salvation ticket.

PICTURING THE WHOLE: FORM, REFORM, REVOLUTION

WALTER BENN MICHAELS

Talking about the political 'Uses of Photography,' John Berger says 'most photographs ... are about suffering, and most of that suffering is man-made'.[1] The reason the point is worth making, he thinks, is because a lot of photography conceals it, his exemplary instance being Edward Steichen's famous *Family of Man* show (1955), which – treating 'the existing class-divided world as if it were a family' – produced a 'sentimental and complacent' vision of that world. It's not that Steichen was wrong to want to think of 'man' as belonging to one family. The sentimentality was in depicting the world as if we already did and hence in obscuring both the political causes of suffering and the cure. By contrast, he offers us Susan Sontag's account of the 'negative epiphany' she experienced on first seeing photographs of Bergen-Belsen and Dachau. Nothing she had ever seen, Sontag writes, 'cut me as sharply, deeply, instantaneously'. His idea is that in order for photography to have any political value, it must – as these photographs did for Sontag – depict the truth of suffering; her idea is that when it does it will cut deep, so deep it's almost a cause of suffering itself, leading the beholder to feel something of what the subject feels.

Indeed, the political potential not only of photography but of art more generally depends, Sontag thinks, on its 'responsiveness to suffering', and here the danger of sentimentality (especially for the art of photography) is even more pronounced.[2] For if the identificatory effect on the viewer – the sympathy produced by feeling something of what the victim feels – is desirable, it is also dangerous, since our sense that we in some sense share the victim's pain may function to repress the recognition that we may in some sense also be responsible for that pain; that 'our privileges are located on the same map as their suffering and may – in ways we prefer not to imagine – be linked to their suffering, as the wealth of some may imply the destitution of others'.[3] Furthermore, because photographs 'tend to transform ... their subject,' photography can make something 'beautiful' 'as an image' when 'in real life' 'it is not'.[4] Thus it 'seems exploitative to look at harrowing photographs of other people's pain in an art gallery', partly because the 'social situation' of the gallery distracts from the 'strong emotion' the work might produce and, perhaps more importantly, because the emotion may be a response to the work as a work of art.[5] In other words, if art photography holds out the promise of producing in the viewer a response to the actual suffering a photograph can depict, it also runs the risk that what the viewer will respond to will be the photograph itself and not the photograph's subject; the art instead of the suffering.

On this model, a model that essentially takes the photographs of the camps as its model, the challenge political photography faces is how to insist on suffering without either aestheticizing or sentimentalizing it. But is this model the right one? I want to suggest that it isn't and, looking at one book by the young American photographer Daniel Shea, I want to argue instead that the point of political photography today cannot be to try to achieve either the right relation with the suffering victim (honoring his dignity, etc.) or the right effect on the compassionate beholder (cutting her just enough to move her in the right way or to the right degree). In fact, I want to say that this interest in the ethical problem of the relations between the photographer and the viewer and the subject of the photograph is itself a kind of sentimentality, and its politics are those of a left neoliberalism: of human rights, diversity, NGOs. By contrast, Shea's commitment is to the aesthetic instead of the ethical, and his understanding of what it means to make art out of photography requires a certain indifference to both his subjects and his audience. It's that aesthetic of indifference that makes possible, I will argue, a certain politics of indifference – a politics that instead, say, of just seeking justice for those who have been treated unfairly by the labour market, seeks to alter the conditions under which that market functions; that instead of focusing on the victims of abuses in what Berger calls 'a class-divided society', focuses on the abuse of class division itself; a politics that, in other words, is not left neoliberal but left.

The photos in Shea's *Blisner, IL* were taken between 2011 and 2014 in southern Illinois (IL is the postal abbreviation for Illinois). Because they're photographs (not drawings or descriptions), what they show us is what was there – in front of Shea's camera – and what it looked like at the moment he made a picture of it. The pictures, in other words, are linked to the thing they are of and to the moment in which they were made in ways that other modes of representation are not. If *Blisner, IL* were a collection of stories for example (like one of its obvious analogies, Sherwood Anderson's short story

cycle *Winesburg, Ohio*), the young man fishing, the train tracks, the statues would never have had to be present in front of the author's pen or even to have existed at all.

And it could be set in the early twenty-first century without having been written in the early twenty-first century. Which is just to say that, as a book of photographs, *Blisner* makes distinctive ontological and historical claims: that those people and those train tracks were really there, and that the photographer was there too.

But Blisner wasn't there. The pictures are of real things but the town is not a real place. So one of the things the book is interested in is how a fiction can be produced out of non-fictional elements. And if Daniel Shea's presence when the photographs were made makes an irreducible historical claim – this is what this wall looked like then, in 2012 – it's also true that the punctuality of that moment is as misleading as it is illuminating. *Blisner, IL* is as much the picture of a process as of a moment. Just as de-industrialization was made possible by industrialization, the photo of an aging wall refers also to a time when it was in better shape. The exhortation painted on this one – why not now? – was painted on it some time ago; 'now,' in this picture, means also 'then'. So one way to think about the multiplicity of times deployed in *Blisner* is that they construct a narrative and, in particular, a narrative of decline, of things that were made a long time ago and that are now crumbling. Sticking with de-industrialization, manufacturing jobs in the US hit their peak in the mid-1970s and have today hit a new low; in the same period, the real wealth of the bottom 60 per cent of the population has declined. More particularly, Illinois has lost 330,500 (5.6 per cent) manufacturing jobs since 1998.[6]

But although there's an important sense in which that's the story *Blisner* tells, there's an even more important sense in which it isn't – in which the book is not about decline and isn't exactly a narrative either. Most obviously, *Blisner, IL*'s opening photographs are not of the declining fictional town Blisner, IL, but of another Blisner book (*Blisner, Ill*, published in 2012) to which this one is a sequel. The object these photos depict was made just a few years ago, and it belongs to the burgeoning (albeit cottage) industry of the photo book. And these new photos were made in a studio in Long Island City, which (unlike the places in Illinois where the others were taken) is in the midst of what the *Commercial Observer* in New York describes as a 'dramatic makeover from an industrial wasteland to a residential destination',[7] just the kind of transformation often precipitated by the arrival of artists like Shea. So one thing the juxtaposition of *Blisner* (the book) and Blisner (the town) asks us to think about is the simultaneity of economic activity and economic stagnation – two aspects of the same thing, connected less by a narrative than by a logic. Or if we want to hang on to narrative, we could say that their juxtaposition begins to inscribe both the history of the town and the history of the book in the history of something else – the history of societies organized by the relation between capital and labour.

And also, the history of art. For if the newly neoliberal 1970s were a crucial economic moment in American capitalism, they were equally crucial in the history of photography, or at least in the history of photography as an art form. Writers like Jean-François Chevrier and Michael Fried have identified the beginning of what Fried calls 'a new regime' of art photography with the emergence in this period of 'a tendency toward a considerably larger image size than had previously been thought appropriate to art photography' and hence 'an intention that the photographs in question would be framed and hung on a wall', to be looked at, Fried adds, 'like paintings'.[8] Today anybody who's interested in photography is familiar with the achievements made possible by this development. But today – as exemplified in Shea's commitment to the photography book – we are also seeing something different. After thirty years of being asked by ambitious art to look at the picture on the wall, we are increasingly being asked to hold it in our hand; not to walk through the gallery but to turn the page. And if, in one sense, this represents a return to what for many years was arguably the dominant, even default, tradition in photography, it also represents something new.

Before the new regime, no one making photography books was expressing a preference for the small image on the page over the large image on the wall; the large image wasn't even an option. But today, for someone like Shea, the photo book is not what it once was – a norm – but what large format photographs have made it – a choice. And it's not only a way of showing your pictures; it's a particular kind of aesthetic object.

This way of putting the point might make some writers on photography a little nervous. In volume three of their invaluable *The Photobook: A History*, for example, Martin Parr and Gerry Badger lament the degree to which photography has been 'colonized by the art museum' and they deplore the 'tendency' of critics to 'discuss photographs in aesthetic terms' and of photographers to forsake the 'documentary'.[9] From their standpoint, the idea that the photobook has been 'reinvigorated' in part as a refusal of the museum wall might look attractive.[10] But the idea that the terms of this refusal are themselves aesthetic would not. In fact, the opening pages of *Blisner* (the photographs of the first book) might count for them as an exemplary instance of a photography they criticize for being 'as self-referential and as solipsistic as a lot of the work currently afflicting contemporary art'.

Their worry is that a commitment to the specifically aesthetic is at best distracting from and at worst incompatible with a real politics. From this standpoint, the photobook that begins with a picture of another photobook – more generally, a work of art concerned above all with itself as a work of art – might seem to abandon the distinctive purchase on the world outside the book that seems to give the photograph whatever political power it has.

But what I'm saying here is just the opposite.[11] The inscription on *Blisner*'s binding reads 'An Index of Work As Labor As Work'. The 'index' registers photography's purchase on the world (the photograph's distinctive causal link to the conditions under which it was produced: no photo of two young men fishing without two young men actually fishing). The redescription of that work as labor points toward a particular understanding of those conditions and of what the photographer does that makes sense of them in relation to capital, and thus makes possible the production of something different – work *as*, or the work *of*, art. And it's this claim to be a work of art that, far from refusing the social and political issues raised by documentary, makes it possible to produce them at a level the documentary in itself cannot quite attain, and with a political vision that, in the current moment, one might even characterize as revolutionary in a way that (for now) no politics can quite be.

I've already begun to describe *Blisner's* claim to the aesthetic by noting that its opening pages thematize the fact that it is a book, with a relation to another book. But the distinctive marks of what it means for it to be a book are everywhere, for example in the difference between the two opposite page photographs of the old movie theatre which you see at the same time, and the two pictures of streetlights which (since you have to turn the page) you can only see separately. More generally, there are many pairings, often but not always of different pictures of the same thing, and the fact of the pairs (more or less inevitable, given the structure of any book) is marked by the further fact that so many photos are not paired, that they appear instead opposite a blank page and that the negative space of the blank page – indeed the negative space of the pages where there are photos – is deployed as something you are meant to see rather than as the background of something you're meant to see. Thus for example with respect to the bridge that bleeds from the left page onto the right (itself a description that depends on the distinctive structure of the book), the white space between the edge of the right page and the edge of the photograph structures the photograph differently from the ones that occupy two full pages, if only because it produces that sense in the photograph itself of motion from left to right.

Why does this matter? It matters because, instead of presenting itself as a collection of pictures a viewer might look at in the same way you might walk around a gallery or look around a website, *Blisner* presents itself as having its own order, its own principle of organization. Interestingly, distinguishing between the experience of the book and the experience of the gallery, Sontag (in 2003) was already speculating on the advantages of the book in the hand over the picture on the wall. Her thought was that because 'one can look privately' and 'linger over the pictures,' the 'weight and seriousness' of photographs of suffering 'survive better in a book' than they do in the 'social situation' of a gallery or museum visit. Her interest in the book, in other words, was in its relative success in producing and maintaining appropriately 'strong emotions'. But the effect on the reader is not at all what's at stake with *Blisner*. Here the reader is free to linger or not linger and, like Sontag's gallery-goer, to look at the pictures in any order we want. But the order they're actually in has nothing to do with us, and it's this assertion of an order that is independent of the reader – that belongs to the book instead of to the reader – that matters. More generally, the insistence that every part of the book is related to every other part of the book is what serves to establish its autonomy – the relatedness of everything inside it, the irrelevance of everything outside it. And it's this autonomy – both the demand that the work be experienced as a whole and the concomitant indifference to how its individual readers experience it (its refusal, more generally, of a certain appeal to its readers) – that not only constitutes *Blisner*'s politics but defines them in left (rather than in liberal) terms.

That's the point of making photographers' studios in gentrifying Long Island City and coal mining towns in de-industrializing southern Illinois elements in a single entity. It's what the communist and literary theorist Georg Lukács used to call the necessity of 'picturing capitalist development as a whole'.[12] And it's even more vividly the point of establishing the irrelevance of the viewer's relation to this whole. Depending on where we are (in southern Illinois or in Queens) and who we are (people who make and buy books like *Blisner* or people pictured in them), we will have very different experiences of our moment in 'capitalist development', and we will naturally feel very differently about them. But if those feelings are inevitable and even sometimes attractive, they are also in the end of secondary interest. In a society organized by class, everybody belongs to one, and if you want to change that society, it doesn't matter which one you belong to. To put the point in the terms usefully introduced by Sontag, this juxtaposition of art flourishing in Long Island City with industry dying in southern Illinois does indeed suggest the way in which 'our privileges' may be 'linked to their suffering', in exactly the way that 'the wealth of some may imply the destitution of others'. But where for Sontag the goal is for the beholder to feel both sympathy and something like guilt, for Shea the question of how we feel (sympathetic or complicit or both) is irrelevant.

More abstractly, the relation between capital and labor is not structured by the way capitalists feel about workers or workers about capitalists, or by any appeal one could make to the other. More concretely, as in this photo of a painting of a child's hands reaching to the grown-up's, the pathos (the plea for compassion) is assigned to the work of art the photo shows (not the one it is) and is offset by the power of the paired photographs that precede it – of the young man with the fishing rod, self-contained, whose hands make no appeal, and of the leaf-like fingers (almost more like fingers than the painted fingers) of the inverted (negative) image that, after a page of negative space, follows it. So what's involved in picturing the whole is not exactly eliminating our feelings about these people, but transforming them into feelings about the work of art that structures the relation between them.

In other words, if one way to understand photography as political art is to see it as soliciting our identification with, compassion for, and perhaps activism on behalf of those left behind in places like Blisner, that's not *Blisner's* way. It's not *Blisner's* aesthetic and it's not *Blisner's* politics. It's not even *Blisner's* idea of what politics is.

We can begin to see this by thinking about the young black man fishing in *Blisner* in relation to the white artist and the statistically white viewer of the picture. What I mean by calling the viewer statistically white is that, just as blacks are over-represented among the poor in the U.S., whites are over-represented among the upper-middle class, the class that cares most about photography as art. So one plausible way to look at this young man is as a victim of the racism that has created those disproportions and a plausible way to understand his presence in this book is as an anti-racist appeal to its readers. But, aesthetically, I've already begun to suggest some of the reasons for thinking he's not there to solicit the complex feelings about black people (guilt tinged with admiration, aversion combined with attraction, etc.) that white (especially upper-class white) Americans have a virtuoso command of. And, politically, the very things that produce that virtuosity – the effects of racism, the disparities between whites and blacks in wealth, in health, in education, etc. – are as irrelevant to *Blisner's* politics as compassion is to its aesthetic. Indeed, the politics of what Adolph Reed and Merlin Chowkwanyun call disparitarianism and the prominence of anti-racism are more the problem than the solution, since they function primarily to articulate the ruling-class view that discrimination and not exploitation is the cause of American inequality. And in the U.S., the ideological success of this argument makes it a weapon against even the slightest move toward a working-class politics (e.g. the Sanders campaign) by insisting, in Hillary Clinton's words, that 'if we broke up the big banks tomorrow' that wouldn't 'end racism' or 'sexism'.[13]

Here neoliberal ethics (holding neoliberalism to its own ideals) are deployed instead of, and against, an anti-neoliberal politics. Instead of the structural change that would, for example, take health care and higher education out of the market, it's structural racism we're urged to worry about, because that deprives many people of a fair chance to be successful *in* the market. It's for this reason that the politics of anti-discrimination today is in no sense a left politics, and that *Blisner* takes the effects of deindustrialization rather than discrimination as its subject. Asked in a recent interview to comment on 'the anti-racist left', Cedric Johnson suggests that it's a mistake to think about phenomena like police violence (including the fact that Black people are disproportionately its target) or the huge prison population (and the fact that Blacks are so over-represented in it) as functions 'exclusively or even primarily' of 'racism'.[14] 'The heart of the problem,' he says, dates back to the process of deindustrialization and its consequences for working people – high levels of unemployment, even higher levels of underemployment and wage discipline in general (even for those who have full-time work). This has been bad news for the working class, and disproportionately bad news for black people for the completely uncontroversial reason that several hundred years of slavery and a century of Jim Crow have contributed to them being 'overrepresented among unskilled workers' and hence disproportionately harmed by the 'elimination of well-paying, low-skilled manufacturing jobs via automation and deindustrialization'.[15] And insofar as the long term response to this crisis has been not to create better paying jobs but to seek to provide equality of opportunity to compete for the few good ones, anti-discrimination has become the hegemon of social justice. It's not for nothing that the neoliberal right[16] and the neoliberal left[17] both love diversity.

In other words, because both racism and now anti-racism have been used to shape the reserve army of labor and to deploy workers for maximum efficiency, it makes no more sense to think of the one (racism) as the problem than it does to think of the other (anti-racism) as the solution. Or to put the point more positively, we can only make sense of either of them, and of the hegemonic status of anti-discrimination more generally, by understanding them as ways of making capitalism work. What the resistance to capitalism thus requires is a certain scepticism about the moral outrage reliably produced by the demonstration of disproportionately raced, sexed and gendered outcomes. More precisely, it requires a certain skepticism about outrage itself, as well as about its kinder gentler cousins, sympathy and compassion.

Hence what's politically important about *Blisner* is the same thing as what's aesthetically important about it – its ability to produce the work's autonomy (its wholeness) as a way of acknowledging without appealing to the experience of its reader, of acknowledging but rendering irrelevant (treating it almost as a kind of nostalgia) the power of the appeal itself. Its imagination of an anti-capitalist politics – one that sought to destroy the class system rather than render it more meritocratic – is embodied precisely in the indifference to both subject and reader that establishes its claim to aesthetic autonomy. In other words, its politics is its claim to be art, a claim we can make more perspicuous by contrasting *Blisner* to another significant (and exactly contemporary but explicitly documentary) photographic project, Matt Black's 2014 *The Geography of Poverty*. Black has for a long time taken photographs of the poverty in California's Central Valley. Several years ago, worried that people tended to think of that poverty as confined to certain areas of the country (as a problem that wasn't, in effect, everywhere), he had the idea for an Instagram project: he would take photographs all around the US, posting them as he travelled, with the goal, as he describes it, of 'get(ing) people that are on Instagram to picture themselves in those places'.[18]

One way, then, to get at what's specific to Shea's *Blisner* is to note that Black's *Geography of Poverty* is explicitly committed to what I have argued *Blisner* rejects, the identificatory structure of the appeal: these people are in need of help, we need to imagine what it would be like to be them, we need to help them. Another way is by noting that Black's understanding of his subject is poverty rather than the process or logic according to which both poverty and wealth are produced; Shea's deindustrialization, by contrast, is a concept. Finally, *Geography of Poverty* has no interest in establishing an internal structure. It's organized around an essentially additive idea of the whole. The problem Black sets out to solve is getting people to see that poverty was not just 'happening in some weird place in the middle of nowhere ... that's just an outlier' but is everywhere. What his project involves is in effect a geographical 'all lives matter'; seeing exclusion as the problem, it establishes inclusion as the solution when, again by contrast, the logic of deindustrialization understands everyone as already included. LIC (if you're looking at nonsite.org, that's the view from Dan Shea's roof) doesn't exclude Blisner, it lives off Blisner; the two are constitutive of each other.

Another way to put this would be to say that Black's idea of the whole is the US and thus the *Geography* project is structured externally by a route that took him more or less around the circumference of the country, a journey that, if it were extended, would take him around the globe, and that, as he notes, isn't really (cannot really be) complete – new possibilities (on the road and, where the project exists, on the internet) are always open. Whereas Shea's idea of the whole is capitalism, an idea that in principle can be made visible without ever going anywhere, and that he makes manifest by the internal, closed structure of the book. That is, the whole that matters in *Blisner* is a whole that must be understood rather than experienced or (more precisely) that must be understood in order to be experienced, and that in a crucial sense exists independent of our or anyone's experience. The idea of this whole is embodied first in *Blisner*'s fictionality (the fact that the real people and real places it pictures are subsumed by an unreal town, so although there's an important sense in which every picture in it is a picture of something, there's an equally important sense in which the book as such is not a picture of anything) and, second, in its declaration of

 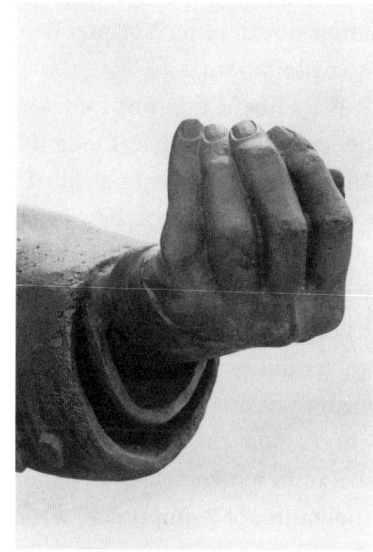

independence from its reader/beholder (the fact that its order belongs to it, not our experience of it, and that it not only makes no appeal to the viewer but even refuses the very idea of such an appeal).

That's what I mean by saying that what distinguishes the politics of *Blisner, IL* from the politics of *Geography of America* is its aesthetics; its claim to be art rather than documentary. My point here is not about the relation of the aesthetic to the political as such. Obviously, they're not identical; even if you think that art is just another way of doing politics, the fact that it's one way among others (different, say, from giving policy speeches) would suggest its distinctiveness. And conversely, they're not entirely separable; indeed the very idea that they can be separated is sometimes thought to imply a certain politics (usually a conservative one), and many works don't even seek such separation. So when, in his *Essays on Photography and Politics*, a writer like David Levi-Strauss asks the rhetorical question 'Why can't beauty be a call to action', his implication that it can be is obviously right.[19]

Just to stick with our current examples, many of Matt Black's photographs are beautiful and they are a call to action, an exhortation to the viewers to do something about the poverty in our midst. But *Blisner* asserts its aesthetics by *not* calling on us to do anything. And today, that particular aesthetic – of the work that seeks to establish its internal coherence, that asserts itself as a whole – is an expression of a particular politics – one that in picturing the world as a whole, pictures it as organized by exploitation, by paying workers less than the value of what they produce. It's as if *Blisner* achieves the form that marks it as having a class aesthetic only by refusing the call to action that would give it a role to play in a class politics. As if it makes no appeal to action not despite, but precisely because it pictures the world as organized by exploitation.

Why might that be? One kind of answer might plausibly gesture toward the critique of what Doug Henwood, Liza Featherstone and Christian Parenti several years ago called activistism. What they were describing was action taken with the best intentions in the world but without recourse to any analysis of the political economy producing the problem the actions were supposed to address, and thus tending to reproduce rather than resist the structures of neoliberal capital. Today for example, the complete compatibility of liberal movements like Teach for America and Black Lives Matter not only with each other but also with the charterization of American schools and the busting of teachers unions suggests the ways in which liberalism lends itself to neoliberalism. More generally, the anti-disparitarian orientation of a supposedly left politics would itself be an exemplary instance of activistism. The problem is not with the motives behind this kind of struggle for equality; it's with the relation between those motives and the consequences of the actions they generate.

And this is equally true of Matt Black's in many ways admirable *Geography of Poverty* project. The minute you understand yourself as 'trying to put forgotten marginalized communities in the spotlight'[20] – as if the problem is that capitalism forgets or marginalizes, as opposed to exploits the working class – you've committed yourself to a conception of both the political and the aesthetic that makes visible the fact of poverty at the expense precisely of the idea of exploitation.

This is why it makes both political and aesthetic sense for Shea – who began *Blisner* out of his anger at the coal industry and because, as he puts it, he 'cared about' these 'people and about [their] struggle' – to say now, about himself as an artist, 'I don't identify as an activist at all anymore'.[21] This disidentification is not just personal, and it's not a sign of discouraged quietism. Just the opposite. At this moment, to assert the difference – indeed the opposition – between the artist and the activist is to assert a conception of the aesthetic as the condition of possibility of action that would not be activistism. If we tend to identify the very idea of political art with the effort to try to get the beholder to do something, it's as if – at this moment – the mark of a truly left political art is that it *doesn't* try to get you to do anything. What it does instead is make it possible for you to understand something.

Leo Panitch has recently suggested that in the twenty-first century, reform 'in terms of the old debate about reform versus revolution' 'is probably no longer possible within capitalism'.[22] And, of course, it's notoriously the case that in the US the very meaning of reform – school reform, welfare reform, pension reform, tax reform – is invoked with increasing frequency on behalf of technologies for facilitating rather than reversing the upward redistribution of wealth. Or, more precisely, on behalf of efforts to identify the public good with the logic of the market. This is true even of reforms that are presented as coming from the left. Reparations, for example (as Ken Warren has pointed out), essentially involve paying people what they'd have if they'd been treated fairly in the labour market, the housing market, the mortgage market, etc.[23] And the identification of reform with access to markets (think of the current revival of the guaranteed minimum income) remains true even though one lesson of the Sanders campaign is that the actual left alternatives – taking housing, health care and education *out* of the market – turn out still to be attractive to millions of young people. So maybe it's not that reform is now impossible but rather that it's been reconfigured; instead of guaranteeing you the right to a house, it seeks to guarantee you the right to compete for a mortgage.

But revolution against capitalism doesn't become more possible just because reform within capitalism (the effort to mitigate rather than legitimate exploitation) becomes less possible. It just becomes more necessary. Which is, I want to say, what *Blisner* understands. Or a little less dramatically, what *Blisner* understands – what the assertion of its form instead of and against the appeal to its beholder insists on, what the insistence on form instead of reform dramatizes – is the necessity of a politics that if it is not fundamentally anti-capitalist, is not anti-capitalist at all.

Blisner's own relation to this necessity – actually the way it produces this necessity – is aesthetic in a Kantian mode, as a form of contemplation rather than an exhortation to do something.[24] In other words, *Blisner* doesn't and cannot say what the politics that I just described as 'fundamentally anti-capitalist' might be. Rather, its inability to say what that politics might be is the condition of possibility of its saying what the point of that politics must be. It's a kind of thought experiment in the relation between form and capitalism where the ambition to achieve the one expresses the desire to end the other. And where, conversely, success at ending the other would make the desire for the one irrelevant. You want form because you don't know how to end capital; if you end capital you won't want form. Or, a little more precisely, the desire for aesthetic form is both the desire to see the world as it is and to imagine the possibility of its being radically different. And if we were to succeed in making it different, the desire for form would become irrelevant; many things would be beautiful, none would be art.

This is why Shea's choosing art against activism (form against reform) matters. The idea that art can be political in the sense of encouraging people to do the right political thing has always been a little problematic. (Sartre loved *Guernica* but 'does anyone think,' he asked, 'that it won over a single heart to the Spanish cause?'[25]) Of course, one reason for this might have been that even if Picasso's aesthetic ambitions in *Guernica* are perhaps less challenging than those of, say, his analytical cubist period, art (especially art since modernism) can be hard; you have to understand it in order to be won over by it, and you have to know a lot and look at a lot before you can understand it. But that's not the only problem; indeed for our purposes that might even be understood as an advantage.

For insofar as the problem with activistism and the difference between the activist and the artist both involve the difficulty of figuring out the right political thing to do, and insofar as today we might say that the difficulty of figuring out what that is is every bit as vivid as the difficulty of doing it (see Syriza), it doesn't make much sense to think of politics as easier than art. Just the opposite. It's hard to make or even understand a masterpiece but harder still to understand what it would take to make a revolution, much less actually make one. Hence part of art's power today is its ability to envision the possibility of (and necessity for) an act that we cannot yet quite identify, much less perform. Indeed, we might say today that for artists like Shea this aporetic relation between art and action can best be understood as the truth of both. Putting the point negatively, a successful revolution would make art unnecessary. Putting the point positively, every successful work of art reminds us that a revolution is what we need.

NOTES

An earlier and quite different version of this essay was first published under the title 'Picturing the Whole' in the book made up of these photographs, Daniel Shea's *Blisner, IL* (London: Fourteen-Nineteen, 2014). I'm grateful to him for permission to re-use some of the original material and, of course, for the work itself. Most of the photos here come from that book. With Shea's permission, they have also been made available on nonsite.org.

1   John Berger, *About Looking*, New York: Vintage International, 1991, p. 61.
2   Susan Sontag, *Regarding the Pain of Others*, New York: Picador, 2003, p. 45.
3   Sontag, *Regarding*, p. 103.
4   Sontag, *Regarding*, p. 76.
5   Sontag, *Regarding*, p. 119.
6   For data on the US and Illinois specifically, see the US Department of Labor, Bureau of Labor Statistics online database at http://data.bls.gov.
7   Al Barbarino, 'Long Island City's Renaissance', *Commercial Observer*, 12 March 2013.
8   Michael Fried, *Why Photography Matters as Art as Never Before*, New Haven: Yale University Press, 2008, p.14.
9   Martin Parr and Gerry Badger, *The Photobook: A History, Volume III*, London: Phaidon Press, 2014, p. 7.
10 Interestingly, Sontag also prefers the photo in the book to the one on the museum wall since she thinks the 'weight and seriousness' of photographs of suffering 'survive better in a book' than they do in the 'social situation' of a gallery or museum visit. The emotions they produce don't fade quite as fast.
11 For a more extensive elaboration of this argument and discussion of many more artists, see Walter Benn Michaels, *The Beauty of a Social Problem: Photography, Economy, Autonomy*, Chicago: University of Chicago Press, 2015.
12 Georg Lukács, *Lenin: A Study on the Unity of His Thought*, trans. by Nicholas Jacobs, London: Verso, 2009, p. 10.
13 David Weigel, 'Clinton in Nevada: "Not everything is about an economic theory"', *The Washington Post*, 13 February 2016. She also pointed out that it wouldn't end discrimination against the LGBT community or 'make people feel more welcoming to immigrants'.
14 Gregor Baszak, 'Marxism through the back door: An interview with Cedric Johnson', *Platypus Review*, 79, September 2015.
15 This is Touré Reed's account of Charles Killingworth's 1968 argument in *Jobs and Income for Negroes*. See Toure Reed, 'Why Moynihan Was Not So Misunderstood at the Time', *Nonsite*, 17, 4 September 2015. Reed goes on to argue that 'racism, though real and relevant, was not the principal cause of black poverty in the 1960s nor is it today'.
16 For example, Goldman Sachs: 'Diversity is at the very core of our ability to serve our clients well and to maximize return for shareholders'. See: http://www.goldmansachs.com/who-we-are/diversity-and-inclusion/.
17 For example, every university in the United States. But here my own distinction begins to look pretty flimsy. When the people pictured on the Harvard website (http://diversity.college.harvard.edu) are just studying to become the people on the Goldman Sachs website, perhaps something even cruder than the distinction between left and right neoliberals is required: rich people love diversity.
18 Olivier Laurent, 'How One Photographer is Mapping America's Poverty', *Time*, 16 July 2015.

19 David Levi Strauss, *Between the Eyes: Essays on Photography and Politics,* New York: Aperture, 2005, p. 9.
20 Brennavan Sritharan, 'Matt Black's "Moral" Photography of America's Sprawling Poverty', *British Journal of Photography*, 28 August 2015.
21 Lucas Foglia and Daniel Shea, 'Interview: Daniel Shea on Blisner, Il', *photo-eye blog*, 12 November 2014.
22 Chris Hedges and Leo Panitch, 'Days of Revolt: We Are All Greeks Now', *The Real News Network*, 15 September 2015.
23 Walter Benn Michaels and Kenneth Warren, 'Reparations and Other Right-Wing Fantasies', *Nonsite*, 11 February 2016.
24 But here the feeling of beauty is imbricated in the understanding of the whole and the concept that in Kant is alien to the aesthetic is made integral to it.
25 Jean-Paul Sartre, *What is Literature,* translated by Bernard Frechtman, Cambridge: Harvard, 1988, p. 28.

ADDRESSING THE IMPOSSIBLE

SLAVOJ ŽIŽEK

It has been claimed that the main reason for the decline of social utopia in the last decades is that, due to technological progress, we no longer need to resort to utopias since in our reality itself (almost) everything is now possible. However, this sense of unlimited possibilities is accompanied by a set of impossibilities: today the very idea of a radical social transformation appears as an impossible dream – and the term 'impossible' should make us stop and think. Impossible and possible are distributed in a strange way, both simultaneously exploding into an excess.

On the one hand, in the domains of personal freedoms and scientific technology, the impossible is more and more possible (or so we are told): 'nothing is impossible'. We can enjoy sex in all its perverse versions, entire archives of music, films, and TV series are available for downloading, going to space is available to everyone (with money ...), there is the prospect of enhancing our physical and psychic abilities, of manipulating our basic properties through interventions into genome, up to the tech-gnostic dream achieving immortality by way of fully transforming our identity into software which can be downloaded from one device to another.

On the other hand, especially in the domain of socio-economic relations, our era perceives itself as the era of maturity in which, with the collapse of communist states, humanity has abandoned the old millenarian utopian dreams and accepted the constraints of reality (read: the capitalist socio-economic reality) with all its impossibilities: *you cannot* engage in large collective acts (which necessarily end in totalitarian terror), cling to the old welfare state (it makes you non-competitive and leads to economic crisis), isolate yourself from the global market, etc. (In its ideological version, ecology also adds its own list of impossibilities, so-called threshold values – no more global warming than 2 degrees Celsius, etc. – based on 'expert opinions'.)[1]

The reason is that we live in the post-political era of the naturalization of economy. Political decisions are as a rule presented as matters of pure economic necessity – when austerity measures are imposed, we are repeatedly told that this is simply what has to be done. In such post-political conditions, the exercise of power no longer primarily relies on censorship, but on unconstrained permissiveness, or, as Alain Badiou put it in thesis 14 of his "Fifteen Theses on Contemporary Art":

> Since it is sure of its ability to control the entire domain of the visible and the audible via the laws governing commercial circulation and democratic communication, Empire no longer censures anything. All art, and all thought, is ruined when we accept this permission to consume, to communicate and to enjoy. We should become pitiless censors of ourselves.[2]

Today we effectively seem to be at the opposite point of the ideology of 1960s: the mottos of spontaneity, creative self-expression, etc., are taken over by the System. In other words, the old logic of the system reproducing itself through repressing and rigidly channelling the subject's spontaneous impetuses is left behind. Non-alienated spontaneity, self-expression, self-realization, all directly serve the system, which is why pitiless self-censorship is a *sine qua non* of emancipatory politics. Especially in the domain of poetic art, this means that one should totally reject any attitude of self-expression, of displaying one's innermost emotional turmoil, desires, dreams. True art has *nothing whatsoever* to do with the disgusting emotional exhibitionism – insofar as the standard notion of 'poetic spirit' is the ability to display one's intimate turmoil, what Vladimir Mayakovski said about himself with regard to his turn from personal poetry to political propaganda in verse ('I had to step on the throat of my Muse') is the constitutive gesture of a true poet. If there is a thing that provokes disgust in a true poet, it is the scene when a close friend, opening up his heart, spills out all the dirt of his inner life.

The two lines from Rudyard Kipling's 'If' seem quite an appropriate guide for those who want to remain faithful to communism: 'If you can wait and not be tired of waiting, if you can dream – and not make dreams your master'. I see Fredric Jameson's 'American Utopia' as a big step in this direction of censoring our dreams. Jameson recently proposed the utopia of global militarization of society as a mode of emancipation: while the deadlocks of global capitalism are more and more palpable, all the imagined democratic-multitude-grassroots changes 'from below' are ultimately doomed to fail. So the only way to effectively break the vicious cycle of global capitalism is some kind of 'militarization', which is another name for suspending the power of the self-regulating economy, and invoking the non-market command provision of goods in the manner of the American military.³

Jameson's achievement here involves imagining a future outside the constraints of the existing order by mercilessly breaking old taboos. These taboos arise from the fact that every historical situation contains its own unique utopian perspective, an immanent vision of what is wrong with it, an ideal representation of how, with some changes, the situation could be rendered much better. When the desire for a radical social change emerges, it is thus logical that it first endeavours to actualize this immanent utopian vision, which is why it has to end in catastrophe. A voluptuous lady from Portugal once told me a wonderful anecdote: when her most recent lover had first seen her fully naked, he told her that, if she lost just one or two kilos, her body would be perfect. The truth was, of course, that had she lost the kilos, she would probably have looked more ordinary. The very element that seems to disturb perfection itself creates the illusion of the perfection it disturbs: if we take away the excessive element, we lose the perfection itself.

It is at this level that we should also discern the mistake of Marx. He perceived how capitalism unleashed the breathtaking dynamics of self-enhancing productivity – see his fascinated descriptions of how, in capitalism, 'all things solid melt into thin air,' of how capitalism is the greatest 'revolutionizer' in the entire history of humanity. On the other hand, he also clearly perceived how this dynamism of capitalism is propelled by its own inner obstacle or antagonism: the ultimate limit of capitalism (of the capitalist self-propelling productivity) is capital itself, i.e. capital's incessant development and revolutionizing of its own material conditions, the mad dance of its unconditional spiral of productivity, is ultimately nothing but a desperate flight forward to escape its own debilitating inherent contradiction. Marx's fundamental mistake was to conclude from these insights that a higher social order (communism) is possible – an order that would not only maintain, but even raise to a higher degree and effectively and fully release the potential of the self-increasing spiral of productivity which, in capitalism, on account of its inherent obstacle (contradiction), is again and again thwarted by socially destructive economic crises.

Which, then, are the taboos to be broken in imagining a future outside the constraints of the existing order? There are (at least) three.

I

First, one should dismiss not only the two main forms of twentieth-century state socialism (the social democratic welfare state and the Stalinist party dictatorship) but also the very standard by means of which the radical

Left usually measures the failure of the first two: the libertarian vision of communism as association, multitude, councils, and anti-representational direct democracy based on citizen's permanent engagement. The truth we have to embrace is that, if we want to move out of representation towards direct democracy, this direct democracy always has to be supplemented with a non-representational higher power – say, of an 'authoritarian' leader. In Venezuela, Hugo Chavez's leadership was the necessary obverse of his attempts to mobilize direct democracy in *favelas*.

For Toni Negri, the dream to be censored is his idea of the goal of emancipatory movements: the state in which the 'dual power' shared between multitude and state organs is overcome and the self-organized multitude completely takes over social reproduction and regulation. It is as if, in the recent Brazilian revolts and mass protests, Negri, a long-time sympathizer with the Lula government, got his own message back in its true form – the government of Dilma Roussef, Lula's successor, spectacularly failed to contain and integrate the protesting multitude. Although the lives of the poor and the middle classes improved considerably, it was as if this improvement, and the very attempt of the government to involve the excluded minorities in a dialogue and empower them as autonomous political agents, backfired and strengthened acts of resistance.

Hugo Albuquerque concisely describes this process in Negri's terms: 'The central issue is less that people *objectively* "improved their lives," as the economists, sociologists, and statisticians … would have us believe, but rather that they feel authorized to desire and, therefore, now desire without authorization.' He goes on to argue that the lead is taken here by a class with 'no name because it does not need one; it is the very expression of many minorities – the poor, blacks, women, etc. – that are sufficient in themselves, that go beyond labels and labeling and simply live. Without a name, this class is in some sense not orderable, since only a subject that has a name, and is thus subject to a regime, is capable of receiving orders.' The future of this nameless class thus 'depends on positively embracing its own internal plenitude and differences. Carnival, with its masks and its lawlessness, not the normalization of bureaucratic seriousness … will allow a future for these lands. … no repressive formula is capable of containing the intense investment of desire – at least not for long.'[4]

There is undoubtedly a moment of truth in this description: it renders the reality of how the protesters experience their situation, and of the despair of the state power which fails to contain protests through 'rational' measures of material improvement. The dimension that prevents the satisfactory non-antagonistic collaboration of the protesting multitude with a 'progressive' state power is correctly characterized as that of *desire* – and to discern the problem, one should give to this term all its Lacanian weight. Desire is always a desire for its own non-satisfaction. Its ultimate aim is always to reproduce itself as desire, which is why its basic formula is always something like 'I demand this from you, but if you give it to me, I will reject it because this is not really THAT (what I really want),' i.e., desire is a gap, a void in the heart of every demand. Is not an exemplary case of this dialectic of demand and desire a protest movement that demands from the government a measure X (say, to repeal a new law or to abolish a new tax), and if the government immediately concedes, protesters feel frustrated and somehow cheated?

But there is another paradox that defines the protesting multitude: the quoted text which talks about the awakened desire among the multitudes also claims that they are 'sufficient in themselves', they 'go beyond labels and labeling and simply live'. How can multitudes be 'sufficient in themselves' while engaged in continuous protesting, provoking the state power, bombarding it with demands?

Maybe one should render problematic the very basic coordinates of this view, and turn around the opposition between fluid life of multitudes and the regulating oppressive power of the state apparatuses: what if the notion of power as the agency which regulates the de-territorialized flux of multitudes should be turned around? What if the basic units of social life, 'sufficient in themselves', tend to 'simply live' in their secluded groups, in their stable territorialized bases, while the de-territorializing agency is the state apparatus itself? The destabilizing logic of desire belongs to the fluid political superstructure – it is this superstructure that is in excess with regard to the base. No wonder then that in an interview from January 2015, Negri made two 'general propositions,' announcing a change in his position:

> The first one is that after 2011 horizontality must be criticized and overcome, clearly and unambiguously… Secondly, the situation is probably ripe enough to attempt once again that most political of passages: the seizure of power. We have understood the question of power for too long in an excessively negative manner.[5]

The critique of political representation as passivizing alienation (instead of allowing others to speak for them, people should directly organize themselves into associations) reaches its limit here. The idea of organizing society in its entirety as a network of associations is a utopia which obfuscates a triple impossibility:[6]

1) There are numerous cases in which representing (speaking for) others is a necessity. It is cynical to say that victims of mass violence from Auschwitz to Rwanda (and the mentally ill, children, etc., not to mention the suffering animals) should organize themselves and speak for themselves.
2) When we effectively get a mass mobilization of hundreds of thousands of people self-organizing themselves horizontally (Tahrir Square, Gezi Park), we should never forget that they remain a minority, and that the silent majority remains outside, non-represented. (This is why, in Egypt, this silent majority defeated the Tahrir Square crowd and elected Muslim Brotherhood.)
3) Permanent political engagement has a limited time-span: after a couple of weeks or, rarely, months, the majority disengages, and the problem is safeguarding the results of the uprising when things return to normal.

There is nothing inherently 'conservative' in being tired of the usual radical Leftist demands for permanent mobilization and active participation, demands which follow the superego logic: the more we obey them, the more we are guilty. The battle has to be won *here*, in the domain of citizens' passivity, when things return back to normal the morning after ecstatic revolts: it is (relatively) easy to have a big ecstatic spectacle of sublime unity, but how will ordinary people feel the difference in their ordinary daily lives? No wonder conservatives like to see from time to time sublime explosions – they remind people that nothing can really change, that things return to normal the following day. In the final scene of *V for Vendetta*, thousands of unarmed Londoners wearing Guy Fawkes masks march towards Parliament. Without orders, the military allows the crowd to pass and the people take over. As Finch asks Evey for V's identity, she replies: 'He was all of us'. OK, a nice ecstatic moment, but I am ready to sell my mother into slavery in order to see *V for Vendetta* Part 2: what would have happened the day after the victory of the people, how would they (re)organize daily life?

One should thus abandon ('deconstruct' even) the opposition between the 'normal' run of things and the 'state of exception' characterized by fidelity to an Event which disrupts the 'normal' run of things. In the 'normal' run of things, life just goes on following its inertia; we are immersed in our daily cares and rituals, and then something happens: an eventual Awakening, a secular version of a miracle (social emancipatory explosion, traumatic love encounter). If we opt for fidelity to this event, our entire life changes, we are engaged in the 'work of love' and endeavor to inscribe the Event into our reality. At some point, then, the eventual sequence is exhausted and we return to the 'normal' flow of things. But what if the true power of an Event should be measured precisely by its disappearance, when the Event is erased in its result, in the change in 'normal' life? Let's take a socio-political Event: what remains of it in its aftermath when its ecstatic energy is exhausted and things return to 'normality'? How is this 'normality' different from the pre-evental one?

II

The second taboo to be broken concerns the problem of resentment. One should totally reject the predominant optimistic view according to which in communism envy will be left behind as a remainder of capitalist competition, to be replaced by solidary collaboration and pleasure in other's pleasures. Dismissing this myth, Jameson emphasizes that in communism, precisely insofar as it will be a more just society, envy and resentment will explode. He refers here to Lacan, whose thesis is that human desire is always desire of the Other in all the senses of that term: desire for the Other, desire to be desired by the Other, and especially desire for what the Other desires.[7] This last makes envy, which includes resentment, constitutive components of human desire, something Augustine knew well. Recall the passage from his *Confessions*, often quoted by Lacan, describing a scene in which a baby becomes jealous of his brother sucking at their mother's breast: 'I myself have seen and known an infant to be jealous though it could not speak. It became pale, and cast bitter looks on its foster-brother.'

Based on this insight, Jean-Pierre Dupuy proposes a convincing critique of John Rawls' theory of justice.[8] In Rawls' model of a just society, social inequalities are tolerated only insofar as they also help those at the bottom of the social ladder, and insofar as they are not based on inherited hierarchies but on natural inequalities, which are considered contingent.[9] Even the British Conservatives now seem prepared to endorse Rawls' notion of justice: in December 2005, David Cameron, the newly elected leader, signalled his intention to turn the Conservative Party into a defender of the underprivileged, declaring how 'I think the test of all our policies should be: what does it do for the people who have the least, the people on the bottom rung of the ladder?' Theresa May said much the same thing on replacing Cameron in July 2016.

What Rawls doesn't see is how such a society would create the conditions for an uncontrolled explosion of *ressentiment*: in it, I would know that my lower status is fully 'justified' and would thus be deprived of the ploy of excusing my failure as the result of social injustice. Rawls thus proposes a terrifying model of a society in which hierarchy is directly legitimized by natural properties, thereby missing the simple lesson an anecdote about a Slovene peasant makes palpably clear. A good witch gives the peasant a choice: she will either give him one cow and his neighbor two cows, or she'll take one cow from him and two from his neighbor. The peasant immediately chooses the second option. As Gore Vidal once put it, succinctly, 'it is not enough for me to win – the other must lose'. The catch of envy/resentment is that it not only endorses the zero-sum game principle where my victory equals the other's loss. It also implies a gap between the two, which is not a positive gap (we can all win with no losers at all) but a negative one. If I have to choose between my victory and my opponent's loss, I prefer the opponent's loss, even if it means also my own loss. It is as if my eventual gain from the opponent's loss functions as a kind of pathological element that stains the purity of my victory.

Friedrich Hayek knew that it was much easier to accept inequalities if one can claim that they result from an impersonal blind force: the good thing about the 'irrationality' of the market and success or failure in capitalism is that it allows me precisely to perceive my failure or success as 'undeserved', contingent.[10] Remember the old motif of the market as the modern version of an imponderable Fate. The fact that capitalism is not 'just' is thus a key feature of what makes it acceptable to the majority. I can live with my failure much more easily if I know that it is not due to my inferior qualities, but to chance.

What Nietzsche and Freud share is the idea that justice as equality is founded on envy – on the envy of the Other who has what we do not have, and who enjoys it. The demand for justice is thus ultimately the demand that the excessive enjoyment of the Other should be curtailed so that everyone's access to *jouissance* is equal. The necessary outcome of this demand, of course, is asceticism. Since it is not possible to impose equal *jouissance*, what is imposed instead to be equally shared is *prohibition*. Today, in our allegedly permissive society, however, this asceticism assumes the form of its opposite, a *generalized* superego injunction, the command "Enjoy!" We are all under the spell of this injunction. The outcome is that our enjoyment is more hindered than ever. Take the yuppie who combines narcissistic 'Self-Fulfillment' with those utterly ascetic disciplines of jogging, eating health food, and so on. Perhaps this is what Nietzsche had in mind with his notion of the Last Man, though it is only today that we can really discern his contours in the guise of the hedonistic asceticism of yuppies. Nietzsche wasn't simply urging life-assertion against asceticism: he was well aware that a kind of asceticism is the obverse of a decadent excessive sensuality.

III

This brings us to the third taboo: democracy. When Badiou claims that democracy is our fetish, this statement is to be taken literally – in the precise Freudian sense – not just in the vague sense that we elevate democracy into our untouchable Absolute. 'Democracy' is the last thing we see before confronting the 'lack' constitutive of the social field, the fact that 'there is no class relationship', the trauma of social antagonism. It is as if, when confronted with the reality of domination and exploitation, of brutal social struggles, we can always add: yes, but *we have democracy* which gives us hope to resolve or at least regulate struggles, preventing their destructive explosion.

An exemplary case of democracy as fetish is provided by bestsellers and Hollywood blockbusters from *All the President's Men* to *The Pelican Brief*, in which a couple of ordinary guys discover a scandal that reaches up to the President, forcing him to step down. Even if the corruption is shown to reach the very top, ideology resides in the upbeat final message of such works: what a great democratic country is ours where a couple of ordinary guys like you and me can bring down the President, the mightiest man on Earth! This is why the most inappropriate – even stupid – name for a new radical political movement that one can imagine is the one which combines socialism and democracy: it effectively combines the ultimate fetish of the existing world order with a term which blurs the key distinctions. Everyone can be a socialist today, up to Bill Gates – it suffices to profess the need for some kind of harmonious unity of a society, for the common good, for the care of the poor and downtrodden.

Linked to democracy is what Badiou posits as the ultimate horizon of emancipatory politics, the 'axiom of equality,' in stark contrast to Marx for whom equality is:

> ... an exclusively *political* notion, and, as a political value, that it is a distinctively *bourgeois* value (often associated with the French revolutionary slogan: *liberté, égalité, fraternité*). Far from being a value that can be used to thwart class oppression, Marx thinks the idea of equality is actually a vehicle for bourgeois class oppression, and something quite distinct from the communist goal of the abolition of classes.[11]

Or, as Engels put it:

> The idea of socialist society as the realm of *equality* is a one-sided French idea resting upon the old 'liberty, equality, fraternity' – an idea which was justified as a *stage of development* in its own time and place but which,

like all the one-sided ideas of the earlier socialist schools, should now be overcome, for it produces only confusion in people's heads and more precise modes of presentation of the matter have been found.[12]

Does this not hold even for today's French political theory, from Etienne Balibar's *egaliberte* to Badiou? Back to Marx, he unequivocally rejects what Allen Wood calls 'egalitarian intuition' – egalitarian justice is unsatisfactory *precisely because* it applies an equal standard to unequal cases:

> Right by its very nature can consist only in the application of an equal standard; but unequal individuals (and they would not be different individuals if they were not unequal) are measurable by an equal standard only insofar as they are brought under an equal point of view, are taken from one definite side only, for instance, in the present case, are regarded *only as workers* and nothing else is seen in them, everything else being ignored. Further, one worker is married, another is not; one has more children than another, and so on and so forth. Thus with an equal performance of labor, and hence an equal share in the social consumption fund, one will receive more than another. To avoid all these defects, right instead of being equal would have to be unequal.[13]

In claiming that it is not just to apply equal criteria to unequal people, Marx may appear to repeat the old conservative argument for the legitimization of hierarchy. However, there is a subtle distinction that has to be taken into account here: this argument is false when we are in a class society in which class oppression overdetermines inequality, but in a post-class society it is legitimate, since inequality is there independent of class hierarchy and oppression. This is why Marx proposes as the axiom of communism 'to each according to his needs, from each according to his abilities'. Wood points out that this maxim, although popularly associated with Marx, originated from Louis Blanc who wrote in 1851 '*De chacun selon ses moyens, à chacun selon ses besoins*,' and can even be traced back to the New Testament: 'And all that believed were together, and had all things common; and sold their possessions and goods, and parted them to all men, as every man had need'.[14]

While this maxim certainly has nothing to do with equality, it poses problems of its own, the main among which concerns *envy*: can any subject define his/her need without regard to what others proclaim to be their needs? As we have already seen, we should reject the predominant optimist opinion according to which in communism envy will be left behind as a remainder of capitalist competition, to be replaced by solidary collaboration and pleasure in other's pleasures.

So, we have to qualify Badiou's thesis that 'equality is the point of the impossible proper to capitalism'.[15] Yes, but this impossible point is *immanent to the capitalist universe*; it is its immanent contradiction. Capitalism advocates democratic equality, but the legal form of this equality is the very form of inequality. In other words, equality, the immanent ideal-norm of capitalism, is necessarily undermined by the process of its actualization. For this reason, Marx did not demand 'real equality,' i.e., his idea is not that equality as the real-impossible of capitalism should become possible; what he advocated was a move beyond the very horizon of equality.

Furthermore, the 'point of the impossible' of a certain field should not to be elevated into a radical utopian Other. The great art of politics is to detect this point locally, in a series of modest demands which are not simply impossible but appear as possible although they are *de facto* impossible. The situation is like the one in science-fiction stories where the hero opens the wrong door (or presses the wrong button…) and all of a sudden the entire reality around him disintegrates. In the US, universal healthcare is obviously such a point of the impossible, in Europe, it seems to be the cancellation of the Greek debt, etc. It is something you can (in principle) do but de facto you cannot or should not do it – you are free to choose it *on condition you do not actually choose it*. Therein resides the touchy point of democracy, of democratic elections: the result of a vote is sacred, the highest expression of popular sovereignty, but what if people vote 'wrongly' (demanding measures which pose a threat to the basic coordinates of the capitalist system)?

This is why the ideal which emerged from the European establishment's reaction to the threat of Syriza's victory in Greece was best rendered by the title of Gideon Rachman's comment in *Financial Times* that the 'Eurozone's weakest link is the voters'.[16] In this ideal world, Europe gets rid of this 'weakest link' and experts gain the power to directly impose the necessary economic measures – if elections take place at all, their function is just to confirm the consensus of experts. (And incidentally, the same feature characterized Communist regimes in Eastern Europe: an apparently modest demand, totally consistent with the official ideology and the existing legal order – like the demand to repeal a certain law, to replace some top politician – threw the *nomenklatura* into a much greater panic than direct calls for the overthrow of the system.)

IV

On account of the necessary inconsistencies of global capitalism, this paradox of the 'point of the impossible' takes the form of self-reference: the point of the impossible of the global market could well be 'free' market relations themselves. A couple of years ago, a CNN report on Mali described the reality of the international 'free market'. The two pillars of the Malian economy are cotton in the south and cattle in the north, and both are in trouble because of the way Western powers violate the very rules they try to impose brutally on impoverished Third World nations. Mali produces cotton of top quality, but the problem is that the US government spends more money for the financial support of its cotton farmers than the entire state budget of Mali, so no wonder they cannot compete with the US cotton! In the north, the European Union is the culprit. Malian beef cannot compete with the heavily subsidized European milk and beef – the European Union subsidizes every single cow with circa 500 euros per year, more than the per capita gross product of Mali. No wonder the comment of the Malian minister of economy was: we don't need your help or advice or lectures on the beneficial effects of abolishing excessive state regulations, just, please, stick to your own rules about the free market and our troubles will be basically over.

Advocates of capitalism often point out that, in spite of all the critical prophecies, capitalism is overall, from a global perspective, not in crisis but is progressing more than ever – and one cannot but agree with them. Capitalism thrives all around the world (more or less), from China to Africa. It is definitely not in crisis – it is just people caught in specific explosive developments that are in crisis. This tension between overall development and local crises and misery (which from time to time vacillate across the entire system) is part of capitalism's normal functioning: capitalism renews itself through crises.

Let's take the case of slavery. While capitalism legitimizes itself as the economic system which implies and furthers personal freedom (as a condition of market exchange), it generated slavery on its own, as a part of its own dynamics: although slavery became almost extinct at the end of the Middle Ages, it exploded in colonies from early modernity until the American Civil War. And one can risk the hypothesis that today, with the new epoch of global capitalism, a new era of slavery is also arising. Although it is no longer a direct legal status of enslaved persons, slavery acquires a multitude of new forms: millions of immigrant workers on the Arabian peninsula (Saudi Arabia, the United Arab Emirates, Qatar, etc.) who are de facto deprived of elementary civil rights and freedoms; the total control over millions of workers in Asian sweatshops often directly organized as concentration camps; massive use of forced labor in the exploitation of natural resources in many central African states (as in the Congo, and others).

But we don't have to look so far. On 1 December 2013, at least seven people died when a Chinese-owned clothing factory burned down in an industrial zone in the Italian town of Prato, ten kilometres from the centre of Firenze, killing workers trapped in an improvised cardboard dormitory built onsite.[17] We thus do not have to look for the miserable life of new slaves far away in the suburbs of Shanghai (or in Dubai and Qatar) and hypocritically criticize China – slavery can be right here, within our house, we just don't see it (or rather pretend not to see it). This new *de facto* apartheid, this systematic explosion of the number of different forms of *de facto* slavery, is not a deplorable accident but a structural necessity of today's global capitalism. Thus a consequent struggle against it can trigger global change.

There is what appears to be a strong counter-argument against this strategy: many times the Left has engaged in a battle against a particular feature of capitalism with the presupposition that this feature is crucial for the reproduction of the entire system, and it was proven wrong. Marx's analysis of the victory of the North in the American Civil War was based on the premise that cheap cotton produced by slaves in the South and then exported to England was crucial for the smooth functioning of the British capitalism, so that the abolition of slavery in the US would bring crisis and class war into England. The premise of socialist feminists and sexual liberation partisans was that the patriarchal family is crucial for the reproduction and transmission of private property, so that the fall of the patriarchal order will undermine the very roots of the capitalist reproduction. In both cases, capitalism was able to integrate this change without any serious problems.

But does this counter-argument really work? It certainly doesn't work today when global capitalism not only cannot afford any widening of workers' rights, but also even has to abolish many of the traditional social-democratic achievements and gains.

V

This brings us back to Jameson's utopia of militarization. An obvious counter-argument to this project of militarization is that even if we concede its necessity we can conditionally endorse it only for a short period of transition: fully developed communism can in no way be imagined along these lines.

However, things here get very problematic. In traditional Marxism, the predominant name for this transitional period was 'dictatorship of the proletariat', a notion which always caused a lot of discontent. Balibar drew attention to the tendency in official Marxism to 'multiply the "intermediary stages" in order to resolve theoretical difficulties: stages between capitalism and communism, but also between imperialism and the passage to socialism'.[18] Such a 'fetishism of the formal number of these stages'[19] is symptomatic of a disavowed deadlock. What if, then, the way to subvert the logic of the 'stages of development' is to perceive this logic itself as the sign that we are at a lower stage since every imagining of higher stages (to be reached through the sacrifices and sufferings of the present lower stage) is distorted by the perspective of the lower stage?

In a properly Hegelian way, we effectively reach the 'higher stage' not when we overcome the 'lower stage', but when we realize that what we have to get rid of is the very idea that there is a 'higher stage'. And that the prospect of this 'higher stage' can legitimize what we are doing now, in our 'lower stage'. In short, the 'lower stage' is all we have and all we will ever get. Jameson goes far in this direction, breaking many taboos, but it seems that one taboo remains: his anti-statal vision, his traditional Marxist idea of dismantling the state apparatus. Perhaps, the army as the universal model for organizing social production is ultimately an *ersatz* for the state; perhaps this last taboo should also fall, and the big task that lies ahead is how to rethink the state.

Let's return briefly to China. A significant feature of Chinese power today is the redoubling of the state apparatus and legal system by Party institutions that have no legal standing themselves. As He Weifang, a law professor from Beijing, put it succinctly: 'As an organization, the party sits outside, and above the law. It should have a legal identity, in other words, a person to sue, but it is not even registered as an organization. The party exists outside the legal system altogether.'[20]

It is as if, in Benjamin's words, the state-founding violence remains present, embodied in an organization with an unclear legal status:

> It would seem difficult to hide an organization as large as the Chinese Communist Party, but it cultivates its backstage role with care. The big party departments controlling personnel and the media keep a purposely low public profile. The party committees (known as 'leading small groups') which guide and dictate policy to ministries, which in turn have the job of executing them, work out of sight. The make-up of all these committees, and in many cases even their existence, is rarely referred to in the state-controlled media, let alone any discussion of how they arrive at decisions.[21]

The front stage is occupied by 'the government and other state organs, which ostensibly behave much like they do in many countries':[22] the

ADDRESSING THE IMPOSSIBLE   353

Ministry of Finance proposes the budget, courts deliver verdicts, universities teach and deliver degrees, even priests lead rituals. So, on the one hand, we have the legal system, government, elected national assembly, judiciary, the rule of law, etc. But – as the officially used term 'party and state leadership' indicates, with its precise hierarchy of who comes first and who is second – this state power structure is redoubled by the party which is all-present while remaining in the background. Is this redoubling not yet another case of diffraction, of the gap between the 'two vacuums': the 'false' summit of state power, and the 'true' summit of the party? There are, of course, many states, some even formally democratic, in which a half-secret exclusive club or sect *de facto* controls the government; in apartheid South Africa, it was the exclusive Boer Brotherhood, etc. However, what makes the Chinese case unique is that this redoubling of power into public and hidden is itself institutionalized, done openly.

All decisions on nominations to key posts (party and state organs, but also top managers in large companies) are first made by a party body, the 'Central Organization Department,' whose large headquarters in Beijing has no listed phone number and no sign indicating the tenant inside; once the decision is made, legal organs (state assemblies, manager boards) are informed and go through the ritual of confirming it by a vote. The same double procedure – first in the party, then in the state – is reproduced at all levels, up to basic economic policy decisions which are first debated within party organs and once the decision is reached, formally enacted by government bodies.

This brings us to the crucial idea of Jameson's utopia: his rehabilitation of the old Leninist idea of dual power. Is what we find in today's China not also an unexpected kind of dual power? And does the same not hold for Stalinism? Perhaps it is time to take seriously Stalin's obsessive critique of 'bureaucracy', and to appreciate in a new (Hegelian) way the necessary work done by the state bureaucracy. The standard characterization of Stalinist regimes as 'bureaucratic socialism' is totally misleading and (self-)mystifying: it is the way the Stalinist regime itself perceives its problem and understands the cause of its failures and troubles. If there are not enough products in the stores, if authorities do not respond to people's demands, etc., what is easier than to blame the 'bureaucratic' attitude of indifference, petty arrogance, etc.?

No wonder that, from the late 1920s onwards, Stalin was writing attacks on bureaucracy, and the bureaucratic attitude. 'Bureaucratism' was nothing but an effect of the functioning of Stalinist regimes, and the paradox is that it is the ultimate misnomer: what Stalinist regimes really lacked was precisely an efficient 'bureaucracy' (depoliticized and competent administrative apparatus). In other words, the problem of Stalinism was not that it was too 'statist,' implying the full identification of party and state, but, on the contrary, that party and state were forever kept at a distance. The reason was that Stalinism (and, in general, all the communist attempts until now) was not really able to transform the basic functioning of the state apparatuses, so the only way to keep them under control was to supplement state power with extra-legal party power. And the only way to break out of this deadlock… here, a new 'seed of imagination' is desperately needed.

Giorgio Agamben said in an interview that 'thought is the courage of hopelessness' – an insight which is especially pertinent for our historical moment, when even the most pessimistic diagnostics as a rule finish with an uplifting hint at some version of the proverbial light at the end of the tunnel. The true courage is not to imagine an alternative, but to accept the consequences of the fact that there is no clearly discernible alternative: the dream of an alternative is a sign of theoretical cowardice, it functions as a fetish which prevents us from thinking through to the end the deadlock of our predicament. In short, the true courage is to admit that the light at the end of the tunnel is most likely the headlight of another train approaching us from the opposite direction.

NOTES

1 I owe this idea to Alenka Zupančič.
2 Alain Badiou, 'Fifteen Theses on Contemporary Art,' *Lacanian Ink,* 23. Available at www.lacan.com.
3 See Fredric Jameson, 'An American Utopia,' in Slavoj Žižek, ed., *An American Utopia: Dual Power and the Universal Army*, London: Verso Books, 2016.
4 See Hugo Albuquerque, 'Becoming-Brazil: The Savage Rise of the Class Without Name,' *The South Atlantic Quarterly*, Fall 2014, pp. 856-7, 859.
5 Antonio Negri and Jerome Roos, 'Toni Negri: From the Refusal of Labour to the Seizure of Power,' *ROAR Magazine*, 18 January 2015.
6 I rely here on Rowan Williams's 'On Representation,' presented at the colloquium 'The Actuality of the Theologico-Political,' Birkbeck School of Law, London, 24 May 2014.
7 See Jacques Lacan, *Ecrits*, New York: W. W. Norton, 2006, pp. 689-98.
8 See Jean-Pierre Dupuy, *Avions-nous oublie le mal? Penser la politique après le 11 septembre*, Paris: Bayard, 2002.
9 See John Rawls, *A Theory of Justice*, Cambridge: Harvard University Press, 1971 (revised 1999).
10 See Friedrich Hayek, *The Road to Serfdom*, Chicago: University of Chicago Press, 1994.
11 Quoted from Allen Wood, 'Karl Marx on Equality,' published online at http://philosophy.as.nyu.edu/docs/IO/19808/Allen-Wood-Marx-on-Equality.pdf.
12 Karl Marx and Friedrich Engels, *Collected Works* Vol. 24, London: Lawrence and Wishart, 1978, p. 73.
13 Marx and Engels, *Collected Works* Vol. 24, p. 86.

14 Acts 2:44-45.
15 Alain Badiou, *A la recherché du reel perdu*, Paris: Fayard, 2015, p. 55.
16 Gideon Rachman, 'Eurozone's weakest link is the voters', *Financial Times*, 19 December 2014.
17 See James Mackenzie, 'At least seven dead in Italian textile factory fire,' Reuters, 1 December 2013.
18 Etienne Balibar, *Sur la dictature du proletariat*, Paris: Maspero, 1976, p. 148.
19 Balibar, p. 147.
20 Quoted in Richard McGregor, *The Party*, London: Allen Lane, 2010, p. 22.
21 McGregor, p. 21.
22 McGregor, p. 14.

ON REVOLUTIONARY OPTIMISM OF THE INTELLECT

LEO PANITCH

[A] man ought to be so deeply convinced that the source of his own moral forces is in himself ... that he never despairs and never falls into those vulgar, banal moods, pessimism and optimism. My own state of mind synthesizes these two feelings and transcends them: my mind is pessimistic, but my will is optimistic. Since I never build up illusions, I am seldom disappointed. I've always been armed with unlimited patience – not a passive, inert kind, but a patience allied with perseverance.[1]

Antonio Gramsci's words here, written in a letter from prison to his brother Carlo in December 1929, provide useful perspective on the famous slogan, 'pessimism of the intellect, optimism of the will' so often wrongly attributed to Gramsci himself. In fact, he borrowed it from Romain Rolland to describe (in an article in *L'Ordine Novo* during the Turin general strike of April 1920) the traits of 'the socialist conception of the revolutionary process' in contrast with those anarchists who presented themselves as 'the repository of revealed revolutionary truth ... letting off steam with the satisfied observation: "We have said it all along. We were right!"'

Gramsci specifically invoked Rolland's motto in the context of responding to one Italian anarchist who, in a classic misinterpretation of the debate between Marx and Bakunin over the state in the transition to socialism, had repudiated 'Marx's pessimism of the intellect ... "inasmuch as a revolution occurring through extremes of misery or oppression would require the institution of an authoritarian dictatorship"'. While calling for the collaboration between anarchists and socialists in order 'to work systematically to organise a great army of disciplined and conscious militants ... ready to take upon itself effective responsibility for the revolution', Gramsci's defence of the Marxist case for a revolutionary party aiming at creating a revolutionary state was classic:

The proletarian class is at present scattered at random through the cities and the countryside, around machines, or bent over the soil: it works without knowing why it works, forced into servile labour by the ever-pressing threat of death by starvation and cold. It does group together in the unions and the cooperatives, but through the necessity of economic resistance, not through spontaneous choice, not following impulses freely born in its spirit. All the actions of the proletariat mass necessarily move in forms established by the capitalist mode of production, established by the State power of the bourgeoisie. To expect that a mass that is reduced to such conditions of spiritual and bodily slavery should express an autonomous historical development, to expect that it should spontaneously initiate and sustain the creation of a revolution, is pure illusion on the part of ideologues.[2]

It is indeed impossible to read Gramsci's *Prison Notebooks* without appreciating how far he actually transcended the dichotomy between pessimism of the intellect and optimism of the will. He did so precisely by applying his stunningly creative intelligence to what really would need to be involved in the creation of a new type of political party, which in homage to another great Italian political theorist who could also be described as a realist with imagination, he called the 'modern prince'.[3] In trying to articulate the form of a party capable of navigating a revolutionary transformation in conditions where the state was deeply rooted in society, Gramsci was doing the very opposite of entrusting it to revolutionary will to usher in the spontaneous transformative 'event' that is rather in fashion among some radical intellectuals today.[4]

Terry Eagleton's recent book, *Hope Without Optimism*, acknowledges the 'voluntarist and even adventurist' dangers in optimism of the will, but for him optimists are usually conservative 'because their faith in a benign future is rooted in their trust of the essential soundness of the present'.[5] He therefore sees optimism as primarily a ruling-class ideology. Eagleton's hero is Walter Benjamin who builds 'his revolutionary vision on a distrust of historical progress, as well as on a profound melancholia'.[6] Although Eagleton disinters an obscure essay by Benjamin that expresses the need to 'organize pessimism for political ends' this does not in fact go beyond the negativity of countering facile optimism. It leaves us bereft of the optimism we need, intellectually tempered by a sober recognition of the great barriers to positive transformative change, to make whatever positive contribution we can to overcoming those barriers, including in ourselves and our institutions.

In fact, when Eagleton tells us it is 'irrational to hope for the impossible' but not irrational to hope even for 'the vastly improbable', he is actually appealing to the kind of optimism of the intellect that believes we can contribute to making the vastly improbable a little less so. Defining hope as 'rational desire', which Eagleton derives from Aristotle, *is* in fact optimism of the intellect.[7] The intellect is not all abstract reason and positivist empirical calculation. Ethics and imagination are also embedded in the intellect. Optimism of the intellect involves bringing reason, ethics, imagination to bear on how to realize optimism of the will.

What many intellectuals today may find troubling about optimism of the intellect is the credit they fear it may lend to all that has emanated from the 'age of reason', with its universalist claims to truth and its evolutionist proclamations of progress. The abdication of so many left intellectuals from the vocation of telling the truth on these grounds was no doubt partly the result of political and intellectual shortcomings on the traditional left. But they have sometimes only generalized what was wrong with the narrow class struggle perspective that crudely labelled truth either bourgeois or proletarian, applying the same type of dichotomy to race and gender, and indeed to any and all asymmetric relations of power.

To insist that knowledge production and claims to justice, whether in the physical or social sciences, or in philosophy and law, are socially situated is one thing; yet to deny all objective validity to the best principles and practices that have emanated from the physical and social sciences, from philosophy and law, is a form of intellectual practice that throws out the proverbial baby with the bathwater.[8] As Meera Nanda put it so well in concluding her essay on 'Restoring the Real' in the 1997 *Socialist Register*, epistemological relativism, even when rooted in a proper sense of injustice, can even be 'antithetical to the cause of justice for "without truth there is no injustice", only so many different stories'.[9] It is the exploited, marginalized and oppressed who most need to go beyond the segmentation of truth, to de-relativize knowledge, science and ethics to secure equality, to realize democracy, to achieve social and ecological justice.

Thomas Dewey published an essay in 1916 simply entitled 'Progress' which presented an argument which captured so well, right in the midst of the slaughterhouse of the First World War, what I mean by optimism of the intellect that it deserves to be quoted it at some length:

> Some persons will see only irony in a discussion of progress at the present time. Never was pessimism easier ... [Yet] never was there a time when it was more necessary to search for the conditions upon which progress depends ... The economic situation, the problem of poverty by the side

of great wealth, of ignorance and absence of a fair chance in life by the side of culture and unlimited opportunity, have, indeed, always served to remind us that after all we were dealing with an opportunity for progress rather than with an accomplished fact ...

Progress is not automatic; it depends upon human intent and aim and upon acceptance of responsibility for its production ... In dwelling upon the need of conceiving progress as a responsibility and not as an endowment, I put primary emphasis upon responsibility for intelligence, for the power which foresees, plans and constructs in advance. We are so overweighted by nature with impulse, sentiment and emotion, that we are always tempted to rely unduly upon the efficacy of these things... [But] since the variable factor, the factor which may be altered indefinitely, is the social conditions which call out and direct the impulses and sentiments, the positive means of progress lie in the application of intelligence to the construction of proper social devices... Practically, this is a matter of the persistent use of reflection in the study of social conditions and the devising of social contrivances.[10]

Dewey very tellingly concluded that what stood most in the way of progress were not the forces of conservatism and reaction but rather the much more common disbelief in the possibility of what he termed 'constructive social engineering'. Today, this common disbelief is once again the greatest barrier that optimism of the intellect faces. Of course the very term social engineering is liable to send chills down the spines of even most leftist intellectuals today. But should we be so afraid of it? 'Institutional engineering' was the term Karl Polanyi used when he insisted against Friedrich Hayek at the end of *The Great Transformation* that democratic planning was not only possible but was actually the necessary condition for realizing genuine individual freedom by connecting it to collective sociability.[11]

Those who invoke Polanyi's 'double movement' to make a case for law-like alternations within capitalism between eras of market deregulation and reregulation, and thus hope to promote a return from neoliberalism to the guiding principles of the Keynesian welfare state, fail to register Polanyi's central contribution to optimism of the intellect, which was to make the case for democratic socialist economic planning not only against neoliberalism but also as a way of transcending the contradictions of the Keynesian welfare state.[12] Polanyi was a socialist, albeit more an Owenite than a Marxist, and the understanding of capitalist contradiction played a central role in his thought. Polanyi saw the imposition of barriers to laissez-faire within capitalism, whether in the form of tariffs or in the form of social welfare measures, and whether coming from above, as with Bismarck, or from the pressure of the newly organized working classes below, as producing contradictions for capitalism's reproduction. And it was the contradictions this double movement actually did produce within late nineteenth-century capitalism which gave rise to what he called 'the great catastrophe' of World War and Great Depression in the first half of the twentieth century.

Polanyi initially had hoped that Roosevelt's New Deal and the state planning in capitalist democracies that underwrote their victory against fascism in the Second World War, and above all the large majority government the British Labour Party secured in 1945, would lay the foundations for democratic socialist economic planning. But he very quickly recognized that the compromises they made with the powerful forces of capitalism, both domestic and international, were reinforcing capital accumulation and commodification even through the construction of the Keynesian welfare state. Here was the problematic double movement again, with regulation and social reform producing the contradictions that would once again lead to crisis, as indeed proved to be so with the Keynesian welfare state by the 1970s. It was amidst the playing out of these contradictions, and the inability of the left to offer a way beyond them via democratic socialist planning, that neoliberalism took root.

Optimism of the intellect does not involve embracing any teleological laws of historical progress. Optimism of the intellect in fact involves being sensitive to contingency in human history, with contradictions and crises not the only variable factors in determining the scope and possibilities of such contingency, but also the capacities of collective human agency as especially crucial variable factors in developing transformative institutional forms. To get to where Dewey and Polanyi, no less than Marx or Gramsci, wanted us to get involves probing the limits of economic and political institutions. And to do this it is also important to pay close attention to such great pessimists of the intelligence as Max Weber on state bureaucracy and Roberto Michels on party oligarchy. This is precisely because we need to identify the actual institutional barriers that lie in the way of replacing the capitalist rationality of market competition with the socialist rationality of collective planning, so we can at least minimize those barriers through articulating the institutional forms that can develop popular capacities for genuinely democratic participation as well as complex representation and administration. The political purpose for this kind of institutionalism is exactly the opposite of validating path dependency, insisting rather on institutional contingency to the end of discovering how to transform institutions in socialist ways.

The need for creating new political parties oriented to developing the agencies capable of this has increasingly become recognized in recent years. The protest movements against global neoliberalism which have punctuated the past two decades, however remarkable and impressive they have been, have also reconfirmed that you can protest until hell freezes over, but without taking and transforming political power you will never change the world. Jodi Dean's recent book *Crowds and Party* makes this case very well. But her image of the new communist party as an 'affective community' is not enough.[13] It needs also to be an 'intellectual community' oriented to developing capacities for complex democratic representation and administration.

We need to learn from our failures in this respect. Watching the Netflix five-part series, *Rebellion* – produced to coincide with the centenary of Easter 1916 in Ireland – brought to mind the famous line written by that quintessential Irish postmodernist, Samuel Beckett: 'Ever tried. Ever failed. No matter. Try again. Fail again. Fail better.'[14] Indeed, *Rebellion*'s compelling dramatization of the uprising – and its defeat – ends by pointing ahead to the spark it provided for the achievement of Irish independence six years later, while also reminding us of the compromised nature of that national liberation victory insofar as it failed – like so many others later in the twentieth century – to realize the socialist goals of the 1916 revolutionaries.

Learning from failures is not just a matter of retrospect. It is a matter of how we go about examining and drawing lessons from contemporary events. Just like the reformist Fabian Society stalwarts, Sydney and Beatrice Webb, who came back from Moscow in the mid-1930s saying 'we have seen the future and it works', so did too many socialist intellectuals of our time go to Brazil, Venezuela and Bolivia in the first decade of the new millennium and come back with the same message. This lack of critical inquiry is characteristic of optimism of the will. What is needed is a careful, sympathetic probing of the barriers which attempts at transformative change are running up against, and the limits and problems being confronted or evaded, the better to learn from them when we come back and have to face the contingencies of trying to develop the capacities to effect political change in our own countries. Had this been the more common approach abroad to the rise of Syriza in Greece, the euphoria which greeted its election as the first and only new government of the radical left since the global economic crisis began almost a decade ago would have been more tempered – and the emotional screams of betrayal, so characteristic of a frustrated optimism of the will, would have been less common.

Optimism of the intellect is perhaps most needed today to temper the catastrophist pessimism that accompanies the all too credible scientific calculations of approaching ecological disaster. When people try to galvanize us into action on this by saying we have only five or ten years left, they are really asserting their pessimism of the intellect in such a way that suggests that optimism of the will is all we need. In fact we need to confront, and think very hard about how to bridge, the very troubling disjuncture between ecological time and political time. This especially applies to the time it will take to develop the institutional capacities, and above all the democratic socialist economic planning capacity, to fully address the full scale of ecological problems.

Ernst Bloch's magnum opus, *The Principle of Hope*, was right to identify the potential for socialism in what he called the 'utopian intention' of the human intellect. As in Gramsci's insistence that 'everyone is a philosopher' since in 'any intellectual activity whatever, in "language", there is contained a specific conception of the world',[15] this intention could be located in the craftsman's eye for perfection, in the worker's experience of alienation when this is denied her, in the glimpses afforded to it by theatre, architecture, painting, literature, and even in a well-crafted essay. 'In contrast to pessimism, a tested optimism, when the scales fall from the eyes, does not deny the goal-belief in general; *on the contrary, what matters now is to find the right one and to prove it.*'[16]

NOTES

This essay draws on my York University Inaugural Politics Emeritus Lecture, 25 April 2016.

1 Antonio Gramsci, *Letters from Prison*, selected and translated by Lynn Lawner, New York: Harper and Row, 1973, p. 159.
2 The full text in English of Gramsci's 'Address to the Anarchists' (which appeared *L'Ordine Novo* on April 30, 1920) is available at https://libcom.org.
3 See Glen Newey, 'The Getaway Car', *London Review of Books*, 38:2, 21 January 2016, pp. 39-42, quoting Muarizio Viroli, *Redeeming 'The Prince': The Meaning of Machiavelli's Masterpiece,* Princeton: Princeton University Press, 2013.
4 E.g., Alain Badiou, *Being and Event*, New York: Continuum, 2005.
5 Terry Eagleton, *Hope Without Optimism*, Charlottesville: University of Virginia Press, p. 13.
6 Eagleton, *Hope*, p. 14. This is indeed what Benjamin's most famous metaphor coveys: 'the angel of history, his face turned to the past and his wings caught up in a storm blowing from paradise and seeing not a chain of previous events but rather 'one single catastrophe, which unceasingly piles rubble on top of rubble ... The storm drives him irresistibly into the future, to which his back is turned, while the rubble-heap before him grows sky-high. That which we call progress, is *this* storm.'
7 Eagleton, *Hope*, pp. 50-51.

8   This was precisely what Gramsci warned against when he wrote that '… it is wrong to conceive of scientific discussion as a process at law in which there is an accused and a public prosecutor whose professional duty it is to demonstrate that the accused is guilty and has to be put out of circulation … [rather than] that his adversary may well be expressing a need which should be incorporated, if only as a subordinate aspect, in his own construction. To understand and to evaluate realistically one's adversary's position and his reasons (and sometimes one's adversary is the whole of past thought) means precisely to be liberated from the prison of ideologies in the bad sense of the word – that of blind ideological fanaticism. It means taking up a point of view that is "critical", which for the purpose of scientific research is the only fertile one.' *Selections from the Prison Notebooks,* London: Lawrence and Wishart, 1971, pp. 343-4.

9   Meera Nanda, 'Restoring the Real', in Leo Panitch, ed., *Socialist Register 1997: Ruthless Criticism of All That Exists*, London: Merlin Press, 1996, pp. 344-5.

10 Thomas Dewey, 'Progress', *The International Journal of Ethics*, April 2016, pp. 311-13, 315-17.

11 Karl Polanyi, *The Great Transformation,* Boston: Beacon Press, 1944.

12 See, for instance Fred Block and Margaret Somers, *The Power of Market Fundamentalism: Karl Polanyi's Critique*, Cambridge, MA: Harvard University Press, 2014.

13 Jodi Dean, *Crowds and Party,* London: Verso, 2016, pp. 218-19.

14 Samuel Beckett, *Worstward Ho*, http://www.samuel-beckett.net/w_ho.htm

15 Gramsci, *Selections*, p. 323.

16 Ernst Bloch, *The Principle of Hope*, Vol. One, Cambridge: MIT Press, 1986, pp. 445-6.

Socialist Register is available online

Individual subscribers:

Permanent online access to the current volume, plus access to all previous volumes for the period of the subscription.

Details at www.merlinpress.co.uk

Institutional subscribers:

Options:
A. To buy current volume only:
1. Permanent online resource
2. Permanent online access plus hardback printed copy. Mixed Media

B. For ongoing subscriptions: ISSN 0081-0606
3. Ongoing online access with permanent access to the current volume and access to previous volumes for the period of the subscription.
4. As 3 plus hardback printed copy.

Prices and other information available at www.merlinpress.co.uk (or order through a subscription agent)
e-mail: orders@merlinpress.co.uk

The Merlin Press
Central Books Building
Freshwater Road
London
RM8 1RX
UK

www.merlinpress.co.uk

Also Available

Socialist Register 2016: The Politics of the Right
Edited by Leo Panitch and Greg Albo

Today the left faces new challenges from political forces amassing on the radical right. The 52nd volume of the *Socialist Register* presents a serious calibration and a careful political mapping of these forces. It addresses pivotal questions on the reordering of the new right. These essays – very broad in terms of themes and places – speak to the global challenges the new right poses for the left at this historical moment. 400 pages.

Contents: Liz Fekete: Neoliberalism and popular racism: the shifting shape of the European right; Richard Seymour: Ukip and the crisis of Britain; Michael Löwy & Francis Sitel: The far right in France: the Front National in European perspective; Walter Baier: Europe at the crossroads: right populism and reactionary rebellion; Geoff Eley: Fascism then and now; G.M. Tamás: Ethnicism after nationalism: the roots of the new European right; Richard Saull: Capitalism and the politics of the far right; Alexander Buzgalin & Andre Kolgonov: Russia and Ukraine: oligarchic capitalism, conservative statism and right nationalism; Aijaz Ahmad: India: Liberal democracy and the extreme right; David Moore: An arc of authoritarianism in Africa: toward the end of a liberal democratic dream?; Alfredo Saad-Filho & Armando Boito: Brazil: the failure of the PT and the rise of the 'new right'; Gavan McCormack: Chauvinist nationalism in Japan's schizophrenic state; Avishai Ehrlich: Israel's hegemonic right; Doug Henwood: The American right: from margins to mainstream; Bill Fletcher, Jr.: 'Stars and Bars': understanding right-wing populism in the USA; Stefan Kipfer & Parastou Saberi: The times and spaces of right populism: from Paris to Toronto; Lesley Wood: Policing with impunity; Reg Whitaker: The surveillance state; Andreas Karitzis: The dilemmas and potentials of the left: learning from Syriza.

Published in paperback in Canada by Fernwood Publishing and the USA by Monthly Review Press, and in paperback in the UK and the rest of world and hardback in all territories by The Merlin Press

Socialist Register 2015: Transforming Classes
Edited by Leo Panitch and Greg Albo

This 51st annual *Socialist Register* completes the investigation of class formation and class strategies on a global scale begun with last year's volume. Deploying an understanding of class as an historical social process – rather than an abstract sociological category or statistical artifact – the essays here investigate the concrete ways that working classes are being made and remade in the struggles against neoliberalism, austerity and authoritarian governments. Taking stock of the changing balance of class forces as well as old and new forms of workplace, household and political organization, they uncover the class strategies being debated and adapted in different zones of the world. 390 pages.

contents: Susan Ferguson and David McNally: Precarious migrants: Gender, race and the social reproduction of a global working class; Lin Chun: The language of class in China; Achin Vanaik: India's landmark election; Supriya RoyChowdhury: Bringing class back in: Informality in Bangalore; Samantha Ashman and Nicolas Pons-Vignon: NUMSA, the working class and socialist politics in South Africa; Fuat Ercan and Sebnem Oguz: From Gezi resistance to Soma massacre: Capital accumulation and class struggle in Turkey: Joel Beinin and Marie Duboc: The Egyptian workers' movement before and after the 2011 popular uprising; Andreas Bieler and Roland Erne: Transnational solidarity? The European working class in the eurozone crisis; Ricardo Antunes: The new morphology of the working class in contemporary Brazil; Timothy David Clark: Class transformations in Chile's capitalist revolution; George Wright: The Olympic ruling class; John McCullough: The middle class in Hollywood: Anxieties of the American dream; Randy Martin: What has become of the professional managerial class?; Hugo Radice: Class theory and class politics today.
Labour and the left in the USA: a symposium:
Kim Moody and Charles Post: The politics of US labour: Paralysis and possibilities; Jane McAlevey: Forging new class solidarities: Organizing hospital workers; Steve Williams and Rishi Awatramani: New working-class organization and the social movement left Mark Dudzic and Adolph Reed, Jr: The crisis of labour and the left in the United States

Published in paperback in Canada by Fernwood Publishing and the USA by Monthly Review Press, and in paperback in the UK and the rest of world and hardback in all territories by The Merlin Press

Socialist Register 2014: Registering Class
Edited by Leo Panitch, Greg Albo and Vivek Chibber

The 50th volume of the Socialist Register is dedicated to the theme of 'registering class' in light of the spread and deepening of capitalist social relations around the globe. Today's economic crisis has been deployed to extend the class struggle from above while many resistances have been explicitly cast in terms of class struggles from below. This volume addresses how capitalist classes are reorganizing as well as the structure and composition of working classes in the 21st century. 352 pages.

Contents: Leo Panitch, Greg Albo & Vivek Chibber: Preface; Arun Gupta: The Walmart working class; Bryan Palmer: Reconsiderations of class: precariousness as proletarianization; Vivek Chibber: Capitalism, class and universalism: escaping the cul-de-sac of postcolonial theory; Ursula Huws: The underpinnings of class in the digital age: living, labour and value; Colin Leys: The British ruling class; Claude Serfati: The new configuration of the capitalist class; William Carroll: Whither the transnational capitalist class?; Bastiaan van Apeldoorn: The European capitalist class and the crisis of its hegemonic project; Virginia Fontes & Ana Garcia: Brazil's new imperial capitalism; Alfredo Saad-Filho & Lecio Morais: Mass protests: Brazilian spring or Brazilian malaise?; Ian MacDonald: Beyond the labour of Sisyphus: unions and the city; Andrew Murray: Left unity or class unity? Working-class politics in Britain; Madeleine Davis: Rethinking class: the lineage of the Socialist Register; Leo Panitch: Registering class and politics: fifty years of the Socialist Register.

Published in paperback in Canada by Fernwood Publishing and the USA by Monthly Review Press, and in paperback in the UK and the rest of world and hardback in all territories by The Merlin Press

Socialist Register 2013: The Question of Strategy
Edited by Leo Panitch, Greg Albo and Vivek Chibber

Socialist Register 2013 seeks to explore and clarify strategy for the Left, in the light of new challenges, and new opportunities.

Socialists today have to confront two realities - that they cannot avoid the question of reforms and a gradualist path out of capitalism; and that the organizational vehicles for socialism will most likely have to abide by different structures and principles than those that dominated left politics in the 20th century. Though solutions are not obvious, *Socialist Register 2013* interrogates these dilemmas and critiques some unhelpful radical thinking that obstructs the reconsideration of socialist strategy for the 21st century. 380 pages.

Contents: Greg Albo: The Crisis and Economic Alternatives; Sam Gindin: Rethinking Unions, Registering Socialism; Jodi Dean: Occupy Wall Street - After the Anarchist Moment; Barbara Epstein: Occupy Oakland - The Question of Violence; Mimmo Porcaro: Occupy Lenin; Michael Spourdalakis: Left Strategy in the Greek Cauldron - Explaining Syriza's Success; Aristides Baltaz: The Rise of Syriza - An Interview; Hilary Wainwright: Transformative Power: political organization in transition; Christoph Spehr: Die Linke Today - fears and desires; Charles Post: What is Left of Leninism? New European Left Parties in Historical Perspective; Steve Hellman: Whatever Happened to Italian Communism? Lucio Magri's The Tailor of Ulm; John Saul: On Taming a Revolution - The South African Case; Atilio Boron: Strategy and Tactics in Popular Struggles in Latin America; Susan Spronk: Twenty-first Century Socialism in Bolivia - The Gender Agenda; Johanna Brenner & Nancy Holmstrom: Socialist Feminist Strategy Today; Joan Sangster & Meg Luxton: Feminism, Cooptation and the Problems of Amnesia - A Response the Nancy Fraser; Eli Zaretsky: Reconsidering the American Left; Alex Callinicos: Alain Badiou and the Idea od Communism; Michael Lebowitz: The State and the Future of Socialism.

Published in paperback in Canada by Fernwood Publishing and the USA by Monthly Review Press, and in paperback in the UK and the rest of world and hardback in all territories by The Merlin Press